THE INSISTENCE

Caputo is a chump. He gives christians
everything they want: a secret priviledging
of unity & oneness at the expense of any
consideration of multiplicity

INDIANA SERIES IN THE PHILOSOPY OF RELIGION
Merold Westphal, editor

THE INSISTENCE OF GOD

A Theology of Perhaps

JOHN D. CAPUTO

INDIANA UNIVERSITY PRESS
Bloomington and Indianapolis

This book is a publication of

Indiana University Press
Office of Scholarly Publishing
Herman B Wells Library 350
1320 East 10th Street
Bloomington, Indiana 47405 USA

iupress.indiana.edu

Telephone orders   800-842-6796
Fax orders   812-855-7931

∞ The paper used in this publication meets
the minimum requirements of the American National Standard for Information Sciences—Permanence of Paper for Printed
Library Materials, ANSI Z39.48-1992.

Manufactured in the United States of
America

LIBRARY OF CONGRESS
CATALOGING-IN-PUBLICATION DATA

Caputo, John D.
  The insistence of god : a theology of
perhaps / John D. Caputo.
    pages   cm. — (Indiana series in the
philosophy of religion)
  Includes bibliographical references and
index.
  ISBN 978-0-253-01001-8 (cloth : alk.
paper) — ISBN 978-0-253-01007-0 (pbk.
: alk. paper) — ISBN 978-0-253-01010-0
(electronic book) 1. God (Christianity)
2. Postmodernism—Religious aspects—
Christianity. I. Title.
  BT103.C3675 2013
  231—dc23   2013004168

1 2 3 4 5 18 17 16 15 14 13

To my graduate students in the
Religion Department at Syracuse University
Where we conceived unruly and unroyal thoughts
Under the very eye of King David

CONTENTS

The Gap God Opens

God as a Highest Being—a steady hand at the wheel of the universe, ordering all things to good purpose, the spanning providential eye o'erseeing all—has had a good run. But in our postmodern condition we acknowledge the instability of traditional foundations, the ambiguities of the old absolutes, and the complexity of endlessly linking systems without closure. The "internet" is very postmodern. The world is neither a neat, divinely run cosmos nor pure chaos but what James Joyce called so prophetically "chaosmos," a dance of probabilities sometimes producing improbable results. That fits with biblical creation: in the Beginning, at the time God was creating the world, the elements were already there, as old as God. The Bible begins with a B (bet, *bereshit*) not an A (aleph). The first is already invaded by the second (just as "deconstruction" would predict). The biblical elements were too feminine for the later *ex nihilo* theologians who preferred a show of divine testosterone. The biblical creator had to do the best he could with what he had to work with, then hope for the best, like the rest of us. Faith is not a safe harbor but risky business. God is not a warranty for a well-run world, but the name of a promise, an unkept promise, where every promise is also a risk, a flicker of hope on a suffering planet in a remote corner of the universe. I do not believe in the existence of God but in God's insistence. I do not say God "exists," but that God calls—God calls upon us, like an unwelcome interruption, a quiet but insistent solicitation. The truth of God may or may not come true. The work of theology is not to spell out the bells and whistles adorning a heavenly monarch but to meditate upon everything we are here called to, everything we are trying to recall, in and under the name (of) "God." In a postmodern world, this monotheistic name does not have a monopoly. God emerges here and there, often under other names, not in the bound volumes of theology but in loose papers that describe a more underlying and insecure faith, a more restless hope, a more deep-set but unfulfilled promise or desire, a desire beyond desire that is never satisfied. I do not know what I desire when I desire God, where that non-knowing is not a lack but the open-ended venture in the human adventure, the promise/risk, the very structure of hope and expectation, not this Messiah or that, but a messianic expectation not immune from secretly hoping the Messiah never shows up. God does not bring closure but a gap. A God of the gaps is not the gap God fills, but the gap God opens. The name of God makes the present a space troubled by an immemorial past and an unforeseeable future. Good, good, indeed very good. Perhaps. That is not a declaration of fact but a promise on which *we* are expected to make good, an insistence whose existence *we* are expected to deliver. And nobody is guaranteeing anything.

ha!.

God brings the Gap!

This is why God is dead!

So good!

The bursting forth through the Godling Membrane Intellectual

An existence whose delivery is contingent.

ACKNOWLEDGMENTS

Most of this book has been previously unpublished, but some sections have appeared in earlier versions that have been rewritten often beyond recognition but deserve acknowledgment:

"God, Perhaps: The Diacritical Hermeneutics of God in the Work of Richard Kearney," in "Philosophical Thresholds: Crossings of Life and World," ed. Cynthia Willett and Leonard Lawlor, SPEP supplement, *Philosophy Today* 55 (2011): 56–64.

"Hospitality and the Trouble with God," in *Phenomenologies of the Stranger: Between Hostility and Hospitality*, ed. Richard Kearney and Kascha Semonovitch (New York: Fordham University Press, 2011), 83–97.

"The Perversity of the Absolute, the Perverse Core of Hegel, and the Possibility of Radical Theology," in *Hegel and the Infinite: Religion, Politics, and Dialectic*, ed. Clayton Crockett, Creston Davis, and Slavoj Žižek (New York: Columbia University Press, 2011), 47–66.

"The Gap God Opens," *Tikkun* 25, no. 2 (March–April 2010): 41.

Review of *The Monstrosity of Christ: Paradox or Dialectic?* by Slavoj Žižek and John Milbank, ed. Creston Davis, *Notre Dame Philosophical Reviews* 2009.09.33.

"The Invention of Revelation: A Hybrid Hegelian Approach with a Dash of Deconstruction," in *Revelation: Claremont Studies in the Philosophy of Religion, Conference 2012*, ed. I. U. Dalferth and M. Ch. Rodgers (Tübingen: Mohr Siebeck, forthcoming).

"The Future of Continental Philosophy of Religion," conference, Syracuse University, April 7–9, 2011.

"Radical Theology as Theopoetics," in *Theopoetic Folds: Philosophizing Multifariousness*, ed. Roland Faber and Jeremy Fackenthal (New York: Fordham University Press, 2012).

"*Voir Venir:* How Far Plasticity Can Be Stretched," in "*Plastique:* The Dynamics of Catherine Malabou," ed. Tyler Williams and Jarrod Abbott, special issue, *theory@buffalo* 16 (2012): 107–123.

My thanks to Sharon Baker, John Burkey, Clayton Crockett, Neal Deroo, T. Wilson Dickinson, Christina Gschwandtner, Brad Jersak,

Katharine Sarah Moody, Michael Norton, B. Keith Putt, William Robert, Jeffrey Robbins, Phil Snider, Eric Weislogel, and Merold Westphal for reading this manuscript and offering many valuable suggestions that sent me back to the drawing board and have saved me from myself several times over.

Above all, I thank my graduate students in the Religion Department at Syracuse University, upon whom the ideas in this book were first tested and to whom this book is dedicated with much gratitude and love.

PART ONE

The Insistence of God

#1) God, Perhaps: The Fear of One Small Word

- "Perhaps" pp. 3-8
- God, Perhaps pp. 8-14
- Insistence & Existence pp. 14-19
- The 3 Pills of a Theology of "Perhaps" pp. 19-23

#2) The Insistence of God

- In Praise of Rogues pp. 24-27
- The trouble w/ God: Projectiles not Projections pp. 27-31
- The Chiasm of Insistence & Existence: God's Prayer's & Ours pp. 31-35
- The Birth of God pp. 35-38

#3) Insistence & Hospitality: Mary & Martha in a Postmodern World

- "Come" pp. 39-43
- Mary & Martha as Postmodern Hosts pp. 43-47
- Hospitable Agency pp. 47-49
- Events: God can Happen Anywhere pp. 49-53
- The Grammatology of Assent pp. 53-55

ONE

GOD, PERHAPS
The Fear of One Small Word

"Peut-être—il faut toujours dire peut-être pour ..."[1]

See, I am sending you out like sheep
into the midst of wolves;
so be as wise as serpents
and innocent as doves.

—MATTHEW 10:16

I dream of learning how to say "perhaps." I have the same dream, night after night, of a *tolle, lege* experience, in which I open a book—I cannot make out the title—always to the same sentence, *"Peut-être—il faut toujours dire peut-être pour ..."* In the morning I cannot remember the rest of the sentence.

I am dreaming of a new species of theologians, of theologians to come, theologians of the "perhaps," a new society of friends of a dangerous "perhaps." I would like to think we are, perhaps, already a little like these theologians we see coming and that they will be a little like us.[2] But, of course, since we cannot see them coming and do not know what they will be like, we can only call, "come."

L o L

"PERHAPS"

There is every reason for philosophers and theologians to fear this one small word, "perhaps."[3] It seems the very antithesis of what we want from them. We expect philosophers and theologians to help us decide, but "perhaps" is the language of indecision and of the suspension of judgment. We expect knowledge and precision from philosophy but "perhaps" is vague and evasive, an admission that we just don't know. We expect faith from the theologians but "perhaps" means we are uncertain, skeptical, too timid to say anything definite. "Perhaps" is the abdication of faith, decision, ethics, judgment and knowledge, of philosophy and theology, a retreat to the safety of the indecisive and uncommitted. "Perhaps" is the motto of the aesthete in *Either/Or*: if you do it, you will regret it; if you don't do it, you will regret it. So, play it safe and stay out of it.[4]

Unless, perhaps, there is "another experience of the perhaps."[5] Unless "perhaps" has another role and belongs to another order, otherwise than the business as usual of philosophy and theology, otherwise than logic, onto-logic, and onto-theo-logic.[6] That is the premise of the present study. I pursue the possibility that "perhaps" belongs to another "regime" than that of mere opinion and hazy indecision,[7] that it enjoys an "irreducible modality" all its own. I am in search of a "perhaps" that is not a category of logic but proves to be of a more subtle disposition, one uniquely accommodated to address the "event," one that is indeed "the only *possible* thought of the event."[8]

"See, I am sending you out like sheep into the midst of wolves; so be as wise as serpents and innocent as doves" (Matt. 10:16).

In an undertaking as uncertain as this, I call upon the animals of Jesus to be my companions. Animal that I am, I am following (*je suis*) an alternate zoology, a zoo-theological order of beasts who distrust sovereigns that is proposed by Jesus and Derrida,[9] and my candidate for such a strange beast is "perhaps." Accordingly, my advocacy of the weak force of "perhaps" must be as innocent as a dove and as shrewd and sly as a snake, able to brave the wolves of philosophy and theology and their love of monarchy and sovereignty and principial order. I am issuing a call for a new species of theologians, weak theologians who must be, just as Jesus says, as wise, shrewd, and prudent as serpents, the wise ones (*phronimoi*) of the "per-haps"—even as they must be as harmless (*akeraioi*) as the doves. This is a combination so odd as even to merit a pink "perhaps" from the Jesus Seminar, which is exceedingly high praise for the Seminar. Even the Jesus Seminar is forced to admit that this is such a strange saying that Jesus might have actually said it—perhaps, in the pink, almost ruby rubric red.

The "perhaps" of which I speak here does not belong to the "strong" or sovereign order of presence, power, principle, essence, actuality, knowl-edge, or belief. The "perhaps," "powerless in its very power," does not belong to the "dominant thinking about the possible in philosophy."[10] "Per-haps" does not mean the onto-possible, the future present, where it is only a matter of time until it rolls around at some later date. It does not belong to the system of categories organized around the binary pairing of necessary and contingent, presence and absence, being and non-being, knowledge and ignorance, belief and unbelief, certainty and uncertainty, actuality and potentiality, substance and accident, theism and atheism. Nor is this "per-haps" a simple compromise between these binaries, a safe middle ground that would maintain a strategic neutrality while still remaining within that order. It belongs to a different register altogether, not the presential order of ontology but a weaker, more dovelike order, what Derrida amusingly (but he is dead serious) calls the order of "hauntology," which means the order of the event which haunts ontology.[11] The event spooks the black-or-white to-be-or-not-to-be of metaphysics and so it unnerves the onto-theologians. The haunting specter of "perhaps" provokes a more radical opening in the present.[12] It prevents the present from closing down upon itself, from being identical with itself, leaving it structurally exposed to the future, not the future present but the very structure of the to-come (à venir). The event (événement) is the advent of what is coming, the coming (venir) of what we cannot see coming (voir venir), the coming of the future (l'avenir), which always comes as a surprise and includes the best and the worst.[13] "Perhaps" twists free (sly as a serpent) from the grip of thinking in terms of the power of the actual, of the prestige of the present, and opens thinking to the weak force of the to-come. I hold my ground on the groundless ground of "perhaps" in order to stay alive to the chance of the event.

"Perhaps" is the only way to say yes to the future.[14] Yes, yes, perhaps. Yes, yes, to the "perhaps." That is an act of faith (foi) that exceeds the simple binarity of belief (croyance) and unbelief, an affirmation more elusive than any positive position, deeper than any positively posited belief. "Perhaps" is thus a non-knowing which exceeds simple ignorance as faith exceeds simple blindness, because it is responding to what solicits us from afar, sensing what might be coming, desiring something beyond desire. The weak force of "perhaps" is more resolute than any simple credo, a knight of faith more unflinching than any firm belief, more ready for the ordeal, for the test. "Perhaps" is not a simple indecision between presence and absence but an exposure to the promise of what is neither present nor absent. "Perhaps" is not the safety of indecision but a radical risk, for nothing guarantees that things will turn out well, that what is coming will not be a disaster. "Perhaps" is not paralysis but the fluid milieu of undecidability in which every radical decision is made, by which I mean a decision that is not merely programmed or dictated by the circumstances.

"Perhaps" is not a simple disinterest but a word of desire for something, I know not what, something I desire with a "desire beyond desire."[15] "Perhaps" does not mean the diffidence of maybe-maybe-not but the hope harbored in what happens. Perhaps, I hope, perchance, there is a chance, a ghost of a chance, in what is happening.

"Perhaps" is not to be confused with the "possible" as the counter-part of the actual, with a merely logical possibility or empirical unpredictability.[16]

To think "perhaps" is to follow the tracks of a more radical possibilizing, of the weak force of a more unpredictable implausible chance that comes quietly on the wings of a dove. To say "perhaps" is to expose ourselves to a possibility that for all the world seems impossible, that may also turn out to be a disaster. To say "perhaps" is to abandon the shield of safety provided by power, presence, principle, and predictability, by actuality and the real. "Perhaps" risks exposure to a spooky, irreal, inexistent insistence, where insistence exceeds existence and existence can never catch up to what insists.

"Perhaps" gives us access to something that eludes the rule of knowledge as certainty and method because it belongs to another register. "Perhaps" is a principle without principle, an anarchic and unmonarchical *arche*, issuing in an odd sort of affirmative, grammatological and "aphoristic energy."[17] It is not a failed way to know but another way to gain access to what is otherwise than knowledge, to what comes otherwise than by knowing. The un-certainty of "perhaps" does not constitute a defect, a failure to attain certainty, but a release from the rule of the certain, an emancipation from the block that certainty throws up against thinking or desiring otherwise. "Perhaps" galvanizes another kind of thinking. "Perhaps" does not signify a simple lack of purpose but a way to stay on the tracks of something unknown, something structurally to come. "Perhaps" is a surmise of the promise, a relation without relation with what is given only as a promise, given while held back. "Perhaps" bends in the winds of what insists without existence, of what withdraws from presence, pointing like the arrow of a weathervane in the direction of the promise, of the flickering possibility of what neither is nor is not. "Perhaps" shelters things from the harsh light of the concept or the program which prevents the event. Instead of constituting a failure of exact knowledge or of determinate decision, "perhaps" represents a greater rigor and a more resolute adhering to what solicits us, a refusal to allow the prima facie claims of the present to take hold, a refusal to be taken in by an accident of birth. Its weakened vision makes for a more resolute listening and heightened attentiveness, which keeps on the tracks of an ever-vanishing trace.

Because it seeks access to the inaccessible, to the unprogrammable, to the uncertain, to the "event," "perhaps" affirms a more obscure and radical faith (*foi*) not a well-defined and positive belief (*croyance*).[18] The positionality of a positive belief shuts down the open-endedness of the affirmation of the future, provoking the formation of schools, camps, cabals, manifestos, doxa, orthodoxies, heresiologies, excommunicative communities, all closed circles, whose seeming decisiveness is in fact a way of avoiding responsibility, in full flight from a deeper and more unnerving responsibility, all for fear of one small word. "Perhaps" does not refuse to make a leap of faith. It recognizes that what passes for a "leap of faith" in "orthodoxy" is an assertion, an assertiveness, that is trying to make contact with the certain, vainly trying to contract a more abysmal affirmation into a creedal assent. Creeds dissimulate a more disconcerting leap, a more disseminated and open-ended faith in something insistent yet indiscernible. The faithful are of little faith; they fear the faith of this small word "perhaps," the faithful being an assembly of believers in beliefs whose contingency they do not quite confront. "Perhaps" harbors a deeper faith while looking for all the world like doubt, like a lamb amid wolves.

"Perhaps" sounds like the soul of indecision, like a lame excuse for an answer, a refusal to take a stand, the safest course possible. I, on the other hand, think it is risky business, a venture into the abyss, a wild and disproportionate risk, exposing us to an excess, opening us to the best while exposing us to the worst, deprived of the mighty armor of metaphysics. "Perhaps" sounds like mere propositional indecisiveness, maybe this or maybe that, who knows which? But I am interested not in the propositional but the expositional, not in what we propose but in that to which we are exposed, in what poses itself before us, imposes itself upon us, posing and presupposing a possibility that leaves us groping for words.

"Perhaps" is not a refusal to engage with reality but a response to the solicitation of the real beyond the real, not the real as the *res*, present and objective, but the real as the insistence of the ultra-real or hyper-real that insinuates itself into what passes itself off for reality.[19] "Perhaps" belongs not to the logic of the present but to the hyperlogic of the *super, epekeina, hyper, über, au-delà*.[20] "Perhaps" unhinges us from the real, making the impossible possible. "Perhaps" is not a refusal to answer but the depths of responsibility, a recognition of the extent to which the question exceeds us and puts us in question. "Perhaps" opens a door that is (perhaps) better kept shut, raises a possibility we would prefer not to think about, opens a question we would rather keep closed, makes a motion that the powers that be want to table.

"Perhaps" sounds like it has renounced all truth and has consigned itself to a regime of opinion. But in truth the society of the friends of "perhaps" is also the society of the true friends of truth, not because they are *in* the truth, which means inside the secure confines of certainty and dogma, but in the sense of befriending it, seeking it, loving it, exposing themselves to its unforeseeable and dangerous coming, to the risk of the "perhaps." They do not claim to be the truth but to be its friends. These friends of truth are "anchorites," solitaries, outside the commonly received opinions of the community, which means they are dreaming of a community without community.[21]

"Perhaps" sounds neutral, like an anemic inability to affirm or deny, whereas in truth it represents what Keats called a "negative capability," an ability to sustain uncertainty and to venture into the unknown.[22] "Perhaps" sustains our openness to the obscurity of what is going on beneath the surface of what is happening. Those who insist on certainty seize upon the actual and close off an obscure but fertile event. They lack the negative capability of thinking "perhaps not."

The decisiveness of "is" and "is not" keeps the real in check, sweeping the border of the present for illegal entrants, putting a lid on actuality, the fragility and rigidity of which is exposed by "perhaps." "Perhaps" is not a retreat to subjectivity or to some safe inner sanctum in which we are relieved of the need for commitment. It is an unnerving relationship to the real, to the real beyond the real, to the open-endedness of the real. "Perhaps" is attuned to what Heidegger called the quiet power of the possible, where the power of the possible consists in the power of the impossible. "Perhaps" does not withdraw but reaches out; it does not refuse the real but reaches out to its outer limit, to the possibility of the impossible, opening itself to the coming of something, I know not what. *Je ne sais quoi. Il faut croire.*[23]

"Perhaps" is not cowardice compared to the "courage to be" (Tillich), but the courage required for what Nietzsche calls the "dangerous" perhaps, the courage for the open-ended, for the fear and trembling before the uncontainable, for the unforeseeable, a way to conquer our ontological agoraphobia, our "khora-phobia." "Perhaps" is not an empty wish or idle fantasy that takes a shortcut that skips the hard work of reality, but a desire beyond desire for something coming, for something that I cannot see coming. "Perhaps" says it is possible when it is impossible, believes when it is incredible, still hopes even after hope is lost. "Perhaps" is a steely, indefatigable, resolute openness to what seems to have been closed off— while looking for all the world like a sleepy indifference. Perhaps is sly as a serpent, innocent as a dove, a lamb among wolves.

GOD, PERHAPS

One clue to what is going on in the present study is as follows:

"Perhaps"—one must (*il faut*) always say *perhaps* for God. There is a future for God and there is no God except to the degree that some event is possible which, as event, exceeds calculation, rules, program, anticipations, and so forth. God, as the experience of absolute alterity, is unpresentable, but God is the chance of the event and the condition of history.[24]

One must, it is absolutely necessary, always say "perhaps" for God: God, perhaps (*peut-être*). Whenever and wherever there is a chance for the event, that is God, perhaps. God can happen anywhere. But history has no future, and God has no future, indeed there is no history or God at all, unless there is a chance for the event. If there is a chance for the event, if the event can happen anywhere, that is God, perhaps. If there is a chance for history, that is God, perhaps.

As the observant reader may have noticed, I have (as is my wont) begun with the words of Jacques Derrida. Perhaps. I admit to having introduced a slight alteration in the text (sly as a snake), a small point, really (harmless as a dove): I have substituted "God" where Derrida said "justice." I assume full responsibility for such audacity. I do not want to blame Derrida for everything I do in this game of jacks. I take it upon myself to show that God, like justice, has to do with a dangerous "perhaps," fully conscious that this will disconcert the philosophers and theologians among my readers. The philosophers want autonomy, not subservience to God, and theologians want the surety of being saved, not "perhaps." So what good can "God, perhaps" do for either cause?

My claim is that a genuine grammar of assent is found in a grammatology of "perhaps," which is the best suited to meet the needs of a coming theology, of a theology of the event, that is, of a weak theology that comes on the wings of doves. Theology in the strong standard version belongs to the sovereign order of power and presence and favors a grammar of great omni-nouns and hyper-verbs. It strides confidently within the assured and strident categories of theism and atheism, belief and unbelief, existence and non-existence, existence and hyper-existence, nature and supernature, presence and super-presence, visible and invisible, changing and unchanging, absolute and relative, true and false. Weak theology, on the other, is content with a little adverb like "perhaps," which can do no more than interrupt or intercept, deflect or modify other, more prestigious substantive and verbal things, introducing modalities, conditions, degrees, and exceptions, focusing on the "how," not the "what," on little prepositions, not big propositions. Weak theology operates in the spooky, shadowy order of the event, where the event is best addressed, and perhaps only addressed, in the fluctuating shadows and spectral grammar of "perhaps."

"Perhaps" provides the grammar of an archi-assent, the grammatology of faith in the event, reinventing theology in the register of a theo-grammatology. "Perhaps" is the watchword of the theologians to come, a messianic sign of their coming.

When I say "God, perhaps" I am proposing the subject matter of a weak theology but I am not advocating agnostic indecisiveness. "Perhaps" is indeed a Janus head, but it is not an attempt to have it both ways, to escape between the horns, to split the difference, to sit on the fence. On the one hand, I am trying to open thinking and practice to God, to the event that is playing itself out under the name of God, to what we desire in and under that name, to the truth of God. I am taking the name of God seriously. I am praying, to God, which sends the philosophers rushing for the exits. I am trying to expose, or to maintain our exposure, or to give a word to our inescapable exposure, to the insistent claim that is made upon us in that name.

But, on the other hand, in saying "perhaps," I am not allowing the claim made by the event to be contracted to that name, to be identified with that name, to be "identified" as "God." At the point at which the event is identified, it is undermined. I am suspending the name (of) "God" in scare quotes. That sends the (strong) theologians heading for the exits, because they are looking for something to save them, to keep them safe. They are not afraid of sheep or doves, but they have a terrible fear of wolves and snakes. Once I say I know the name of the event, once I can say, this is God, the event is God, then the event ceases to be an event and becomes something that I have added to my repertoire, brought within the horizon of my experience, knowledge, belief, identification, and expectation, whereas the event is precisely what always and already, structurally, exceeds my horizons. What I mean by the event is the surprise, what literally over-takes me, shattering my horizon of expectation. God is *a* name for the event, but the very idea of an event prevents us from saying the event *is* God, because the very idea of the event is that I cannot see it coming. For the event, names are always lacking, even the name of God. But that is not because the event is a *hyperousios*, the unnamable hyper-presence of mystical theology, with which deconstruction is sometimes confused, but because the event is still coming, is structurally to-come, *à venir*, while I am always saying, praying "come," *viens*. That is the very idea of a religion without religion, as opposed to the strong religion that reposes on the power of principles and propositions, the prestige of proper names, of properly sacred names, of sacred proper names found in sacred books.

The event that is harbored within the name of "God" does not belong to experience in the usual phenomenological or Kantian sense of the sphere of possible experience, which is the order of presence, and that is because it lies on the border of that experience, slyly eluding its horizon of expectation, which it is capable of shattering. To shatter the horizon of possible experience is to be impossible, to belong to an impossible experience, to belong to an experience of "the" impossible. That in turn introduces a new or second sense of experience, the experience proper to the event, whose grammar is the grammar of the "perhaps," which does not refer to the merely possible but to the possibility of the impossible. The second sense moves from the impossibility of experience to the experience of the impossible. The possibility of the impossible is one of God's most venerable biblical names, the proper referent, if there is such a thing, of "perhaps," maybe even of God, perhaps.

"Perhaps" provides not the logic but the grammatologic of the "weakness of God," where the might of God Almighty turns out to be the subjunctive might of "maybe" or "might be," whose reach extends all the way to the impossible.[25] "Perhaps" provides a grammatical, rhetorical, poetic, strategic, syntactic, and semantic alternative to the militant logic of omnipotence, to the imperial logic of onto-logic and theo-logic. Onto-theologic trades in the hard and fast, the dogmatic, the decisive scission that cuts off being from non-being, which occludes the may-being of "perhaps." "Perhaps" is the weak force of a possibility (of the impossible) not the strong force of actuality, the weakness of a solicitation not the strength of a command, the faintness of a suggestion not the power of an imperative, the fragility of a call not the audacity of an order. The discursive form that can accommodate itself to "perhaps" is not a logic but a "poetics," so a grammatology is a poetics of "perhaps." "Perhaps" is like a sheep among wolves, or like a dove charged with keeping the low profile of a snake.

To gain some sense of what I mean when I say "God, perhaps," let us contrast it with what it could quite legitimately mean within classical ("strong") theology. There saying "perhaps" of God is a function of the sovereignty of God, of the unlimited possibilities of Almighty God, all that the Almighty is able to do, all the Almighty may be, which is quite a lot, considering that with God nothing is impossible. If God is the God who is, who already is all that God is able to be, the plenitude of being, the hyper-plenitude of overflowing being, then God will always be God. The "I am who am" (Exod. 3:14) as it is understood in medieval theology will provide metaphysical support for the biblical God who will always be faithful to his people. The lion of Athens can lay down with the lamb of Jerusalem, as the rock of ages, the immutable, unshakeable warrantor of a promise. The biblical God who always will be there for us in the future is the God who always was and always is there in the first place, *per omnia saecula saeculo-rum*. God is the God who will be just because God is the God Who Is, in the classical and rather Greek, or Greco-Latin terms of Aquinas, *ipsum esse per se subsistens*. God is now, always was and always will be, and will always be faithful to his promises, his word, can always ultimately be counted upon in the future, and in so doing and so being God brings peace to our hearts.[26]

But when I say "God, perhaps," I am inscribing the Tetragrammaton in a general grammatology, inscribing God in spacing and timing *without remainder*. I am signing on to the futural, to becoming, while confessing that this becoming is not underwritten by some divine steadfastness or providential warranty, as it is in Hegel. My "perhaps" is not an appositional appendix, an appresentation added to a prior presence. My "perhaps," "maybe," *peut-être* cuts deeply into the name of God so much that the name (of) "God" takes place in the very element of the *peut-être* itself, of the "event" of the promise which is no less a threat, of the maybe which is also a maybe not. We are not the least assured that God will be there, not the least assured that God may be at all, not the least assured that the "name" of God offers anything more than a hope, a prayer, a faith in something coming, something I know not what, a hope that may turn out in fact to be a nightmare, a monster, which happens time and time again when people act "in the name of God."

The name of God is the name of a hope, which means of a promise/threat which also licenses murder. If we made a list of all the names in the name of which murder is committed, the name of God would, perhaps, head the list, in close competition with "truth" and "justice." Every promise is inscribed in *khora*, in the groundless ground of the trace, of the play of differences, of spacing-and-timing. That means that every promise is structurally inhabited by a threat. We rely upon promises in the face of a threat even as a threat can be posed only if something is promised, and "perhaps" means there is no guarantee about how things will turn out. In face of *khora* we can only hope against hope, since it is only when things are impossible that real hope is possible.[27] Then what? Then we must, as Derrida says, go where we cannot go; know that the gift is impossible, then *give*. That means that the name of God is the name of a call in which we are called upon to respond, which we may or may not do, whether or not we think there is anyone or anything out there making such a call. The name of God is the name of a deed, of what is to be done, something that may or may not be done, something that demands to be done with or without God, something that may be done under other names, something structurally to-come where what happens rests upon our response and may end up being a disaster.

The poetics of "perhaps," of the possibility of the im/possible, implies that the conditions under which we trust also undermine our trust, so that trust is trust in a radical "perhaps," a God who may or may not be, who may or may not be trusted, which is after all what "perhaps" must surely mean, even as a trust in what is completely trustworthy is little or no trust at all but a surety. *Khora* is nothing human but neither is it a monster, and this because "she" does not belong to the order of presence, but serves only as a nickname for the spacing of *différance,* the play of traces within which anything—void or plenum, fear or hope, good or evil, ground or abyss, monster or angel—is inscribed. Without *khora* there is no "perhaps," no maybe/maybe not—and hence, to refer back to ethics, no risk in opening the door to a stranger. *Khora* is not a monster, not a thing at all, good or bad, but the spacing of *peut-être,* the slash between maybe/maybe not, the distance between these binaries, which means these binaries are provisional inscriptions, contingent unities of meaning, constitutable and substitutable in *différance.*[28] Our hopes and fears are linked to each other, and neither the one nor the other can break loose from its radical hermeneutic concatenation with the other, break free, break out into the open and declare itself triumphant. We pray and weep, hope and fear, within the play of traces, hoping against hope, which is, I would say, the very being of maybeing, the very *être* of the *peut-être* harbored in and by the name of God. When I say "God, perhaps," this God is not receiving secret funding from the God Who Is.

I have in mind the unconventional idea that God, like Zarathustra's great star, is not really and truly God without us, that the insistence of God requires our existence and so depends on us. The divine life is incarnated in us, and God's weakness requires that we do all the heavy lifting. God insists, while we exist. I treat the name of God as the name of an inexistence, an insistence, a call that is visited upon us and demands our response, so that God and the divine omnipotence are more radically emptied into the world. "God, perhaps" means that the name of God is the name of the chance of the event, one of the names, one of the events, which are innumerable and impossible.

The name (of) "God" harbors the omnipresent beckoning of the "perhaps," like a spirit that insists and insinuates itself into everything, that breathes where it will, the possibility of the impossibility that inheres in still and small things. God does not exist; God is a spirit that calls, a spirit that can happen anywhere and haunts everything, insistently. I have found it necessary to deny existence in order to make room for insistence. I have found it necessary to deny omnipotence in order to make room for an omni-potentializing, to make the way clear for an omni-possibilizing, or impossibilizing, an insistent "perhaps" that insinuates itself in all things, great and small. I have found it necessary to deny omnipotence in order to re-invent the omnipresence of an omni-"perhaps."

Far from being a full-scale retreat into the safety of agnosticism, "God, perhaps" names a new theology with the courage of an eerie non-conviction, that calls for a new species of theologians, for venturers upon the turbulent seas of a perilous "perhaps," equipped only with the thinnest of protection, like a sheep amid wolves, theologians of risk, whose subject matter is the irreducible danger of life. This is all contracted in the small word "perhaps," which inspires fear even among sovereigns, for fear that the being of God lies in may-being.[29]

INSISTENCE AND EXISTENCE

When I speak of the "insistence of God" I mean that God does not exist or subsist but that God insists, while it is the world that exists. God's insistence requires God's inexistence. The world's existence requires God's insistence. The name of God is the name of an insistent call or solicitation that is visited upon the world, and whether God comes to exist depends upon whether we resist or assist this insistence. The insistence of God means that God insists upon existing. If I say that God's essence lies in God's insistence, I mean that while metaphysics turns on the distinction between essence and existence, what I am calling here a "poetics" of the "perhaps" turns on the distinction between insistence and existence. God is an insistent claim or provocation, while the business of existence is up to us—existence here meaning response or responding, assuming responsibility to convert what is being called for in the name of God into a deed. So where metaphysics theorizes the distinction between of essence and existence, a poetics describes the "chiasm," the "intertwining," of God's insistence with our existence.[30]

In a chiasm, each depends upon the other, neither one without the other. God needs us to be God, and we need God to be human. The insistence of God needs us for strength, even as we draw strength from God's weakness. God's insistence needs our existence to make any difference. Our existence needs God's insistence in order to have a difference to make. God comes to exist in our response; our deeds constitute the "effects" the name of God has in the world. But we should be very careful not to attach any metaphysical baggage to such talk or confuse ourselves with God. A theology of the event is not supposed to end up in pantheism or reinventing "panentheism," which is a fetching idea and close to my heart, but in the end a bit too far-fetched, still more metaphysics. A theology of the event is instead a poetics, a post- or quasi-phenomenological undertaking trying to avoid the traps and trappings of metaphysics. A poetics that takes up the name of God is a theopoetics. On the whole it is better just to say that God insists and to leave the existing to us, where the question of "existing" is a matter of human responsibility. The chiasm shows up in expressions like "the people of God," but God is God and people are people. God insists; people exist. (I confess that the chiasm sounds excessively anthropocentric and humanistic, but that is a problem I reserve for part 3. First things first.)

But if God is "weak," how can God be insistent? If the insistence of God is so insistent, why speak of the insistence of "God, perhaps?" What is the link between "insistence" and "perhaps?" Is not "perhaps" the very lack of insistence? Perhaps what? Why "perhaps?" I have several things in mind in saying "God, perhaps" when I speak of the insistence of God, but for a start I single out only the three most important. The first has to do with insistence itself—something is calling, or rather something is getting itself called, in and under the name of God, of "God—perhaps," inasmuch as the caller in the call is structurally inaccessible, unidentifiable.[31] It may not be God. It belongs to the very nature of responsibility that the caller of the call is unknowable, unnamable. That is the only way to assume real responsibility. Once we claim to know "this is God," "this is the Law," "this is Nature," then we can always plead that we are just obeying orders, just doing our duty, and thereby avoid responsibility. The call, I will say here, always takes place in the middle voice, meaning we go too far if we presume to identify the caller. If we are called upon in a radical way, we don't get to call out the caller.

The second reason I am saying "God, perhaps" has to do with existence, since it is altogether possible that what is insisted upon will be resisted; a solicitation can be ignored, and a call can go unanswered. The call is after all only a call and as such structurally "weak." It has the force without force of "justice," not the real force of law; there are no police to enforce it. The response is up to us and we may, perhaps, respond, which means that perhaps we may not. God may, perhaps, make a difference. Thirdly, when the insistence of God is translated into existence and made to make a difference, the difference God makes may, perhaps, be a disaster. In the case of the name of God, justice may flow like water over the land or perhaps what will flow will be the blood of injustice, the worst violence, which happens time and again with names like "God." The name of God, like "justice" or "love," is a high-velocity word, a speeding projectile. As such it elicits the best and the worst, and so it is invoked for better or for worse.

"Perhaps" spooks everything insisting and existing. "Perhaps" haunts everything inside and outside "theology" or "philosophy," ethics and politics—the list goes on. That is why "perhaps" is indissolubly linked with prayer, which emerges from the tension between the insistence or inexistence of God and existence. In a certain sense, I keep writing one book after another about prayer, which seems to be my only topic. The insistence of God refers to the insistence with which God calls upon us, while prayer means calling upon a God who calls. The insistence of God means that the being (*l'être*) of God is may-being (*peut-être*), the "maybe" or "perhaps" of an ambiguous promise/threat, which may be leading us into grace or into the worst evil, and prayer means we are trying to hang on. I will say more about prayer below, but here at the start let me warn the reader that when I use the word "prayer," this has nothing to do with the pieties of religion. Indeed I fear it will bring small comfort to the theologians of piety, peace, and quiet. I am thinking of expressions like "being left without a prayer," meaning we have no chance, the odds are long, the chance is slim, the situation is dangerous and impossible. I am thinking of "hanging on by a prayer," of someone reduced to pleading, praying, which is the root of the word in Latin, *precari,* to plead, to beg, to entreat. The English word "precarious" means what is "obtained by entreaty, hence uncertain" (OED). To "serve at the pleasure" of a leader means one's position is literally "precarious," dependent on the favor of the leader, which is why those who profess unorthodox things that displease the leader need "tenure," from *tenere,* "holding on" (for dear life, by a prayer).

As a matter of grammar, grammatology, and weak theology, they only pray whose situation is precarious, who are surrounded on all sides by uncertainty, who are at the mercy of events, at the mercy of "perhaps"— and who is not? Our physical life is precarious, at the mercy of the natural elements that sometimes rise up against us and upon whose favor we depend. Our lives are lived at the pleasure of a little planet which has provided us with a favorable environment, unless or until it does not, a point to which I will return in the final part of this book under the title of "cosmopoetics." Events are merciful, perhaps, *merci,* unless they are not, which means we all live lives of prayer, praying for mercy, living off their promise, fretful of their threat, dependent upon their good graces—even if we never go near a house of prayer. They pray who are in an uncertain situation—and who is not?—unable to see what is coming, hounded by the wolves of unforeseeable forces, praying for the grace of an event. They pray who appreciate the precariousness of life, the fragility of what we love or desire, which is made all the more precious by its precariousness. In the most rigorous linguistic and etymological sense of the word, the only sensible response to being surrounded by wolves is to pray for an event, for the grace of an event, for an event of grace. When you pray, be as harmless as a dove and as wise as a serpent. Prayer requires a *phronimos*—this is Matthew's word—of the *peut-être*, which is Derrida's word. Praying in a precarious situation is all a basic matter of phenomenology and etymology and it does not necessarily have anything to do with theology. The theologians arrive at a scene that has already been constituted in human experience. Prayer is older than theology and it is not the private property of the long robes who make a profitable living out of saying "Lord, Lord." My interest in theology stems from an interest in something much older than theology, older than the hoariest theologian, something that can do with or without theology, and would be at best the business of a new species of theologians.

I would understand it if, at this point, the orthodox theologians feel rejected, if they get up and leave, before my lecture has even started, rejecting out of hand the very idea that this is theology at all. I share their suspicion. Indeed, such a suspicion of what I am doing is the condition under which I do it, under which I conduct what I am calling a "radical" theology. I would publish this book under protest if the orthodox theologians did not protest it. If this "theology" were not suspect, if it did not threaten a walkout by the pious, I would not be associated with it. What I call theology is possible only under the condition that it might not—perhaps—be theology, that it might be impossible for it to be theology, that it might be impossible, plain and simple. If it could sail smoothly and identifiably, without running up against the impossible, it would not be what I am talking about. So I can only pray for the patience of the orthodox. But they are right, and I readily admit it, the Bible would never have broken all the records for book sales if Exodus 3:14 read, "I am, perhaps, who I am, but then again I might not be. It might turn out that, after all, I am not who I say I am, or that I am not who you think I am."

The insistence of God in a thin theology is not for the risk-averse—but then again how can the risk-averse pray? As with God, so with theology, so with prayer: one must always remember to say "perhaps." The fortunes of one are tied to the others, all chiasmically intertwined. When Derrida started talking about "the possibility of the impossible" there must have been echoes of the Bible they made him read as a child bouncing around in his head.[32] The impossible just might be possible, perhaps. Is that not our constant prayer? Is that not why we pray? Is there any other reason to pray?

Is that not God, perhaps? Is that not the sort of thing that is always going on with "God," in one way or the other, what is happening in the name (of) "God," what is always being insisted upon in and by this name? That is my question, my thesis, my hypothesis, my presupposition, my concern, my faith, my wager, my prayer.

Think of this book as a prayer, a prayer to be faithful to God, perhaps, where "perhaps" is the element of prayer. I believe in prayer. I am a man of prayer. I am praying all the time. I am dead serious about this, but I cannot conceal a smile as I say it.[33] I am always praying and weeping, but I am also smiling throughout, laughing through my tears. I am saying this, I shamelessly admit it, in part to win over the pious, to make peace with them and offer them something "edifying," at the sound of which the theologians of peace and piety will bow their heads in devout assent, as is their wont whenever someone says, "let us pray." But I will not conceal the fact that my prayer is slightly impious, for I admit I am saying that to pray is to pray to God, perhaps, which is the part I fear will empty the pews. I am praying for the chance of an event, for the possibility of the impossible. Pray I say, pray to God, perhaps, but pray, with or without God, with or without religion, with or without a book of prayer, because prayer is for the precariousness, and who among us is not in a precarious situation? I invoke prayer and grace and the name of God, all of which is highly reassuring to the pious, but I also fear I am going to lose their confidence. No matter; I must take the risk. I can do no other. For it is always necessary to say "perhaps" when it comes to God, to let a certain cloud of unknowing and uncertainty settle over sacred names, like grace and prayer, theology and God, over all the divine names, omninames too powerful and intimidating to be trusted by doves and sheep.

There is no God except insofar there is a chance of an event, which we cannot see coming, the unforeseeable come-what-may which may be the grace of a new beginning. Unless it is a disaster. There may be grace or there may be dragons and monsters. The "may be" is the problem. God, who is the possibility of the impossible, may happen anywhere, may arrive unannounced, a knock on the door in the middle of the night, and that may be trouble. No one, especially not God, is guaranteeing anything. It's not in his nature! It may be in his "essence," which is a dogma of metaphysics, but it is not in his "insistence," which is why I restrict myself to a poetics and maintain that theology has to clear its head of metaphysics. Hence, in this essay, "perhaps" will serve as a dim but guiding light, a slightly anarchic quasi-principle, a principle without principle, whose flickering lead we are asked to follow with fear and trembling. We are called upon to be the *phronimoi* of the "perhaps," on the off chance that this may be theology, perhaps.

If the faithful stick around and hear me out to the bitter end, they will overhear that my faith is placed in what is going on *in* the name (of) "God" and of "theology," which is the insistence of the event, or the chance of the event, and the corresponding faith that God can happen anywhere. My faith is deeper than faith in God and cannot be contracted to faith in God. What corresponds to insistence is a deep and structural faith; what corresponds to existence is a belief that some being is or is not there. My faith is faith in faith itself—it's faith all the way down, and there is no bottom—which is what is involved in having faith in the event. Insistence is a pure trembling, a specter, almost nothing, like a spirit. There's no one out there, no hyper-entity, to ensure it will all turn out well in the end. According to my hermeneutic principle—which is never to avoid the difficulty in life[34]—the event that is going on in theology only emerges once we set loose this dangerous and problematic "perhaps," which sets loose the trouble with God, the auto-problematizing character of God, problematizing both insistence and existence, opening up a chasm, a chiasm, a chaosmos.

THE THREE PILLS OF A THEOLOGY OF "PERHAPS"

In what follows I will present my case for a theology of "perhaps" in three steps. I would call these steps my three pillars except that that is too strong and erect, too edifying and foundational a thing to say in deconstruction. So as opposed to proposing three pillars of a strong theology I will speak instead of the three pills of a poetics of "perhaps," three pills that theology has to swallow in order to get over its fear of this small word "perhaps." Think of these pills as pharmaceuticals in the Derridean sense, as in his famous essay bearing the hilarious title "Plato's Pharmacy," where a *pharmakon* means a drug that may make you better, provided it does not poison you (a promise/threat, a dangerous perhaps).[35] Taking a *pharmakon* is taking a chance on an event. So, at the risk of killing off my readership altogether, I will argue that a genuinely radical theology can only be launched by downing a potentially lethal cocktail, three doses that a more devout theology will consider quackery and will in any case find difficult to get down. The side effects may be intolerable and I do not guarantee a cure.

The Insistence of God

The first step, the one I have already begun, is the elaboration of what I am calling the "insistence of God." That involves delineating the strange grammatology or poetics of the "perhaps." This discourse I claim is cut to

fit the insistence of God, which results in the odd locution or circumlocu-
tion, "God, perhaps," which leaves God hanging by a prayer (ch. 1). Then
I single out the structure of "insistence," which I have begun to identify as
the "chiasm," not a double bind but a double binding or mutual intertwining, of God to us and of us to God, each in need of the other, each praying
like mad, prayer being the precarious way God's insistence finds its way
into existence—for better or for worse (ch. 2). Next I illustrate this chiasm
with the structure of "hospitality," and here I have recourse to Meister Eckhart, who read the fabulous story of the hospitality of Mary and Martha
in an eccentric way (ch. 3). I take special note of the wisdom of Martha,
to which I will return throughout the book. Eckhart's Martha is a clue to
everything I say.

Theopoetics

In the second step the accent shifts from the insistence of God to the
insistence of the discourse called for by the insistence of God. In an effort
to weaken theology in order to make room for "perhaps," I formulate an
idea of a "radical theology" as a "theopoetics," that rethinks the logos in
theo-logy as a poetics. This step addresses the insistence of theology, of
a radical theology, and follows the traces of the name (of) "God" in confessional theological discourse. I agree that this will upset the digestion
of orthodox theologians, who ever since The City of God have enjoyed a
steady red-meat diet of logic and onto-theo-logic, which is chided by Derrida as "carno-phallo-onto-theo-logo-centrism." In this chapter and the
next I make a distinction between confessional theology and radical (or
circumfessional) theology, one which I will also turn on and bring under
attack, trying to make the one porous to the other. The two have rocky
relations (ch. 4). This discussion provides the occasion for the introduction of my postmodern version of Tillich, my own "two types of (postmodern) philosophy of religion," in which I will come out of the closet
as a kind of Hegelian whose theopoetics is opposed to the Kantians (my
"two types"). This no doubt will come as a surprise to my readers who,
ever since Radical Hermeneutics, are used to hearing me hold forth that
the radical element in hermeneutics lies in getting rid of the closet Hegelianism of Gadamer and Ricoeur. I still believe that, but I have since been
born again about Hegel, given a new grace, having chanced upon a way to
think of myself as a Hegelian. The Kantians, I will argue, are serving up an
abridged postmodernism, a postmodernism light, which avoids anything
with a higher alcoholic (deconstructive) content. They have no taste for

the radical innovation and renovation of a theology that comes of thinking of religion as a *Vorstellung,* where it is *Vorstellungen* all the way down, a
theology that, lacking a logic, being bereft of a *Begriff,* is at best a poetics of
the "perhaps" (ch. 5).

If I treat Hegel as the hero of radical theology, I also show him a terrible ingratitude by complaining that he has himself cut off the chance of
the event, the possibility of the *peut-être.* So I serve up a heretical version
even of Hegel, claiming we truly bring the Spirit down to earth only when
the Spirit alights on the plane of the "perhaps." There can be no "events" in
Hegel himself, not finally, not in any really robust sense, because Hegel's
Geist supplies an underlying "logic" that undergirds or oversees and hence
in some way or another "foresees" what is coming. Hegel's God on earth
is still too powerful and "providential" a divine force for my new species
of theologians and for my weak and spectral "perhaps." I clarify my view
of Hegel by way of a dialogue with two of the most interesting heretical
Hegelians of the day: Catherine Malabou, who proposes the possibility of
the event in Hegel, à la Heidegger and Derrida (ch. 6), and Slavoj Žižek,
who thinks that the Spirit is just a spook and who promotes instead a radically negative dialectic spelling the death of God. That will also allow me
to say a word about John Milbank's extremely militant theology of peace,
Žižek and Milbank being two good examples of "strong" or "sovereign"
thinking, who happily play the wolves to our sheep (ch. 7). Hegel prevents
the event from above, by elevating it into the movements of the *Aufhebung.*
My argument here is that the Hegel of both Malabou and Žižek fails to
restore the prevented event. Malabou's Hegel does not face up to a more
rigorous *adieu,* to the exposure of God to the radical "perhaps" of death
pure and simple. Žižek, on the other hand, prevents the event from below
by killing off the old God by way of a massively metaphysical overkill, no
maybes about it. He suppresses the *peut-être* not from above, by installing negation within a divine economy, but from below, by consigning the
event to a fatal forsaken Lacanian *Lama sabachthani.* Malabou's Hegel is
not far from process theology; Žižek's has resurrected the death-of-God
theology of the 1960s.

Cosmopoetics

In the final part, I criticize my theopoetics as having been thus far too
humanistic and anthropocentric and so I turn to the cosmic dimensions of
my "perhaps." I return to the figure of Eckhart's "Martha," whom I treat as
the mother of a new religious realism and materialism, and I accuse myself

of having been in the first two parts of this book, perhaps, too much on the side of Mary and her "beautiful soul." I correct this by widening the perspective from the chiasmic to the cosmic, shifting from a theopoetics to a "cosmopoetics," extending the analysis to the insistence of the real and material world itself, where I will describe the "grace of the world" and the subject matter of a cosmo-theopoetics. A cosmopoetics takes root in a contemporary cosmology and it requires us to start by rethinking the distinction between the human and the inhuman, which is, perhaps, not as rigorous as we think (ch. 8).

The new cosmology is taking our breath away with speculative leaps that have opened up a cosmological "perhaps" that has stolen philosophy's thunder (which is wonder). It has rendered obsolete the old pre-Copernican mythopoetics to which theology has too long been wedded and shaken our most basic presuppositions about "human" and "life" and "matter," exposing them to a "perhaps" we never imagined. This cosmopoetics helps us answer a contemporary movement, led by Quentin Meillassoux, who argues that Kant effectively undid the real Copernican Revolution and replaced it with a phony one in order to leave the door wide open to "fideism," to the "theological turn" and the "return of religion." If that is what continental philosophy leads to, these *enfants terribles* conclude, it is not worth the trouble! They want to replace Kant's phenomenal/noumenal dualism with real being, not "being for us" but "being in itself," where we and our "religion" are destined to cosmic death. Given my distinction between "two types" of continental philosophy I agree with this critique of the Kantian version of postmodernism. But inspired by Martha's realism and materialism, and by a certain heretical Hegelianism, I propose that if we stay with the difficulty of being-nothing all the way down there may be (cosmic) grace on the other end (ch. 9). This requires, first, that we correct the caricature of continental philosophy upon which this argument depends, which I do with the help of Bruno Latour (ch. 10).

That leads to the concluding proposal of my theopoetics of "perhaps," a cosmo-theopoetic realism and materialism that turns on what I call the "nihilism of grace," in which I locate another albeit unnerving sense of "resurrection," as "more life," not "eternal life." Hearing this, the orthodox will by now suspect (rightly) that they are being invited to dine on a mushroom the host is not sure is edible. The grace is the edible or edifying part, but a nihilistic grace is the part that is hard to get down, a perilous pill for theology, which I will maintain has always been too short-tempered with nihilism. Nihilism is very close to the pure gift, and so, while any form of nihilism sounds like terrible trouble, my wager is that being-nothing will turn out to mean being-*for*-nothing, life "without why" (more Meister Eckhart), which I propose constitutes the grace of the world (ch. 11). I illustrate what I am talking about by introducing what I call a cosmo-theopoetic Jesus, a kind of pagan/Jewish "Yeshua," in whom the cosmic grace I am describing is concentrated in a particularly felicitous and vivid way. In the end, I ask, what is it that calls in the sounding of our "perhaps"? Is it the insistence of God, of life, of the world? Perhaps what is coming is "perhaps" itself. Perhaps, all that will remain of "religion" and "God" will be left clinging to the grace of "perhaps" (ch. 12).

If perchance the orthodox can swallow all this, they will afterward feel exceedingly odd, not sure if they are healed or done for. But that, in the unaccountable system of accounting of a poetics of "perhaps," is exactly the unforeseeable result they should have seen coming. Is this the best chance for grace? For God? Perhaps.

Amen. *Ite, missa est.* Go, it is ended, but I pray you, do not go in peace. Remember always to say "perhaps."

TWO

THE INSISTENCE OF GOD

As he came near and saw the city, he wept over it, saying,
"If you, even you, had only recognized on this day
the things that make for peace!
But now they are hidden from your eyes."

—LUKE 19:41

IN PRAISE OF ROGUES

Allow me to put my cards on the table right at the outset. My criterion of truth is how well we have learned to deal with the fear of one small word, "perhaps." That, I would say, is a general problem for us all. No one gets a pass. But in this book I am singling out theology and calling for a new species of theologians, theologians of the future. That means I measure theology by the extent to which it avoids the pitfalls of a too-comforting piety—of pious prayers and pious theology portrayed on gilded postcards. I avoid piety like sin itself. I confess up front to having had a long-standing love/hate relationship with religion and theology, which is why the measure of religion for me is that it be without religion. About religion *simpliciter* I worry about what Lacan says in a precious little book called *Le Triomphe de la Religion*. Religion is out to soothe hearts (*d'apaiser les coeurs*), to pacify and appease, and, no matter how grim the forecast, how bad the news, religion will come up with something—"It's absolutely fabulous." Religion can give sense to anything, "juicy sense" (*sens truculents*), no matter what. That is what the priests are trained to do.[1]

Still, while I am driven mad by the bowed heads who have confused themselves with the God before whom they incline, I have also been madly in love with theology for as long as I can remember. To this day I have a weakness for theology, or at least for something that is happening *in* theology, for events still unnamed that stir within its breast. So I bear witness to my love of theology by searching for a theology to come, with or without theology, with or without God, or religion, all along praying like mad, with or without a book of prayers, praying for courage in the face of one small word, "perhaps." Were I called upon to give a homily—never fear!—I would preach in praise not of peace but of the sword of "perhaps." I am trying to stage a coup that steals the word "theology" out from under the nose of the palace theologians and use these stolen goods to haunt the house of the pious. I am following the traces of an unruly, anarchic, unfettered, altered, and contaminated theology that will send the royal theologians running for cover. I will variously give this theology without theology, this theology of the "without" (*sans*), odd, irregular, scorching, and polemical names—although none as wicked as Johannes de Silentio's quip about "rouged theology"[2]—calling it weak when theology wants to be strong, impious when the theologians are at their pieties, calling it trouble when the pious are praying for peace, allowing it to frequent the company of sinners, prostitutes, and tax collectors to the scandal of the long robes.[3]

Make no mistake. The "theologians" for whom I mean to make special trouble are the house theologians, the palace guard, the keepers of the keys, not the rascals and the rogues of theology who earn their wrath. The American Catholic Bishops' Secretariat for Doctrine issued a statement in 2011 that academic theologians can be a "curse and an affliction upon the church."[4] That I take to be high praise, excellent evidence that the theologians in question are on the job and doing something right. They are a curse and affliction to the patriarchal and homophobic power of the powers that be but a blessing to the people of God, with whom the hierarchy has tragically confused itself. The research and relentless interrogation of scripture, doctrine, and tradition undertaken by such theologians expose the contingency and historical constitution of beliefs and practices that the hierarchy wants the faithful to consider eternal and handed down by God. Such a God, as it turns out, clearly privileges men and excludes women from ordination and just as clearly prefers medieval monarchical power to the community of the Holy Spirit. Indeed, anyone who is a curse and an affliction upon such an institution, one that continues to this day, after repeated exposés, to be accused of protecting sexual predators from the law, is a blessing to their victims. So let there be no mistake about the "theologians" who are my special target. They are the ones, as Kierkegaard said, who are making a profitable living off the Crucifixion—while trying to keep the dissident theologians out of work.

In pursuing this course, I believe I am following "in his steps" (1 Pet. 2:21).[5] I am following the traces of a well-known rogue, a famous outlaw who was turned into the Law itself by the palace theologians, even though my guess is that he would have made them blush with shame, thrown them into a rage, had they met him in the flesh, in his flesh. They say his flesh was assumed by an Über-Being come down to earth for a bit of heavenly business on earth, but I can imagine what they would have called him had they met him in the flesh—a "homosexual," out to destroy "family values," a flag-burner, a libertine, a "socialist," out to raise our taxes—in short, a "curse and an affliction upon the church." So I gladly take my stand with the outlaw and ask what theology would look like were it written by the outlaws, the outliers, the out of power, the troublemakers, the poor, the rogues. Like him, I say I am trying to bring not peace but trouble (Matt. 10:34), and as I keep a dove I also collect snakes. I am out to put the sword to theology, to feed it pills that will turn it a little green around the gills, not to feed it more pacifiers. My idea is to break the crust of piety, to call out the princes of the church and shame them into doing honest work, to break the idols of religious authorities wherever they rear their head, whether under the cover of a book or an institution.

I seek a breakthrough to something that seeks to break out from theology, something stirring within theology, some theological event, some archi-theological eventiveness, something theology contains but without being able to contain, something calling that will call out a new species of theologians. Breaking through to something uncontainable that is itself breaking out is what might be called a deconstruction. I thus conduct these impious exercises in the name of the deconstruction of theology. As an exercise in breaking of any sort, deconstruction qualifies as rogue thought, but deconstruction is not necessarily all bad news for the Good News. Still, deconstruction is trouble, and something of a sword or a bitter pill. I wager that the palace theologians would have taken the original outlaw in whose memory Christianity takes place to be bad news, a destroyer of temples, a deconstructor, and they would be more right than wrong about that. He is lost in the fog of history, buried under centuries of piety and power, of ontologizing, theologizing, Neoplatonizing, quasi-Gnosticizing councils, in constant need of being recovered by historical and terrestrial quests trying to unearth an empty tomb. I am praying for his return, praying for him to come back in an earthier form, before he was hoisted high into the skies of the celestial, celestializing theologians, from whence they said a heavenman descended to earth, at that time the center of the universe (the universe has since moved on). At the end of this book (ch. 12) I will propose a sketch of how much a man of earth and flesh he was. The keepers of the keys piously assemble in his name, assuming their seats in solemn conclave, proudly presiding under the cover of humility, of course, while an appointed doorkeeper keeps constant watch lest he actually return in the flesh and interrupt the proceedings. Žižek wants to be more Christian than the Christians. I wish him well but I entertain no such aspiration. I am more interested in Yeshua than in Christianity.[6]

THE TROUBLE WITH GOD: PROJECTILES NOT PROJECTIONS

The insistence of God means that God insists upon existing, and this in turn is tied up, to the point of being identifiable with the question of prayer. Prayer emerges from the distance between insistence and existence. Prayer is the precarious way God's insistence seeks existence. The "insistence of God" refers to the insistent way that God calls upon us, while "prayer" refers to the act of calling upon and responding to God's call, remembering always that the name of God is the name of trouble.

So I insist that we will get nowhere in theology unless we see how perilous it is to pray, how deep the shadows are that engulf what the pious call prayer, how much trouble is stirred up by calling upon the name of God, upon which theology is an extended meditation. I do not merely refer to how much double-dealing and self-deception prayer involves, how much prayer is a power play, how much the will of God is a cover for willful men, for power and domination, plain and simple. That is surely peril enough. But I am no less concerned with the trouble "God" causes even when we are earnest, or think ourselves earnest (for how would we ever know?). I focus on the abyss of trouble upon which the small craft of prayer opens up when we assume the best of intentions, when we are doing our best to expose ourselves to everything that stirs within that name. But I am interested in still more: how much God's own "being" is rocked by trouble, how deeply troubled is God's own tumultuous makeup, how precarious is God, the name of God, the event that insists in the name of God. So the precariousness falls on both sides—God and us. We ourselves along with God, we are all in trouble, all in this together, each dependent upon the other, all intertwined in a precarious prayer. Theology has been happy to allow God to preside over trouble but disinclined to draw God into trouble, disinclined to concede the precariousness of God, reluctant to see God in such radical straits, in such radical solidarity with us. Theology has usually preferred to think that God oversees the churning seas or commands them or walks on them, whereas I see the both of us together, praying and weeping together in the same sea-tossed ship.

It is, accordingly, an easy misunderstanding and a superficial criticism of religion to reduce it to a human "projection," which is Feuerbach's rendering of religion. Or rather, as our citation of Lacan shows, that is a perfectly good criticism of a superficial religion. But it is a failure to see that, more deeply considered, the name of God arises not from a projection but from a projectile coming right at us, a *problema* in the original Greek sense, which literally means something thrown up in our way, a hurdle to be scaled, a barrier to cross, a rock aimed right at our heads. To speak of the insistence of God is to say that God is a *problema*, a provocation, an insistent disturbance, a solicitation, a visitation by a stranger, like a call calling I know not what, or an insistent knock on our door in the middle of the night. That makes prayer an exposure to a projectile, a willingness to stand out in the open in the middle of a storm, where there are projectiles everywhere carried by the wind, hence the extreme opposite of a projection. Levinas calls it a trauma, by which he means not a psychopathic trauma that results in narcissism but an ethical trauma *to* our narcissism, and that is well said.[7] We are too inclined to write off religious trauma as a right-wing tactic meant to scare the faithful with the fear of hell and of apocalyptic destruction and to advocate instead a kind of liberal de-traumatized life. But in radical theology we make room for another trauma, the bracing trauma of the event, of the other person and of everything *tout autre,* which assaults our narcissism and draws us out of ourselves. If the name of God is not causing us a great deal of difficulty, it is not God we are talking about. That at least is so in a theology of "perhaps," a theology radically considered. So it is the more pious theologians who have brought down this criticism on the rest of us. All of us theologians, orthodox and rogue alike, agree that everything depends on God. But for the pious that means it all comes back to the rock of ages, whereas for us rogues it means to watch out for rocks flying at our skulls. It all comes back to a rocky and precarious *peut-être,* meaning it just all depends. To pray, to pray to God, perhaps, is to invoke and call upon, but only because we are first of all provoked and called upon, asked to respond, for better or for worst, to either extreme. Sometimes our response is a disaster. God is trouble.

To put it in a way calculated to rattle the faith of the faithful, to pray to God is to acknowledge that God too is praying, on his or her knees, weeping over the world, as much in need of help, as much in trouble as are the rest of us, praying like mad for a response. That means that when I speak of "prayers and tears," I do not merely mean the prayers and tears of Saint Augustine, or of Jacques Derrida, beautiful as these are, but also God's own tears and prayers. God, too, is praying and weeping over a good outcome for Jerusalem, for the world. I am always writing about prayers and tears, up to and including, especially, the prayers and tears of God. If we go along with the traditional, if suspect, etymology of "religion" as a binding, then in my view religion is a double binding, a double-sided bind, including both God's insistence and our existence. Each is bound to the other, we to God and God to us, each in need of the other, like two lovers who depend upon each other for everything. We and God together, both dependent, both precarious, both in need of prayer, both praying and weeping over the future, over the dead. Abyss calling out to abyss. So if we invoke the name of God, if we call upon God, we call only because we are first called upon by God, each "accused," as Levinas liked to say, each put on the spot, addressed, called out, "interlocuted" (*interloqué*). Accordingly, God needs our help, prays and weeps that we come to the divine aid, as much as we need God's. God's eyes too are blinded by tears, like the women weeping at the foot of the cross. The significance of the double yes, the yes, yes, is that this is both our yes and God's. The yes of the call or the solicitation initiates and is echoed by the second yes of the response. God calls; we respond. This is at the far remove from projection. It is a willingness to be exposed to the worst. It is looking for trouble. Later on (part 3), I will argue that the horizon of trouble is to be widened lest the chiasm become a closed circle, too anthropocentric, too unmindful of the non-human, of the theo-zoological and theo-cosmological.

God is great, God is good. Yes, yes. Perhaps. That is the promise and the risk. It's all quite precarious and God knows how much damage can be done by that kind of talk, which is just as famous for spilling blood as for letting justice flow like water. God *is* great—great trouble, a great question, a great problem. So it all depends. Remember that in Greek *problema* means something that gets in our face, that "puts it to us," poses a task we have to solve, a conflict we have to resolve. To employ a Deleuzian trope, I treat God as a problem—not only for us but for God—to which the world is a solution, a series of solutions, provisional, tentative, throwaway solutions (which in other contexts go under the name "history"). To switch to a Derridean trope, that means the world is "deconstructible," while God, on the other hand, *s'il y en a*, is not deconstructible. That does not mean that God is an Eternal Being, God forbid. It does not even mean that God exists, which gives you an idea of how much trouble besets God. God's problem is that God insists, is an insistent problem that won't go away, that God is in permanent trouble, just like us, and it is up to us to deal with it, since we are the ones who do exist. We are the people of God, the ones assigned or singled out to respond to what is being called for in the name of God. In my vocabulary, the insistence of God means the insistent problem, task, challenge, obstacle, hurdle, question, and barrier that goes under the name of the "event," an idea I keep coming back to, circling around, refining and defining, but without trying to be too confining. The name of God, I keep saying, is the name of the chance of an event, a chance for grace, but that spells trouble, a problem, to which the world, and our being-in-the-world, are a series of shaky solutions.

The denial of God, garden-variety atheism—there are more exotic hybrid forms cultivated by a more advanced horticulture—is the foolishness of thinking that the world is the whole answer where there is no question. The fool says in his heart, there is no question. But on my impious accounting, garden-variety atheism is just the flip side of garden-variety theism, and one is as intolerable, intolerant, and shortsighted as the other. These two combatants, who bear such deep odium for each other, share a common illusion; they both mistake an event for a being, or a Super-being, a ground of Being, beyond or without being, a mighty being that does things, or mysteriously decides not to, an agent-being in the sky, all familiar growths cultivated in pre-Copernican fields. On the "theist" side, those who affirm such an entity; on the "atheist" side, no, no. You get the atheism you deserve, depending on the theism you are serving up, which usually turns out to be God as a projection instead of a projectile. So I cultivate an unorthodox horticulture which prays for an exotic and hybrid species, a new species of theologians practicing a "theology of the event." That means to cause the orthodox a certain amount of trouble because they are sure that this is atheism, while causing no less unhappiness among the infidels who are sure it is theism. If that is so, then the theology of "perhaps" is on to something because it spells perfect trouble to both, slipping and sliding with serpentine skill on the slash between both sides, like a lamb of "perhaps" between the wolves of theism and atheism.

Theism and atheism are symmetric idols, similar contractions of the genuine *problema,* idle distractions when it comes to an insistent God, who has no time for such diversions and is interested in deeds. So I am saying, do not separate the doer from the deed. There are events, events happen, events get themselves said and done, in the middle voice, in and under many names. "Obligation," for example.[8] Or "God," for example. Deeds, like everything else, require a corresponding discourse, which I fit out as a "poetics" of the event that they contain according to the logic and alogic of the possibility of the impossible. But the "God" example is exemplary for me. "God" is a paradigmatic name because it is a paradigm of "perhaps," of the prayers and tears brought on by "perhaps," a name that harbors more insistent trouble than we can imagine or conceive, that than which nothing more troubling and troublesome, nothing more problematizing and problematic can be conceived. "God" is the name of the chance of an event, of an eventiveness of the *peut-être*, an eventiveness that, while often enough traveling under other names, happens with unfailing regularity in "religion" and "theology," which give harbor to the insistence of "God."

THE CHIASM OF INSISTENCE AND EXISTENCE: GOD'S PRAYERS AND OURS

Prayer is the chiasmic intertwining of insistence and existence. In religion, the insistence of God becomes effective, and things get done, but that decidedly does not mean that prayer means asking God to do things for us. The weakness of God means that God is not an agent who does things or fails to. We are the agents and so we are also the ones who fail. God's perfection is that God does not do anything wrong, but that is only because God is not a being who does things in the first place. That does not mean that a great deal does not get done under the name of what is called for in the name of God. Things are done in the middle voice; they get themselves done, and the agents involved are hard to identify. So when I say God is praying, I am speaking of God's calling, God's insistence. When I say that we are praying, I am saying that we are calling upon God and also that we are responding, answering in the name of God, in the name of something, God knows what. Our prayers are our response. God's praying and our praying, God's calling and our responding, God's tears and ours, belong together, are bound together, like a problem and a solution. "Religion" is a chiasm,[9] a mutual ligature (on the old etymology of "*religio*") of God's prayers and ours, each bound to the other, rigorously (the alternate etymology), an intertwining of God's need for us and our need for God, a binding of the precariousness of our existence together with the precariousness of God's insistence, the chiasm of insistence and existence, of inexistence and existents. In prayer, we are made strong by the insistence (or weakness) of God, and the insistence of God is made strong by our existence.

In prayer, the sheer fortuitousness of things is released; the chance of an event is put in play. For Augustine, prayer gives words to our *cor inquietum*, to a restlessness in our hearts, to which I add that it also releases a parallel restlessness in God's own heart. "Come," the paradigmatic prayer, the archi-prayer of which other prayers are inflections, making every season an advent—of something, I know not what. "Come," the deepest confessional, or circumfessional, word we have, cannot be insulated from come-what-may, even as being cannot be insulated from may-being, from come-what-may-being. Prayer is asking God for help while at the same time God is asking us for help, each petition intertwined with the other over the fate of a contingent world. The path of prayer is a two-way street, precarious in either direction. Prayer arises *de profundis,* from a doubly profound discontent, God's and ours. Prayers are sighs issuing from the abyss of being and its discontents, from being made porous by becoming, made to tremble by the event. In what metaphysics imagines to be a perfect world, one in which the distance between insistence and existence has been closed (*per impossibile*), prayer is perfectly unnecessary. Prayer proceeds from a profound suspicion of everything that poses as presupposed, from a suspicion of the whole order of presence, essence, substance, subject, being, truth, with its long legacy of self-legitimation and intimidation. Prayer inches its way to the outside of this order, feeling around its edges, groping in the dark.

In rogue theology—as opposed to de Silentio's rouged theology!—prayer pits itself against the built-in call for pacified tranquility and infinite respect for the order of presence. Camel breeding, Zarathustra called that, while his prayer begins like a lion and ends like a child. I propose a merger of Zarathustra's animals with the animals of Jesus, trying to produce a menagerie of grace and the gift. In such a theo-zoology, prayer is the opposite of letting sleeping dogs lie and it keeps a safe distance from the bulls and bears of an economic exchange. Prayer represents a call for being otherwise, for renewal, for a new and unruly rule, for another and more anarchic "kingdom," for a rule of another kind, another way to be. That is why making such a call can cost people their lives even as the name of God provides our most ancient alibi for murder. God prays and weeps along with us, praying over what is coming, seeking to find a footing in the world, praying for a good outcome, to produce divine effects among all creatures great and small. Prayer emerges from the vertigo of "perhaps," from the tension between hope and threat, between faith and incredulity.

Prayer is the risky business of disturbing the present with the prospect of an unforeseeable future and the memory of an immemorial past, with the chance of the event. Prayer does not close its eyes to the obvious problem that this prospect (literally "fore-sight") and this retrospect have to do with what is precisely unknown, which is what imposes upon us the cruel rule of the "perhaps." Prayer is always blinded by tears, up to and including God's tears, God's blindness. To pray, to pray to God, perhaps, is to embrace, yes, eyes wide open, yes, yes, all the unnerving trouble, all the hope and fear, all the fearing to hope, all the hoping against hope installed in the perhaps and perchance, in the maybe and might be. To pray is to say "come" to what we cannot see coming, none of us, including God. Divine "providence" arises from the assumption that somebody must know what is going on, and if not God, then who? Who, indeed! Suppose no one knows what is going on? That is the event. Is there not an event in God? Is not God an event? Is that not what is going on in that name? Is that not what we always mean? Is that not the genuine subject matter of a theological thinking that is rigorous enough to proceed without the pretense of a visitation by a celestial revelation?

I am always trying to learn how to say "perhaps" and "yes, yes" in one breath, two breaths in one. The primal phenomenon in my conception of prayer is the chance of grace, which is the chance of the event, of the "perhaps." The undecidable fluctuation between grace and chance, between these two gratuities, is the very element of prayer and theology and God. "Perhaps" is the very air of this double breath, the thin air of a weak theology, of prayer and God. In an impious theology such as this, "perhaps" and "may-being" are the very element of God, of the precariousness of God and of the ambiance of prayer, let's say the "quasi-transcendental" field upon which they all sink to their knees, where it is the "quasi-" that spells all the trouble. True transcendentals hold things firm; quasi-transcendentals are open-ended.

The insistence of God is persistent, spreading like a mysterious vapor or dark energy—shall we say specter or a ghost?—that sets things in motion, leaving them ajar, destabilized, "solicited" in the literal sense of shaking (*sollicitare*). The name of God is a provocation and an interruption, venerable but dangerous, healing but quite poisonous, grounding but no less destabilizing, an ancient *arche* but very anarchical. From of old, it has perplexed us and driven us quite mad—with love and justice, with passion and rage, with madness of almost every kind. It gives the urge to kill or to risk being killed a perfect alibi. There is no better way to save the world than with religion, and also no better way to burn it down. The ambiguity and undecidability in this name are not accidental, not a simple slip or fault in an otherwise pure essence that can be cleaned up and eliminated. They are constitutive, built right in, because the name of God—like the name of death—is the name of a limit-state, an extremity, a name in which we are driven to an extreme, a name we call upon *in extremis*. Our faculties are stretched beyond themselves, as Deleuze would say, beyond the possible to the impossible, as Derrida would say. The people of God are, for better or worse, impossible people, people with a taste for the impossible, with a taste for the worst violence and for the most radical justice.

The pious pray for peace and quiet, asking God to make things easy for them, to spare us all this trouble, to make us safe, praying to be relieved of the precariousness of things. They want God to save us, not cause us trouble. But such safety would spare us of God, preventing the event that is harbored by the name of God. They are praying to be spared a visitation from God, in exactly the opposite sense intended in Meister Eckhart's famous prayer (I pray God to rid me of God). I am suggesting something unsafe and out of order, slightly anarchic, hier-anarchical, an-archeological, un-saving. I favor a kind of impious anti-theological theology, with anti-dogmatic doctrines, where infallible institutions and inerrant books are the only heresy, because they contradict the "essence" of God, where God's essence lies in God's insistence. Accordingly, I think of God as a disturbance of the peace. Old Spinoza, following Scotus Eriugena, treated God as a *natura naturans* and *natura naturata,* and that caused both these philosophers considerable trouble in their own lifetimes. But I pursue the experiment of thinking of God as the source of irregularity, of disordered and displaced orders, of God as *natura unnaturans* and of the world as *natura unnaturata.* No one who reads the New Testament slowly would ever come up with a theory that associates God with "natural law," not when irregularity, interruption, and lawless miracle are the very occasion of the appearance of God. God is the force or element in things that interrupts their current drift. If "nature" means the drift (*dérive*) of what is happening (*arriver*), the "event" diverts and sets things adrift. The "event" means what we cannot see coming (*voir venir*), no one, God or human. The name of "God" has the effect of setting things on a new course, of making things new—for better or for worse. "For better or for worse"—the traditional words of the wedding ceremony—is the hallmark of a theology of "perhaps." There is nothing to guarantee that to make things new is to make them better. No one can warrant that the new order will not be a disaster. Indeed what monstrosity has not introduced itself as the "new order"? Nothing can insure us against that. That is why, on my unaccountable accounting, to pray is to invite trouble, to put yourself at risk, to expose yourself to the worst.

The "undecidability" of the name of God means translatability; it means that when we say "God" we might have something else in mind, or that others might have other names for what we do have in mind. But I go farther and say that for "us," for the cultures of the great monotheisms and religions of the Book, who speak in Greek of "theology" and in Christian Latin of "prayer" and "religion," the name of God is the name of undecidability itself, a paradigmatic name of this instability, of all the unstable transitions and unsteady passages that transpire between things, between words and things, between words and other words, between words and deeds. That is the permanent lesson of mystical theology and of the *docta ignorantia*, which is why Derrida says he does not trust anything that does not pass through mystical theology. I am using "perhaps" appositionally, "God, Perhaps" (as in New York City, the Big Apple). "Perhaps" is my candidate in the competition over the divine names, however much a long shot and a dark horse. The God Who Is "Perhaps" itself, provided we can say such a thing, is a way to name the irreducible restiveness of our lives no less than of the restiveness of God's own restless heart. The name of God is the name of an insistent dream and a desire, of a prayer and a tear, God's no less than ours. I say *a* name, not *the* name, not the first, last, or only name. It is only one of many first names in multiple domains, caught as it is in a chain of substitutions from which it can break loose only by ceasing to be a name at all. The name of God is intertwined with every name, with naming itself, where naming means to call for a response, where "come" opens up the field of naming, dreaming, desiring, praying, weeping.[10] "Come" is a first word, a word for words, one of them, at least, just as it is the very form of prayer.

THE BIRTH OF GOD

The chiasm of insistence and existence is not a new idea. It is as old as God. As Angelus Silesius writes:

> *God Does Not Live Without Me*
> I know that God cannot live an instant without me;
> Were I to become nothing, He must give up the Ghost.[11]

Silesius is putting to verse an idea that goes back to Meister Eckhart, who wrote:

> It is God's nature to give, and His being depends on His giving to us when we are under [submissive to Him]. If we are not, and receive nothing, we do Him violence and kill Him.[12]

God needs us to be God, and God's life depends upon it. Otherwise we will all be complicit in killing God. Notice what the "death of God" means in the chiasm: God dies unless we come to God's aid and let God be God in our lives. What has been traditionally called death of God theology is a headline grabber but it is a misleading misnomer—it should have been called the birth of God.[13] God's death does not consist in God becoming human but in *not* becoming human. The death of God means that the insistence of God is a seed sown in rock, that it withers on the vine, that it goes unheeded, that God does not come to exist, that the name of God fails to be the name of a deed and is nothing more than a tinkling cymbal. That is why I never speak of the death of God but of the birth of God or the desire for God (desiring *sans* all that Lacanian lament and lamentation over the lost phallus) and why Eckhart's account of the story of Mary and Martha (ch. 3) is one of the inspirations of my theology of the event, as will become more and more clear as we go along. God is what God does, and what God does is what is done in the name of God, which is the birth of God in the world. The death of God means that God's call goes unheard, is stillborn. The birth of God means the prayers and tears of God gain a hearing in the world and God comes to life in the world, in the people of God, in deeds, in the way the world "worlds," as Heidegger would say. Thus the counterpart of the weakness of God is the responsibility this weakness imposes upon us to be strong, to assume responsibility for ourselves, to take charge of our lives, to answer the call that is issued in the name of God. When God calls, we are put in the accusative, put on the spot, made responsible.

It is interesting to note that, as a historical-exegetical matter, Eckhart's intentions in speaking like this were perfectly orthodox; these were sermons and he was speaking *emphatice*, existentially, to the heart. He had in mind the existential implications of Aquinas's doctrine of sanctifying grace. But the Inquisition was not convinced since, if nothing else, it said that this was a risky way to talk and could lead to misunderstanding when Eckhart was no longer around to explain his good intentions. The Inquisition understood something about the death of the author and the iterability of texts, and, as far as its own institutional self-interests went, it had good reason to be concerned. I am not saying there is anything good about an Inquisition or the death it can bring to authors, but only that the Inquisitors were not stupid. Eckhart's sermons stand at the head of a tradition that leads up to German Idealism, in which there is a "death of God" in a stronger and more literal sense and a great solicitation of orthodoxy to which I will return in later chapters.[14]

As a metonym for the event, the name (of) "God" can happen anywhere, but God *needs us* to happen at all. God calls upon us to let God be God in us, Eckhart says. The responsibility for God's existence falls upon us and has to be cast in the future active participle: it remains to be seen whether God will have been or whether God will be stillborn, whether what will have been will be called God. Does God exist? It remains to be seen. It depends upon the event that is harbored within the name of God and whether we make ourselves worthy of that event or bring shame upon it. We will only be able to determine whether God exists after the fact, that is, whether this name will have brought justice or shame or have made no difference at all. We are not able to see God coming. God must take his chances like the rest of us, *in* the rest of us. We will only be able to tell afterward if God has come. So theology will always be after the fact, and God's providential foresight will all be reconstructed retroactively, after we see what has come, even while the name of God will always contain the inexhaustible reservoir of the unforeseeable to-come. In the meantime—and it is always the meantime—the event that takes place in the name of God is quiet and invisible and it remains to be seen if anything will happen. God's insistence can be heard by anyone with the ears to hear, but God's providence remains to be seen. God's existence is still coming. God's position is a question still in the posing, a problem always being posed, a question put to the world, an insistence that may be resisted.

It all depends, perhaps, *peut-être*. Calls can go unanswered, imperatives can be unheeded, solicitations ignored, promptings repressed, messages lost or misinterpreted, according to Derrida's postal principle, which is here put to work in understanding divine missives and angelic deliveries. Nothing is guaranteed. There is a resistance corresponding to every insistence. Calls can be misunderstood, misheard, misleading, mistranslated, miscommunicated and the results can be a disaster. God's being is as precarious as ours, and we are both praying like mad because of the precarious and iffy being we share, the being of may-being, where *peut-être* is the medium and the message.

The weakness of God becomes strong in the response we make to the event, rather the way that Bonhoeffer called for a "mature" and "religionless" Christianity made mature by human beings who are not waiting for a God to save them; in the way that Kierkegaard said that the name of God is the name of a deed; and in the way that Walter Benjamin said that *we* are the messianic generation, the ones that the dead are waiting for to bring them redemption. The call is only made manifest in the response that is made to it. The response is what exists and bears the only witness we have to what insists.

If God did not need us, as orthodoxy contends, then why is God constantly trying to get in touch with us? If God did not need us, the name of God would not have given rise to so many messages in the mail, to such voluminous scriptures in which we are insistently entreated to fill up what is lacking in the body of God. The "words of God" means God's prayers, in which we come upon God weeping over the world, entreating our help. We are all praying to make ourselves worthy of the events that happen to us, God included, all of us intertwined, all laboring under a spectral and dangerous "perhaps." We and God together, bowing before the same prayer wall, in a remote corner of the universe, bound together like a question and a response, a problem and a resolution. We together are praying and weeping for the coming of the Messiah, for something, I know not, something or someone none of us can see coming.

A chiasm woven from a double prayer, a double binding, and tears redoubled where the meaning of prayer, and God, and "coming" are all interwoven with "perhaps." Come, for better or worse. Yes, yes, perhaps. *Viens, oui, oui.* To pray is to enter an abyss of provocation and perchance, where God's abyss is our abyss, a double abyss, in which no one can see what is coming.

If I were ever invited to be a guest curator of an exhibition meant to honor a theology of "perhaps," I would announce a collection of representations of Jesus weeping over Jerusalem (Luke 19:41–42).

THREE

INSISTENCE AND HOSPITALITY
Mary and Martha in a Postmodern World

Now as they went on their way,
he entered a certain village,
where a woman named Martha
welcomed (hypedexato) *him into her home.*
—LUKE 10:38

"COME"

The name of God is the name of trouble. The insistence of God means that God calls for a response or, since God is not somebody who "does" things like call, it means that the calling takes place in the middle voice, in and under the name of God. God calls in the middle voice. The call is perfectly figured in an unexpected and insistent knocking on our door. A disturbing visitation in the night is an uncertainty in which all the sting of "perhaps" is perfectly concentrated, in which the dynamics of "perhaps" and a theology of insistence is both modeled and put in play. Hospitality means to say "come" in response to what is calling, and that may well be trouble. We might say that hospitality is an example of an event, but if so it is an exemplary one, a paradigm, maybe even a surname for any and every event, which can come at any moment, like a wayfarer in need of a cup of cold water unless, perhaps, he is a thief in the night. As an ancient virtue in the Bible, where the very life of the desert traveler depended upon being made welcome, hospitality cuts deeply into the fabric of the biblical name of God, where the invisible face of God is inscribed on the face of the stranger, as if God were looking for shelter. Well beyond its status as a particular virtue, hospitality is a figure of the event, a figure of the chiasm of insistence and existence, of call and response.

Hospitality means welcoming the other, saying "come" to the other. But as Derrida's well-known analysis shows, normally it ends up meaning welcoming the same, inviting a short list of insiders while discretely keeping the uninvited (the other) in the dark. Hence instead of "inviting" the same, what Derrida calls "unconditional" hospitality can only be found in an unexpected "visitation" by the other, by the *tout autre*, that is, taking a chance on the event, which may be trouble. Hospitality in its paradigmatic sense requires putting ourselves at risk instead of creating a closed circle of friends (the same). It is the effect of a visitation by the *hostis*, the "stranger," who might be hostile. Hospitality, like the chiasmic insistence of God— or is it the other way around?—means to say "come" to what we cannot see coming, to what may or may not ("perhaps") be welcome, to welcome the unwelcome, which is why Derrida coined the word "hosti-pitality,"[1] and Jesus said that it is easy to love our friends but loving our enemies can be dicey.

The inability to identify the one who is coming, who may perhaps be here to do us harm, and to predict or control this coming is not a passing problem with hospitality that will hopefully be corrected at a later time. It belongs to the very structure of insistence. That failure to be certain is not a failure but a "negative capability," a power to sustain uncertainty that structures the insistence of hospitality. The "come" of hospitality and the "come" of prayer are isomorphic; in both cases, "come"—like the "yes" of a vow—is addressed to what we cannot see coming. If things had greater clarity and security and a more certain outcome, we would not need to make vows or to pray or, better, we would be unable to, as the vow and the prayer would suffocate with self-complacency. If there were no events there would be nothing to promise, nothing to pray for, nothing to which, for which, or in the name of which to say, "come." Just so, the uninvited knock at the door could be trouble, and the "could be," the "perhaps," is constitutive and irreducible. The non-knowing is the more radical side of mystical theology that has always unnerved the churches.

The insistence of God is the opposite of a Platonic model of piety, which turns on the preexistence of God, the presupposition and prepossession of God, instead of an abrupt visitation. In Platonism we have merely forgotten what we are calling for and the knock at the door simply serves as an aid to recalling, the occasion of the recollection of what we always already possess, reactivating the re-union of a primordial union that has been temporarily interrupted. As Kierkegaard's Johannes Climacus pointed out, "midwifery" is a pagan model, not a biblical model.[2] It is one of the most pacifying theories in the history of philosophy, which all of Aristotle's instincts rightly resisted. In the theory of recollection and all its variations, there are no events, which is why Kierkegaard opposed recollection to what he called "repetition forwards" and Deleuze tried to reinvent another and amazing version of Platonism under the name of repetition.

In recollection, nothing would be truly at risk, nothing uncertain, strange, uncanny, unnerving—and consequently nothing "new" would "happen." There would be no events, no ghosts. If you say "come" and you comprehend it, if you know whom you are addressing, then it is not God, not a stranger, not a risk, not trouble. If you can see it coming, Derrida said, it is not an event. If you already know who is on the other side of the door, it is not hospitality, or only half. If you can foresee the future, it is already present, only the future present, not the absolute future. I hasten to add that, while I take the name of "God" in the cultures of the great monotheisms to have paradigmatic value, I am also saying this name is an artifact, a constituted effect, of those cultures. "God" does not have exclusive rights to this property.[3] *Tout autre est tout autre.*

The trouble with hospitality, the trouble that is hospitality, is its commerce with the possible, and the trouble with the possible is its commerce with the impossible. To say "come" to the ("merely") possible is to play with dice loaded in our favor. Things only get interesting when we come up against the insistence of the impossible. Things really happen *by* the impossible.[4] Hospitality kicks into high gear (is "unconditional") when it is impossible, when we suffer a visitation *by* the impossible, that is, we are asked to welcome the unwelcome; otherwise we are just admitting the same. Jesus's favorite example was love, which comes to a head when we are asked to love the unlovable. Kierkegaard's example was faith, which acquires teeth when it means to believe the unbelievable (the absurd). Paul said hope means hoping against hope. To be sure, I am not calling for stupidity but for a judgment that is willing to take a risk. I am not saying that we have to open the door every time someone knocks, to say yes to everything that happens. That would simply result in another rule which would avoid the responsibility required to respond to the singularity of the event. As Derrida says, sometimes the only way to keep the future open, the only way to say yes to the future, is to say no to this or that.[5]

These are all so many fetching variations on the "possibility of the impossible," which is perhaps as good a way as any to describe what we mean by "God," by the insistence of God, by the event visited upon us in and under that name. The possibility of the impossible is both a biblical and a Derridean trope. The Bible refers to an almighty super-existent, and in Derrida it refers to an insistence, a weak force without existential punch. The impossible is the trace of God in a theology of "perhaps." Where there is the impossible, there is God (for better or for worse). The "perhaps" that trembles in the name of God is the might and may-being of the impossible. The "come" that is common to both prayer and hospitality is made possible by exposing the serene horizon of the possible to the obscene shock of the impossible. The "come" is not possible without putting oneself "out," outside, exposed to the danger, to the stranger who shatters the horizon of the familiar. The first words of prayer are yes, yes, *oui, oui,* come, amen. But that is risky business. It could perhaps be trouble. When to resist what is strange? When to welcome it? That's the thing, the issue, the *Sache*—there is no formula by which to tell. That is the chance of the event. Although welcoming the stranger involves a certain death to the self-same, it need not mean certain death, pure and simply. Hospitality is not supposed to be just plain suicide. I do not deny that. I just deny that there is a program that will decide for us which is which, a formula for the chance of an event. We do not have the software yet to make this decision for us, to monitor the chaosmic play of the "perhaps." That's the *Sache* of my thinking, *s'il y en a.*

I am tempted to say that "come" is the first word in a theology of the insistence of God. But if "come" comes first, it is because it comes second, in response to an insistent knock on the door. The first word is already an answer, an *Ant-wort,* made in response to an address. In the beginning is the *Ant-wort,* rather the way the rabbis like to point out that the first letter in Genesis, "in the beginning," is the second letter (*B, bet, beta, bereshit*). "Come" comes in response to the beckoning of what is "to come," which is unforeseeable. "Hosti-pitality" means that the *hostis,* the stranger, the unknown, however it is translated, may be a friend or foe, a traveler in search of lodging or a rogue. The stranger is both a venerable figure and dangerous, risky business, putting the circle of the same at risk. Without the risk, it is just more of the same. The stranger is maddening, trouble, like God; undecidable, like God. Are strangers and undecidability figures of God? Or is God, perhaps, a figure of the undecidability of the stranger, of openness to the other? Of the irreducible riskiness that is built into things, of the "perhaps," which is the condition of possibility and impossibility of moving forward. *Tout autre est tout autre*—that is my candidate for the postmodern contribution to the medieval list of transcendentals, my version of the *aliquid.*[6] Each and every thing is a something, is constituted by I-know-not-what singularity, a this-ness (*haecceitas*) or strangeness, which is the seat of the spell it casts upon us and what sends us all falling to our knees, God included.

What we call in Christian Latin "religion" may be thought of as offering hospitality to God, answering to what is going on in the name of God, making room for God, welcoming God, receiving God, and then keeping our fingers crossed. Think of God as a divine stranger who needs food, shelter and clothing, where the insistence of God is in need of our assistance. Hospitality is not a character trait of the pious, not just a virtue to be cultivated, or one of several virtues, but the field in which everything we do transpires. Hospitality describes not a particular part but the very structure or movement of life, not our "essence" but the explanation for why every attempt to prescribe our essence is always already outstripped. Essence is undone by insistence, which is why existence is never merely a matter of actualizing a formula prescribed by essence.

MARY AND MARTHA AS POSTMODERN HOSTS

I am not just making all this up. This is not just all of my own devising, the issue of an overexcited imagination. I am just repeating what Meister Eckhart says, whom I will call upon as my authority and a witness for the defense if I am called before the Inquisition (since he has experience in such matters). The Meister was a master of the insistence of the event, which means, of course, that he provides a magisterial account of our lack of mastery in the face of the unforeseeable.

Meister Eckhart famously said, I pray God to rid me of God.[7] That is one of the most famous prayers ever made, one of the most radical, and also one of the greatest contributions to the poetics of "perhaps" and a theology of trouble, which in turn visited upon Meister Eckhart himself quite a great deal of trouble. The court theologians viewed this disturbing saying with Inquisitorial alarm. But this was the peculiar piety of a master of impious sayings. He was earnestly praying, asking the God who can never be mastered and domesticated, the one we can never see coming, to rid us of the God whom we think we have in our sights, under our control. I pray the God whose coming is always the coming of the stranger to rid me of the God who serves to keep guard over the circle of the same.[8] I pray the God who exposes me to trouble to rid me of the God who keeps me safe, who functions as a guarantor of tranquility and order. I pray the groundless ground of the "perhaps" to rid me of the rock-solid ground of the certain and foreseeable (which is what "providence" literally means). It is not hard to see what made the "Curia" curious, what it found so unnerving in the nervy sermons of Meister Eckhart, who was a master of a very nervy hermeneutics. As the Meister liked to say, "I go further" and I say that this prayer is God's own prayer, that God, too, is striving to be rid of God and to break through to the divine abyss. The insistence of God means that God too is asking to be rid of the God of peace and quiet.

Meister Eckhart said, "I have begun with a few words in Latin that are written in the Gospel; and in German this means: 'Our Lord Jesus went up into a little town, and was received by a virgin who was a wife.'"[9] As usual, Meister Eckhart, who was not a Fundamentalist, takes some liberties with his text, which reads in the more prudent translation of the New Revised Standard Version: "Now as they went on their way, he entered a certain village, where a woman named Martha welcomed [*hypedexato*] him into her home" (Luke 10:38). Luke is telling the story of Mary and Martha, widely treated in the Middle Ages as an allegory of the contemplative life and the active life. By the little town, Eckhart says, the Gospel means the soul itself, the ground of the soul, which must make itself ready for God's arrival, for the coming of God, for the event of God's advent. An advent takes place on the plane of the event. Whatever the liturgical season, Meister Eckhart's sermons are all "Advent" sermons, which take as their subject the advent of God into the soul, the birth of the Son in the soul, and hence the readiness of the soul for this coming.

Advent takes place on the plane of the "event," of the insistence of God, which Eckhart stages as a scene of the hospitality the soul extends to God. For Eckhart, advent is a double event, a double birth, both God's and the soul's: the advent of God in the soul is the birth of the Son in the soul and the rebirth of the soul in the Son, with the result that if we block this event, we kill God, by cutting off God's birth, and we kill the soul, by cutting off its rebirth. That, as I said above, is my complaint with the vocabulary of the "death of God" theologians, who need to consider becoming birth-of-God theologians. In my vocabulary the death of God would mean the desistence of insistence, the resistance to insistence, the refusal to come to its assistance. So God needs the soul, needs a little town in which to be born, even as the soul needs God. Both God and the soul are on the way to the little town, *unterwegs,* Heidegger would say, in order to be born and reborn. God's birth is the soul's rebirth. It is a double birth, a double event, a double prayer, a double yes. So I read the story of Mary and Martha not merely as an allegory of contemplation and action but as an allegory of the chiasmic intertwining of the insistence of God with existence.

Eckhart's reading of this famous story is unorthodox and defamiliar-izing. Not fearing to contradict Jesus's literal assertion (in the Middle Ages, a literal reading is but one of several ways to read the scriptures) that Mary has chosen the better part—traditionally taken to be the gift of divine contemplation from which Martha allows herself to be distracted by her worldly duties (Luke 10:41–42)—Eckhart paradoxically privileges Martha over Mary on the grounds that Martha has a double gift. Martha is busy about the many works, the many material things—meals, clean linens, a swept house—that are needed to welcome Jesus and make him comfortable (*vita activa*). Her attention to these duties is not a distraction, Eckhart says, but a gift she enjoys beyond Mary who has only one gift, who knows only how to languish at the master's feet (*vita contemplativa*). Mary only understands God as peace and the promise, but she does not come to grips with unrest and threat. She is the beautiful soul who lingers over the beauty of God's insistence. But when Jesus says, "Martha, Martha," Eckhart claims that is a mystical symbol that Jesus secretly prefers Martha's world because Martha understands that the name of God is the name of a deed. Martha has two gifts to Mary's one. Mary has the gift of hearing God's insistence, but Martha knows that insistence requires existence, so she utters a double yes, *viens, oui, oui.* Martha seeks peace, as does Mary, but Martha also knows that peace comes packaged with trouble. Martha knows that to ask for Jesus to come is to call for peace and accept trouble, both the promise and the threat, and that peace cannot be purchased separately. Martha knows that the insistence of God is not merely to be savored at the feet of Jesus but urgently requires our assistance, the assistance that translates God's insistence into existence. Mary savors the name of God, which is edifying but still languishing in inexistence, while Martha responds, which actualizes God's birth and the soul's rebirth, which are one and the same. In Martha, God happens with all the robustness of mundane existence. She knows that if Jesus is coming there is food to prepare, a house to be cleaned, because Jesus is a not a heavenman but a man of flesh and blood with human needs. There is a realism and materialism in Martha that is missing from Mary's beautiful immaterialism that is never made real, and Jesus secretly prefers her materialism. Martha's world is real and existing, while Mary's world is world-less, free from the cares of the world, an inexistent worldlessness.

Martha is an emblem for me, a figure in whom all the dynamics of the event, of the insistence of the event, are contracted, and I will come back to her throughout this study, especially in the third part. At this point it would suffice to say Martha recognizes that Jesus has human needs, which if we are frank are animal needs. So now we reach a delicate zoo-theological point, scandalous to our sensitivities. Jesus has not only animal companions but animal needs because, after all, Jesus is an animal, a human animal to be sure, but it is the animality that Jesus assumes that is the scandal of the Incarnation and the scandal by which Martha is not offended. So Martha is a figure of hospitality in its most elemental form, as hospitality to the flesh, in all its weakness. By the weakness of the flesh I mean that while the "body" is an active and transparent agent, easily forgotten or lost sight of because of the ease with which it navigates about the world, "flesh" draws attention to itself, for better or for worse, in sickness and in health, in *jouissance* and suffering. Flesh is opaque and burdensome, a site of strain and difficulty, constantly calling attention to itself, and however glorious quite inglorious. The many weaknesses of the flesh—from our most humble animal needs to incapacity, disability, disease, and death—co-constitute the life of flesh; they do not contradict it. The weaknesses of the flesh intensify life, raising its pitch to the limits. They do not refute the provocation of God but constitute so many occasions for the invocation of the name of God, so many invitations to respond to the name of God, where the name of God means to say yes to life in all its tumult and difficulty, joy and sorrow, promise and risk.

That is why it makes perfect sense to speak of a "disabled God" (Eiesland), or a "mortal God" (Derrida), of "the body of God" (McFague), or of a "suffering God" (Bonhoeffer), or even of the God of "indecent theology" (Althaus-Reid). Difficulty, disability, indecency, disease, and death itself are features of life, part of the way the multiple forms of life are etched, part of its dance, and not a lasting punishment for a fateful exercise of bad judgment in Eden, not the "residue of Eden," as Sharon Betcher describes Augustine's woeful misunderstanding of disabilities.[10] They no more constitute refutations of life than they constitute contradictions of the divine nature or attributes incompatible with the divine being requiring the urgent attention of theodicy. For God is God as *natura unnaturans et unnaturata*. They are not a fall, or a sign of a fallen life, but life *in extremis*, so many twists and turns of life, bearing witness to the extremity of the event, the event of excess and exceeding that is discharged in and under the name of God and that commands our response. The idea behind the theology of hospitality to the event is to make ourselves worthy of the events that happen to us, however humbling and disabling they may seem to be. "For better or for worse" is the inscrutable and uncircumventable equation, the unavowable vow of our marriage to the flesh of the world, to the world of the flesh, where "flesh" is both the substance and the figure of this nonstable matrix, this autodeconstructive and autopoetic and primal pool.

Eckhart introduces another interesting chiasm in this sermon. The soul in a state of radical prayer (who impiously prays God to rid her of God) is said to be both a "virgin" and "wife," which is an aporia that Amy Hollywood has explored with great resourcefulness in reference to the Beguines to whom Eckhart preached and from whom he learned a thing or two.[11] By a "virgin," Eckhart means that in order to receive God into its home the soul must be pure of all attachments, not only to worldly paraphernalia like wealth and power, but even to religious paraphernalia. By the latter he means what I have been calling piety, the pieties of religion, the pieties of the prescribed prayers, ascetic practices, fastings and vigils, to which I would add the paraphernalia of creedal and doctrinal assertions, which can deprive the soul of its purity and freedom for God just as surely as can worldly concerns.[12] So virgin purity signifies religion without religion. But the purity of the virgin side must be intertwined with the fruitfulness of the wife, with a life of works and with all the accompanying trouble of giving birth. The soul as virgin has an inner purity of intention; the soul as wife has an outer fruitfulness born of an intercourse with the world. The soul must work like Martha, like a busy and fruitful wife, while also and at the same time being pure of attachment to its own works. Its sole interest lies not in being applauded for its prayerful pieties but in exposing itself to the advent of Jesus, to his coming, come what may. But, in virtue of Eckhart's doctrine of the chiasmic event of the birth of God in the soul and the rebirth of the soul in God, whatever happens on the side of the soul must also happen on the side of God. God too must divest himself of his divine properties and names, like "his" and "creator" and even "God" itself, stripping the divine being to the nudity and inexistence of the Godhead, in order to release the event of the birth of the Son from the divine abyss, coming into existence in the soul, in the world. God must be stripped of existence in order for the divine inexistence to bear fruit in the world. Abyss joins to abyss in the birth of God. God must be reduced to the inexistence of the call, to the virgin purity of insistence, which calls for a response in the order of existence, to be born in the world.

No matter what the official calendar in Christendom may say, in the kingdom of God it is, as a structural matter, always Advent, the advent of the event, preparing our hospitality for the event without adorning ourselves with the pieties of religion and ascetic practices. The sermon concludes with a perfect advent prayer, "That we may be a little town into which Jesus may come and be received . . . may God help us to this. Amen." In my unauthorized translation this reads, *Viens, oui, oui.*

HOSPITABLE AGENCY

Eckhart's interpretation of Martha as both virgin and wife lays to rest the familiar objection that mysticism is a form of quietism and that religion is lost in the unreal and immaterial, a point to which I return in part 3. It is important is to see that Martha works not of herself, out of her own autonomy and resources—there is a sustained critique of the "humanism" of the "ego" in Eckhart—but in collaboration with God, whom the soul has received into its ground. That corresponds to what Derrida calls the decision of the other in me. Martha's work is a response, already coming second, as a second yes, responding to the coming of Jesus into the little town. Martha's word is first of all an answer, an *Antwort*. It is first of all second.

We must be clear that the insistence of God does not imply that God is an agent who calls, prays, insists, or *does* anything. The insistence of God means that God is a solicitation or provocation, not an agent, because agents take the form of Martha: they respond to provocations, making the decision of the other in me. The provocation of God, then, takes place in the middle voice, and the only thing that is manifest, the only thing we can see, is the response. That is the philosophical wisdom and realistic concession behind the adage "God helps those who help themselves." A strong theology, a theology of an agent-God, requires ventriloquists, people, up to now almost invariably men, who authorize themselves to speak in the name of God. Strong theology is a megaphonic device used by men to amplify their voice and to disguise their human all too human will as the will of God. In a theology of the insistence of God, the theology of an entirely new species of theologians, agency is left to actual, mundane, and identifiable agents, whom no one should confuse with God and who, above all, should not confuse themselves with God. There is no more salutary offspring of the theology of events than the recognition that it is human beings who claim to do things in the name of God, which is why the history of religion is inevitably also a history of violence. It is the very essence of the mythic, the magical, the mystifying to treat an event as an entity, to treat the insistence of God as an existing agent, an acting being, even and especially the First or Highest Being. It is a mystification to treat God as an Über-being with mysterious powers to do things which to the "infidels" are the doings of more mundane powers. In a theology of "perhaps," we side with the infidels and we think the true faith requires more infidelity and less mystification.

We take as a model the agency of Martha, the wife who was a virgin. Martha acts, but she acts from the ground of the soul, which is one with the ground of God. That means she is an agent mobilized in response to a provocation, to an event, who gives existence to an insistence, and that existence takes the form of the most material and quotidian reality. That is figured in the language of deconstruction as the decision of the other in me. It is figured in Meister Eckhart in the images borrowed from both the Christian narrative (the birth of the Son) and Neoplatonism, where the action of the soul proceeds from the unity of the ground of the soul with the ground of God. The virgin part of the soul (the Neoplatonic discourse) is to keep ourselves free from the illusion of an autonomous subject—that is the critique of the humanist subject—while the wifely part (the Christian discourse) is to replace it with a responsible subject, an agent who gives birth to and incarnates the Son in the world. Action is the agency of the other in me, a hospitable agency, as when Paul says, I live now not I but Christ lives in me. Just so, Christ lives now not in himself, in eternity, but in me. If the Christic is a chiasmic figure, as I treat it, then the soul needs Christ and Christ needs the soul in order to live and move and be. Pantheism says that our existence is God's. Panentheism says that God's existence is *in* ours and ours in God's. But in a theology of "perhaps," God does not exist; God insists, and it is our responsibility to bring about something that exists.

Agency is responsibility to the insistence of the event, and a failure of responsibility is resistance thrown up to the event, inhospitality to the event. If the name of God is the name of an event, theology is a caretaker of the event, entrusted with the cultivation of the eventiveness of that name. God is not a powerful doer and mysterious undoer but the power-less power of the event. That is why it is futile to blame God for doing us wrong and unnecessary to exonerate God's ways before human courts. It is human beings who belong in human courts, human beings who are capable both of attacking and defending the stranger in the name of God. In the ambiguity of this unstable middle, across the uneven plane of immanence, the proportionately ambiguous power of agency and freedom makes its wary way. The hoary theological "problem of evil" thus has nothing to do with all the choices that a sovereign omnipotent and omniscient God could have made but failed to make, thereby leaving us in our present sorry and befuddled state. The problem of evil has to do with the ambient and chaotic play of ambiguous beings, an ambience beyond mere ambiguity, since our choices rarely boil down to two. The ambience of our being is its greatest if riskiest resource.

EVENTS: GOD CAN HAPPEN ANYWHERE

The insistence of God is the chance that God can happen anywhere. The insistence of God is the inexistence of God, but the existence of God is liable to break out at any time, in great and world-historical events, like Paul on the road to Damascus, and in the smallest things, like the rose that blossoms unseen. No one can see God coming, including God. The insistence of God is a metonym or surname for the event, and the existence of God a metonym or surname for the response to the event. By "the event," which is the motivating idea in everything I say, I mean the advent of what we cannot see coming. Events break out (*e-venire*), break in (*in-venire*), and interrupt the course of things. When something comes, something unexpected, that is the advent of the event and that is the Derridean side of the event. But events also have a Deleuzean side. Events, Deleuze says, are not what happens but what is going on *in* what happens.[13] I have no interest in staging a contest between Derrida and Deleuze. I am running these two senses together when I speak of the insistence of God. When the unforeseeable breaks in and interrupts the course of things (the Derridean sense of event), that means that the event hitherto simmering as a virtuality (the Deleuzean sense) has broken out, meaning the possibility of the impossible just broke out (Deleuze) or just broke in (Derrida). "Breaking out" (*e-venire*) means that names contain events for Deleuze as virtualities that may irrupt. "Breaking in" (*in-venire*) means that names contain events for Derrida that may interrupt, as promises of something coming or calling that may take us by surprise. These two work together. For example, if I speak of the democracy to come, of the promise of democracy (Derrida), that means there is something virtual simmering *in* what we today call democracy (Deleuze), something getting itself promised in the middle voice, that solicits us from afar. When Deleuze speaks of a virtuality, Derrida speaks of a promise.[14] Either way, names contain what they cannot contain, irrupting from and interrupting anything that tries to contain them. God can break in or break out anywhere. *Tout autre est tout autre.* When I say that names "harbor" events, I am bringing Deleuze and Derrida together instead of pitting them against each other. Events are expressed in names and realized in things for Deleuze, which is why we are never imprisoned by names but always already delivered over by them to the virtualities stirring within them. Things are never simply, baldly, and immediately "given" but always already named, interpreted, construed (the hermeneutics of events). Radical thinking—including radical theological thinking—is conducted on the plane of the event, on an anonymous quasi-transcendental field, a primal khoral, ankhoral site of movement and rest, life and death, joy and suffering, friend and foe, on a groundless ground, shaken, shocked, solicited.

For the new species of theologians of which I dream, to "think" the name of God means to expose ourselves to the insistence of the event that is contained in that name, to give it its head, all the while eluding the police of "religion." The confessional orthodoxies seek to head off the event, not to welcome but to domesticate it, to fence in the anarchic and aphoristic energy of this name, to police the event by means of normalizing propositions, books, councils, and institutional forces with considerable political muscle, and to use it to their own ends. To no avail—which is why orthodox theology is *also* a veritable breeding ground of radical theology. For the name of God is not subsistent but insistent. It contains what it cannot contain, contains the uncontainable, like the *Khora akhoraton* (a figure of Mary, the mother of God), which is not purely and simply isolable from *Khora* pure and simple, the nameless name in the *Timaeus*. That is why I use the word "theology" while always qualifying it impudently— calling what I do "weak" or "radical" or "rogue" theology or a theology of "perhaps," all meant to torture the word half to death while offering me protection from the police of piety. When I say theology, I am trying to rewrite orthodoxy's favorite word and produce something impious. I am not interested in "religion" in the sense that Meister Eckhart warns us against—fasting and vigils and observances and doctrines—which is why I speak of religion without "religion." I am not finally interested in "religion" but in God. I go further: I am not interested in God but in the name of God. I go still further: I am not interested in the name of God but in the event that insists in the name of God. For the name of God, as dangerous as it is saving, as life-giving as it is death-dealing, contains the uncontainable event of a provocation and a promise, which leaves us hanging on by a prayer, left without a prayer, which is the only way to pray. I pray God to rid me of God, of what I expect God to be. I pray for the coming of the event promised and provoked by the name of God. I go further still: even God is not interested in "God." God too is praying to be rid of God, insisting on becoming God without God.

In a theology of the event, the name of God is inscribed on the plane of the event, like a figure in the sand, like a cloud in the sky, or even like a form inscribed by the Demiurge in khoral space. As the name of an event, God can happen anywhere. The name of God is entangled with the course of mundane life, with the rhythm of its joys and fears, with the terrors of the night and the exaltations of the day, which is not to say that it is any less inscrutable, any less a matter of an absolute secret, any less *tout autre*.

The insistence of God spells the end of the spell that the figures of "transcendence" and "eternity" have cast over religion. The insistence of God enables and disables the classical distinction between transcendence and immanence. What theology was searching for under the figure of the "transcendence" of God—"transcendence" is not a bad word!—as a force arching over or "crossing beyond" the world, is here redescribed as a modality *of* the world, an unforeseeable worlding of the world, as a way the world catches us up in its sweep, makes itself felt in all its intensity.

Transcendence is not the opposite of immanence but another way to con-figure the plane of immanence, another way the lines of force that traverse the field of immanence are redrawn, intensified and made salient, the way the plane of immanence is bent or warped. Such transcendence can hap-pen anywhere—in Eros or art, in politics or everyday life, in the transcen-dence of the exceptional or the quotidian.[15] What is coming is not another world but another coming *of* the world, another worlding of the world, a coming otherwise. Transcendence is the insistence or the promise of the world. This promise, as Derrida says, which represents a kind of constitu-tive disorder, is not a speech act or any kind of anthropological or egologi-cal effect. "It is not in the world, because the world 'is' (promised) in the promise, according to the promise. It is not a promise of man to God or of God to man, nor of man (as being in the world) to himself, but the finite promise *of* the world, as world."[16]

"Transcendence" describes in my vocabulary the way a horizon of fore-seeability is shattered by the coming of the unforeseeable. It is another way of running up against the impossible, up against the possibility of the impossible, against its limits. In transcendence the distinctive forces of immanence are shattered, pushed to the limit, underlined, figured, and this shows up in limit-words and limit-cases, like God and death, *tout autre*. It is the world that transcends us.[17] Transcendence is a category of the world, a mundane species, a particular mode of transpiring on what is called in metaphysics the plane of immanence, in virtue of which the flow of immanence intensifies and forces itself to the surface. The figures of transcendence, which readily assume the form of literature or mythol-ogy, of dreams or desires, are ways of retracing the lines of the world in imaginative form, ways of reclaiming the world in all its richness and inten-sity. Such a "reversal" of transcendence into a promise of the world, as I am describing it here, invites the consequent "displacement" of the binar-ity of immanence and transcendence, meaning we need a new vocabulary because this one is dualistic and distortive of mundane existence.

Just so, I treat the "eternity" of God as a figure of a radical temporality. The insistence of the event issues from a certain recess, is nestled among the obscure secrets of the world, from the secretive time of the world, which I describe as the stirring of twofold retreat. On one side, a withdrawal into a past that was never present, into time immemorial, and on the other a withholding from the present of an unforeseeable future. The present thus is doubly displaced, doubly stretched out, pulled apart in opposing direc-tions, opened by opposing forces. The present is thereby structured by the unpresentable so that by the present we mean the space that is opened

You mean late too

up between two unpresentables. On one side, the present is drawn out of itself by the invitation of something promised, and on the other end it is drawn out of itself by the solicitation of something immemorial that has all along been stirring. Not time and eternity, not this world and some other sphere where time does not flow, but two modalities of time, two ways time temporalizes, two ways the world "worlds," to deploy a couple of early Heideggerianisms. Time is co-constituted by a structural too late and too early. Coiled like a serpent within the settled time of the present there stirs the unsettled and unsettling time which is out of joint, which disjoins the world, which prevents the closure of the world, which the metaphysical-theological imagination confuses with the eternal or other worldly.

One might say that this disjuncture creates an opening for the event, except that the event is the event of the disjuncture, the disruptive force of which is contracted into the notion of the insistence of God, which means that God can break in or break out anywhere. The disjuncture is the space-time of the provocation, where what is provocative is the event. That is why, *pace* Heidegger's famous analysis of the Anaximander fragment, Derrida locates justice in a disjunction, making justice's place a certain dislocation.[18] As with justice so with God, with the insistence of God, which is an interruption, a solicitation, a promise, occurring in a disjunction or dislocation. Disjoining is the work of the event, which does not mean what the event "does," but the way the event opens the space in which things get themselves done. The "axiom" of any hauntology of the event, were such a thing possible, is that when it comes to events, to be is to provoke. Events are not present, but what is provocative about what is present. The tendency of the settled present is to prevent the event while the tendency of prayer is to evoke the event. We would not say that the event is, but that the event provokes. We would not say that God is but that God calls, constituting a provocation that the confessional religions instantiate in some Hyper-being or other, which is the business of the confessional imaginations and no business of ours. The event is not what happens but what is going on in what happens, what is provocative about what happens. The provocation means that we can never see God coming. God can happen anywhere. Even God cannot see God coming.

THE GRAMMATOLOGY OF ASSENT

The insistence of God requires its own grammar or grammatology, all the oblique and indirect resources of language, like the middle voice and the subjunctive and the adverbial. This book is caught in the tension between using "perhaps" adverbally and mentioning it nominally, which of course substantivizes it, making insistence into an essence. So while I have been speaking of the provocative possibility that the name of God contains, we must not forget that every name harbors a provocation and a promise, which is why any and every name is deconstructible. Furthermore, it is also important to remember that this talk of "names" is not meant to privilege nouns or even verbs. Following the advice of Meister Eckhart, who says we must make ourselves "adverbs" of the Word (God), I have made the very subject matter of this book an adverb, "perhaps," while trying to avoid turning it into a substance or a subject. I am arguing that whether we treat God as a noun or a verb (*ipsum esse*), a substantive or a process, everything turns on the "how," on the adverbial "perhaps," which is an attribute of an attribute, a mode of modalizing adjectives, nouns, and verbs, disturbing their tranquility, making room for qualities, degrees, manners, circumstances, conditions, and exceptions. My love of adverbs follows an ancient proverb, "God is a rewarder of adverbs not of nouns," meaning of the how not the what.[19] To this I add that the inquiry made by thinkers such as Levinas and Marion into the role of prepositions is indispensable. Nor should we overlook Michel Serres, who says that angels operate as our prepositions.[20] These all belong to an irregular grammar of assent, to a general grammatology of saying yes to the event, which is an inflection of a standard-form grammar of substantives.

That is also why I have been emphasizing the middle voice as a resource to displace supernatural agency.[21] It is also why I insist that the insistence of God occurs in the subjunctive. We might say, following the dizzying exchange between Cixous and Derrida,[22] that prayer, the "come" we address to "God," prayer as the call for the coming of the event, turns on the undecidable play of the "might," the suggestive slippage from the powerful "might" of God, the power of God almighty, to the powerless power of the "might" as in "might be" or it "might have been," which requires our collaboration. The insistence of God belongs to the power of suggestion, not in the sense of a psychoanalytic reduction of this name to a trick of the unconscious, but in the sense of a suggestive or subjunctive force, the power of a possibility or a perhaps, of an invitation or solicitation. It is why Derrida prefers the performative to the constative, or rather the per*verf*ormative to the performative: the name of God is the name of perverformation. To adapt a Deleuzeanism, we ought to ask not what God 'means' but how we are to play it.

The insistence of God is expressed in a grammatological slippage from the indicative to the subjunctive mood. This is the mood grammarians call the *modus irrealis,* not because it is unreal but because it would like to be real, what we would like or love to believe (from *lieben*), where to believe is literally to be-love. "Irreal" here means a non-reality restless about becoming real, an inexistence that insists on existing. That is why I like to think of deconstruction not as anti-realist but as hyper-realist, a point to which I will return in chapters 9 and 10. Weak theology, like deconstruction, should be written in the subjunctive, because it is all about subjunctions, modifications of the ontological into the "hauntological," spirit-seeings which include the de-ontological, the me-ontological and the pre-ontological, every possible mode, manner, or strategy available to us to deflect and inflect the ontological into the spectral. The insistence of God belongs grammatically in the subjunctive, which subverts the settled nominations and conjunctions of the present.

However maddening this theology, however strange the look of this new species of theologians, however bent I seem on ruining my reputation, I am trying in my own perverse way to write an edifying discourse, the perversity of which is that the edification is built up by deconstruction. I begin with the name of God, again and again, from childhood to old age. All my life I keep starting over again, beginning at the beginning, with the name of God. I am trying to pray, trying to utter a prayer, to God, perhaps, trying to perform or play the insistence of God, to say "come" to what I cannot see coming. Am I using or merely mentioning the name of God? Am I playing with it? Is it playing with me? I do not know, as I do not know if these distinctions hold up, although I do know that the theologians of orthodoxy do not enjoy exclusive rights to this name and do not get to decide what counts as serious and what counts as play when it comes to the name (of) "God." Whenever Derrida was asked questions like that, he would say, if he knew such things, he would know everything.[23] Either way, when it comes to the coming of God, when it comes to saying "come," I am trying to remember to say "perhaps." I am trying to begin with God, with the insistence of God, without forgetting that the name of God is only one of many beginnings, depending on who and when and where you are, "one possibility in the syntax and in the game of first names," as Derrida said many years ago in an early commentary on *Le prénom de dieu,* the first book of Hélène Cixous.[24]

Yes, I said, yes, come, *viens, oui, oui*—that is the opening prayer of a theology of "perhaps," the paradigmatic prayer by which we are constituted, the prayer that insists itself into our existence. "Come" is the perilous prayer of a religion without religion, the passion for God in a disjointed world, the prayer for God, perhaps, the prayer of God, perhaps.

PART TWO

Theopoetics
THE INSISTENCE OF THEOLOGY

FOUR

THEOPOETICS AS THE INSISTENCE
OF A RADICAL THEOLOGY

I mean, brothers and sisters, the appointed time has grown short;
from now on, let even those who have wives be as though they had none,
and those who mourn as though they were not mourning,
and those who rejoice as though they were not rejoicing,
and those who buy as though they had no possessions,
and those who deal with the world as though they had no dealings with it.
For the present form of this world is passing away.

—1 CORINTHIANS 7:29–31

At the end of his 1920–21 lecture course on the letters of St. Paul, the young Heidegger wrote:

Real philosophy of religion arises not from preconceived concepts of philosophy and religion. Rather, the possibility of its philosophical understanding arises out of a certain religiosity—for us, the Christian religiosity.[1]

We cannot start with a stable concept of "philosophy" and a stable concept of "religion" and then "apply" "philosophy" to "religion." We must allow what are called "philosophy" and "religion" to tremble together under the force of their mutual contact, letting each push back on the other. That contact can be made not in the abstract, but rather from out of the original sources of the experience of "religiosity," out of the concrete experience of the religious traditions. Heidegger continues:

Why exactly the Christian religiosity lies in the focus of our study, that is a difficult question; it is answerable only through the solution of the problem of the historical connections.

That is, the privileging of Christianity arises from what he calls "our own historical situation and facticity," which forever throws into doubt both the possibility and desirability of the so-called objectivity of the historical "in itself." We always begin where we are, with an accident of birth, whether we like it or not. Unfortunately, Heidegger speaks as if it were self-evident that this factical situation is constituted by a single and homogeneous "for us," that there were no non-Christians among "us," in Germany or elsewhere. That is fatefully prescient of terrible times ahead for Heidegger and for Germany and for "us." But that should not obscure Heidegger's point. In a theology of the "perhaps," the very ideas of philosophy and religion come into question and reconfigure under the impact each makes upon the other. The new species of theologians of whom I dream attaches a coefficient of "perhaps" to both "philosophy" and "religion." Such work may be undertaken only on the condition that we speak not "about" religion but from out of the experience (*aus der Erfahrung*) of phenomena we judge in a preconceptual way to be "religious," starting out from where "we" are, but not necessarily ending there, all the while worrying more than Heidegger does about how much has been prejudged by resorting to what "we" call in Greek "philosophy" and "theology" and in Christian Latin "religion."

THEOLOGY: CONFESSIONAL AND CIRCUMFESSIONAL

Theology is bottomless. It swims in a sea whose surface is tossed and turbulent, whose depths it never plumbs. Theology is haunted and it is this haunted condition that I want to ponder under the name of the insistence of something in theology that theology cannot see coming. Now, in the second part of this study, the accent shifts from God's insistence to the insistence of the more radical theological thinking it implies, a thinking that does not exist but insists, exposed as it is to an event that calls for a hearing, that solicits what exists. What exist are the concrete "confessional" theologies, Christian or Islamic or Jewish theologies, for example, the theologies of real historical communities. I am interested in theology first as it functions in the confessions, where it is "factically" found, but finally in the event that stirs *within* historical theological reflection. That event-driven thinking is what I am calling radical theology, preserving the name "theology" but under a certain erasure. I start with confessional theology while trying to expose it, to expose myself, to its own excess, to hold us all open to the event. My interest in theology, like my interest in the name of God, is focused on the dynamics of the event that is calling in theology—an event that is calling on theology, that is getting itself called and recalled in theology, that theology is calling for. That is the event, which is God, perhaps. What I call the insistence of the event, or the happenstance of "perhaps," belongs to the insistence of a more searching theological reflection, which continues the workings of confessional theology in another register even as it solicits it, indeed precisely because it solicits and pressures it.

By attempting to give words to something insistent, something that insists on being heard, radical theology is always to come. It is what is coming, what calls "come" in any existing theology, which is why it calls for a coming species of theologians. When I say it does not exist, I mean it is not framed by a body of theses and doctrines and not supported by an institutional form of life even as it haunts the corridors of institutional power. It is not the theology *of* some concrete or confessional community but the theology *in* it, which is why its practitioners are more often than not found there. Indeed, it is not clear where *else* they would be found. It is not another entry in the competition of theological systems, not another existent or entity alongside others competing for existence. Radical theology and confessional theology do not differ as do two competing doctrines, as two existents, but as an insistence and an existent, as a spook or spectral shadow and an actuality. They differ not as two beings but as a being and a may-being, or even as a thought differs from what disturbs that thought. The distinction between radical and confessional theology is thus far from clean and binary. In making this distinction I am at least as interested in *un*-making it. My idea is not so much to oppose them to each other as to allow the one to haunt the inner thoughts and sleep of the other.[2] Radical theology is what confessional theology is dreaming of, even and especially if it wakes in a start and complains about nightmares. If there is a difference between them, then I am trying to situate myself in the distance between them.

My ultimate subject matter is radical theology, but that in turn might be more properly described as the becoming-radical *of* confessional theology. I am not saying anything that confessional theologians would not in a certain way already know, by which they are not already solicited in a midnight hour of restlessness. Were a confessional theologian to ask me how I know this or that, I would answer that it is because you know it and I have learned it from you. I am simply trying to engage confessional theologies, to engage myself, to engage us all in a more radical confession, or circumfession, of what we "know," not with a formed and explicit knowledge, but with a spooky sense of something unknown *in* what we know, of something stirring in our restless hearts (*cor inquietum*), of something coming. We all want to belong to the generation of coming theologians, even when we do not, or so we should. That is my thesis.

In that sense, the project of a radical theology is ultra-Augustinian and deeply confessional, and I am simply marking off the gradients in a scale of more and more confessional, circumfessional thinking. Radical theology is rarely more than confessional theology in a radically circumfessional mode. My proper subject matter is the becoming-circumfessional of confessional theology. So all my talk of spectrality does not imply that radical theology is nowhere to be found. It exists in fragments and asides and apostrophes within confessional theology, a point in which I will take some interest. Its real existence is testified to every time confessional theologians come under attack as heretics or atheists, whenever they touch a nerve in the powers that be that know their power is being put at risk. For example, when confessional theologians start writing "God Herself," it is quite startling how much starts to shift, as a series of brilliant feminist theologies and other progressive confessional theologians have demonstrated. That is why "the Church"—the Boys—thinks that feminism spells trouble, the Boys being seminary-trained ventriloquists who identify themselves with the Church, who cultivate the art of pleading that it is God who is against ordaining women, not them; they are just doing their duty, which as Derrida says is the classic way to avoid responsibility.

Radical theology also exists in occasional exercises such as the present one in which attempts are made to articulate it "directly," which is in the end impossible on its own terms. For any "radical" theology inevitably betrays its own historical roots, its confessional and existential pedigree, thereby exposing the parasitic nature of radical theology, if it is possible to be both root and parasite. As a theology focused on the insistence of the event, radical theology represents a way to get at something spooking confessional theology, some specter of the "perhaps" transpiring *in* theology that haunts the halls of theology, all the while calling for a new species of theologian. To the old species of theologian, radical theology looks like it is just playing around with theological language; to a radical theologian, the old species of theologian looks like someone afraid of the dark. Radical theology, the becoming radical of confessional theology, feels about in the dark for something the old theologians would just as soon keep under wraps, something that steals over them in an idle moment, a thought that perhaps all this *really is* through a glass, in the dark, and perhaps the darkness goes all the way down. Perhaps we *really do not* know at all what we mean. Radical theology is confessional theology confessing "perhaps," yielding to the pressure of "perhaps," to the insistent stirring of the event. The full force of the insistence of my weak "perhaps" is felt precisely in the pressure it puts on what enjoys the prestige of presence and of seeming to be well grounded.

By thus sticking resolutely and decisively with the insistence of "perhaps," by following the dark at the end of the tunnel, by advancing another way to think about God and prayer and religion, I am in turn seeking another way to think about theology, about what is insisting within theology, which is God, perhaps. That is what I am trying to spell out here, in the second part of this book.

MARTHA'S WORLD—AND THE VERY IDEA OF "RADICAL" THEOLOGY

I admit there is a lot of brio and bravado in "radical," especially for a theology that styles itself as "weak" and admits it is parasitic. But what I mean by "radical" is not foundational but non-foundational. I do not mean radically grounded but radically exposed. Radicality for me refers to our inescapable exposure to the unforeseeable, which requires having the spine for the "perhaps," the willingness to be a sheep among wolves, innocent as a dove, savvy as a serpent. These exotic tropes signify the hermeneutic art of seeing in the dark, the dark art of seeing what we cannot see coming. Radical theology is a memoir of the blind. Like Meister Eckhart, one of the patron saints and inspirations for this spooky art, I pray to the "God" that such a "theology" seeks, which is God, perhaps, or all the God, perhaps, we are going to get, to rid me of the God served up in the propositions of orthodoxy.

In the present chapter I argue that a theology such as this, turning on the insistence of God, a resolutely un-sovereign and anti-imperial and un-monarchical theology, a theology that insists without quite existing, will take the form of what I will call here a theopoetics. I invoke theopoetics in order to explain the discursive shape, the grammatological genre required by radical theology. The "radical" in radical theology goes to the roots of classical theology and uproots them, pulling up by the root the *logos* of the old theology and replacing it with a poetics. In the process it uproots its piety, its celestial demeanor, along with the mythological and quasi-gnostic drift of its *logos*, exposing it to the events that underlie and undermine it. Or, to put it another way, the old "logos" of theology is replaced with "events," which are addressed by a poetics, not a logic. To put it in Paul Ricoeur's terms, it is not a *logos* but an event that the *mythos* gives us to think. I will undertake this work not in the manner of an "apophatics"—of silence and non-knowing as a way to show our respect for the *hyperousios*—but in the manner of a discursive poetics. I proceed by way not of silence but of an alternate discursive formation designed to elude the constraints of *logos*. I am interested in not the *logos* of classical theology, which is lured by a dualistic logic of two worlds that provides its mythic architecture, but in the event that is harbored in classical theology.

So conceived, classical theology is charged with conducting negotiations between these two worlds, cutting the best deal it can get on behalf of sublunary beings below (us) with a celestial Über-being above, arranging a fair exchange of a vale of tears for a mountain of peace. The being of the troubled world—Martha's world—is being *for* another world where trouble is left behind—Mary's worldless world. *Requiescat in pace.* That puts Christianity in particular in a double bind. Tempted as it may be, Christian theology has never been able to entirely deal away the body, in virtue of its memory of the bodily Jesus and his human-animal needs to which Martha attends. But it also has never been able to explain why anyone would really need the glorified body Christians finally get on the other side in eternity, where there will be no household duties. The "body" in Christianity is haunted by the specter of a "glory" that, contrary to its central doctrine of the glorified "bodies without flesh," never succeeds in leaving flesh and animality behind, which shows up in the confusion in scriptures about whether or not to include "flesh" in eternal life (see ch. 12, below). Glorified bodies will live in a world without elements—no need of water to wash with, of air to respirate, of fire to be warmed by, of earth to stand on. It will be an entirely worldless world, Mary's worldlessness run to a fantastic completion, like a Kantian idea.

Once the world of time, suffering, and death—Martha's world—becomes the coin in trade for Mary's world, for eternal peace, the curtain parts to reveal a fantastic scene: impassible, subtle, agile, light, and airy bodies darting about a heavenly sphere released from the tides and tempests of the temporal world below, disincarnate bodies (*s'il y en a!*), bodies without flesh, whose antics result in the hilarious conundrums confronted by a deadpan Augustine and other Church fathers: teeth that do not chew, digestive systems that do not eat (or do other unmentionable things that Agamben and Žižek do not hesitate to mention), sexual organs that do not make love (more unmentionables), multiple generations all the same age (speculated to be thirty!), so that you and your grandmother must learn to deal with being contemporaries, and other equally ludicrous fantasies that add up to the obvious question of why we should need bodies at all.[3] *Pax aeterna. Requiescat in pace.* The peace of death, the quiet of the grave. God is death, and death is not a dead end but a key that unlocks celestial doors. O death, where is thy triumph? (The question, it should not go unnoticed, is met with the unbroken silence of the dead.) The logic of the old onto-logic is best addressed not by a logical counter-argument but rather the way Johannes Climacus addressed Hegel: not with logic but with laughter, with the comic, like the hilarious holy cards of unctuous saints.

A more radically uprooting theology of "perhaps" checks this quasi-gnostic drift, calls off these negotiations and explains that the whole thing has been based upon a misunderstanding. Theology should have been unlocking other doors and should have set out in search of other keys and indeed should be sung in another and more mundane key. Radical theology switches keys, changes the conversation, redescribes the terms of theological debate, demystifies two-worlds theory and exposes it as a bipolar disorder, a form of double vision, terrestrial and beatific, which can be traced to its ungodly fear of one small word, "perhaps." In its weak, sheepish but serpentine form, radical theology returns us to the multiplex plane of the world, with all its tempests, time, and trouble. The pulse of radical theology is taken by whether it has an impulse for the world, the stomach for flesh, the spine or heart—I multiply as many carno-corporeal animal images as possible—to displace the *logos* of two worlds, to transfer the funds of its heavenly treasures to earthly accounts.

In radical theology, theology is redirected to Martha's world and the promise of the booming, buzzing world below. By the world "below" I mean "this" world; by "this" I mean "the" world, the only one we know; by "we" I mean us all, anybody any of us ever met. Deleuze calls it the plane of immanence. I simply say the world tossed about by shifting tides and changing circumstances of space and time. This world is here, *diesseits,* and not *for* another one there, *jenseits.* It is not *for* anything because it is everything there is and there is nothing you could get for it in return if you decided to trade it in. That means having a heart for trouble is part and parcel of the promise of the world. To affirm the promise is to acknowledge that the world is under threat and that the world may, perhaps, come to grief. Pain, grief, and misery are all part of the promise, and the promise is the chance of an event, which is God, perhaps. They constitute the substance, the *Sache,* of another spectral theology, one that is, perhaps, secretly suspected in confessional theology. If I am asked what proof I have for radical theology, I plead for a little sympathy: how is one supposed to prove there is a ghost? My only proof is that you already know it, meaning you have been spooked by it, so my poetics follows something like the "method" employed by Zarathustra: you know it but you will not say it. I must suspect that Mary suspects that Martha had chosen the better part. I will return to this complex of questions about the promise of the "world" under the title of a "cosmopoetics" in the third part of this study.

My appointed task in the present chapter is to weaken or dilute the old *logos,* which I here undertake under the flag of "theopoetics." This may be regarded as a kind of heart transplant in which the celestial and moribund *logos* of classical theology, always close to death, *memento mori,* its beat barely detectable, is replaced with a heartier "poetics." If the quasi-gnostic tide is stemmed by redescribing the *logos* of theology as a *poetics,* the poetics turns out to mean having a heart—a *cor inquietum*—for the travails of the "perhaps," which brings us to the circumfessional cut that, as I claim, is already inscribed *in* confessional theology. If the *logos* is the tranquilizing agent, the poetics is the radicalizing agent, resulting not in the il-logical but the alogical, the displaced logic, the specter of "perhaps." Far from fearing one small word, theopoetics presents its papers as the poetics of the "perhaps." In radical theology (confessional theology becoming circumfessional, theo-logy becoming theo-poetics), the logic of transcendence is displaced by a poetics of the quasi-transcendental. But if a poetics is not a "logic," neither is it an "aesthetics." A poetics is not a theory of art or sensuous feelings; it is not a work of art and it does not mean "poetry,"[4] even as it does not fall back upon a feeling of dependence (Schleiermacher). If we were speaking German, I would say a poetics concerns *Dichtung,* not *Poesie,* a theory of a creative discourse, not of verse.

A "poetics" is a discourse cut to fit what I have been calling the insistence of the event and as such provides a perfect candidate for the grammatology of the "perhaps." I argued some time ago that what does the work of "ethics" in a theology of the event is a "poetics of obligation," which gives up looking for deep metaphysical foundations of obligation and learns to appreciate the groundlessness of what is happening in obligation.[5] Here I am arguing that theology undergoes a parallel transmutation, learning to serve as a poetics of the event insisting in the name (of) "God," to appreciate what it insists in the name of God so as to bring it to words in an alternate genre or discursive form—without heading for the hills of apophatic silence and without straying on to the bombastic battlefields of theism and atheism.

But there is still another leg to the argument that I will reserve for the next chapter. I find common cause with all postmodern theories of religion intent on "overcoming onto-theology," which reject the classical metaphysical logic by which traditional theology has been sustained. These theories have variously taken a linguistic, cultural, or hermeneutic turn that concedes that we have no access to overarching ahistorical pre-linguistic metaphysical principles with which to buck up the classical faith. We are forced to proceed on foot, having conceded that when it comes to the eagles of metaphysical knowledge, we want for wings. But I intervene at just this point by introducing a distinction between two types of post-modern philosophy of religion, to adapt a famous strategy from Paul Til-lich, where this time the prototypes will be Kant and Hegel, not Augustine and Aquinas. The first type thinks that postmodernism plays the role of Kant in the philosophy of religion. This I will applaud as marking a certain (postmodern) advance but I will go on to complain that it is an abridged edition of postmodernism, a postmodernism "light," like a nonalcoholic wine. In the end, I will object it works like a retrenchment, an apology for classical and confessional theology, in which classical metaphysics is able to survive by going dark. So the first type, the Kantian one, I will argue, fails to get as far as radical theology because it really is a division of con-fessional theology known as "apologetics" using postmodern resources to defend the present species of theologians. This is not bad because it pro-duces valuable results on its own level, and if everybody got at least this far we would be all better off. But it could do better. This distinction will also prove useful in the third part of this book, when I take up the current attack on the so-called theological turn taken in continental philosophy, which I view as largely an attack on its Kantian mode.

The second type, which is where I place my hope in a coming species of theologian, thinks postmodernism plays the role of Hegel in the philoso-phy of religion. That, I hope to show, is the only way to effectively uproot the *logos* in classical theology and clear the way for a new species of theo-logians. So I frame theopoetics by situating it within Hegel's differentia-tion of art, religion, and philosophy, where a poetics is located between the realization of the absolute in the work of art (transcendental aesthetics) and a realization of the absolute in the philosophical concept (logic). In this version of postmodernism, religion is taken as a *Vorstellung* that can only be appreciated in a poetics. But my poetics lacks a Concept, which is the point at which this ceases to be a Hegelian point and swerves off into a Hegelian apostasy. It is at best a weak Hegelian type, a headless Hegelian-ism, in a weak or quasi-transcendental postmodern poetics. My argument, in short, is this: radical theology is the becoming radical of confessional theology, and this is only possible as theopoetics, and theopoetics turns out to be a poetics of the event. The argument comes to a head in the next chapter, when I get to my distinction between two types of continental philosophy of religion.

THE BECOMING RADICAL OF CONFESSIONAL THEOLOGY

The first step is to show that theology, by which I mean at the start confessional theology, yields radical theology if it allows itself to yield to the insistence of the event, to the pressure the event puts on confessional theology. Confessional theology becomes circumfessional if it is willing to fess up to the event by which it is spooked. The confessional theologies are the only theologies that exist, while radical theology, which does not exist, insists or haunts the confessional theologies.

To sort this out in an orderly way, let us distinguish between religious actors and theological reflection. The actors belong to a first-order operation of religious beliefs and practices, prescinding for present purposes from the debate about which of these two comes first.[6] Some of these practices are cultic in which, as Hegel says, the community deepens its sense of a common spirit, its sense of identification with the Spirit, and in which it engages in a common reading of the sacred scriptures around which the community is organized.[7] To these works of worship we must also add the works of love, of "doing justice" in the name of God, of doing the truth, making the truth of the scriptures come true, making the words of worship into deeds. But in addition to its practices, there are also first-order beliefs—the five pillars of Islam, the seven sacraments of Catholicism, the ten commandments of Judaism—the itemizable assertions and basic creeds that circulate in a more or less common and popular form among the faithful. The vagueness of the popular belief is the reason the community takes up theological reflection, which is a second-order operation where the community does its thinking. Theology conceptualizes the beliefs of the community, regulates its practices, and subjects its scriptures to a critical reading that establishes the guiding interpretation that defines the community and its traditions. But theology does not have unilateral authority, for in all such theological reflection the community must in its turn be able to recognize itself. Theological reflection must reflect the community, and the community must be able to see its own reflection in the theology. The theologians report back to the community and receive authentication by the way in which they make explicit what was all along implicit in the community's beliefs and practices. When they do not, either the theology simply disappears because it has no purchase on the community, or the community attaches itself to the theology and reconfigures or else it just splits (schism).

Confessional theology is a local process, one that goes on in a concrete, historical existing community, where there is a body of received scriptures and a "confession" or "profession" of inherited and specific beliefs (*croyances*) commonly shared by the community. But it proves necessary or unavoidable—under the sheer pressure and momentum of theological questioning—to press on further to a still-deeper order of reflection that continues the work of analysis and conceptualization but one without ties to a confessional community, one which to that extent questions in a more free and unfettered way. It is necessary, or unavoidable, to cross the borders of confessional theology and engage in a more "radical" theology. Radical theology does not report back to the confessional community or seek its authentication there, and reserves for itself the right to ask any question, without regard to whether it fractures or divides the community or causes schismatic conflict and confessional breaks or engages in revisionist readings of classical scriptures. Radical theology emerges both as a demand of thought, which has the right to ask any question, and as a demand of praxis, which seeks to suspend any claim that privileges an inherited legacy, which is an accident of birth (a historical community).

But then, we might ask, to whom does the radical theologian report? In principle, to everyone, to "humanity" at large, which gives radical theology a more universal look or cosmopolitan flare. The first form this took was too strong. It is found in early modernity in the Enlightenment, where radical questioning took the form of the "rational theology" of the seventeenth- and eighteenth-century Rationalists, who were feeling the oats of the new defiance of tradition and authority. One thinks for example of Spinoza's principles of biblical criticism or of Kant's analysis of religion within the limits of reason alone, in which Kant concludes that the universal and rational element of religion is ethics, reducing the rest to superstition. But as modernism is complicit with the classical metaphysical sense of radical as foundational and with strong transcendental principles, the version of radical theology that I defend is not modern but postmodern, and neither is it rationalist nor does it deal in strict Kantian transcendentals. It is quasi-transcendental, non-foundational, and hermeneutic, proceeding from the radicality of what I like to call a radical hermeneutics and from a new sense of reason.

Postmodern radical theology sets out in search not of rational universality but of hermeneutic universality, let us say the universal of universal hospitality, where "universal" means being willing to talk to anyone, anywhere, anytime, and "rational" means that there is nothing that cannot in principle be discussed. Hermeneutic universality means accepting universal risk, being willing to put one's own presuppositions at risk, as Gadamer said,[8] and to give a hearing to anything that puts them into question, to say that *perhaps* the other one knows something I do not know and is going to say something I did not see coming. The risk-averse avoid adverbs like "perhaps." So we can see at once that this is heartier stuff, with a heart for hermeneutic trouble, which concedes that "universality" means not that we all speak with one voice (modern univocity) but that we all get a chance to speak (postmodern plurivocity). That is the universality and rationality implied in Derrida's notion of the right to ask any question, implying the right to pose any answer,[9] which he variously describes as the characteristic trait of philosophy, the university, literature, or the "new humanities."[10] If the "radicality" of the modern is to seek a single universal and common root (*radix*) of the multiple contingent and historical particulars, the very idea of the postmodern is to deny that there is any such thing. Postmodernity puts such radicality radically in question, uproots this common root, so that postmodern radicality lies in a kind of ultra-rationality which passes through the rational while leaving its trace behind in a new concept of the rational. Postmodern theory thus is not pre-modern, pre-rational, or anti-rational but questions standard-form (modernist) rationality, radicality, and universality. It recognizes the universality and multiplicity of "singularities," which are never simply particulars included under a universal, even as it thinks the origin is divided, never a simple source, so that its root system is as Deleuze liked to say "rhizomatic." The latter is the root system of weeds for which the "heresiology" of orthodoxy theology means to be the herbicide.

Thus the premise that theology always "reports back" to the religious community is repeated with a difference in radical theology. This time the religious community is a "community without community," that is, one that is completely open-ended, since what the radical theologian has to say is addressed in principle to anyone willing to listen, with or without a confessional affiliation, anyone at least who is not stampeded by the word "theology," as most philosophers are. But I must furthermore admit straight off that this is a bit of a fiction, which is the same thing as saying that radical theology insists but it does not exist. I slipped in "in principle" because in fact reflection always begins where we are and when we reflect we always reflect our beginning, which is why radical theology is confessional theology in another and rather more heretical mode. So the fiction embedded in the hermeneutic universality of radical theology is exposed by conceding that those of us who meddle in radical theology are just like everybody else and are always already in the middle of some confessional community and a complex of other communities. We have not been granted a special pass on the human condition. We too have a community or meta-community to report back to, from which we are seeking "authentification," and we submit to a vast and complex system of protocols and censorship, just like everybody else.

To begin with, to the extent that a radical theology could ever be formulated, it would typically report back to a specifically Western community. It would normally be situated within the Western monotheisms and have recourse to Western philosophical discourses steeped in deep-set notions of presence, essence, idea, substance, subject, up to and including the very notions of "religion" and "philosophy" and "theology," the whole constellation of what Heidegger liked to call "metaphysics," meaning not an academic discipline but the entire historical, cultural, and intellectual framework of Greco-European civilization. Secondly, as the becoming radical of confessional theology, radical theology will inevitably reflect a certain confessional pedigree, background, and tradition, the existing traditions from which the radical theologians emerged. I for example make no bones about having broadly biblical and specifically Christian concerns, mostly because that is where I am—meaning that is the confessional tradition I have inherited, by which I have been formed, and about which I am the least ignorant. Radical theology is parasitic upon confessional traditions, feeling about for the events that take place in such traditions. (It would be hard to tell the difference between "radical Christianity" and a corresponding radical theology by a "recovering" Christian theologian.) Finally, almost any kind of theology today, confessional or radical, will be the product of an "academic" theologian, which means that it "reports back" to a powerful disciplinary system of academic protocols. Theology is written by career-minded, university-hopping academics for "peer-reviewed" conferences, journals, and academic presses, by academic candidates in search of employment, tenure, promotion, and a long list of academic honors like endowed chairs, research grants, and prestigious lectureships. However much we like to think that thinking belongs to the order of the gift, that it is a vocation, and I am not saying that it is not, it *also* is rigorously inscribed within the increasingly corporate economy of "academe," with the result that its freedom and hermeneutic universality are something less than it likes to think. Its unfettered freedom is also fettered to earning a living, something to which the throng of young jobless PhDs we have produced can testify better than can I.

The interesting point in this distinction (like any distinction) is its soft spots, the points along the borders where it breaks down and become porous and does not hold up. Having made a distinction like this, the first order of business in deconstruction is to turn on it and attack it, to break it down and weaken it, to make each side porous to the other. So the lines I am trying to draw become particularly grey and ambiguous in the case of confessional theologians who are also academics, whose work is marked by a tension between reporting back to the confessional community to which they belong and to the scholarly community to which they also belong. In my vocabulary, the historical, critical, and doctrinal research they undertake, which starts out by trying to give theological voice to their confessional tradition, often ends up making contact with the events that burn through the confessional beliefs and practices and that thereby expose the relative, contingent, and constituted character of the confessional community. These theologians are on their way to a radical theology, but if they follow that way too far, the confessional community concludes they have lost their way, which is a good way for them to lose their job in the confessional institutions which employ them. They are as good an example of confessional theology becoming radical as we will find. So a good deal of what I mean by radical theology is confessional theologians pushing up against their confessional limits and confessing they have run into events that cannot be contained by the usual confessional containers.

I take radical theology to be a matter of radical honesty or what Nietzsche called truthfulness. I posit that there are midnight moments when confessional theologians toss and turn with the haunting thought that what they call a gift of grace is in fact an accident of birth—that, had they been born in another time and place, they would have entirely different things inside their heads than the things they defend in their daytime theologies. That radical confession is what I mean by confessional theologians becoming circum-fessional, in which the accent switches from *confessio* as professing a creed to *confessio* as confessing how deeply exposed to events we are. By the same token, the so-called radical theologians, who are often people who grew up in and then parted company with a particular confessional faith, may all along be simply transcribing an underlying confessional theology into other words and at a higher degree of abstraction and in a more open-ended way.

Inasmuch as hermeneutics is always interested in interpretive presuppositions, another way to sort out the differences between confessional theology and radical theology is to pick out their differing presuppositions. The presuppositions of the confessional communities are the founding scriptures and the continuing traditions of the community. Such foundations are historical. The presuppositions of rationalist theology are transcendental and ahistorical, invoking a so-called "pure" reason which proclaims its universal immunity from any possible "perhaps." Inasmuch as postmodernists are dubious in the extreme about the latter, the presuppositions of postmodern theology are either hermeneutic or deconstructive. Hermeneutics in the sense of Gadamer or Ricoeur presupposes the "truth" of the religious tradition or classic, its enduring viability, its continuing power to fuel the tradition in ways that are ever changing yet ever "true" to itself. The "truth" of the tradition does not lie in a changeless body of beliefs but in a changing but enduring form of life.

Hermeneutics in the more radical sense, which is one way to think about deconstruction, is more dubious of such truth and in search of a more ruthless truthfulness. Having taken trouble as its criterion of truth, the trouble that ensues upon saying "perhaps," it seeks a more deconstructive version of postmodern theology, presupposing only what Derrida calls the "secret," where the secret is that there is no Secret, no privileged access to the Secret Code that explains everything. That produces a more challenging and truthful notion of truth, which has nothing to do with producing sophistry and confusion. It insists upon the radical contingency of any historical tradition as an effect of the play of traces; it denies that any such tradition has a privileged access to the essence or *Wesen* of things and hence to any deep truth, and settles instead for the insistence of the event. That means it settles for a more contingent truth and is more nominalistic about beliefs and more pluralistic about traditions. It takes beliefs and practices to be but relatively stable and hence also relatively unstable, and provisional unities of meaning inscribed in *différance* or, as Derrida liked to put it later on, inscribed in the desert sands of *khora*, of khoral spacing, and productive of "chaosmic" results. If the assumptions of hermeneutics are always those of risk and hospitality and exposure to the "perhaps," deconstruction puts us (or more precisely concedes we are ourselves always already put) more deeply at risk, asking us to undertake a more unconditional hospitality. In other words, a deconstructive or radical hermeneutics is more braced for trouble than garden-variety hermeneutics. But deconstruction must not be mistaken as something destructive or merely skeptical because at its heart deconstruction arises not from negation but from a deeper affirmation of something, I know not what, from a faith (*foi*) in an event, heeding a call, an exigency, a summons, an injunction, an imperative.

If, one might ask, what I mean by "radical theology" is simply another way of describing what I have been calling radical hermeneutics, but this time with a theological or religious accent, why not stick to "radical hermeneutics"? Why buy all the trouble that comes by introducing "theology" or "religion," which will only succeed in clearing the room of the philosophers? As a philosopher friend of mine asked me recently, can't you say everything you want to say by talking about "Being" and "finitude," and never bringing up religion?[11] The answer is that I could, but once we step outside the academic building in which we are having this conversation, the massive cultural fact of "religion" is all around us and practically nobody out there is much interested in or moved by academic terms of art like *Being* and *finitude*. Furthermore, whether we like it or not, the demands of truthfulness are such that we philosophers have to admit we have here crossed the threshold into a certain archi-religion or religion without the trappings of religion, without the intrigues of the bishops and the cost of buying candles.

We have to do here with something like a "religious confession," but this time a circum-fession of the absolute secret. As opposed to the relative secrets we keep from one another which can, in various contexts, be revealed, either because of a court order or because we cannot keep our mouths shut, the absolute secret can never be revealed and this because it is absolutely and in principle unknown. We can't disclose it because we don't know it. We don't know in any deep way what we desire, what we desire with a desire beyond desire, which leads us to a more radical confession, or circumfession, that we are radically cut off from the secret, meaning that we do not know who we are, which is the enduring truth of Augustine's *Confessions: quaestio mihi magna factus sum*. We are hanging on by faith, hanging on by a prayer, left almost without a prayer, praying a prayer without a prayer, without knowing whether there is anyone to pray to. That is the real trouble with prayer, which is why we pray when we are in trouble. The trouble with prayer is that it brings with it even more trouble, the way praying for faith implies we lack faith. With this introduction of prayer, we have crossed the threshold of a certain religion. Where there is religion there is prayer; where there is prayer, there is religion, even and especially if it is a religion without religion, or a faith without faith, which is also why a radical theology is a theology without theology, a radical theology without confessional theology. So my radical hermeneutics cannot keep itself safe from a radical theology, which is also why the new species of theologians of whom I dream is in for trouble.

PERHAPS NOT—SPOOKING THE FAITHFUL

Now we come to a crucial point for radical theology, to a border crossing, where we seek to cross the threshold from confessional theology to

grammar

radical theology. Here we are ask how to cross over from what exists to what does not; to pursue the way what exists yields to the weak pressure of what merely insists. But how can there *be* such a crossing if one of the terms does not exist? Let me give an example of what I mean. "Confessional" theology is more or less the only theology that exists because it addresses the only kind of "religion" that actually exists, the concrete confessional or historical traditions of religious beliefs and practices. Kierkegaard described this in wonderfully polemical terms as the religion that comes replete with "a full staff of bishops, deans, pastors," with "a complete inventory of churches, bells, organs, offering boxes, collection boxes, hymn boards, hearses, etc."[12] That is what exists. What does not exist for Kierkegaard, what only insists, is the Christianity of the New Testament. His entire work as an author consisted in situating himself as a Christian Socrates in the distance between what exists and what insists, but only insists, under the name of "Christianity." My idea of radical theology is to go one step further and pressure Kierkegaard to think what insists, what is still insisting, which Christianity in all its apostolic fervor cannot contain.

So the two must not simply pass each other like ships in the night. For then what I am calling radical theology loses its point and its point of departure, because radical theology is an exploration of the events that are taking place *in* confessional theology. If radical theology does not exist but is parasitic on the existing theologies of the existing communities, then, if the radical theologians are not talking to the confessional traditions, they run the risk of talking only to themselves. In their effort to speak to everyone they may well end up speaking to no one but themselves, impaneled on imponderable panels at annual meetings of the AAR.[13] They may achieve tenure and promotion that way, but not much else. So as I conceive it, there is or ought to be a crucial and critical interaction between the two, and radical theology must find a way of burning through or bleeding into confessional theology, even as confessional theology must expose itself to and embody the disturbance of radical theology. Radical theology is confessional theology becoming radical. As we have already seen, this is most likely to take place in the case of confessional theologians who are also academics, where the intersection of and tensions between the two very often take place in the same skin—skins that need to be quite thick, I might add, because of the arrows directed their way by the more conservative members of the confession.

In my view, radical theology, as a second-order work of reflection, an even more radical work of reflecting on the reflection engaged in by the confessional theologians, produces something of a double effect on confessional theology, which I will describe as one of both displacement and affirmation.

Displacement

The first effect of radical theology is one of displacement and delimitation or, in Derrida's more impudent vocabulary, "haunting" or spooking the confessional traditions with one small word, "perhaps." Radical theology is not the theology of a mundane religion, a rival candidate in the competition for membership and funds that goes on among the confessional communities. It has no national headquarters, holds no councils, has no dogmas, takes up no collections, neither ordains nor excommunicates, and sends out no missionaries to knock on doors (altogether an ideal religion!). Taking up no earthly room, existing in or as no earthly institution, it acts somewhat more like a hovering spirit that haunts the living confessional traditions, as a ghost that spooks their closed confessional assemblies, a specter that insists in what exists, insisting on being heard. It is not trying to produce a competitor, a rival body of beliefs (*croyances*), but to etch the outlines of an obscure faith (*foi*) in an event. Its effect is to modify the "how" of the confessional traditions, not to produce another "what." It is not a competing creedal body but the specter of a coming spirit, an *arrivant*, as well as a ghostly reminder of the dead (*revenants*). Radical theology insists its way into the confessional communities, disclosing their historical contingency and the mundane multiplicity of the confessional traditions, exposing thus the deeply cultural valence of any body of historical beliefs and practices. It whispers insistently from offstage a little "perhaps" in the ear of the actors in the several traditions, making them acutely conscious of the extent to which their roles have been written by the fortuitous effects of history rather than an dictated from on high, and of the extent to which the "gift" of their personal faith is an accident of birth. It insistently raises the suspicion that one's inherited tradition, the "gift of grace," is *perhaps* the chance of an event, an event of happenstance, and that the only difference between the two is that a "grace" is the event that has happened to us, where the main task is to make ourselves worthy of the events that happen to us.[14] But there are many such graces, many gifts, because the event can happen anywhere, here perhaps, or maybe there. God, perhaps, can happen anywhere.

"Perhaps" is a ghost that issues in a thin theology of a nearly invisible but insistent body of faith, not a full-blown and corpulent body of beliefs defended by the long-robed in Gothic chambers while choirs swell with pious hymns in the background. It is the ghost or whisper of something both unforeseeable and immemorial, something going on *in* the confessional theologies, God, perhaps, and if here then why not, perhaps, elsewhere? In so doing it exposes the "mythic" content at the core of any mundane confessional theology, by which I mean its character as a local narrative, a contingent happening. In a mythic thinking, the distance between the event and the mundane formation is closed down, and that closes off the hermeneutic opening to the event that radical theology seeks to uncover. The hauntological effect of radical theology is thus to distance, dislodge, and disengage the actors from their mundane roles, to raise the suspicion of the event in the actors, to attach a coefficient of historicizing irony to their beliefs and practices, to insert a distance between their mundane vocation and the more obscure prompting of the event. Do not lace the garments of contingency too tightly, Kierkegaard says. Under the insistent influence of radical theology, to live in a confessional community is to have a vocation that is simultaneously subject to revocation, to live out a calling under constant recall by the event. This produces the acute discomfort in these actors born of the realization that had they not, perchance, been born here and now, had they perhaps been born at another time and place, they would be acting out very different roles, speaking in different tongues, singing songs to other gods, telling other sacred stories and taking their cues from other paradigms.

The deeper confessional academic theologians dig into their respective traditions, the more they uncover its time-bound and contingent makeup and the more they make contact with the underlying and insistent events by which they are nourished. As they think through the events that are at work in their confessional theologies, they often think their way right through them, thereby passing through the confessional theology and coming out the other side. That lands them in the middle of radical theology. Indeed, that is not only possible; it may be the *only* possible path to radical theology. This capacity of what I am calling radical theology to bleed into the work of confessional theology explains the friction between confessional theologians and the confessional authorities. That is the reason that the latter can conclude that the theologians are a "scourge and an affliction upon the church,"[15] even as, from the point of view of people trying to freely think through their faith and experience, it is the bishops who scourge and afflict the people of God. So we all begin where we are, where we exist, with an act, conscious or not, of historical association with our legacy, with the tradition we have inherited. Where else could one possibly begin? Even if in the spirit of radical critique you deny that, it just means

that you have inherited a legacy of radical critique, of suspicion and questioning—that you were taught to ask questions. But this act of association
is followed by an ironic distancing, an act of historical dissociation, which
prevents one from being identified with what one inherits, which leads to
an appreciation of the utter contingency of the situation of inheritance.

This dislocating dissociation is what I will call the *"perhaps not"*: here I
am, in this body, in this body of inherited beliefs (*croyances*), but perhaps
not. Had I been born elsewhere, I would be and believe otherwise, without damage to a more obscure faith (*foi*). The adverbial shift introduced
by "perhaps" displaces the nominal or substantive what-I-am by means of
a how. God rewards the how, not the what (if you're after rewards). In virtue of the weak force of *perhaps not*, I am able to sustain a negative capability, to sustain an uncertainty, to unplug lovingly and respectfully from
the order I inherit without simply being disinherited. This is what Žižek
calls "uncoupling," suspending the order I inherit and the place I occupy
in it. Žižek links this with Paul's *hos mē* or *quasi non* ("as if not") injunctions (1 Cor. 7: 29–31),[16] following up an extended discussion of this text in
Agamben's *The Time That Remains*, which itself goes back to Heidegger's
commentary on Paul's letters in his early lectures on the phenomenology
of religion (1921–22).[17] Paul was saying that the present form of the world
is passing away and that the *kairos*, the exact appointed time of the second
coming, has been foreshortened (*synestalmenos*), meaning it has already
begun and has therefore become all the more imminent. If the present
order is beginning already to be swept away and the time is short, what are
we to do in the meantime? Paul's answer is a set of emergency measures
for this exceptional moment, all of which come down to not launching
any new projects. He recognizes that life goes on and the saints are pressed
by the straits or constraints (*ananke*) of the present, and his advice is to
remain as they are: if you are single, do not marry; if you are married, stay
married, but live as if you were not married; buy things (as you must) but
as if you had no possessions; deal with the world (as you must) but as if
you were not dealing with it. For the world is passing away and the present life of the Corinthians will be transformed into a new life in which the
value of marriage and possessions will be dwarfed by the new being. In the
meantime such mundane things should not become a distraction.

Heidegger in turn took up these texts as a way to sort out the "factical
life" of primal Christianity from the factical roles Christians were given to
play ("thrown" into). The difference between Christian factical life and the
life of non-Christians is not found in the content (*Gehalt*) of their lives.
They may be rich or poor, tinkers or tailors, single or married, master or

slave, just like everyone else. The difference lies in what Heidegger calls the meaning of their "enactment" (*Vollzug*), the way in which they enact the lives they have been given, or, as he would put it in *Being and Time,* the way they project upon the situation into which they have been thrown. That meaning is found in the "as if not": they must defer or "retard" their enactment, not be absorbed by it, and have it or live as if they did not, because the *kairos* that will change everything is fast approaching.[18] Their life is not a frozen or suspended animation but a living and animate suspension of their worldly vocations. They suspend the worldly condition of life in order to release its Christian factical life in Christ. There is no better example of this than Kierkegaard's brilliant riff on the knight of faith who looks like a tax collector, where the worldly vocation is constantly subject to revocation under the pressure of faith in the absurd, so that the right way to be a tax collector is to be one as if one is not. Later on, in *Being and Time,* this becomes the basis of the distinction between inauthentic life, in which Dasein allows itself to be absorbed by worldly concerns and its mundane place in the world, and authentic Dasein, which is free for its ownmost possibility for being. But that does not mean that authentic Dasein changes jobs or takes up residence somewhere else: it appropriates its being in the world authentically, which means that it has its mundane role as if it had it not. Authenticity is a modification of inauthenticity, as Heidegger points out.[19] For all the world the knight of faith appears to be nothing more than a tax collector.

I suggest a further extension of this Pauline figure, one that will surely displease the faithful, because I think the *hos mē* counsels, which are a form of *peut-être,* are a good model for what I am calling dissociation and Žižek calls uncoupling, which models the relation between radical theology and the confessional religions. In my view the call of the event subjects the call of the mundane confessional vocation to recall; one inhabits the belief as if not, weakening the belief in order to release the event. We weaken the intimidating prestige and enormous power of belief (*croyance*) in order to release the pressure exerted by the soft voice of the event of faith (*foi*). As Heidegger interprets Paul to say that we suspend the enactment of the worldly condition to release the quality of factical life, I would say that we suspend the mundane circumstances of "belief" in order to release the event of "faith." A self must never allow itself to be consolidated into the selfsame, never allow its identity to become identical with itself. We must deprive our worldly vocation of its power to provide ease, comfort, closure, and security—it is just when we say "peace" that destruction overtakes us (1 Thess. 5:3)—in order to weaken its defenses and allow it to release the experience of the event. We suspend the comforts of the community of inherited beliefs (*croyances*)—we have them as if we have them not—in order to release the event of faith (*foi*). Those of you who are Christians or Jews, Hindus or Muslims—to which I would add the warring parties of theists or atheists—or whatever you are, should remain as you are. But live as if you were not, live knowing that had you been born elsewhere life would be different, with no damage to the workings of the event of faith. So the first effect of radical theology is subversive, exposing confessional theology to the "perhaps not" or the "as if not." It disarms the powerful apologetic armatures of the various confessional traditions so that one can continue (or not!) to belong to the confessional community but only with a considerable unease, with a good deal of trouble because the real trouble lies not in a troubled faith but in an untroubled belief. One may continue to participate in the community, or perhaps not. Remain loyal to the community, if you wish. The community is not destroyed but it is put at risk, a little spooked by the shadows of "perhaps not," by the fear of one small word, or two. One remains a Christian, perhaps, or perhaps not. One rightly passes for a Christian or a Jew or one rightly passes for an atheist, while living with the unsettling suspicion that something else (the event) is running quietly and softly in the background.

In the view that we strike in weak theology, the *mē* in *hos mē* corresponds to the *mē* in *ta mē onta* (1 Cor. 1:28), when Paul says that the things that are not are stronger than the things that are. The "event" corresponds to the things that are not, that insist without existing, their voice ever soft and low, having no worldly standing, while "the things that are" (*ta onta*) refers to the order of presence, essence, and actuality. That means that the weakness and non-being of the event are stronger than the power and prestige of presence and actuality (the worldly vocation). The event is the call that recalls or revokes the mundane vocation. The call insists, but it does not exist (*mē onta*). For Heidegger, potentiality is higher than any actuality, just as the silent call of weak and withdrawn Being is deeper than manifest and showy beings. For Deleuze, the virtual is deeper than the actual, the flux of life more important than its particular fluctuations, the event of life deeper than accidents of birth.

Affirmation

While the work of radical theology is critical and subversive of what the actors embedded in first-order beliefs and practices are doing, its effect is not, at least not ultimately, negative. Nothing is worth our trouble if our only aim is to make trouble for it. In the end, radical theology is deeply affirmative—not of the confessional beliefs (*croyances*) and practices, but of a deeper insistence in things, a deeper faith (*foi*) in the event they contain.[20] Radical theology is a delicate art that requires the equipoise of being able to say in one breath, "yes, yes, but perhaps not," of being something as if not. Thus the exposure of the creedal structure to the archi-faith of the "perhaps" can result in its radicalized counterpart, say a "radical Christianity," a "Christianity, perhaps," a "weak" or even a "spooked" Christianity, which shows the influence of its exposure to the insistence of the event. We see this when Kierkegaard's Johannes Climacus declines the compliment of "being" Christian and prefers to speak of "becoming" one, when Bonhoeffer speaks of religionless Christianity, and when Levinas speaks of loving the Torah more than God. I also think it alive and well in movements today like "Emergent Church," and in the prophetic paradoxes preached by Peter Rollins, who lets Derridean and Žižekian conundrums roll off his tongue—like "heretical orthodoxy" and "faithful infidelity"— in the name of a radical Christian life. At such points the creedal system has been weakened enough to let a certain archi-faith eventuate, and the certitude of "being-Christian" is weakened enough to free up a "Christianity, perhaps," which also implies a "perhaps not." We also see it in Derrida's famous saying that he "rightly passes" for an atheist, meaning that atheism is a "belief" that must be weakened and made porous so as not to close off the underlying insistence of the event of faith.

The events that are contained *in* a concrete tradition but not contained *by* it show up in the confessional scriptures from time to time, like wormholes between one universe of religious discourse and another one, like tunnels dug under confessional borders. In the story of the good Samaritan it is the stranger, the non-Jew, not the priest or Levite, who does the truth, which exposes a more radical underbelly of per(ver)formativity underlying the creedal faith overhead. In another story, it is a Canaanite woman who tests the limits of being Jewish by challenging Jesus's claim that he was sent to the Jews alone (Matt. 15:21–28). At the end of Romans, Paul signals that everyone must be grafted onto the tree of Israel, but perhaps not. Either way, since God cannot be frustrated, everyone must be saved, regardless of whether they are grafted onto the tree of Israel or not, although just how is a great mystery to him. In every case, the creedal structure is weakened in favor of the event while the creedal faith is not simply jettisoned, so one remains in the creedal structure, as if not. One lives in it as if one did not. So what radical theology displaces it also opens up. It puts into question but it is not negative; questioning is not a negation but a way of exposing the actual to the event and the confessional to the circumfessional. It says "perhaps not" to the belief just in order to say "yes, yes" to the event. Nothing is worth our time if our only aim is to drop acid on it. In the end, a radical theology of "perhaps," even of "perhaps not," is deeply affirmative, "yes, yes," of the confessional beliefs (*croyances*) and practices, but not as such; it is ultimately an affirmation of a deeper faith (*foi*) in these beliefs, in the event they harbor, in the chance of the event that underlies the beliefs, a chance we are maintaining will always have to do with grace.

In short, radical theology does not exist; it insists. It is a specter, un-dead, homeless and *un-heimlich*. No "death of God" allows it to rest in peace, nor can it make a home amid the comforts of the life-world. Hence it wanders the world as a spectral "perhaps," whispering a reminder of the may-being of being, a "maybe" that wends its way into everything that we would otherwise liked to have described as substance, essence, and presence, as knowledge, science, and truth. The foxes have their holes, the birds their nests, but radical theology has nowhere to lay down its head. It haunts the halls of philosophy and theology, infiltrating them with a quiet but overwhelming unease over the insufficiency of their categories and of every project of objectification. It may be that the disciplinary distribution of academic bodies in the university to come will be deconstructed—not only scattered and disturbed but also opened up and released—in such a way as to allow the formation of new objects and modes of inquiry, that is, to allow the event instead of preventing the event. Perhaps, a university to come will not so much give radical theology a home—its very character as a specter, which means as something *un-heimlich*, prevents that—but will prove to be more welcoming of specters. Perhaps, a thinking to come will be more willingly haunted, more ready for anxiety, more easily exposed to the disturbing specter of a certain groundlessness, of a certain uncertainty that gives life its intensity.

EVENTS

We keep coming back to the event. But what are these events? Events do not exist; they insist. It is we who are called upon to give them existence. What are they calling? To what are we responding? By what are we addressed? For what do they call? To what are we saying yes? In what can we have a faith if it is not fixed in creedal terms?

Events, we have been saying, have two characteristic features: first, events are what we cannot see coming, and secondly, events are not what happens but what is going *in* what happens. So an event is the sense of what is to come that is going on in what is happening. What is happening is what exists, while the event is what insists. In what we in the academic study of religion call the philosophy of religion, what happens, what actually exists, is "religion," or rather religions in the (Christian Latin) plural. By this we mean the concrete confessional communities and cultural-historical traditions, including both the first-order religious beliefs and practices and the second-order theological traditions in which the former achieve conceptual articulation. The theological reflection that goes on within the confessions is critical and conceptual work, to be sure, but it remains within "religion," within the compass of the *croyance*, explicating what happens without tapping into the event, which is something of a quasi-transcendental operation. We might say, using an expression of Husserl's, that both the first-order creedal beliefs and practices as well as the second-order theological reflection that goes on within the confessions together belong to a common theological "natural attitude" or naive belief in the confessional body, to a straightforward "doxic" attitude toward its founding sources. That falls short of the radical event-driven reflection undertaken in radical theology as the natural attitude falls short of the transcendental attitude. From the point of view of radical theology, a confessional theology is working within an existent tradition that is already "constituted," in which it has a naive belief (*croyance*), since what "constitutes" a religious tradition is the insistent event to which it arises as a response. Events are not constituted but constituting, but they are only found in what is constituted, which serves as their transcendental clue. Hence the work of radical theology is to "think" (used as a transitive verb) the event, to explicate the more radical faith (*foi*) in the event that is taking place in what is happening in the historically constituted and existing traditions of belief. (Of course, the very idea of a strong transcendental is undone by being inscribed in *différance*, by being described as an effect of *différance*.)

As everything depends upon being able to explain what we mean by an event, let us here approach the event as an event of *desire*, where we gain access to what we mean by desire only by asking "what do I desire?," or still better (in the middle voice), "what is getting itself desired in my desire?" What do "we" (among whom "I" too am also found) desire with a "desire beyond desire?"[21] I am distinguishing two orders of desire. In the first place, I mark a straightforward or first-order desire, which is conscious and present to itself, which desires something identifiably itself, whether in "terrestrial" goods, like money or prestige, or even in "celestial" ones, like "heaven" or "eternal salvation." This desire has proper names with which it can name its desire and so up to a point can know what it desires and desire what it knows. I distinguish such desire from a "desire beyond desire," the mark of which is that it lacks any proper names, that it does not know what it desires, or who is desiring or how, that it desires something *je ne sais quoi,* something going on *in* what I desire. In desiring this or that identifiable good thing I open myself to the realization that *perhaps* something else is getting itself desired, so that the first-order desire simulates while also dis-simulating something desired beyond desire. That is the trouble. The rea-son I do not know what I desire is that there is always something *coming* in what I desire, always a radical exposure to the future, something *promised* that is disturbing my present desire, so that to say I desire some identifiable thing, this or that, here and now, is to say I desire what is promised in and by this or that, that something is getting itself promised in what I desire. In a thinking of the event, nothing is ever identifiably itself, which is why it is trouble. Nothing can be contracted to itself and one can never claim to "know" "what" it "is," not because of some limitation on the part of the knower, but because this thing itself is not what it is; it is perhaps more than itself, otherwise than itself, a how not a what. It is not yet what it perhaps can be, or how. It is solicited, made to tremble, by what it promises to be, which resonates in what I desire. Everything is at once a promise made and a promise unkept, and what we desire is not what it is but what it prom-ises to be, or rather what is being promised in the desire. First-order desire is directed at something formed and constituted, while a desire beyond desire is elicited by the event that has been contracted into the first-order object of desire. Desire beyond desire is sparked by the eventive energy or eventative force that is getting evoked in and by the determinate object, by the event that is troubling first-order desire. (If I were under orders to come up with a theory of the *objet petit a,* that would be it.)

One of Derrida's favorite examples of how these two orders of desire interact is "democracy," where it would be the height of injustice, a mark of the most undemocratic injustice, to identify "democracy" with any exist-ing democratic state. For "democracy" does not exist; it calls. Democracy is not what it is; it is not the pretense of democracy made by any existing democracy, but what it promises to be, what is being promised in and by and under the word "democracy." This is what Derrida calls the "democ-racy to come" (*à venir*). The *à venir* is not the "future present," that is, some future state of democracy that will eventually become present, if we are lucky.[22] The *à venir* ("to come") is the ongoing structural demand, the exi-gency, the call, the promise of democracy which presses in upon the pres-ent and makes the present tremble with insecurity, solicited and shaken by the call of the *à venir,* the call to which we respond in trying to make democracy happen, the call which re-calls anything that pretends to be democracy.[23] If deconstruction is the analysis of the event, we might think of the analysis of the event as the process of subjecting a given empirical reality to pressure, to an infinite pressure of insistence. By this I mean the pressure of the infinitive—the *à venir*—which is the white light of an infinitival exaction which refuses to content itself with what presents itself in the present, so that we are only content with the radical discontent provoked by the promise, by what is coming, by what is to come, which is the event. In whatever identifiable content we desire there stirs the restless discontent of the event, which is what we desire with a desire beyond desire. The *à venir* brings all the pressure, the infinite pressure, of the "perhaps" upon the present.

In any (finite) identifiable content, there is contained something that it cannot contain, which is the source of the (infinitival) discontent and the specter of the "perhaps." When these considerations are brought to bear upon the question of theology we can see that the concrete confessional traditions are communities of desire of the first order. In them the infinitival event is contracted to a finite and historical content, an identifiable form that has a proper name, that is inextricably embedded in the contingency of its particular cultural form of life. That means that the confessional traditions have a built-in tendency to close ranks, to close the circle, to make things easy for themselves, to excommunicate the "perhaps it could be otherwise." Radical theology, on the other hand, spells trouble because it is interested in the event, in what is being promised in these proper names, which threatens to be shut down in the confessional theologies, in the uncontainable that is going on *in* the concrete confessional traditions, in what is getting itself desired in their desire, which we desire with a desire beyond desire.

That means that the event is also decisively marked by a certain *excess* or uncontainability. The basis of the radicalization to which the confessional religions are subject is that they contain something that they cannot contain, something uncontainable, something that insists in what exists, something that exceeds what is as the promise exceeds presence, something "undeconstructible." What is undeconstructible (*s'il y en a*) is not something actually infinite and indestructible, nor some transcendental ideal, but the urgency and pressure exerted by the infinitival to-come in the name of which deconstruction takes place. The undeconstructible is what demands the construction of something in its name whose deconstruction it simultaneously demands, the way justice demands laws which enshrine justice and at the same time demand—in the name of justice—the deconstruction of the very laws that were constructed in the name of justice. Justice demands what must be and cannot be; justice demands laws whose possibility depends upon the very same thing that makes it impossible to ever meet this demand. Whatever law comes to be in the name of justice is annulled by the very demand for justice that brought it about in the first place.[24] As "in the name of justice," so "in the name of God." The subject matter of radical theology is God, the name of God, the event that is sheltered—both concealed and kept safe—by that name, the event that insists and disturbs us in that name. The subject matter of radical theology is the insistence of God, perhaps, which demands names whose possibility depends upon the very same thing that makes it impossible ever to meet that demand. Its "*Sache*," as Heidegger liked to say, its stuff and substance, is what appears not, the promise and the uncontainable excess that is harbored by the name of God, what is asked and solicited, desired and demanded, promised and threatened, in and under the name of God (for better or for worse), which is God, perhaps.

TWO TYPES OF CONTINENTAL
PHILOSOPHY OF RELIGION

Kierkegaard's Johannes Climacus reports the case of one Dr. Hjortespring, who was converted to Hegelianism by a miracle on Easter morning at the Hotel Streit in Hamburg.[1] My own story is not as dramatic. Still, if truth be told, in the present work I fear I will shock my friends by declaring myself a born-again Hegelian, and this in order to distinguish myself from the Kantians. My reasoning is as follows. The event is an event of truth. The insistence of the event may also be called its insistent "truth." The "democracy to come" means the truth that insists on coming (true) *in* democracy, that is trying to come (true) *as* democracy. Just so, the name of God is the name of an event that is trying to come true in and under that name. It is at this point—truth—that I call upon the approach to religion and religious truth taken by Hegel, who is, by my lights, the father or (if Tillich is the father) the grandfather of radical theology and the predecessor of the new species of theologians for which I am calling. Hegel offers a new analysis of Christian theology and a new paradigm for the philosophy of religion by formulating a new idea of religious truth that constitutes for me a predecessor form of the theology of "perhaps" and consequently of theopoetics.

We can now turn to the question of two types of continental philosophy of religion.[2]

HEGEL ON THE REVEALED TRUTH

Before Hegel—which is not to say that this paradigm is not alive and well today—the distinction I am making between confessional theology and radical theology was treated as a distinction between "revealed" theology and "rational" theology, each of which provided access to a stratum of truth proper to itself. Revealed theology had to do with the truth of revelation, with all those truths that were revealed to humankind by God that humankind by its own lights, by the light of unaided human reason (*lumen rationis*), was unable to know. Thus the Trinity and the Incarnation are the content of *theologia sacra,* of a sacred or revealed theology, whose ultimate presupposition is faith in the Word of God. "Rational" theology (*theologia rationalis*) gets what is left over, the relatively small core of "rational" truth that is not off-limits to reason, the bit that unaided human reason can come up with on its own—which mostly reduces the philosophy of religion to a bad infinity of endless anthologies of proofs for the existence of God, the immortality of the soul, and resolutions of the problem of evil. "Rational" theology meant the tradition of seventeenth- and eighteenth-century scholasticisms that reached their most famous systematic form in Christian Baumgarten, which Kant labeled "onto-theology," a term later made famous by Heidegger, who to the unrelieved joy of almost everyone wanted to "overcome" it. Kant rightly and famously criticized these rationalist excesses and proposed instead an alternate radical theology that cut through to the taproot of religion in reason alone, albeit in practical reason, in the sole fact as it were of pure reason, the unconditional givenness of the Moral Law. In the Moral Law we can have a rational faith, with the result that for Kant religion is reduced to ethics and the rest is superstition.

Hegel on the other hand took the opposite view.[3] He was interested in exactly what rational theology ruled out—above all in the Trinity, Incarnation, Crucifixion, Resurrection, and Ascension—in which he said everything truly interesting about Christianity is to be found. He thought rational theology removed the chicken from the soup. So far from treating these defining Christian themes as supernatural mysteries that needed to be delivered to earthlings by an Über-being come down from the sky, Hegel treated them as a *Vorstellung*, an imaginative-sensuous presentation—or what for me will be the stuff of a "poetics"—of something that required conceptual clarification. "Christian" then would refer to something not of "supernatural" but of figurative (or as I will argue poetic) provenance, as a certain imaginative presentation of the truth. "Christianity" would be a determinate historical formation whose so-called mysteries are mysterious not because they "transcend" natural reason and require a dispatch from a supernatural source and angelic messengers, but because they elude rational argumentation in the same way a work of narratival imagination eludes a formal argument. They acquire their "force" not from having a Divine Warranty, enjoying all the "good faith and credit" of God himself, as if God were the World Bank, but from supplying the matrix of a viable form of life, of which there are of course innumerable alternatives. So Hegel branded the theologies of all the rationalist philosophers as arid exercises of *Verstand* (understanding). *Verstand* was something of a term of abuse for Hegel, meaning barren and boring, one-sided and lifeless, reducing reason to mere conceptual thinking, to abstract, formal ahistorical concepts.[4] *Verstand* is all about entities, propositions, and proofs and it misses the living organic matrix by which genuine theological thinking is nourished. It cannot see the forest for the trees. Everything that is truly interesting about religion, everything substantive and enlivening, Hegel said, is being left out—all the warm blood and vitality, all the "spirit," all the "revelatory" force, all the *Sache* of Christianity. Hegel was a serious Christian philosopher for whom Christianity was the revelatory religion par excellence, the complete revelation of the consummate truth, and Hegel insisted that we take its most characteristic teachings—its *theologia sacra*—with the utmost seriousness *as philosophers*, for these are the carriers of its "revelation," the bearers of its truth.

While Hegel nearly drove Kierkegaard out of his mind, Hegel could get away with saying this because of his idea of truth as the process of becoming true of the truth, that is, the becoming true of the Absolute Spirit, or the becoming true of what in religion is (figuratively) called "God." So my talk of the becoming radical of confessional theology parallels the Hegelian idea of the becoming true of the religious spirit in the domain of absolute knowledge. For Hegel religion is a pivotal—one might even say, quite literally, "crucial"—stage in the becoming true of truth, which means for him the development or maturation of what can be variously called the Absolute, God, or Spirit. Religion occupies the middle region of this process, midway between art and philosophy. In religion, the Absolute pivots between art, the presentation of itself in the mode of immediate sensuous feeling, on the one hand, and philosophy, the presentation of itself as present to itself absolutely, in self-knowledge, in which the Absolute becomes truly itself, the self-thinking thought (Aristotle), thought conscious of itself absolutely, on the other hand. Religion occupies this middle space because in religion the purely sensuous is lifted up to the higher, more narrational and pictorial form of the *Vorstellung* without achieving the absolute clarity of the self-conscious thought Hegel calls the *Begriff*. A *Vorstellung* is a figurative presentation, a representation of the truth in the form of a narrative or a theological figure, an image of the truth that is not a mere feeling. Take the "story" of the birth of the Savior of the world in a stable because there was no room in the inn, heralded by the angels on high to lowly shepherds in their field, the presence of the animals at the scene, the visit of the wise men from the east to a mere babe in a manger, and so forth. For Hegel, that is "the greatest story ever told." That story (prescinding from its present capitalist incarnation in shopping malls) functions on several levels all at once: it is one of the most beautiful stories in the scriptures, a popular Christian belief, a joyous feast on the liturgical calendar of the Church ("Christmas"), and the "Incarnation," a doctrine subject to deep and complex theological reflection within the Christian tradition. (The same thing could be said about "Easter.") A *Vorstellung* is the way the truth takes place in a figurative or narratival, mythic or symbolic space. It is in truth a figure but it is a true figure. Thinking is bound to respect the truth of the figure because the figure presents thinking with the absolute truth in an imaginative form.

Hegel's point is that something important, which means for him something "conceptual" (*begrifflich*), is getting itself said and done in these religious figures. A *Vorstellung* has a "subjective" side—it occurs in figural form, as artistically constructed narratives, textual allusions, symbolic references, mythic beings, theological Leitmotifs, miraculous events, etc.—but it also has an objective side—this is the Absolute Spirit expressing itself—which means it is latent with conceptual content. It is both "subject" and "substance." One thinks of the distinction in contemporary physics between "picture" theorists and "equation" theorists, between the visualization of the Big Bang on the "Discovery" Channel and the mathematics behind it. So what is "revealed" *in* the religious imagination is made conceptually clear in philosophy, namely that the Absolute *an sich* ("God," the "Father") is a one-sided, abstract understanding of the fullness of the truth of the Absolute.[5] Ultimately, the Absolute is *an sich und für sich* which is pictorially figured in the "Trinity" (the dynamics of the life of God), Incarnation (birth of God), Crucifixion (death of God), Resurrection and Ascension (the afterlife or people of God). All of those dogmas have to be "thought," conceived in a *Begriff*, grasped in the grip of the philosopher's concept, where they take the form of *Philosophie, absolutes Wissen, Wissenschaft*. The good news for the Christian "Good News" is that Christian revelation is the revelation of the absolute truth and Christianity is the consummate religion. That is Hegel being innocent as a dove. The bad news is that the "Good News" is the absolute truth only in a pictorial form, only a stage in the development of truth, a relatively true but therefore still relatively untrue form of the becoming true of absolute truth, of its complete and consummate revelation. Each and every "doctrine" of Christian revelation is true, is a stage of truth in the making, where truth is a work in progress, and so each element merits philosophical respect and demands a philosophical analysis. The truth needs philosophy but philosophy needs religion. That is Hegel being shrewd as a serpent.

Notice how Hegel has turned everything upside down. The traditional distinction is a regional schema that draws a border between rational and revealed theology and denies philosophy access to revealed theology where reason runs up against unyielding border guards. Rational theology is therefore subordinate to revealed theology as reason is subordinated to faith. But Hegel's distinction between *Vorstellung* and *Begriff* is not a regional distinction but a distinction of standpoints yielding different stages or degrees of clarity, with the result that *philosophy is given access to everything in theology*. Nothing in theology is off-limits. So, in Hegel, "revealed" religion is subordinated to philosophy as the figurative is to the conceptual. But in subordinating revelation to philosophy, he has expanded the workload of philosophy. What was previously off-limits to philosophy ("revelation") is now the heart of the matter revealing the richness of *Vernunft*. What was previously taken to be its province, the narrowly philosophical content of theology, its so-called "rational" element, is dismissed by Hegel as mere *Verstand* and logic chopping, which is pretty much what continental philosophers today criticize under the name of "onto-theologic." Hegel criticizes rational theology as abstract knowledge and one-sided rationalism, while claiming that the "faith-based" contents of "revelation" are precisely what is philosophically the most interesting and nourishing, the most "revealing" of all for thought.

In so doing, Hegel has invented radical theology. That is because he has, at one and the same time, effectively moved beyond rationalism and made the "revealed" theological content the subject matter while also cutting off the Gnostic (two-worlds) drift of classical theology. He reveals the truth of revelation while undermining the mythic supernaturalism of classical orthodoxy. He demystifies the two-worlds dualism institutionalized in early Christianity under the influence of Neoplatonism, most famously and triumphantly by Augustine, by which mainstream confessional theology has allowed itself to be fenced in ever since. In its place he puts forth an antecedent of what we would today call, using the language of Deleuze, a plane of immanence where differences are marked by distinctions of degree, by gradations of intensity, and stages of becoming, with the result that "sacred doctrine" or "divine revelation" acquires worldly (meaning this-worldly rather than other-worldly) significance. Religion is about what Derrida called the promise of the world (Martha's world),[6] and the world is no longer divided between time and eternity, revelation no longer divided by a qualitative difference between the natural and the supernatural, and knowledge no longer divided between the rational and the supra-rational. Instead, revelation is treated as a stage of our experience of the becoming true of the truth, a moment in the passage from the sensuous through the pictorial to the conceptual grasp of truth. Hegel has undermined the subordination of reason to revelation, of philosophy to revealed theology, and in the process made the contents of revelation part of the business of philosophy. Hegel thinks that religion is a *Vorstellung* of absolute knowledge, an imaginative mirroring of transparent truth, the trace the self-thinking thought makes in the world.

A HEADLESS HEGELIANISM

If, in Hegel, radical theology means bringing philosophical conceptuality to bear upon religious *Vorstellungen*, the postmodernists complain that Hegel is here being overbearing.[7] Kierkegaard introduced the first postmodernism when his Johannes Climacus quipped that according to the metaphysics of absolute knowledge God came into the world in order to schedule a consult with German metaphysicians about the makeup of the divine nature. There is thus a considerable *Gnosis* still clinging to Hegel, an unmistakably Gnostic insistence on knowing, on *Wissen* and *Begriff*. That is why, as I said at the outset, what I am calling a theology of the insistence of the event is a heretical version of Hegel, a variant postmodern Hegelianism, a kind of hybrid or even headless Hegelianism without the Concept according to the strange logic of the *sans*. The trouble with my Hegel is that it has no *Begriff*. If my religion comes without religion, my Hegel comes without the *Begriff*. If, as we will see below, the critique of Hegelian "totalization" is overblown, inasmuch as there is real contingency in Hegel, I do not think the critique of *savoir absolu* is overblown. I regard the notions of Absolute Knowledge, Absolute Concept, and Absolute Spirit as so much metaphysical inflation, the *parole soufflée* of Idealist metaphysics. My own idea is that religion is a *Vorstellung* of which there is no Concept, a figure that does not admit of metaphysical elucidation. My *Vorstellung* is headed for decapitation not recapitulation, having nowhere to turn for a Final Explanation of itself. In short, I have found it necessary to delimit Kant in order to make room for Hegel, but then to delimit Hegel in order to make room for the event.

Unlike the Hegelians of the strict observance I am only mildly distressed by this because I think we get the best results in the long run by dealing with trouble up front. For it is precisely by weakening the grip of the *Begriff* that it is possible to release the event. I accept Hegel's characterization of religion as a *Vorstellung*, but I think that what is going on *in* religion is not the *Begriff* but the event. The general procedure in weak thinking is to weaken the hold of existence in order to release insistence. Alternately one might say that, when it comes to religion, the concept (lowercase) is that there is no Concept (uppercase), only *Vorstellungen*, only the several "presentations" or "figures" of truth, but without a (capitalized) Truth to police or monitor their staging. So I favor the idea of a truth without Truth, a becoming true of truth without Truth. As the radical in radical theology can always be fitted out in the spectral logic of the without (*sans*), where it reappears in a ghostly *sous rature*, I am presenting a ghostly Hegel. Here is where I call upon a poetics for aid in my distress, a poetics that, as for Hegel, is midway between an aesthetics (art) and a logic (philosophy), but with a difference.

On the view that I take, in the wake of Hegel, a "revelation" is not a supernatural intervention from another world that interrupts the course of history and nature with a disclosure of which the world itself would not be capable. Of course, a revelation is "special" and "beyond reason"—not because it exceeds all human faculties, but because it eludes the faculty of reason by way of other faculties. It is beyond reason the way any work of imagination[8] lies beyond reason: it eludes reason's formal-logical skills by flying beneath its radar and opening up the world in another way, in a more singular and preconceptual way. If we say a revelation is *tout autre*, that does not mean that it breaks in upon us from *another world* but that it comes as *another worlding* of the world, another world disclosure, another way the world itself opens up, is reconfigured, is "revealed" in an unforeseeable and unanticipated way. The unforeseeability is the revealability; we were blind and now we see. A revelation is a world disclosure, which re-veals by disclosing a singular and idiomatic world, a life-world, a form of life, a linguistic and cultural framework, everything we mean by the disseminated but concatenated complex of the "world." A revelation does indeed break in upon us as a *tout autre* interrupting our lives, unsettling settled beliefs and practices, not because it comes from outside space and time but because it interrupts the spacing and timing of the given world with a new form of spacing and timing, a new and unforeseen way to be. A revelation is not a message from another world but a new and unforeseeable messaging of the world itself, of history itself. Revelation is an in-coming, a breaking-in upon the world that takes the world by surprise. That is not "super-natural" but a part of the amplitude of the way world works (its *physis* or *natura*, so to speak). To live in history is to be structurally subject to surprise, to unforeseeability, to the future. The interruptive disclosure that breaks in *upon* the world in a revelation is the interruptive disclosure, the disclosive interruption, which *is* the world. That is what we mean by the "world," by the idiomatic and singular constellations that the world is endlessly undergoing. A revelation is a provisional and local fulfillment of the promise of the world, of the promise that gets itself made in and as and through the world, and it does so in a way we didn't see coming, which is what we mean by time and history.

In short, a revelation is an event, *l'invention de l'autre,* the possibility of the impossible, and like every event, one we did not see coming, whereas in orthodox Hegelianism the Spirit is Absolute Knowledge and can in principle see everything coming (which is why there is only a limited chance for a genuine event in orthodox Hegelianism, a point to which I will return in the next chapter). The in-breaking power of the Sermon on the Mount does not consist in being a supernatural revelation delivered by a heavenman come down from the sky, proffering some account of things that lies beyond the ken of humankind. It lies "beyond the reach of reason" in the sense that it lies outside the circle of its "logic," outside the sphere of influence of the "principle of sufficient reason," as Heidegger says about poetic thinking.[9] It represents an insight into a form of life structured by the "rule of God," let us say, by the ruleless and unruly rule of the gift as opposed to the logical rules of an economy. The Sermon on the Mount does not belong to the circle of logic but to the open-endedness of poetics. It is a shocking re-envisioning of human life, of an unprecedented form of life. But by a "poetics" I do not mean poetry or verse, free or rhymed, or any form of poetic ornament or adornment of some preestablished belief. A poetics is not an aesthetics adorning a prior religious belief or practice (*croyance*) but a creative-discursive evocation (*poiesis*) of an unnamable faith (*foi*) to come.[10] A poetics is a constellation of puns and pictures, of parables and paradoxes wilder than anything imagined by Lewis Carroll, of reversals and antinomies, of tropes, figures, narratives, of striking and even outrageous images like being both a dove and a snake in order to be like sheep among wolves, moving stories, miraculous events, visions, dis-seminations, evocations, solicitations, and imperatives that nominate and record an event. A poetics is a repertoire of strategies, discursive and rhe-torical, constative and performative, semantic, syntactical, and pragmatic, all loosely assembled, like the mobile army of metaphors and metonyms to which the young Nietzsche refers, an army on the move, trying to gain ground on the plane of immanence.[11]

In short, in a poetics all of the aphoristic and anarchistic energy of what Derrida calls *différance* is joined with what Hegel meant by a *Vorstellung,* as a sensuous-pictorial embodiment of the truth, not a conceptual-logical one. A *Vorstellung* is a world-picture, a world-praxis, a world-formation, a world-creation, an event of *poiesis,* of the creative and recreative, by which I do not mean the origin of the universe in the Big Bang, or the *creatio ex nihilo* doctrine created from almost nothing by the second-century theologians. The "world" in the poetics of the "world" is the life-world, a form of life, a vision, a disclosure, a paradigm, a revelation, and the "poetics" is the constellation of discursive strategies and practices, the grammatology or theo-grammatology, in which and through which the world is forged or formed. A genuine "revelation" is always "special," which means the idiomatic trait, the structure of singularity of a world, the singular way the world is revealed in the formation, rather the way we speak of the "world" of Milton or Shakespeare, of Renoir or Picasso, the way the world is revealed in different ways in different writers or painters, or in different languages, where a language is, as Merleau-Ponty once said, a singular way to "sing the world." A revelation is a world disclosure, a constellation of elements—linguistic, cultural, economic, social, political, ethical, religious, and who knows what else. It is because every authentic revelation is special that there is no such thing as "revelation" in the singular, but many revelations in the plural, as many as there are cultural forms of life, which is the trouble built right into the idea of revelation.

In my hybrid headless Hegelianism the *Vorstellung* is a presentation or representation, a figure or an image, not of the *Begriff*—I have no head for the *Begriff*—but of the event. A poetics is neither an aesthetics of the work of art nor a logic of the concept, but a poetics of the event. The event is not what happens but what is going on *in* what happens, where what is going on is the promise of the event, not the finality of the *Begriff*. The event is not what exists but what insists, what is being promised and mourned, called and recalled, desired with a desire beyond desire, contained without being contained, in what happens—in Torah or Christ or Sharia no less than in the lava rock of native Hawaiians. A genuinely radical theology is a poetics of the event, a theo-poetics, not a theo-logic, of the event that is harbored in the name of God, which is a "natural" name, meaning a name in a "natural" (or "historical") language, which makes its appearance in the various confessions and confessional theologies. A theopoetics is a deployment of multiple discursive resources meant to give words to the event, but without miscasting it as a gift coming down from the sky (supernaturalism) and without laying claim to the high ground of the Concept (metaphysics) which dominates it from above, without asserting that one knows the secret, the code, the rule that governs events. There is no event of events, only so many events, so many eventive traditions, so many promises, so many calls, so many plural ways in which events insist upon existing. The traditions that we in the West describe in Christian Latin as "religious" are so many ways of figuring the event, so many ways the event takes the form of narratives, parables, figures, images, and sensuous presentations of the promise, of the gift, of the call, all more or less taking the form of the "possibility of the impossible,"[12] which is a venerable name of God in the Abrahamic traditions, which does not so much "define" them as point to why they cannot be defined but simply treated as complexes of overlapping cultural practices.

Religion is a *Vorstellung* not of a metaphysical substance but of the insistence of the event. A *Vorstellung* is a way to poetize the pressure exerted by insistence, what is called the "event" by several continental philosophers—Heidegger, Derrida, and Deleuze foremost among them, although I also think much of what Badiou has to say about the event in Paul's letters can also be cautiously incorporated into this account. I displace and replace the Hegelian philosophy of the Spirit with the poetics of the event.[13] The event is nominated without being finally named even as events are effects of names, the comet's tail of memories, hopes, and promises being made in and by the name. The event is called, called for, called up, even as we ourselves are called upon, all in the name of God. The event belongs to what it summons up, an appellatory, messianic, vocative, valorized space in which we are called upon or visited *by* "the" impossible. The event takes place as the insistence of the possibility of the impossible. When I claim that theopoetics in particular is a poetics of the possibility of the impossible, which is one of the most familiar and perplexing names of God in the Hebrew and Christian scriptures, this reflects my earlier delimitation of how genuinely "free" radical theology is, seeing that, as a "theology," it is inextricably tied to Western philosophical and Jewish, Islamic, and Christian monotheistic traditions. It is as difficult to free a pure radical theology from confessional theology as it is to remain within a pure confessional religion without being exposed to a radical theology or theopoetics of the event. That is why the most precise way to describe religion without religion is to redescribe it as religion with/out religion, inside and outside religion and to situate oneself on the slash between them, and the best way to describe radical theology is in terms of the becoming radical of confessional theology.[14]

Of course, as we have seen, Hegel does not deny that there are "concepts" in the confessional theologies, but he regards them as the conceptualization of a mythology, as the logic of a mytho-logic, which retains the conceptual architecture of the mythic world, hence as uncapitalized concepts of the understanding, not the Concept (*Begriff*). (One could, for example, work out in some detail the logic of the technology and cosmology in *Star Wars,* or the logic of the world of *Harry Potter.*) Orthodox confessional theology is the literalization of an event; it is mythology taken seriously and thought through, a second-order reflection on and the logical conceptualization of a symbolic vision of the world, that is, of a world of beings and super-beings and super-mutations, where events are given the form of entities and super-entities. The fundamental tendency of mythic thinking is to turn the insistence of events into beings who do the insisting—turning the call of justice into the Just One calling, the injunction of the good into the Good One enjoining—and to locate them as immaterial entities inhabiting another world. In a myth, an event becomes an Über-being. A hermeneutic or poetics of the event moves in exactly the opposite direction.

I am thus distinguishing a theopoetics from a mythopoetics. Theopoetics is not mythopoetics just because it is mytho-poetics demythologized and re-poeticized in a poetics of the event. In theopoetics, everything turns on *rejecting* supernaturalism, that is, the cluster of distinctions between natural and supernatural, transcendence and immanence, reason and faith, human knowledge and divine revelation, and time and eternity. In mytho-poetics, an omnipotent Superbeing in the sky, who outknows, outwits, outwills, and outmans us has to our good fortune intervened in terrestrial life and equipped us with the "secret," with the hidden "answer" to the question that we could never have come up with on our own (at least those of us who happened to be lucky enough to be standing in the right place at the right time to receive the revelation as the divine motorcade goes speeding by). The several "religions"—if it is not time to give up on this word—are for me so many ways to "poetize" or "sing" the world (Merleau-Ponty), and they differ from one another in ways that are broadly similar to the ways that languages differ from one another. It would make no more sense to ask what is the true religion than to ask what is the true language. They differ as do different modes of "being-in-the-world" (Heidegger), different "forms of life" (Wittgenstein), different measures of intensity within the plane of immanence (Deleuze), and different vocabularies doing different things (Rorty).

TWO TYPES OF CONTINENTAL PHILOSOPHY OF RELIGION

I come now, after this considerable preparation, to the second leg of my claim. In the view that I am defending, there are two forms of postmodern philosophies of religion, the one descending from Kant and the other from Hegel, which is the form I am advocating here under the name of theopoetics. By "continental philosophy of religion" I mean post-metaphysical approaches to religion starting with Kierkegaard and culminating in the post-structuralist theories of the *soixante-huitaires*. These approaches turn on a critique of metaphysics and logico-formal thinking and variously look for more material, experiential, existential, embodied, gendered, historical, linguistic, cultural, and interpretive ways of thinking about religion in terms stretching from the "existing individual" to the "plane of immanence," regimes of truth and *différance*.

Kant

The first type of continental philosophy of religion thinks that postmodern critiques of classical metaphysics play the role of Kant in the philosophy of religion. Taking its lead from Kant's famous statement that he has found it necessary to deny knowledge in order to make room for faith, postmodern theory is treated as an epistemological critique that delimits the pretensions of the various forms of reductionism brought forth in modernity.[15] The "modern" tradition under fire in this "postmodernism" culminates in the masters of suspicion, the atheistic reductionisms of Marx, Nietzsche, and Freud, which reduce religion to the sigh of the economically distressed, the resentment of the weak against the strong, or a desire for one's mommy. Such critiques of religion hold up if and only if they are backed by sustainable metaphysical claims. But the several versions of postmodern theory have discredited such metaphysical claims by denying that we have access to overarching ahistorical, disinterested, and purely objective principles independent of the linguistic and historical soil in which they spring up. For example, even Nietzsche's own atheism, if accorded metaphysical status, would be undermined by his theory of perspectives, which undermines metaphysics. In this case, postmodern theory is being taken as a subdivision of confessional theology known as apologetics, the epistemological delimitation of atheistic metaphysics that leaves the field open for confessional theology, for religious belief in the God of classical metaphysical theology. So instead of the becoming radical of confessional theology we have the opposite, the becoming confessional of a radical impulse. The first type of postmodern theory employs a safe "perhaps," a perhaps meant to keep us safe and sound; it claims that the most severe critiques of religion are overreaching and so we are perhaps safe after all. The first postmodernist on this account is Kierkegaard, when he has Johannes Climacus say that the world is not a system for us, but that does not mean it is not a system for God.[16] Climacus's distinction between "for us" and "for God" steps up as the successor form of Kant's untenable distinction between appearances and things in themselves and it makes it possible for us to have faith in the way things are for God even though we are deprived of the God's-eye view ourselves.

In the Kantian version, postmodernism ends up as a way to contain the trouble that irrupts in modern materialism, a way to limit trouble in order to allow the old Augustinian dualism to emerge in a different form. Postmodernism is incorporated into confessional theology as an epistemological critique and an exercise in (1) "apologetics," a defense of faith, a "skepticism" that fends off atheistic "dogmatism," that deflects attacks on religious faith by casting doubt on the metaphysical presuppositions of atheism and (2) an epistemological "humility" that we are not God. Postmodernism implies not that there is no God but only that we are not God. Postmodernism bars the door to objectivistic reductionism while leaving another door wide open for the possibility of faith in the God of metaphysical theology, or of the various confessional theologies, but without the pretense of achieving metaphysical knowledge. It is content with a draw: in exchange for blocking the way to a metaphysical refutation of religion it is happy to surrender any claim to a metaphysical defense of religion and to retreat to epistemology. It is a faith-first approach that reminds us of what Meillassoux calls fideism, a word that historically has meant something arbitrary and decisionistic, which is the polemical value of the word for Meillassoux. I think the Kantians can give a reason for the faith that is in them, and it is not irrational, but it remains a kind of soft fideism that refuses the harder look at religious phenomena taken by the more Hegelian posture I advocate, on which Meillassoux and I would agree.[17] At the end of the day, confessional theology remains standing, its head bloodied—it cannot itself lay claim to metaphysical support—but unbowed—it cannot be refuted by an opposing metaphysics, and it may still be defended. So in the first version of postmodernism religion is defended but it is not radicalized. The walls around Augustine's *City of God* are still standing—what I am calling the two-worlds theory and the soft Gnosticism—all made safe from reductionistic critique. The trouble has been contained and the negotiations with modernity are satisfactorily concluded. But it does not pursue a more radical course or expose itself to a more unnerving "perhaps."

I do not mean to deny the merits of the Kantian version of postmodern philosophy of religion or to underestimate its advantages over classical apologetics, which are modernist to the core. I am not ungrateful for the considerable advance it makes in dealing with two very intemperate forms of thinking. Its epistemological humility is well aimed against two very deserving targets, each of which could stand a little humility: on the one hand, atheistic critics who mount disdainful eliminationist critiques of religion (one thinks of the popular but polarizing intellectual temper tantrums of Christopher Hitchens, Richard Dawkins, and Daniel Dennett) and, on the other hand, religious fundamentalists who think that by believing in God they themselves have become God, or at least have acquired the status and authority of God and are authorized to speak for God. Absolutism in either guise, theistic or atheistic, falls before the Kantian scythe. Within confessional theology itself, the approach to religion taken in what I am criticizing as an abridged postmodernism belongs to a progressive wing eager to absorb the insights of radical thinkers from Nietzsche to Žižek in order to engage in serious self-criticism and to undermine the demonization of atheism by theology. If we criticize theologians for not reading such writers, are we then to criticize them when they do? Postmodern theology results in a serious criticism of the violence and fundamentalism of religion from *within* theology itself, which is vastly more effective than any external criticism of theology. It is part of an auto-deconstruction of theological imperialism, militarism, patriarchy, racism, and homophobia, drawing upon a theology of peace and justice stretching from Amos to Martin Luther King (which is why religious people are so regularly found working among the most destitute people on earth) and calling down upon itself the fire of conservative religious authorities who are out to purge the seminaries of all such postmodern personnel. If such theological thinking were the coin of the realm in religion today, religious violence would not be in the headlines and issues of social justice would be.

So I am saying that the post-Kantian version is good but it could be better. Whatever its critical merits, and they are considerable, the Kantian version resists the becoming radical of confessional theology that I am calling radical theology. A more searching version of postmodern theory requires a more searching (and post-Hegelian) analysis of what is going on *in* religion and theology. The post-Kantian version is at bottom an apologetic for and an epistemological defense of confessional theology—the conservatives fail to appreciate that the Kantians are actually conserving orthodoxy—not a critical analysis of it. It is at best a thin postmodernism, an abridged edition, or, if you will excuse a certain flippancy, a postmodernism "light," like a nonalcoholic wine. It makes the way clear for a classical two-worlds piety, innocent as a dove but insufficiently serpentine, better at delimiting the pretensions of objectivistic reductionism than at delimiting the pretensions of confessional theology. It is a Kantian or pious version of postmodernism that has provoked Meillassoux and the "speculative realists" to undertake a widespread critique of continental philosophers from Kant to the present as a form of fideism. The right response to the speculative realists lies in pointing out to them that they are half right, but they have neglected the other and Hegelian version of continental philosophy of religion. I will come back to this point in part 3, where I will deal with the lingering residue of Kantianism in continental philosophy (of religion or of anything else).

In the version that descends from Hegel, postmodern theory is neither an epistemology nor an apologetics but a genuinely radical theology which mounts a heartier critique of confessional two-worlds theology. Postmodern philosophy is not restricted to building epistemological levees to contain the rising waters of materialist critique; instead, it fully embraces the floods that rush across the plane of immanence. But by sailing the insistence of the event under the flag of Hegel we have not thereby ended up in metaphysics after all, for the event is introduced precisely to do non-metaphysical service for what Hegel called *Geist*, which was in Hegel himself the metaphysical plane of absolute Being, which is still marked by transcendence. Like the Kantian type, the Hegelian version of postmodern theory comes after metaphysics. It is not metaphysics, but unlike the Kantian type it is not merely epistemology. Having no metaphysical pretensions, it devotes all its time to time and to everything that takes place in space, to the various intensities and lines of force of the events that traverse the plane of immanence. Of course, if one dials down the word "metaphysics" a notch or two and takes it to mean an account of the deep structures of our *experience*, the work of going beyond a description of what is happening in order to reach an interpretation of what is going on *in* what happens, then a poetics might by quite a stretch be called a certain "metaphysics." But this would be of so radically muted and experiential a kind that it would be far better described as a "phenomenological ontology," and then it would need to be muted one more time as a quasi-transcendental post-phenomenological ontology-cum-hauntology.

That will not appease the classical appetite for metaphysics. Theopoetics is certainly not a metaphysics if by that one means the faculty of producing arguments and drawing conclusions about what absolutely transcends experience, which I treat as a captive of the mytho-poetics of the "two worlds" famously theorized by Augustine. In the Hegelian type, there are not two worlds but one, which has nothing to do with denying the alternate universes theorized by contemporary physics. The plane of immanence is, thus, not a monochrome but a rainbow of multiple modes of the insistence of events, a multiplex plane of differences, of endless multiplicity and becoming, of the endless becoming true of the truth, in all the modes and modalities which can be expressed on the plane of the "perhaps" and its army of adverbs. The space-bound and time-bound character of our understanding is never denied in theopoetics, but that bond is not treated as a limitation and made to serve the purpose of clearing a path for faith in a God outside space and time who sees and knows all and manages all things unto good. The worldly limits of our understanding are instead the way we have access to what is going on in and under the name of God.

In the postmodern approach to religion that descends from Hegel, where religion is taken to be a *Vorstellung*, it is *Vorstellungen* all the way down, unlike the Kantian version, where a *Vorstellung* has a more limited and strategic role. In the Kantian version one could still say that religion is a *Vorstellung* so long as that is restricted to meaning that religion is a finite, historical, and created human institution which should not be confused with God Almighty, with God "in his heaven." Postmodern theory on the Kantian approach then turns out to be a critique of idols, where religion's *Vorstellung* of God is to be sharply distinguished from God's own being, the Eternal Creator of heaven and earth. That is pretty much what Karl Barth has to say and so we would on this approach end up calling Barth a postmodern theologian, which should give us pause. But in the Hegelian version, where the *Vorstellung* goes all the way down, it is not merely the case that religion is a *Vorstellung* of God, but that "God" too is a *Vorstellung*, not just the God of the philosophers but also the God of Abraham and Isaac, God being a way, one of the ways, to name the insistence of the event. At a certain point, on this Hegelian approach, confessional theologians ask themselves in a radical way whether they need God to describe what they think is going on in the name (of) "God." The Kantian version seeks to delimit knowledge to make room for faith in the transcendence of God. The Hegelian version delimits transcendence and redescribes faith and God. Postmodernism takes a distinct turn in the direction of the "philosophy of religion" when it recognizes that the name of God is, indeed, not just one more name, but a paradigmatic name, where what is going on *in* that name, what I am calling the event, takes place in a paradigmatic way.

The difference between the two versions shows up in a revealing way in the contrasting ways they deal with hard-line atheism and fundamentalism, both of which are strong, wolfish ways of thinking compared to them. The Hegelian version agrees with the atheists. Like Tillich, the Hegelians think that if God is taken to be an entity, even a prime entity, "the right religious and theological reply is atheism."[18] (Or as Bruno Latour says, if by atheism you mean "a general doubt about mastery," then since we have had enough of masters we are all for atheism.)[19] There is only one world. But the Hegelians chide dogmatic atheistic metaphysics for having a tin ear for the poetics of religion, for being ham-fisted, inept, and insensitive with religion, like computer geeks trying to understand poetry by writing a program to generate poems or trying to understand a poem by formalizing its argument. The Kantian version, what I am calling an abridged version of postmodernism, on the other hand, agrees with the Fundamentalists: the basics of *what* the Fundamentalists believe is "fundamentally" right, but it chides them, not for their "what" but for their "how." It chastises them for confusing themselves with God and for having allowed themselves to be stampeded by the deracinating effects of techno-capitalism into biblical literalism and authoritarianism, and it counsels a more cautious course while applauding them for not negotiating away the fundamentals.

In the Kantian version, to say "God, perhaps" comes down to saying that the "perhaps" allows the God of classical theology to still stand and such faith to be still possible. In the Hegelian version, to say "God, perhaps" is to link God with the perhaps, to let "perhaps" cut into the very name of God, as the possibility of the impossible. In the Kantian version, "perhaps" keeps God safe from trouble; in the Hegelian version, "perhaps" signifies the trouble with God.

THE NAME (OF) "GOD":
AN APOLOGY TO THE ORTHODOX

I am aware how disconcerting the becoming radical of confessional theology is to the orthodox; how deeply unsatisfying the "God, perhaps" of whom I speak is to orthodox theology. I do not depict a recognizable empirical church with candles, liturgies, and doctrines. I do not describe a God who is a refuge, an agent capable of stepping in when needed. The insistence of God, which does not refer to a First Being or even to a Tillichian ground of Being, may turn out to be a disaster and may "perhaps" not be at all (existence depends on us). "God, perhaps" contradicts in one fell swoop the classical divine names of necessity, omnipotence and omni-benevolence while introducing a new and most unwelcome addition, "perhaps." I am aware that, for orthodox theology, God is most certainly an agent of the very highest sort, having created the world from nothing, compared to which intervening in this or that sublunary scene is small potatoes. Furthermore, in orthodox theology God's intervention in the world could never result in a disaster since God is all good and all knowing. The most we could say is that sometimes we are not sure how God has intervened and we cannot understand the wisdom of God's ways, for God's ways are not our ways. My God looks like thin soup, of no use to man nor beast nor climate control. The more honest thing for me to do, the orthodox are likely to think, is to just admit that I am not speaking of

God at all but am simply defending some notion of my own devising that the faithful cannot recognize.

I take this line of objection seriously because I myself would find it deeply unsatisfying if the results of these pages would be merely to supply more fodder for academics talking to themselves at the AAR. I do not mean to say that such strictly academic and technical discourses do not have an important, indeed irreducible, role to play, but rather that my interests are both broader and deeper than that, which is why I keep stressing that radical theology is deeply interwoven with confessional theology. That is why it belongs to my own circumfessional project to confess that the distinction between radical and confessional theology is something of a fiction, that each side is more porous to the other than I am letting on. The whole idea is to *haunt* confessional theology, to expose it to what it contains but cannot succeed in containing, to expose it to an event it cannot prevent, after which it will continue to be, perhaps, but it will never be the same. So I want to be very clear here about my intentions.

My position is radically "grammatological," which means that the root source of the discrepancy between radical and confessional theology can be traced to the *trace,* something that shows up in the series of scare quotes that mark my version of theology, by which everything in radical theology is suspended (*points de suspension*). The discrepancy is rooted in my speaking of the "name" of God, the name (of) "God," to my practice of saying "God" not God, or the "event" that is contained in the name of God, not God. This I do because of my conviction that *no one has access to anything else.* The "scare quotes" cannot be removed, and if they are removed, then things get genuinely scary and we are exposed to the worst violence. Everything I have to say about radical theology turns on the irreducibility of the scare quotes. The difference between "radical theology" and "theology" in a more orthodox sense, the whole idea behind this hauntology, is that the scare quotes haunt (scare) everything we say when we say "God." What we have to do with, inside theology or outside, inside religion or outside, is the constituted effect "God," the name by which we nominate an event, or a cluster of events, for better or for worse. This all goes back to Derrida's argument in the early writings that there is no "transcendental signified," no "naked thing" or *res* to which we are hardwired, or with which we somehow make "naked contact." Such a supposed transcendental signified would magically stand free of the play of traces in such a way that, after having delivered us over to the thing itself, we can thank the signifier for its services and relieve it of any further duties, throwing away the ladder it provided. The mark of radical theology is that in it "God" does not get a pass. The meaning of "God" *is* the meaning of God. But I am emphasizing that this meaning has been constituted not only in theological discussion but also in deeds and actions, in rituals and practices, in ongoing historical traditions, in forms of life and modes of being in the world, which are the organized around that name, making up the real response to what insists in that name. What we mean by God is what *we mean* by God, what and how religious traditions have constituted it, the "interpretation" this name has been given, not only in words but also in deeds, not only in theological traditions but also in the way this name is translated into historical institutions and practices. This word has not dropped from the sky into our laps.

My position is *radically* "phenomenological," issuing from what I have called the "reduction" to the event or to the call, an *epoche* in which I "reduce" or "suspend" (in the phenomenological sense) the name (of) "God," hanging it from its hauntological scare quotes, in order to release the event.[20] By undertaking a reduction of God to the insistence of God, to the insistence of the event, I treat confessional theology as still operating in the "natural attitude." By sticking with "God" I am, like any good phenomenologist, sticking strictly to what is given. But my position is also radically *hermeneutic*, because I claim nothing is simply given; everything is interpreted. Interpretation goes all the way down. So I claim, on the one hand, that the name (of) "God" has been historically constituted by historical communities, in historical beliefs and practices which make up what it means. But, on the other hand, and as I have taken pains to emphasize, I am not saying this name is a "subjective projection." It is not the effect of a projection but the name of a "projectile," of an event by which we have been visited as by a thief in the night, an event which invades us and overturns the tables of our lives, and this event is given word and deed under the name (of) "God," for better and for worse. When someone says they have encountered the living Christ, I take them with deadly seriousness. I think they are talking about something real. I take them to be describing something that overtakes them, something transformative, to which they are giving words. This is hermeneutics; this is not Feuerbach. This is a theory of interpretation not a metaphysical anthropologism, and its antecedent is in Hegel's notion that the name of God has both a substance and a subject side. In chapter 10 I will argue, following the analysis of Bruno Latour, that there is nothing about what we have constituted (an "artifact") that condemns it to being a fiction, a fantasy, or a merely subjective occurrence. To insist upon a mediated contact with the real does not destroy contact with the real; it explains it, including explaining why we have considerably richer and more complex contact with the real than does the tree outside the window with the breeze bending its limbs. This is hermeneutics, seeking an interpretive angle of entry into the world, not a theory of linguistic idealism or a claim that we are locked inside a prison house of signifiers.[21]

So then why not simply drop "God" and talk about "justice" or "love?" That choice is not mine to make; it has never been made available to me. God, "God," haunts me, hounds me:[22]

> I fled Him, down the nights and down the days;
> I fled Him, down the arches of the years;
> I fled Him, down the labyrinthine ways
> Of my own mind; and in the mist of tears
> I hid from Him, and under running laughter.

I cannot shake God, "God," the name (of) "God," capitalized and in the singular. This is not merely an autobiographical observation on my part but a matter of a massive cultural fact. This name, as the work of Hent de Vries shows so well, is not just any name, but one of paradigmatic and pressing significance, which announces the very possibility of the impossible. It is the name of a desire beyond desire, the very heart of everything that interests and grips those who have a heart, the very heart of life itself. At least that is so for "us," for those who live in the tracks of the Christian Latin trace *religio*, Greco-Europeans' descendants who have been saturated by the monotheistic traditions, their scriptures, liturgies, and narratives, their metaphors and metonyms, who "find themselves" (*Befindlichkeit*) in such a world as soon as they open their eyes. I say all this without saying that the name (of) "God" functions in that way everywhere or for everyone. God forbid.

Then, perhaps, radical theology might be a postmodern version of negative theology. The distinction between "God" and God is standard fare in the Jewish critique of idols, and in negative or apophatic theology. For example, Meister Eckhart distinguished between God, meaning what we human beings mean when we say "God," and *Gottheit,* meaning what God is in God's own naked being. But as I have been saying for as long as I can remember, deconstruction is not negative theology; it is not a way of inscribing a zone of absolute respect around the transcendence of God. It is a radical hermeneutics of the immanence of the trace. The closest thing to grammatology in classical theories of language and knowledge is nominalism. That is why I argued some time ago that Eckhart's distinction between *Gott* and *Gottheit* is a function of *différance,* a discrimination internal to language that never for a moment makes naked contact with the naked God (without the scare quotes).[23] The tree outside the window has non-linguistic contact with the wind. But we will not find non-linguistic contact in the linguistic distinction between *Gott* and *Gottheit* in the *sermones* of Meister Eckhart, the master of *Leben und Lesen,* one of the veritable founders of modern German and a formidable linguistic genius. Meister Eckhart was arguing that certain experiences authorize us to remove the scare quotes. I beg to differ with my beloved master. I would say that certain *events* authorize us to in-vent new differential effects; that certain experiences overtake us, take us by surprise, leaving us "lost for words," "groping for words." That does not mean that these events reduce us to silence or wipe away language. On the contrary, they return us to the very springs of language, discourse, and action, which is what they did for Meister Eckhart, resulting in a genius whose towering linguistic achievements belong to the story of the very creation of the German language.

Consequently, when I deny that God is an agent-being who does things, I am saying that the only thing we know about agency is human beings doing things under certain names, in response to certain claims made upon them. As a matter of hermeneutics and phenomenology, the history of the agency of God is the history of things that human beings do that are interpreted to have been done by the "grace" of God, and in the name (of) "God," in just the way that people in other cultural or religious traditions would describe their actions in other terms and with other graces and other proper names. No one has seen God and lived; the only thing we see are people doing things under the name of God, which to those who dismiss the name (of) "God" looks quite foolish. They see people dancing but cannot hear the music.[24] In such cases I am claiming that such actions come in response to events that are harbored in those names, events that insist, that lay claim to us. It is no part of my "weak theology" to deny the power of such action, the strength of such deeds. My whole idea is to single out such events in terms of their insistence and to point to the history of what exists as a result, for better or for worse. The weakness of God means that what is done in the name of God is done by human beings in the name of "God." When we speak of the agency of God in terms of natural events, such as tsunamis averted, then what is interpreted as the grace of "God," an event of grace, is otherwise described in radical theology as the grace of the event, an important point to which I will return in the conclusion of this study.

I should also add that as the author of a book titled *Against Ethics* I am *not* arguing that religion is just ethics under another name. I reject Kant's reduction of religion to ethics. It is no part of my meditation upon the insistence of God to argue that the events underlying "religion" are only or even primarily "ethical," for which I have repeatedly criticized Levinas. I regard religion instead in more Hegelian terms as a *Vorstellung* of a broader and more culturally rich cluster of events underlying a rich weave of beliefs and practices, ideas and images, institutions and traditions. The events that interest me certainly include justice and democracy, which I claim are impoverished if they are described as "secular" values, marked as they are by a deeper religious impulse. But these events extend well beyond that and have to do with a richer affirmation that extends to life itself, to a broader and wider celebration of life, to a joy in everyday mortal life. I am speaking of a generalized *viens, oui, oui* to life and the future, extending beyond the "moral virtues" and belonging to the "theological virtues," to an underlying faith and hope and love of life itself, which I regard as a magnificent condensation of the very life of "religion." This a point to which I will return in chapter 11 when I address the question of nihilism.

But why, then, this association of "God" with the threat of disaster, when religious people seek God in order to avoid disasters? My point is that whatever they are seeking when they seek God, what they reach is "God." I am not saying that the reduction to the insistence of the event is a matter of words; it is a matter of events, of both the events that words nominate and the events to which words give rise, and these events are risky business. The history of "God" includes the history of the worst bloodshed, persecution, and injustice. To this, the orthodox respond, but that is not God; that is simply how some people have misused the name of God or made it serve their selfish purposes, as opposed to others from whom the name of God has called forth a life of sacrifice for others. But my whole point is that this is a recourse which we are denied, that we do not get to lay aside "God" and seek entry through the back door to God. The scare quotes cannot be lifted. The fluctuation between the sacrifice of others to my own will and the sacrifice of my will in the service of others is built into the name (of) "God" in just the way the best and the worst are built into other high-velocity words like justice and democracy, truth and love. The higher the velocity at which these words speed along, the higher the stakes for good and for evil. The name (of) "God" calls forth the best *and* the worst. It is the riskiest name we know and you cannot simply decontaminate it of its undecidability.

The reduction to insistence, the impossibility of removing the scare quotes, is for me the condition of the possibility of *faith*, which I am distinguishing from confessional *belief.* Faith is faith only when it is not secure, when it is not firmed up by having made contact with some sort of naked uninterpreted fact of the matter or naked necessity. Faith is faith when it is groping in the dark, seeking to nominate something, I know not what, something by which I have been overtaken, just the way prayer is really prayer when I am hanging on by a prayer, not knowing whether there is anyone to whom to pray. I am meditating upon the name (of) "God" not trying to debunk or dismiss it. I am seeking out its truth. I am trying to find out what is going on *in* religion, feeling about for the events that give rise to effects like "religion," "prayer," "God." I am engaged in a radical phenomenological and hermeneutic rumination on this name, on what insists in this name, on what is trying to come true there, whether we like it or not.

As I have already indicated in my discussion of the good done in the abridged version of postmodernism, I want to make clear that I do not for a moment think and do not mean to imply that the "orthodox" are political reactionaries or right-wing ideologues. I do not identify religion with the religious right. On the contrary, I have been arguing from the start, from the first time it hit me how singularly "religious" deconstruction is. Biblical or Abrahamic "religion" contains the most intense and concentrated version of what postmodern philosophers call "openness to the other" and the affirmation of "singularity," and there is a good argument to be made that this is where such ideas originate. That is why I have argued that this is not an accidental convergence; postmodern continental thought draws directly upon a cluster of what Derrida calls "unavowed theologemes,"[25] upon biblical sources like the Jewish prophets and Paul, theological sources like Augustine and Luther, religious thinkers like Kierkegaard and Levinas. These religious motifs are closely interwoven with politically radical tendencies in a postmodern secular thinker like Derrida or Lyotard (even as there are theophantic sources behind Deleuze). By the same token, these radical political motifs show up time and again in progressive religious thinkers and activists like Dorothy Day, who was completely orthodox in her beliefs. That explains my interest in the "working church" in *What Would Jesus Deconstruct?* where I was following the work of a very orthodox pastor of a Catholic Church in the worst neighborhoods of North Philadelphia. That is also why I have said we would all be better off if orthodoxy would *at the very least* embrace what I have called an "abridged postmodernism," which calls for a modesty, tolerance, and open-endedness that would put to shame the mean-spiritedness of the religious right and put an end to religious violence in general. That affection for religion is why my work invites attack by the secular left. But I have also argued that we should not be satisfied with an edited version of postmodernism, for all the reasons I have been giving in the present study and elsewhere. That is why my work invites attack by orthodox religious thinkers, left or right.

Radical theology is called into existence by the insistence of the event by which orthodox theology is pressured from within. But for the most part, I do not think radical theology *does* exist—except in the crevices and interstices of confessional theology, among "radicals" within the confessional traditions, who are constantly being harassed, called out or just outright fired by the confessional powers that be. These thinkers have my unalloyed admiration. Radical theology is always inside/outside, always parasitic upon confessional theologies, which it means to invade, disturb, transgress, and haunt. It does not pose a rival God in a rival religion meant to out-recruit confessional traditions for members. It is not a rival existent but an insistence, a ghost that haunts what exists. If so, the present essay on radical theology is meant to offer these confessional theologians a word of encouragement. Heidegger says that inauthenticity bears witness to authenticity, that the very flight from the call of anxiety testifies to that very call—because it is clear that something has sent us scurrying for the cover afforded by average everydayness. That, I am tempted to say, is what motivates the violence of confessional authorities against their own theologians: these authorities have been spooked and they are running like hell from the call of the event while a more radical theology keeps its ears peeled for what is calling and what is called in order to own up to, to expose us all to a deeper affirmation, to confess a more uncertain faith and hope, a more dangerous love.

THEOPOETICS IS NOT METAPHYSICS

But if we say it is *Vorstellungen* all the way down, and that postmodern theory is not merely an epistemology, then how does the Hegelian version of postmodernism manage to avoid being an ontology or a metaphysics? If it is not merely a theory of the limits of our knowledge, is it not then a theory of being? Can there be anything in between?

To answer that question I must first make it plain that I am making use for my own ends of a schema with a Hegelian inspiration, of aesthetics, poetics, metaphysics, which derives from what Hegel called the dialectical stages of art, religion, and philosophy. My own irregular form of Hegelianism is to privilege not the dialectic, not even a negative dialectic, as does Žižek, but a non-dialectical version of these three stages, so that the schema has been de-hierarchized, or an-archized, or disseminated, so that now there are three "equi-primordial" forms, not an ascending ladder. They are not three "stages" of "ascent" to the "absolute" but three perspectives, three non-absolutes, three truth events, truth effects, both separable and inseparable, both distinct and porous, both unique and interactive, and ultimately not just three and ultimately not "ultimate," just the most interesting currently available. The division is not Kantian, critical, and modernist but deconstructive, differentialist, and postmodernist. So I am defending a view that a poetics is neither an epistemology nor a metaphysics but a certain irregular form of phenomenology.

As we will see below (ch. 10), Bruno Latour has shown in his many works that the very dichotomy between "epistemology" and "ontology" or "metaphysics"—is it really real, out there, or is just in our head, in here?—is an invention of modernism, a function of the subject/object duality, a product of the fiction/fact split with which modernity opens its doors. It is ultimately a way to blackmail and bludgeon us into a kind of foolish realism. What we need is a third thing, neither the one nor the other, or perhaps better, the first thing, the thing that was there before the iconoclastic hammer of modernity was visited upon the integrity of what we might in a simpler time have called "experience," which is a chiasmic intermingling, intertwining, and ongoing series of negotiations between the human and non-human. That I take to be the motif of "phenomenology," properly understood, although Latour would like to write off phenomenology—to "freeze frame it," as Don Ihde says—as a philosophy of "consciousness," or of "deconstruction," although his so-called nonmodernism differs very little from the "postmodernism" he belittles, choosing to deprive these movements of the very history he asserts belongs democratically to everything (else!).[26]

So I see a poetics to be a thoroughgoing post-phenomenology or quasi-phenomenology or radical heretical phenomenology, having passed through and altered the transcendental pretensions of classical Husserlian phenomenology, transpiring not under the heading of transcendental subjectivity but in a headless anonymous quasi-transcendental field. In my vocabulary, for example, Merleau-Ponty has provided us with a "poetics of embodiment." Accordingly, the Hegelian version of continental philosophy of religion regards the two-worlds theory with unvarnished "incredulity," to take up Lyotard's quite precise choice of words, lying as it does beyond any possible experience, still embedded in a mythic pre-Copernican imagination, and doomed to long-term extinction. The Hegelian version does not try to knock out the two-worlds theory with dogmatic this-worldly metaphysical counter-arguments. It has sworn off metaphysics the way people swear off fatty foods; they are tempting, but ultimately they are bad for you. Rather than mounting a rival metaphysical polemic against the old metaphysics it tries to demythologize the classical two-worlds theology and to understand it differently, to offer a more persuasive alter-nate account. It submits the old theology not to the hammer of modernist refutation but to a postmodern hermeneutics of reinterpretation. It does not smash it into smithereens but weans us off it hermeneutically, savvy as a snake not mean as a wolf, reading the old two-worlds theology carefully, productively, in the style of deconstruction, which adopts a style of read-ing, not of razing, which employs a stylus not a hammer, which is what I was trying to do throughout *The Weakness of God*. It wants to heed all of theology's voices, to hear what is happening in classical theologians like Augustine, to cherish theology by feeling around for the "events" that are unfolding there, and not to hammer away at it in the ham-fisted way we find in Hitchens and Dawkins.

The version of postmodernism that claims Hegel as its antecedent is not trying to strike a knockdown anti-metaphysical blow, marshaling a metaphysics of immanence that wages war on the metaphysics of tran-scendence, engaging a battle to the death with the two-worlds account. *There are no non-circular arguments against a world outside space and time, no arguments that do not proceed from the assumption that all being must be spatial or temporal.* Because all of our resources are drawn from space and time, we have no resources to disprove the existence of something out-side space and time. There is no negative ontological argument, no radical or demonstrated atheism. The arguments against any such extra-worldly transcendence are at best indirect, that we really do not require such tran-scendence, that it looks more and more unlikely, unbelievable, with each passing day, whence the precision of the word "incredulity" as opposed to "refutation." Weak theology eludes the wolves of metaphysics with a sim-ple wager that, in its literal form, the two-worlds theory has had by now a good run and been given ample opportunity to prove itself and is now about to turn tail. After putting up a fierce resistance, the old pre-Coperni-can metaphysics is about to fold its tents. Its pre-Copernican imagination is just going to turn out to look so bad that we will give it up. In denying that there is a metaphysical disproof of the existence of a being called God I do not draw the Kantian and fideistic conclusion, that it is now safe to have faith in the old metaphysics, but the quasi-Hegelian and radical con-clusion that this God requires a rethinking whose focus is on the event harbored in the name (of) "God."

At a certain point, the phenomenological evidence will weigh so heav-ily against the two-worlds metaphysics that it will be greeted as sheer fan-tasy, as imaginary as the light and airy risen bodies flitting about in eternity about which it fantasizes. Rather than offering a this-worldly metaphysics that refutes an other-worldly metaphysics, the Hegelian version thinks that the latter is becoming so phenomenologically implausible as to be destined to simply die off. The Hegelian version has absolutely no interest in advancing the cause of the God of the gaps. No effort or energy is expended on epistemologically delimiting contemporary physics in order to make room for supernatural interventions in space and time. Following the advice of the Dalai Lama, it is at peace with contemporary physics.[27] It thinks that Copernican astronomy lays to rest the distinctions between "heaven above" and "hell below" (with earth in the middle!), that the convertibility of energy and mass in Relativity lays to rest the distinction between spirit and matter, and in general that the borders between human and non-human animals, or between life and non-life, or between nature and technology are a lot more porous than the old-time humanism, anthropologism, metaphysics, and religion like to think. It thinks that technology is fast overtaking theology in terms both of imaginative power and of making miracles happen, and that in general the "supernatural" must make a graceful exit and allow itself to give way to software and "superstrings," all matters to which I will return in the third part of this book.

If the Hegelian version provides a poetics but not a metaphysics of religion, what about metaphysics itself? If, as I think, "metaphysics" means an account of what is called "mind-independent being," that amounts to an account of the way things are *when we are not there*. As Derrida says, if you want to think about things "as such," that means to think of them as if you were not there, "as if I were dead":

> To perceive the object *as such* implies that you perceive the object as it is or as it is supposed to be when you are not there. . . . So to relate to an object *as such* means to relate to it as if you were dead. That's the condition of truth . . . the condition of objectivity.[28]

Metaphysics speaks of a world that is mindless of us, a world that has no mind for us, that would be what is whether or not we were there. If that is what we want, then we need to learn a great deal of mathematics. We need to figure out what contemporary speculative cosmologists are saying about the macrosphere as well as figuring out what quantum physicists and string theorists are saying about the microsphere. Physics is pretty much all the metaphysics in the strong sense that we are likely to get. Metaphysics nowadays pretty much amounts to microphysics and macrophysics, particle physics and astrophysics, made possible first by microscopes and telescopes, and now by computer-driven microscopic and macroscopic

Heidegger on Aristotle's physics

Foucault

instruments that probe the unimaginably small and the unimaginably large, the likes of which would have startled Cusanus himself who first noticed their *coincidentia.* What has been called "metaphysics" in the history of philosophy up to now is turning out to be reasoned arguments for impressionistic accounts of the dominant features of the medium-sized objects of experience found in the middle, midway between the micro and the macro, part of the tailor-made fit between the size of the world and the size of our bodies. These accounts, as Kant said, generate endless and irresoluble debates just because they try to extend their limited impressions beyond the limit, beyond any "possible experience," meaning beyond experimental controls. But I am getting ahead of myself. (Again, I will return to all this in part 3.)

A poetics, on the other hand, is neither an aesthetics nor a metaphysics. It is not an attempt to write a poem, make a painting or a sculpture, or engage in elegant decorative language. Its medium is neither the material-sensuous substrate of art nor the formal symbols of mathematics. It is more abstract and less sensuous than art and more concrete and sensuous than mathematics. A poetics is a grammatological production, making its home in language, which as Derrida argues in *Of Grammatology* is non-formalizable and non-programmable, open-ended, and theopoetics draws upon all of the anarchic and "aphoristic energy" of *différance.*[29] If poetics paints a picture, the picture is made with words, and poetics is not afraid of an argument. It is committed *ex professo* to the thousand words, not the picture, while appreciating that the pictures are precious beyond words. But by itself, by its very vocation, which is evocation, a poetics is called upon to be evocative and provocative, to provide a discursive resource, an "account" (which is one way to translate *logos*)—perhaps, if you like, even a certain very hauntological "ontology"—of how things are *where we are* and *when we are there,* as if we were alive, which we half are, since this *vita mortalis* is always marked in part by death. A poetics describes the chiasm, when there are "minds," when mind-independent beings emerge into minded beings, and when we mind how things turn out, which is what Heidegger called *Sorge,* which could be very loosely translated as trouble.

To speak of the chiasm should not lead us into the temptation of thinking that being depends upon thinking in order to be. The chiasm should not induce the critics of poetics to rashly conclude that this is idealism. It does not make being into something mind-dependent, as in Idealist metaphysics. It just means that when there *are* minds, when minds are real, they need to be properly taken into account—which is the broad answer to Meillassoux's caricature of continental philosophers. A poetics is not an ornamentation, a decoration, but a thinking that tries to put itself (*stellen*) forth (*vor*) in a discursive formation, or rather to put forth an event, to formulate an image, a picture, a story, a body of tropes that gives word to the event, to provide insistence with a discursive existence. It takes up the lived, experiential intertwining, the chiasm, of life and world, of the "life-world," of the sphere of life, but without the anthropocentrism characteristic of such attempts in the past or their resistance to the invasion of life by the formal and technological. As the work of Catherine Malabou exemplifies, in putting forth the event it has no need to put down the neurological, a point to which I will return in the next chapter. It situates itself midway between the lush and sensuous life of art and the abstractions of mathematics. It is all for art and mathematics; it calls for art and mathematics, and it cannot have enough of either, lest it be blinded by its occupation to everything else. But it takes its own role to be *sui generis,* irreducible, which is to give words to the "world" (Heidegger), to the world of "incarnate" life (Merleau-Ponty), to the "plane of immanence" (Deleuze), or to the effects of grammatological energy (Derrida).

A poetics has a mind for how things are when we are there, when there are minds, when being is also filled with minds, and when the distinction between minds and bodies collapses. One of the first points in such a poetics, thus, would be to insist that "mind" is a word that leads us astray, leading us into the temptation of the "mind–body" problem and so should be straightaway put on mothballs and replaced with a more interesting and helpful vocabulary. That has been one of the strong points of the continental tradition of philosophy. What are words like *Dasein, Existenz, Lebenswelt, Sorge, différance, tout autre, événement,* and *Ereignis* except marvelous imaginings, extravagant terms of art, exotic and suggestive constructions of these venturers and adventurers on the plane of immanence, implorers and explorers of the insistence of the event? A theopoetics is an "account" of the event, and as such a kind of "logos," not a logocentric or theo-logocentric one, but a creative discursive construction (*poiesis*) which as such is ever liable to deconstruction. We need not jettison the notion of a "logos" but only think it differently. Heidegger got us started down that road by thinking it in terms of its root sense of "gathering," which is good, because a poetics is an ensemble of discursive resources. But it is not good enough, as Derrida pointed out, because what is even better is dis-juncture, the opening, the gap God makes, not the gap God closes by gathering things together. Justice, Derrida said, lies in discerning the differential, not gathering the essential. Theopoetics lives on the edge of the gaps opened by the insistence of God. Theopoetics treats the event as a "call," and every account of a call must include an account of the response. Theopoetics is the poetics of the particular events insisting in the name of "God," in which it hears a weak call, discerns a solicitation, yields to a certain pressure, a certain insistence. A solicitation calls for a response, which is why I say that God does not exist but God insists. God exists only insofar as a response is made in the world to what is called for in and under the name of God. In a theopoetics, the name of God is the name of something to do. In a theopoetics, the weakness of God must be addressed by the strength of a response, which is its chiasmic partner. God needs us as much as we need God, and therein lies all the trouble with God, all the trouble God is (calls) and all the trouble God causes (calling upon us).

In a theopoetics, "God" is a paradigmatic word, echoing in a semi-transparent way events transpiring on the plane of immanence, events I have summoned up under the guiding trope of "perhaps." That is why, it is my contention, religion provides a paradigmatic, telling, and "revealing" phenomenon, and represents a veritable "revelation," a "religious" revelation of the becoming true of the truth, which means a certain post-phenomenological poetics of the event of truth becoming true. For when there are minds minding what's going on, then there is "truth," and when there is truth, there are "events" insisting on becoming true, and when there are events, there are promises and prayers—and then there is what we call in Christian Latin "religion." Religion, we are arguing, is a *Vorstellung* of the insistence of the event, of a cluster of events, and the philosophy of religion, the one that descends from Hegel, provides a poetics of the event that is being nominated and denominated, performed and perverformed, in the name of God, in the historical name (of) "God," that is, a theo-poetics. Consequently, radical theology is possible only in the Hegelian version of continental philosophy of religion. Having uprooted the *logos* in theology, radical theology properly so called turns out to be an improper theology, a theology without theology, theology turning not on the existence of God but on God's insistence, theology as theo-poetics. Radical theology thus is a theopoetics of the event or, if you prefer, theopoetics is radical theology.

Theopoetics is how I combine being innocent as a dove with being savvy as a snake, how I hope to heed the insistence of God, perhaps, how I pray to stay in play with the "perhaps" that portends the trouble with God's coming. If the angels who service my weak theology and who announce the coming of a new species of theologians were to appear on some blue-black winter night, they would break the bad news to the shepherds that they are to send their sheep out among the wolves, proclaiming not peace on earth but trouble.

SIX

IS THERE AN EVENT IN HEGEL?
Malabou, Plasticity, and "Perhaps"

Where the corpse is, there the vultures will gather.
—LUKE 17:37

HEGEL, PERHAPS

Let there be no mistake. I am following Hegel where he did not quite mean to lead, marching to a drum he did not quite beat, taking up a cause he did not quite advocate. I am proposing, as Heidegger would have said, to "repeat" Hegel, to repeat not what Hegel actually said, which has already been said by Hegel, but to repeat the possible in Hegel, remaining loyal to the possibilities Hegel opened up for us by being faithfully disloyal to Hegel. To repeat Hegel in a productive way is, of course, to repeat Hegel's own prodigious ability to repeat his predecessors, above all Aristotle.[1] I am feeling about in the dark for the "perhaps" in Hegel, and for the first sightings of a coming species of theologians, seeking thus the future of Hegel, the future in Hegel, to borrow the suggestive title and thematic of Catherine Malabou's book on Hegel, which I will examine below.

So I proceed by posing the question: Is there an event in Hegel? Is there—against all odds—the chance of the insistence of an event in Hegel? Does Hegel still have a chance? Is there is a true future (*avenir*), something truly to come, *à venir*, in the Absolute, in Hegel's Absolute, in "Hegel"? I say "against all odds" because, ever since the merciless mockery launched by the magnificent Kierkegaardian pseudonyms, Hegel has been treated as the Absolute Professor, the maestro of Totalization, who has extinguished the event by absorbing it into the System, reducing the poor existing individual to a paragraph entry in the *Encyclopedia,* as Johannes Climacus constantly complains. But that makes a mockery of Hegel, rejoins Žižek, who regards it as a "scarecrow" Hegel, which means for me such a Hegel as will scare not only crows but the doves and snakes and sheep favored by Jesus. As I persist in insisting that everything depends upon the insistence of the event, my dialogue with Hegel will seek to find a place for the event in Hegel, a place for this little word "perhaps" in the *Encyclopedia,* and so to insinuate its humble grammatology of the event into the great halls of his *Logic.*

In this chapter and the next, I continue to put myself at a distance from the Kantians and to expand upon the sense in which radical theology seeks the reinvention of the event in Hegel. I do this by turning to the work of Žižek and Catherine Malabou, who I judge are the two most interesting contemporary neo-Hegelians. Malabou rereads Hegel in reference to Aristotle with Heidegger and Derrida uppermost in her mind, precisely so as to pose the possibility of a Hegelian event. Slavoj Žižek, whom I will address in the next chapter, reads Hegel in reference to Lacan, resulting in a fierce and fearless negative dialectic, in the face of which I timidly inquire if Žižek is not himself afraid of one small word, perhaps. I pose the same point to John Milbank, Žižek's partner in their ferocious dialogue, a veritable *gigantomachia* that pits the Christian Olympian Champion of Cosmos against the dark forces of a Lacanian Alcyoneus defending Chaos to the bitter end. The sheer noise of this combat will put the doves and snakes and all the surrounding wildlife to flight. In the end, I will argue, the insistence of the event in my Hegelianism will forever be a heresy for the Hegelians. In Hegel there is an alliance with the monsters of the old theology that would overwhelm a weak theology of "perhaps," which consorts with monsters of a lesser sort, with events of a lesser god (ch. 7).

I am doing all this in order to further the cause of a new species of theologians of "perhaps," of the insistence of a new theology and to further confirm my loyalty to Martha's world. All along I am trying to refine my idea of radical theology—learning how to think the insistence of God, which means learning how to give events a chance and learning how to say "perhaps"—as a theopoetics of "grace." I am linking what theology calls grace with the chance of the event as the chance for grace. So to that end, before engaging Malabou and Žižek, I will begin with a quiet word about this guiding and beguiling question of "grace," whose voice is ever soft and low, at the sound of which every pious knee will bend. This will all come to a head in the final part of the book, under the title of a nihilism of grace, where I will speak of a "being-for-nothing" and thereby bring this inquiry into the strange logic of "perhaps" to such conclusion as inquiries like this can tolerate.

GIFTS, GRACE, AND MIRACLE

The gift, in Derrida's famous analysis,[2] descends upon us unexpectedly, out of nowhere (almost), a convergence of unforeseen lines of force that produce a surprising effect, beyond anything we thought possible. The gift is an event, which cannot be planned, programmed, calculated, or counted on. It appears by chance, like an irruption, like a miracle or a grace. My hypothesis is that the underlying experience that funds our theologies of grace, that funds theology itself, if there is such a thing, something that the theologies obscurely desire with a desire beyond desire, is the gift, which in religion goes under the name of grace. The gift is grace, with or without religion, God or theology, already there before the theologians arrive on the scene. Miracles, as a kind of gift or event, have to do with the possibility of the impossible, not with the myth of a transcendent supernatural being swooping in on natural life and giving it a lift. The gift of transcendence is already there in the world, and the miracles of grace are events transpiring on the plane of the gift; they are ways that the plane is warped and bent. There is a kind of anonymous eventiveness already inscribed in things, which the Greeks called *tuche,* which in a poetics is called the aleatory, like the throw of the dice. In metaphysics this goes under the name of "contingency," but in religion it is called grace. Our lives are a series of ongoing run-ins with the aleatory, where "free" and "conscious intentions" run up against the anonymous play in things. We are asked to stay in play with this play, to play along with its open-endedness, to keep open the space of the gift, to release the forces that make possible miracles large and small, that make possible a visitation *by* the impossible, like Martha preparing for the visit of Jesus. That is the fabric of life. When we speak of the "meaning of life" we mean its fabric.

Nothing says the miracle will not turn out to be a disaster, that the gift will not be poison, or the event a catastrophe. That is why the most appropriate name for the gift, which has no proper name, no proper law, no principle or program, is *peut-être,* the possibility or may-being of the impossible, for better or for worse. To call for the event, to respond to the insistence of the event, to give events a chance, to pray for grace—all synonymous terms in a radical theology—is to be drawn into a high-risk game. We are playing poker late into the night, praying that our luck will change. So my proposal to think of life itself as a grace includes explaining why it so often is a curse.

Life comes to us without asking, out of nowhere, as it were. To be born is to answer a call we never heard, Levinas says. Why was I not first consulted? Constantine Constantius complains.[3] If we are lucky or graced enough to be able to say that life is priceless, we are saying that we desire life for itself, not for what it can bring in trade. If it does not have a price, it is a grace, *gratia,* gratuitous, something that can only be given and enjoyed freely, not bought or exchanged—something that the Roman Catholic Church learned at a very great price. A grace is for nothing, a being-for-nothing. A grace can only be given, like a gift, and the gift can only be affirmed. [4]

But why, perchance, would we ever think of Hegel in this regard? The Hegel who is a hero of the theology of "perhaps" has inscribed the fortuitousness and troubles of time and space into the very heart of God, a point pushed even harder by Schelling. But the remains and residue of the old theology still cling to Hegel inasmuch as the providential knowledge of the Spirit threatens to pacify the aleatory quality of the event, which does not have a chance up against the *Begriff.* So I seek to weaken his Spirit into a more spectral ghost, into the specter of the *peut-être,* in order to give events a ghost of a chance. I treat the insistence of God as a new version, or perversion, of the absolute, softening it into a kind of quasi-absolute, an absolute perhaps, *s'il y en a,* which gives grace a chance. Truth to tell, my absolute is not exactly absolute, not precisely being but becoming, and what is becoming, pure and simple, is the world. If "perhaps" is a saving power, it is one that also means that nothing is safe. Where there's life, there's hope, we say, but where there's hope there's trouble.

If I place Hegel at the center of a theology of "perhaps," I do so in virtue of a double displacement. First—in dialogue with Malabou—I seek to free up the perhaps, the chance of the event in Hegel. Secondly—in a debate with Žižek—I seek to displace the "dialectic" and its logic. My Hegel is the philosopher of the *Vorstellung* where art, religion, and philosophy are not the royal way of the Spirit on the way to Absolute Knowledge but the unroyal and irregular ways of a specter in a crowned or sacred anarchy, three forms among many in a pluri-form imaginative life giving shape to the restlessness of the world. The only concept—in the lowercase—that interests me is the concept of the event, a weak concept that does not "grasp" (*capere, greifen*) anything while insisting upon a response. I number theology among the several discourses—and there are more than one, more than three—that contain such concepts, that suspect an inner restlessness in things and feel called upon to give it voice.

If I tried to pass myself off as a real Hegelian, I would pose as philosopher of the concept, indeed of the absolute, but then I would add one small word, whispering softly so as not to be heard by the border guards, the concept of an absolute "perhaps." I frankly admit I am in search of another Hegel, of the specter of another Spirit, of a still more troubling and troublesome Hegel, a spectral Hegel, whose Spirit suffers from exposure to the insistence of the event. I admire the work of Malabou and Žižek because they seek to repeat Hegel, to rewrite as they read, or to reinvent what they read. Malabou's Hegel has evidently been given a copy of the works of Heidegger and Derrida, whereas Žižek's Hegel seems to have spent some time on the couch with Dr. Lacan. I am not criticizing that. I applaud all such anachronisms in the name of releasing the anakairotics, the *kairos* of the event, which is our only chance for grace, our only hope, our hope in hope itself, *s'il y en a.*

HEGEL AND THE DEATH OF GOD

Is there an event in Hegel? In *The Future of Hegel,* Catherine Malabou offers an engaging argument for precisely such a possibility.[5] She disputes Heidegger's contention that in Hegel the eyes of the Spirit are turned toward the past, that the Spirit has no future, and that absolute knowledge is the end of time. She worries that, having been convinced by Heidegger that Hegel bids *adieu* to time, contemporary philosophers have bid *adieu* to Hegel (4). Under her signature concept of "plasticity," Malabou tries to reverse that trend by showing that, for Hegel, Spirit admits of the event (*événement*; 103), that Hegel respects the contingency of the event as something radically to come (*à venir*; 162). The Spirit, Hegel's Spirit, and Hegel—the name of the thinker is the name of a matter to be thought— do indeed have a future (*avenir*). Her reading is organized around a central trope, *voir venir*, an expression she has adopted from Derrida, which wavers undecidably between foreseeability, fore-seeing what is coming, and unforeseeability, as when we say in English let's "see what comes" of doing this or that. For when it comes to the event, in Derrida, we are calling for the coming of something that we can't see coming, preparing for something for which we cannot be prepared. Does the Absolute have a chance? Does Hegel have a chance—or has he been left without a prayer?

In an adroit comparison of Hegel and Aristotle, Malabou shows the way in which Hegel takes up the self-thinking thought of Aristotle and sets it forth (*vor-stellen*) in history, translating it into the progressive stages of the education of the Spirit. The Spirit moves through time along a series of auto-transformations of its stored-up virtual energies (*hexis*) as it makes its way on its long journey home through the world. American theologians say Hegel invented "process theology," because he "dynamizes" the Aristotelian *theos* (52–53). But by setting God in time and time in God, by putting the virtual into God (45), Hegel earned the wrath of traditional theologians, who accuse him of reducing God to something needy and imperfect (91ff.). They object that Hegel robs God of transcendence, and thereby robs God of his free gift-giving generosity and his future. If God is reduced to a needy and necessitarian process, where everything that happens in God is prescribed by the essential laws inscribed in the *Logic,* then nothing can really "happen" in Hegel's God. There can be no "event" of God's free self-giving advent.

Malabou defends Hegel against this charge by arguing that God's activity is not a lack but a "plasticity." God is not a static act but a dynamic activity (*Tätigkeit*). Malabou reproduces almost exactly the argument that has been going on for decades between American process philosophers and traditional Thomists, about the relative superiority of temporal action (*actio*) versus a timeless pure act (*actus*).[6] In an impressive account of the "death of God," she argues that Hegel describes a "double kenosis": God is "presented" at a "distance" (*vor-gestellt*) by human beings only because God presents the divine being to humans at a distance (112).[7] The image of the distant God in religious representation (*Vorstellung*) is not the result of a human limitation but the issue of God representing something going on in God. Just so, Heidegger maintained that the various metaphysical epochs are not constituted by the "theories" of "metaphysicians" but by the way Being has granted itself to their thinking. Religion is not a figure of our imagination but the way God figures divine being in the world, gives divinity form in space and time, God's plasticity. Christianity is the pivot of history in which this double *kenosis* (Phil. 2:7)—literally "emptying" but importantly translated by Luther as *Entäußerung,* externalization or alienation—is overcome with a single blow, a *coup de grâce.* God rises to self-knowledge in the same act in which human beings rise to a knowledge of God. Each rises to a knowledge of their unity with the other. As Meister Eckhart said—in a text that caught Hegel's eye—the eye in which I see God is the same eye in which God sees me.[8]

Christ then is not merely a Greek "plastic individual"—in English, we would say a "role model"—the "becoming essential of the accidental," but an ontological event in the history of the *Geist,* the "becoming accidental of the essential." For Hegel, Christ is not the model of an ideal life, a gifted and charismatic man, a genius, a spell-binding preacher, a magnetic personality, like Pericles or Socrates. That is pure paganism. Christ is the *Vorstellung* of the Absolute, God's self-presentation in time and space, who presents himself not as an aristocratic Aristotelian *phronimos* but in the form of a servant. Christ was not a great man; he was the God-man, the "monstrous compound,"[9] the becoming subject of substance, expressed artistically not in the stone-blind figures of sculpture but in painting, which can alone capture the heartbreak in his eyes (117). Christ is the way

God sees himself coming (118), a temporal intuition of the Absolute (121), the way the Absolute is "schematized" in time. God is dead—long live God. The death of (the distant) God is the birth of (the immanent) God, of God's authentic and unalienated life in time. It is like the king's two bodies, except that it has to do with incarnation itself, with being embodied in the first place.

SPECULATIVE HERMENEUTICS

The only "end of time" in Hegel, therefore, is the end of the time of alienation (127–28), but that end is the beginning of the time of plasticity, of the auto-transforming life of the Absolute in time. The future is only beginning. That future is comprehended in philosophy, which is "absolute knowledge," the "speculative" process. Malabou calls this "speculative hermeneutics," meaning the speculative art of interpreting historical forms of life as forms of the life of the Spirit, seeing how the outlines of the Absolute emerge from the materials of multiplicity and contingency. The speculative hermeneut reads the book of the Absolute; the Absolute opens like a book to the hermeneut (167). Where Heidegger's hermeneutics of "facticity" means there are only interpretations, not absolutes (no "absolute knowledge"), Malabou's speculative hermeneutics refers to the power to discern the form of the essential (absolute) in the figures of the accidental (contingency) and the ability to locate the figures of the accidental within the form of the essential. Speculative hermeneutics unites the becoming essential of the accidental (the Greek "model") and the becoming accidental of the essential (the Christian "Incarnation"). The hermeneutic eye of the speculative philosopher can see the ways that Spirit condenses itself into a succession of historical forms into which its previous forms have vanished only to be recapitulated and contained there *virtualiter*. Each figure of the spirit is a *hexis* of the Spirit, ready to be deployed in a new context.

The speculative hermeneut can discern the same self-transforming Spirit, can stay in play with the play between its necessity and contingency (161). That, says Malabou, allows for the event, for the "fundamental truth of Hegelianism," which is the mutual support the necessary and the aleatory lend each other. Her speculative hermeneutics is a hermeneutics of "absolute" facticity, of what she calls the "absolute fact": it "assumes as an absolute fact the emergence of the random in the very bosom of necessity and the fact that the random, the aleatory, becomes necessary" (163). Absolute knowledge thus "cancels the tendency to question whether a wholly different origin might have been possible, whether there could have been a wholly different destination from the one that actually came to pass" (163), all of which would be so much alienation, the idleness of having too much empty time (Kantian time) on one's hands. Thought overcomes alienation by seeing the necessity in the contingent, by saying with the later Heidegger that we cannot inquire into the possibility of another destiny of Being, other than the one we received. I am also reminded of the Heidegger of *Being and Time* who says that authentic resoluteness drives out all accidentality from the tradition because it chooses what we have inherited, which gives it the sense of a fate.[10] Heidegger, Malabou comments, could not have said such things without Hegel—unless perhaps Malabou could not have said such a thing about Hegel without Heidegger. Necessity is the felt or experienced necessity of the contingent once it is actually given, after which it seems it could not have been otherwise. In that way, the event of the future and the tradition are put back into play (190).

HEGEL'S TELESCOPE

Malabou provides a welcome relief from the "scarecrow" Hegel, from the caricatures of Hegel that have proliferated from the searing stylus and scorching wit of Kierkegaard's pseudonyms all the way up to humorless Levinasianisms about totality. What is a criticism of Hegel for others—the seeming arbitrariness of the transitions in the *Phenomenology of the Spirit,* which occur almost by a wave of the phenomenological wand—is for her the strength of the dialectic, an exhibition of Hegel's tolerance of the play of the accidental. The transitions from epoch to epoch are not programmable, rule-governed, and predictable, but are precisely spiritual, that is, plastic. If they were predictable or programmable, they would be mathematical, formal, and dead. The Spirit cannot see what is coming. Its movements are events.

The problem, I think, arises when we consider that, then again, the Spirit can see what is coming—after it has come, at dusk. This may seem like small consolation, like someone who proudly announces that she has been given the power to predict the past, but there is more to it than that. Things come as a surprise and we cannot see them coming. But once they have occurred, afterward, when the dust has settled at dusk, we can see how they came. They are certainly not the only things that could have happened, and we could not have predicted them, because they are contingent events. But once they have happened, we can see then how they could have been foreseen; we can afterward make actual the implicit logic, detect the movement of the Spirit, and feel their necessity. So the unforeseeable and contingent events of world history have a kind of counter-factual foreseeability and necessity, and this because of the element of necessity in the life of the Spirit. If we knew beforehand (which we did not and could not) what we would know afterward, we would have seen them coming. So all that we do know in advance, all that we can say we saw coming, is that *whatever* happens, *whatever* will have happened, it would sooner or later, by the time its gets to be dusk, eventually be possible to see how and why they would have been coming.

My claim is this: nothing is going to happen that does not fulfill the destination of the Spirit. If "eventually" the Spirit can see these unforeseeables coming, this undoes the "event." Husserl spoke of an a priori history: even without doing empirical research, we know certain things must have been. Hegel offers a kind of deferred a priori: after they have happened, we can see not how these things in particular must have been but how they implement what must be always going on in whatever is or has been. However unaccountable the contingent is, we can count on that much necessity. However unaccountable Hegel's "perhaps," we know in advance that "perhaps" will always have been enlisted in the service of "must be." Nothing in history can be protected from the destination of the Spirit.

So I think Malabou's argument can go only so far because we can go only so far with Hegel. *In the end*—meaning both in the long run and in its *telos,* in its destination, taking a long teleological telescopic look—this argument does not succeed. There is no deep or radical *destinerrance* in its destination, only a contained contingency and deferred necessity. The destiny of the Spirit drives out the *destinerrance* to which the event is always exposed. There is indeed a relative and contained errancy in Hegel, a measure of waste and proliferation in the contingent. But there is no absolute errancy in Hegel, no absolute waste, no errancy that reaches as far as the absolute itself. In my view, what all this real contingency really amounts to is that the Spirit can achieve its destination (*telos*) in many different ways. Whatever arbitrary chance befalls it, the Spirit will always and necessarily achieve its destination. There is no chance that it will not.

The comparison with Aristotle is telling. For Aristotle the *ousia* of a man—and he clearly meant a man—might be actualized in many different ways, as a poet, a statesman, or a philosopher, say; there are multiple plastic individuals, and each *polis* has its own. But *in the end* the *ousia* sets the limits, the ends, the parameters: the man will never surprise us and become a bird. Or more pertinently, the bird will never become a man,

which was the shocking surprise visited upon Aristotelians, upon everyone, by Darwin who brought time to bear upon the species, not simply
upon the individual (a surprise they still have not absorbed in primitive
religious communities all over the United States—the problem is not con-
fined to Kansas). The form is fixed and unchanging and so therefore is the
telos. The species are eternal in Aristotle. Individuals come and go, but the
species does not. There are innumerable fluctuations and unpredictable
variations *within* the form. But when it comes to the species, Aristotle sees
eye to eye with Plato's *eidos* and he cannot fly with Darwinian becoming.
The essential form does not mutate. The form insures that the end is always
coming. We can see that, as surely as we can see anything, but we just cannot see how. It is like reading a novel in which we know that the hero survives the crisis, even though the threats by which he is surrounded in the
next to the last chapter seem inescapable. For Aristotle, there are various
accidental variations, several of which can play prominent paradigmatic
("plastic") roles for us to model ourselves after, but the essential form is
unchanging, and that is as much of the becoming essential of the accidental as the form can tolerate. Anything more than that and it would burst or
explode! There is *no chance* the essential form will mutate under the force
of a plastic individual, no chance of the event of the plastic explosion of the
form itself.

Just so, the virtual energies of the Spirit may be actualized in any number of contingent ways, but whatever way it chances upon it will inevitably find its way home and become itself, the self-thinking thought. The
Spirit insures that the end is always coming. There is *no chance* that will
fail to happen. We know that. We can see it coming, but we have to wait
until dusk to see how. I think it is at precisely this point Malabou engages
in an anachronism, which I applaud, so long as we are frank about it. At
this crucial point, in dealing with the essential necessity, she invokes a
kind of felt necessity of the particular tradition we have ended up with. In
this way, Malabou tries to suppress what cannot be suppressed in Hegel:
there cannot be an "absolute fact," or a hermeneutics of facticity in Heidegger's sense, and the only way we can obtain one—here we are reinventing Hegel—is by surprising us with the name of Heidegger just when
we expected the name of Hegel. We really did not see that move coming,
but afterward, when you view the replay slowly, you can catch her in the
act. That I think is a "gratuitous" move, which can be a grace, a gift, but
I would be frank about that. Malabou substitutes the open-ended "play"
of the epochs in Heidegger's *Seinsgeschichte*, the Heraclitean child play
"without why"—the epochs are because they are, they are such as they

are, without why, although there is a common destiny running through them—for the more Aristotelian and Hegelian interplay between necessity and chance.[11] At the most, Heidegger is speaking of a phenomenological necessity, the felt, lived, experienced necessity of the tradition we have factically inherited by an accident of birth. Heidegger is practicing an existential-phenomenological hermeneutics, not a speculative hermeneutics. Thus would Malabou rewrite Hegel via Heidegger.

Hegel, on the other hand, is speaking about the logical necessity inscribed in the essence of the Absolute and the speculative proposition that is laid out in the logos of the *Logic.* There can be no "absolute fact." That would require an absolute being, a necessary entity, that the absolute *be* an entity, a particular entity at a particular time and place, rather than merely setting itself forth *in* an entity (*Vorstellung*).[12] The absolute could no more appear as a fact than the infinite could ever take the form of a finite being. Individuals, entities, facts, finite things come and go and only the infinite matrix abides. Being is not a being—that is both a Hegelian and a Heideggerian principle. There is no absolute event. Events are always contingent. In my view, one can go very far in this direction. The truth of the matter in Hegel is that the Spirit does not require Greeks or Romans, Christ or Christianity, Descartes or the Reformation, Napoleon or even, *mirabile dictu,* German philosophers. That whole constellation, the totality of the empirical course of actual history, could have been quite different, and these names, cultures, languages, and particular stages of the Spirit might never have seen the light of day. Of course it is "factically" difficult to imagine what the alternative course of history could have been, and even more difficult from Hegel's point of view to imagine how we could have gotten along without the most felicitous accident of all, Christ, the "monstrous compound," the monster of grace, who is the most telling sign of all of the workings of the Spirit. Still, it could all have been different and we might even have been forced to do without the Christian Incarnation.

But even then something else would have done duty for the Spirit, and *whatever* that would have been—we know this in advance, we can see this coming—the same mega-story, the same story of the Spirit becoming itself, unfolding its essence, overcoming its alienation, explicating what is implicit in its substance, would have taken place, but by other means. That is as much of the becoming accidental of the essential, of the chance of the event, as the philosophy of Spirit can tolerate. Any more and it would burst or explode! But the Absolute cannot explode. If Absolute thought cancels our capacity to imagine a wholly different destination for history, as Malabou says (163), that is because it does not permit a different destination, only different, indeed infinitely different means. The Spirit admits of alternate courses but not the radical alterity admitted by *différance* and *destinerrance*.

I hasten to add that I am not in the least ungrateful for Malabou's Hegel, for the grace of her rereading. She has demonstrated a considerable contingency, a great deal more than Hegel is usually given credit for. So we are in the debt of Malabou for her gift, for liberating Hegel from a good deal of perfectly ridiculous readings while also allowing us to avoid the totalitarian reading, even if that will always remain a risk. Hegel is not a totalitarian insofar as the totality could have been totally different. But my claim is that no possible alternate could be so different that it would not still have finally served the essence and purpose of the Spirit, of the Spirit becoming Spirit. This is not a matter of a faith in the impossible, in the incredible, of a hope against hope, but a matter of absolute knowledge.

I say this because if Hegel is not a totalitarian, Hegel is an essentialist, as is Aristotle. For Hegel the play of differences plays by the rules of the Spirit. The measure of contingency that Hegel provides is strictly set in advance by the essence of the absolute, just as for Aristotle individuals contingently come and go while the limits set by the eternal species abide forever. Thinking for Hegel bears an analogy to the hermeneutics of discerning the essential forms (in the nominative) of the static species amid the changing variations of appearance in Aristotle. For Hegel, thinking is a hermeneutics of discerning the essence, the "essencing," the *Wesen* in the verbal sense (Heidegger), of the movements of the Spirit in time. The movement from Aristotle to Hegel embodies a grammatical shift from nouns to verbs, from form to movement, which is one of the reservations I have about the primacy of form in Malabou, which is too likely to contract the aphoristic energy of *différance* to nouns. Philosophy for Hegel is a hermeneutic skill of bringing to bear upon history the speculative presupposition of the essence of the Spirit and looking for its traces. But this hermeneutical skill is essentially a work of deferral. The "perhaps" reaches as far as the means, not the telos. Philosophy can only be conducted at dusk because, while the philosophers can see that the Spirit is coming, they cannot see how it is coming until after it has arrived. In religion we say "God" has promised us that he will come, that all will be well in the end, and we know that God is all good and true to his word, imagining God (*vorstellen*) to be an infinitely reliable and powerful fellow. In philosophy, we comprehend what they are saying in religion, which means that in philosophy we know the same but we know it better. Speculative hermeneutics is not merely a matter of understanding differently, but of understanding better.

So we philosophers explain to the people in the pews that when they say in their prayers and hymns that God is faithful to his promises what is really meant is what the philosophers say in their books, that the "Absolute" is true to its *Wesen.* The Absolute is the Absolute, which means that if the Absolute is put into time, it is absolutely necessary that it be faithful to itself; it cannot implode or explode. What we don't know (and the Absolute does not know, either, since the "Absolute" is not "somebody" who "knows" things) is how the Absolute is going to do this, or rather, how this process in and of the Absolute will be carried out, in the middle voice (nobody is "doing" anything). We have to wait, to defer till dusk.

There is a future in Hegel's Absolute up to a point. The Spirit is flexible enough that what is going to happen next is an open question. But *in the end,* no matter what happens, there will have been an explanation and a necessity. *In the end,* there will have been only so much "future" in that sense. Dealing with the future in Hegel is an exercise in patience, as is speculative hermeneutics. It requires both a taste for the contingent and a high tolerance of the unexpected—Malabou shows this—but it also requires the ability to see how the Spirit writes straight with crooked lines, which Hegel *just like the traditional theologians* is always telling us. Speculative hermeneutics is conducted by means of a world-historical telescope equipped with a zoom lens. It needs the ability to zoom in to see the Spirit's self-unfolding when it happens very explicitly and transparently in a text or a deed of singular and emblematic importance—the Crucifixion, or the World-Spirit showing up in Jena on horseback—and the ability to zoom out, to take the long look and see how, over a great deal of death and destruction, of detours and dead bodies, "finally," in its *finis,* in the end, it ekes its way forward. It requires a taste for trouble, the heart for enduring the death-dealing power of the negative, but "in the end"—in the long run, in its *telos,* in the long teleological telescope of Hegel—no matter how twisted and terrible the course, Spirit does what Spirit is. In that sense, there is no chance and no event and no future in Hegel.

HOW FAR CAN PLASTICITY BE STRETCHED?

So just how plastic is plasticity? Just how plastic is the Spirit? The divine plasticity has to do with the means, which concerns the particulars, but not the *telos,* which is necessary and inflexible. God always, essentially, and irreducibly sees himself coming (118). God does not bend on that point. That's what we mean by God. There is no chance that God is not going to come to the end. The plasticity of the Spirit is like the plasticity of Aristotle's *phronimos:* there are a lot of different ways to be good, and there is no one standard form or formula, but the *phronimos* will always find a way that is just right. Just so, there are a lot of ways for the Spirit to be the Spirit, but in the end the Spirit is the Spirit, which means it always eventually comes home. No manner of harm befalls the Spirit itself. Individuals come and go but the species and the Spirit are unchanging, just as in Heidegger no being can hold sway over Being. No matter how negative the course of the Spirit, the Spirit is not finally going to fail to come. Individuals are finite, but the Spirit is infinite. This or that individual, nation, language, religion, art form, or culture may come and go, but it is all for the cause, for the sake, for the *Sache* of the Spirit. Individuals cannot be this patient, but the species and the Spirit can.

There is an end, a limit and a *telos,* to the Spirit's plasticity. In Hegel, the Spirit is always open to the future, but it is not open to no more future, to absolute death, to telic frustration or catastrophe. In the end, it never ends in a simple bad infinity. The Spirit can never mean no more Spirit. There is no law of entropy hanging over the Spirit's head. In the end, in the *telos,* Hegel is not talking about the event, which we cannot see coming, but about a range of events that we cannot see coming within a larger and unbreached horizon of expectation, of what we can see coming. The Spirit includes the chance of death within a larger rhythm of life in which the purposes of its life are served. God is dead—long live God. The Spirit includes the death of this or that finite individual or formation, but it does not include the chance of infinite and absolute death, of the death of the absolute. There is no death of God in Hegel in that sense. That is as absurd to Hegel as it is to classical theology. The Spirit is not exposed to absolute death. The "necessity" in the "play" between the necessary and the aleatory rules that out, absolutely. The *logos* or *Wesen* of the Spirit is infinite and immortal; after all, in religion it travels under the name of God. The spirit can never drop dead, or be stopped dead in its tracks, blow up, wither away, go astray, get lost, fail to eventually come home, suffer absolute amnesia, forget absolutely who and what it is.

So we can stretch plasticity only so far.[13] A plastic Spirit *cannot explode.* Contrariwise, if "plasticity" includes explosion,[14] the Spirit *is not plastic.* It belongs to the very *Wesen* of the Spirit not to forget that it must be about the Spirit's business (*Sache*). There are many ways for the spirit to come and go, many ways for it to come home, but it would never not come home, never not complete its circle, and never explode in mid-course. Heidegger himself left the homecoming open: the future is "dark" and "uncertain" and the evening of the *"Abend"-land* might last forever.[15] But in Hegel, while there are many ways in which the Spirit cannot see what is coming, or see itself coming, as to the contingencies, the empirical actualities of itself, still it always and essentially sees itself coming inasmuch as it knows what it is. Whatever happens, we know that it is the Spirit doing what Spirit is. It is only what it does (it's not a Super-Person); it does only what it is (abides by its *Wesen*). But it (we) cannot foresee how it will do what it has to do, that is, how what must be done will be done. Still, there is contingency on the micro-level of the Spirit, but not on the macro-level. As to the big picture, the large course the Spirit traverses, the large circle it always cuts, there is no maybe about it; it must be what it must be. The Spirit must do what must be done but we must always remember to say "perhaps" as to the particulars.

DERRIDA'S QUESTION: IS THERE AN EVENT IN HEGEL?

God is dead. Adieu to God (*à Dieu*). But is this adieu really just an *au revoir*, or *voir re-venir*, because God's going under is really the only and best way for God to come home, to become God, to see himself come, to return to himself? Or is it an *adieu* to God, because God is dead and gone forever?

Let us put it this way: Is the "death of God" all part of an inscrutable— or if you are a German metaphysician, perhaps not so inscrutable—divine plan, all part of a Providential design, part of the wisdom of God? Is the death of God the *felix culpa,* a terrible thing that happened to God but nonetheless that happened for the best? Was it the one and only way God could become God, could overcome his abstract one-sidedness and make his entrance in the world and finally come home to himself in the Spirit? Was the death of God part of the larger divine life? Was it part of the unfolding of the implicit divine being into the fullness of the divine being? *Or* could there really be a pure accident that puts an end to the divine being? Could the divine Providence be blindsided? Could God, unawares, step on an explosive? Could God be blown to bits without so much as knowing what hit him? Could God just be destroyed, blown up, *adieu,* no more God, dead and gone, *requiescat in pace*? Could the whole thing have been avoided had God been a bit more cautious, watched where he stepped, exercised some divine foresight?

That is question posed by Derrida—with infinite discretion, courtesy, caution, and respect—to Hegel and to Malabou reading Hegel, at the end of "The Time of *Adieux,*" his preface to *The Future of Hegel.* Derrida begs to disagree, pleadingly. Prithee, give me leave to raise a question to which he says he does not know the answer. Two *adieux,* two times. The one *adieu* a final parting, an undisguised good-bye, like two estranged friends or lovers who part ways for good, or like the parting of death, especially at death. The other *adieu* is an *au revoir*, a "till we meet again," *à bientôt*, see you later, see you again, soon, I hope, but sooner or later, in the end, we will meet again. The absence makes their hearts grow fonder and when the separation has ended the two are reunited, closer than ever, their love made more perfect by the ordeal. In the first case the separation is permanent; the time of the *adieu* is forever. In the second case, the time of the *adieu* is temporary; the lovers are apart "just for a time." In the second, the going away is inscribed within a return, a seeing again, *voir re-venir*, and the lovers can see a return coming. The death of God is inscribed as a moment within the larger life of God, like a stage in the divine development.

Derrida puts this question to Malabou reading Hegel almost rhetorically, with the obvious implication that Hegel is talking about *au revoir*, an ultimate reconciliation, as if the lovers had a quarrel and got over it and were all the better for it in the end, which is the logic of the dialectic, the power of the negative, the way the "necessity" in things works for Hegel. In the end, there can be no future, no event for Hegel, not in the truly radical sense. True, there are contingent events but only up to a point. Events happen in the Spirit, but the Spirit is not eventive. Contingency is not radical; the Absolute is not contingent. There is a future, there are events, in a circumscribed sense, and it is a caricature of Hegel to fail to see that, which is the strength of Malabou's presentation of Hegel. But there cannot be a future in the sense of the more radical time of the more decisive *adieu*, the *adieu* which is issued in a condition of *destinerrance*, a point that is occluded or transmuted in *The Future of Hegel* by transforming Hegelian necessity into Heideggerian facticity. In Heidegger, the oblivion of Being in the *Abendland* may just go on and on, perhaps, and there may never be another beginning, perhaps, and this "perhaps" is the *Weltspiel* thought by Heraclitus. But for Hegel God cannot fail to become God, the divine life cannot finally end, since the very essence of God lies in his infinite and imperishable life. Finite things end, but the infinite is the matrix or womb in which they come and go. The life of God can be transformed, which is the meaning of God's plasticity, but the plastic life of God cannot be ended, dashed, snuffed out, exploded, blown to bits, for then the absolute would not be absolute, God would not be God and the dialectic would not be the dialectic. God is not flexible about being God.

But the more radically risky temporality of *destinerrance* is the condition of the event, of the chance of an event, and the only way for there to be an event and a future—for God. Allowing the chance of the event in this more radical sense would be true only of a *certain* Hegel, a Hegel repeated with a difference, altered and circumcised, one that Hegel himself would not recognize, recollect, or be reconciled with. It would come as a shocking surprise to Hegel, explosive news. For there to be a future for God, a future in the radical sense, God would have to be at risk, and God would have to face the future just like the rest of us, with fear and trembling, uncertain of and unable to see what was coming, no guarantees, praying and weeping over the future of God, forced to make a leap of faith with an uncertain outcome. For there to be a future for God, God would have to be exposed to the final and uttermost risk of death, where death would be something more than a moment in a metaphysical transition, more than the plasticity of transformability, but the possibility of extinction, of entropic dissipation, of a thermal equilibrium overtaking the divine fire, where there would be neither form nor transformation, where the logic of the dialectic would be exploded by the logic of death and utter irreversible extinction.

As Derrida aptly asks:

> Who could or would possibly be ready or able to subscribe to such a history, I ask you? Neither Hegel, nor the theologians or thinkers of faith who believe they are opposed to him. (xlvii)

On this point in particular—ascribing a radical future, the chance of an event to God—Hegel and the theologians who think they oppose Hegel are actually on the same side. The theologians do not oppose Hegel. Hegel is one of them, and he is like them a champion of the infinite life of God. When it comes to history, Augustine and Hegel are on the same side. They agree about what the theologians call Divine Providence, which means foresight, and about a long list of other and venerable divine names, omniscience, benevolence, omnipotence, at the head of the list. Hegel's radicality is to have reinscribed the divine names in space and time and forced them to become themselves in and through the painful work of negativity. In Hegel, the divine being is set forth, *vor-gestellt* and exposed to a certain (limited) play of chance. Up to a point. Hegel's radicality is to have set forth the death of God in time, indeed *as* time, but only in the sense of the time of *adieu* as *au revoir*, where the dialectic has planned a rendezvous for God with God in the Spirit. The death of God is a transitional moment in the indestructible life of the Spirit in space and time, the way maturation demands putting away the things of a child, the way the seed dies to allow the plant to grow. But in the end (*telos*), the future of Hegel is the future of the infinite Spirit, and that is not the future of the event. That prevents the event. The future is the eventiveness within the life of the Absolute, which is not as such an event, but a necessity, an Absolute. The future of Hegel's Spirit, in the end, in its *telos*, is *le futur present*, not the *à venir* in its infinitival exposure to the chance of an event (*événement*). For that we would require a new species of theologians, whom I am calling here the theologians of "perhaps," for whom I am calling here, who would produce a new theology that insists in the classical one, that insists itself within and so disturbs the classical theologians, pressuring them into confessions they would soon repress.

Derrida himself remains infinitely circumspect in this regard, in regard to Malabou, from whose work he has learned so much. So he poses this rhetorical question to himself and responds, "I don't know anymore." He is praying to be excused from outright disagreement. He has his doubts that the notions of the "essential" and the "accidental" can be of further use when it comes to the event, which represents a deeper play in the future of God than their simple interplay (xlvi). For accidents are accidents relative to essence and conversely. If either notion is displaced, both are displaced—in *différance*—so that the distinction between the becoming essential of the accidental (Greek paradigms) and the becoming accidental of the essential (Christian incarnation) is displaced along with it. Neither accident alone, even a "pure" accident, nor its interplay with essence, can accommodate the chance of an event. I am no longer able to understand this idiom, Derrida says. I have not embraced one or the other of these times, he says, because *adieu*, "as the *peut-etre*"—*adieu* is like *peut-être*, *adieu* is *peut-être*—leaves him unable to understand "my own incomprehension, a certain increasing and stubborn non-intelligence, on this stubbornness precisely, of an idiom, of more than one idiom, perhaps (*peut-être*) ..." I do not understand. I prithee excuse my failure to understand.

Perhaps God's death means "God is dead—Long live God." Or perhaps God is dead and gone forever. To be sure, the *peut-être* is the question: to be, but, perhaps, not to be. The Spirit cannot tolerate this deep "perhaps," the real possibility, the real exposure of God to possible death, to final extinction, to the possibility of bidding a real, rending, and final *adieu* to *Dieu*. The very possibility of the real and final death of God undoes the dialectic, the *Aufhebung*, and by so doing makes the chance of an event—the *peut-être*—possible. The chance of the event goes back to what in the language of metaphysics we would call an archi-accidentality that displaces the dialectical equilibrium of necessity and chance, essence and accident. The chance of the event gives God a future by exposing God to the risk of death and hence to the risk of the future. As to the chance that God, perhaps, could be killed in an explosion, be finished off once and for all:

> would that be the condition of a future, if there must be such a thing called the future? The very condition for something to come, and even that of another God, of an absolute other God? (xlvii)

That would make for a God, perhaps, which would be the subject matter of a new thinking of theology and a new species of theologians. A *tout autre* God is God as the *tout autre*, where *tout autre est tout autre*. So the chance for God is, metonymically, the name of the chance of an event, of the coming of the other, of the wholly other, of everyone or everything wholly other. The chance for God is the chance for the "perhaps," for God, perhaps, which is the chance for grace, where what is coming is "perhaps" itself.[16] That would include the possibility of another God, perhaps a wholly other God, a successor God whom we would possibly not want to call "God" at all, but something else, in a wholly other idiom or discourse, a wholly other time or *à Dieu*. For in the expression the "God to come," or the "coming God," the "to come" is more important than the "God,"[17] and the coming God might be otherwise than God, the coming theologians otherwise than theologians, the coming theology otherwise than theology.

That, Derrida is saying ever so politely to Hegel, and to Malabou reading Hegel, and to Malabou reading Hegel reading Heidegger, is something Hegel could never see coming.[18]

That in turn brings me back to the chiasmic intertwining of the insistence of God and God's existence in the world. God happens, the event insisting in the name of God takes place in the form of a solicitation, a call, to which we are the response, provided that we respond. We may not respond, and then what is lacking in the body of God will go unfulfilled, the event will go unheeded, and we will have ignored the lesson of Martha. We will have killed God, cut off the life of God in the soul, as Meister Eckhart said, which is the death of God that really matters. *Adieu* to God (*à Dieu*). The name of God is the name of a promise, but promises are only promises if they threaten not to be kept.

That is the chance of the event and of God, perhaps.

SEVEN

GIGANTOMACHEAN ETHICS
Žižek, Milbank, and the Fear of One Small Word

And about three o'clock Jesus cried with a loud voice,
"Eli, Eli, lema sabachthani?" that is,
"My God, my God, why have you forsaken me?"
—MATTHEW 27:45–46

Žižek's rereading of Hegel is more radical and disruptive than Malabou's. Žižek sees the Hegel of the *au revoir* coming, the Hegelian Absolute inching its way home through its peregrinations through world history, and he stops it in its tracks. In its place Žižek puts a more deeply doubly negative dialectic, where the Spirit does not come home, where it never had a home, where there never really was a "Spirit." Adieu to the Spirit, good riddance. No, we will not meet again. No, no, we never met in the first place. Stop trying to recollect something that never happened. In Žižek, the death of God takes the radical form of a Lacanian Good Friday, neither Christian nor speculative-Hegelian, a Calvary of confronting the cold truth the Real deals to us, that nothing is coming to save us and we are on our own. Inasmuch as the chance of death is built into the event of life, this is of no little interest to a theology of "perhaps," especially as there is the promise of another more spectral Hegel here, of a displacement of the Spirit by a specter, a spectral undead, Žižek's own *es spukt.* Hegel prevents the event, the *peut-être,* from above, by raising it up into a higher divine economy. Malabou finds a way around this only by replacing Hegel with Heidegger at the crucial moment. Žižek prevents the event from below. He unquestionably releases the event from the grip of an overarching divine providence, but he does so by means of a massive metaphysical attack on the old God. He introduces a radical negation so deep that it ends up suppressing the *peut-être* not from above, not by safely installing negation within the divine economy, but from below, by consigning the event to a fated loss, a fatal forsaken Lacanian *lema sabachthani,* and to metaphysical violence, constituting a kind of predestination *ad infernum.* The question Žižek poses for us is this: if as he likes to say "postmodernists" have created a purely "scarecrow" Hegel, has Žižek created a scarecrow of his own? Is Žižek in his own perverse way afraid of one small word?

ŽIŽEK AND THE DEATH OF GOD

Žižek's version of Hegel is sufficiently heretical for anyone's taste. He denies that the death of God is a moment in the life of God that leads to ultimate reconciliation, resolution, and rebirth. For him, it is atheism redoubled, doubled down, a double negation that does not mean affirmation, but a doubly reinforced negation: no, I repeat, I really mean no. No, and it is worse than that. God is dead and furthermore there never was a God to die anyway (MC, 72).[1] If by identifying the plasticity of the Aristotelian *theos* Malabou has reinvented twentieth-century process theology, Žižek's double negation has resurrected the atheistic death-of-God theology of the 1960s, which is why he has recently been citing Altizer (MC, 260–67). But Altizer is a much more orthodox Hegelian than Žižek. Altizer is not a Lacanian and he does not share Žižek's theory of double negation. In Hegel and Altizer, the death of God is God's coming to life in space and time, the death of the transcendent otherworldly God and the birth of the God with us, the immanent infinite womb of divine life that sustains us. God is dead—long live God. The *au revoir* of the Father and Son are superseded in a final rendezvous in the Spirit, which is an imaginative religious way to visualize what we philosophers can conceptualize as the movement that takes place in the Absolute, by which *an sich sein* and *für sich sein* are mediated and reconciled in the *an und für sich sein* of the Spirit.

But Žižek will have none of that. In Hegel the Spirit is not "somebody" (it's not a finite being) who "does" things (it's not a personal agent) but rather an undergirding substance (infinite Being) expressing itself in the subjectivity of human history (becoming accidental of the essential). That much is just good Hegel. But Žižek goes one step further, diving deeper still down the black hole of negation, like a young Hegelian on the couch with Lacan. The next step he proposes is to realize that there never was what Hegel called the Absolute or what religion calls God. Conflict and contradiction—and now the voice is rather more Schelling than Hegel himself—are not the means the Spirit employs to make its way home; they are the very stuff of the Real where there's no home to go to. There are only human agents who, at the end of the session, are made to realize that there is no Big Other and they are on their own. Deal with the disenchantment. Deal with the Real. Mutual antagonism is all there is and we are going to have to work through it. The unreconciled is real and the real is unreconciled. The only reconciliation is to reconcile ourselves to the irreconcilable by admitting that there is no reconciliation. The antithesis is already the synthesis (MC, 72). He denies the "scarecrow" (MC, 26) Hegel where a reconciliation is all the while going on up above, in a higher "Mega-subject" called the "Spirit" (MC, 60–61), the "totalizing" Hegel mocked by postmodernists who he rightly thinks makes a mockery of Hegel's respect for contingency and individuality. This he replaces with something genuinely scary. Žižek sees an owl-of-Minerva Hegel who devises an after-thefact rationale for what has in fact unfolded contingently (246–47), whose genius lay in his gift of finding a pattern in contingency, while conceding that a good deal of blood was spilled in the process. Far from describing the movements of a Super-Subject-Spirit, Hegel confronts us with the cold and merciless realization that things are what they are, where instead of raising up the real into the rational, the rational is reduced to the real. On this point, he and Malabou are agreed: history is contingent, and necessity is introduced after the fact, and that makes possible a Hegelian event—at least in the sense of a contingent happening.

Žižek's critique of the "big Other" is an important part of the work of "weakening" in my idea of radical theology. As I have argued in *The Weakness of God*, the Crucifixion is not a settling of accounts between God and humanity, in which humanity vicariously pays off an infinite debt by means of the execution of Jesus. That I consider a corrupt mystification of God. On the contrary, the weakness of God, the withering away of orthodox omnipotence, translates into an assumption of human responsibility. Žižek and I are agreed on this point, and he is right to point out our convergence, although for him this is a scene in psychoanalysis:[2]

> Contrary to all appearances, this is what happens in psychoanalysis: the treatment is over when the patient accepts the nonexistence of the big Other. The ideal addressee of our speech, the ideal listener, is the psychoanalyst, the very opposite of the Master-figure that guarantees meaning . . . the patient accepts the absence of such a guarantee. (MC, 55)

Contrary to all appearances, that psychoanalytic scene is also the "very core of Christianity," a Christianity for which "My God, my God, why have you forsaken me?" (Matt. 27:46) has become the watchword:

> The "Holy Spirit" is the community deprived of its support in the big Other. The point of Christianity as the religion of atheism is not the

vulgar humanist one that the becoming-man-of-God reveals that man is the secret of God (Feuerbach et al.); rather, it attacks the religious hard core that survives even in humanism, even up to Stalinism, with its belief in History as the "big Other" that decides on the "objective meaning" of our deeds. . . . That is the ultimate heroic gesture that awaits Christianity: in order to save its treasure, it has to sacrifice itself—like Christ, who had to die so that Christianity could emerge. [3]

The supreme moment of dark Lacanian lucidity is Jesus's lament, "My God, my God, why have you forsaken me?" At that point, the horizon is wiped out and the cold black truth is exposed that no one (save ourselves) is coming over the horizon to save us, that we are sustained by no overarching cosmic support. There is no "big Other": God or Man, Nation or Party, Father or Big Brother, Lacan's symbolic order or what Derrida called the "transcendental signifier." We are on our own.

The debate between John Milbank, the leading Anglo-Catholic theologian of the day, and Žižek, which is staged in *The Monstrosity of Christ,* is instructive on this point. The odd title of the book, which proffers a new Christological title ("monstrosity"), goes back to the line from Hegel's lectures on the philosophy of religion cited above, which describes the expression "God-man" as a "monstrous compound" (MC, 74).[4] For Milbank, this expression means that Christ represents a magnificent show or monstration of God's love for the world which takes the form of the excessive "paradox" of "God become man." For Žižek, it means that Christ is the monstrous moment of the death on the cross in which God himself loses faith and confesses the death of God, which is the theological result demanded by the negative dialectic. The book is framed in terms of a theological and Christological bidding war aimed at deciding whether paradox (Aquinas's theory of analogy) or dialectic (negative) holds the most chips when it comes to making matter matter more. In this corner, Primordial Peace, in that corner, Primordial Conflict. In this corner, Milbank's radically orthodox theology with a straight face, in that corner Žižek's radically ironic, heterodox, and subversive death-of-God theology. Žižek has to work harder because the match takes place on the theologian's field. But Žižek is undaunted; he is used to being the visiting team and knows no limit to the cultural material he can consume and transform. Žižek's readings of G. K. Chesterton and Meister Eckhart, of the Trinity and the Incarnation, are obviously more eccentric than those of Milbank, who clearly holds the home-field advantage.[5]

THE SPIRIT AS SUBJECTIVE PRESUPPOSITION

One new twist Žižek introduces on the death of God is to radically revise the notion of the Spirit. The last words on the cross represent the expiration not only of the orthodox version of the Holy Spirit in Nicene Christianity but of the standard reading of Hegel, where the Spirit is the transcendence-in-immanence of the Absolute that undergirds individuals and their passions:

> The point this reading misses is the ultimate lesson to be learned from the divine Incarnation: the finite existence of mortal humans is the only site of the Spirit, the site where Spirit achieves its actuality.... Spirit is a *virtual* entity in the sense that its status is that of a subjective presupposition: it exists only insofar as subjects *act as if it exists.* Its status is similar to that of an ideological cause like Communism or Nation: it is the substance of the individuals who recognize themselves in it, the ground of their entire existence, the point of reference which provides the ultimate horizon of meaning to their lives, something for which these individuals are ready to give their lives, yet the only thing that really exists are these individuals and their activity, so this substance is actual only insofar as individuals believe in it and act accordingly. The crucial mistake to be avoided is therefore to grasp the Hegelian Spirit as a kind of meta-Subject, a Mind, much larger than an individual human mind, aware of itself: once we do this, Hegel has to appear as a ridiculous spiritualist obscurantist, claiming that there is a kind of mega-Spirit controlling our history.... This holds especially for the Holy Spirit: our awareness, the (self)consciousness of finite humans, is its only actual site ... although God is the substance of our (human) entire being, he is impotent without us, he acts only in and through us, he is posited through our activity as its presupposition.[6]

When Žižek says that the Spirit is a virtual reality, and it only exists if we enact it, this is extremely close to my distinction between the insistence of God and God's existence. But there is a difference. Žižek is offering a ruthless demythologization of Hegel's Spirit, in which we find his account of the event, which is drawn not from Derrida but from Badiou. The Spirit is a "virtual" community, by which Žižek means neither "online" nor a Deleuzean virtuality, but an "imaginary" community, individuals bound together by their "subjective presuppositions," which they discover that they themselves have posited to begin with and must sustain. But instead of a simple "positing," which is something purely subjective (that is as far as Feuerbach got), Žižek offers the notion of a contingent multitude that organizes itself, self-mediates, engendering and positing its own immanent necessity. It retroactively posits its own essence or presuppositions. The subject sees it has itself posited what appears to it as its own presuppositions (MC, 76). Rather than saying that individuals organize themselves immediately into collectivities, Žižek describes a transubjective "it" that organizes itself, which corresponds to how I myself want to deploy the "middle voice." So we are very close on this point.

For Žižek, this cannot be done immediately. As Hegel says, it requires a "mediator," some singular individual, like the King, the Leader, or the Christ, each of whom is a "monstrous compound" of some sort—this is not just a miserable ill-tempered man, but His Majesty, not this carpenter's son but the Son of God, and so forth—whose role is to provide a mediation between the individuals and the collectivity. The mediator is the existential occasion, the "event," upon which something gets itself organized in us and we collaborate in the larger event of the formation of the collective. Released from the Necessitarian Spirit, the collective is an event of freedom. The result is that there is neither a mere assemblage of atomic individuals, as in liberal individualism, nor an absolute Mega-Spirit, as in Stalinism or Nazism, where there are no individuals but only the Party, History, the "big Other." Liberal individualism and Stalinism are the recto and the verso of each other; what they both miss is the auto-organizing or auto-emergent—my "middle voice"—collectivity, which is a necessity recognized after the fact (MC, 76–78). The necessity is not just lying there waiting to be discovered by us, as in a pre-critical idea of truth, but constitutes our way to truth, which is part of the truth process itself. Our discovery of eternal truth generates eternal truth, as a retroactive appearance or constitution of necessity after the fact (MC, 78). We construct what we discover; we produce what organizes us. We participate in an event. This is, I think, a literally crucial point.

Milbank is in substantial agreement with Žižek's reading of Hegel as a negative dialectics (MC, 112) but it will come as no surprise that he thinks that Žižek goes too far with the idea of pure contingency. Žižek misses the "uniquely revelatory" power of Christ himself (MC, 114), which is Milbank's way of saying that he is a Christian and that the birth of Christ for him is a contingent historical event which happens to bear the absolute truth, representing the decisive point of entrance of the Eternal Truth upon the contingent stage of time. This is not to fall back on Hegel after all, but on Kierkegaard. It rather perfectly reproduces the question posed by Johannes Climacus: how can eternal happiness be based upon a contingent historical event? According to Milbank, Hegel is a dualist, holding at once to a purely formal and necessitarian account of the logical advance of the categories while treating the material content of actuality as wildly contingent (which is actually Hegel's own criticism of natural religion). Actualities are not the organic expression of absolute life, not the gradual realization of an unfolding logic, but a random outburst of contingencies forced into an after-the-fact formalism, blind nominalist actualities submitted to a pure formal logic. In short, Hegel is a Scotist, and Scotus is the root of all evil. For this reason Milbank thinks Žižek cannot escape between the horns of individualism and totalitarianism. Going back to Gillian Rose's *Dialectic of Nihilism*, Milbank treats negative dialectics as manifest nihilism, a philosophy of the void and negativity, an ontology of violence, which issues in a politics of the violent war of all with all, around which, in his view, all modern political, social, and economic theory revolves.[7] The negative dialectic is complete when we see that all there is, is the plurality of contingencies (MC, 152), which represents a kind of positivistic demythologizing reading of Hegel. This is like a demythologizing reading of the "destiny of Being" in Heidegger where *es gibt* is taken to mean "there is what there is—and that is all there is." For Milbank, Žižek is not a Romantic Schellingian but a Hegelian rationalist, lacking a sense of mystery, of any excess beyond reason, of the untapped reserve of the symbol or of poetry, for whom reason exposes "the inscrutable absurdity of reality taken as a whole," offering us an atheism that takes every opportunity to mime theology (MC, 158). On that, I think, Milbank is not far from the mark. There is no poetics in Žižek, or if there is it is a poetics of the void of the sort we will see below in our discussion of Ray Brassier.

In the place of Hegelian and Žižekian war Milbank puts an ontology of Primordial Peace and reconciliation, "the (unreachable and untraceable) prelapsarian golden age" (MC, 171), made possible only by means of supporting finite things with a metaphysics of analogy. By invoking the analogical standpoint, we are able to see that the tempests that brew here below in time and space, the oppositions and conflicts we everywhere encounter, sometimes dialectical, sometimes not, are more deeply grounded in the ground of being. These conflicts send us hurtling into dialectical opposition, into war, only if we do not look up and see these opposites in their point of "coincidence" (Eckhart and Cusanus—whom Milbank pits against Scotus as the beginnings of an alternate modernity), in the subsistent being of God (Aquinas)—of which they are themselves finite and partial reflections, from which they themselves derive their own being, through which they are finally reconciled. The medieval metaphysics of analogy supports the modern rhetorical trope of paradox. If we are to learn from Hegel, who would take us beyond modernity (Enlightenment), it can only be by reading him back into what lies before modernity, the Trinitarian theology of Augustine and (even more so in Milbank's recent work) the metaphysics of participation of Thomas Aquinas. In Aquinas, dialectics yields to analogy, to the tripartite logic deriving from Thomas's commentary on the apophatic theology of Pseudo-Dionysius, of which Hegel's negative dialectics is the corruption. In Dionysius, affirmation (God is good) yields to negation (not good in the way we know good), which passes into eminence (but with a higher goodness).

For Žižek, and here I could not agree more, Milbank's ontology of peace is an embarrassing exercise of fantasy. Does Milbank actually think that there really was a prelapsarian age in which our ancestors lived naked and innocent, for which we have thus far not come up with any archeological evidence? Does he really think there was a garden of Eden of which, unfortunately, no archival trace has been left behind in the evolutionary record? Are we to take this seriously? Such theologizing is an unchecked exercise in what Lacan called the imaginary (MC, 245–46), or of Nietzsche's observation that the power of an idea to soothe us is no guarantee of its truth. We require a more merciless view of reality (and the Real), a colder truth, if we are going to make it through the day. Žižek is a realist in the sense that he is encouraging us to realize that help is not on the way, that no one is going to save us, save ourselves. This realism springs from his Lacanian notion of the Real, of the deep cut in our hides, the profound trauma by which we are constituted, the impossibility of a deep and fulfilling *jouissance* and its replacement by the endless and futile search for precisely what we cannot have. In Hegel we are being teleologically prompted toward the precise parousiological fulfillment that Žižek says we are denied. In Lacan we must confront the cut, the trauma, and realize that the incision is decisive. But Žižek is not a realist in the epistemological sense—far from it. What matters for him is our ability to sustain our fantasies, to act as if we have a grip on things. What produces the event, what keeps us going, what organizes collective action, is to embrace the "cause," to love and serve it fiercely, for that is what mobilizes subjectivity and produces results. That is why St. Paul is an important paradigm of the event for Badiou, whom Žižek is following on this point. The actual content of Paul's preaching, the resurrected Christ, is a complete myth, to be sure. Nobody's perfect. But the form of Paul's conversion is the very paradigm of the constitution of the militant subject and of the (apostolic) resoluteness to spread the revolution around the world. Paul is the paradigm of Lacan's injunction to remain true to one's desire. But we should have the good sense to realize that "the Lord is my shepherd, I shall not fear" means that we are sustained by sustaining our fantasies, not by the invisible hand of God.

DID SOMEBODY SAY RESPONSIBILITY?

To sum up: the ridiculous thing (the scarecrow) is to say that the Spirit is a "Super Somebody" who does things and cunningly makes use of individuals to do it. The philologically proper Hegelian thing to say is that the Spirit is the underlying ground (substance) upon which individuals (subjects) freely draw their deep resource. (Tillich is a good Hegelian on this point.) The Žižekian thing—which goes all the way back to his *Sublime Object of Ideology*—is to say that the Spirit is nothing but a subjective presupposition, an "as if," in which we recognize ourselves, but which we all recognize is a fiction, even as we still hope it works.[8] I myself say that, by claiming that the Spirit is a *virtual* entity, and by recognizing the *impotence* of God as an actual entity, Žižek comes very close to what I propose in *The Weakness of God*, but with one overriding difference.

Žižek's view of "virtuality" and hence of the event is too much taken with subjective events, too much trained on subjects and their "belief systems," and not enough turned to *the event itself,* what I am calling the insistence of the event that lays claim to us, that evokes a more deep-set "faith" and "responsibility" in the more spectral setting of the "perhaps." That is, the insistence of God is a call for a response, a call for existence. *The event is not the decisiveness of the decision, but the insistence of what calls for existence in a decision, which is the decision of the other in me.* The event is not reducible to subjective beliefs, even auto-organizing collectives, sustained by fantasy. "Subjective beliefs" arise in response to events; they give words to events, and are translated into deeds and institutions by believing subjects. The insistence of God translates into the depths of human responsibility, into *responses* to the subsistence of the events which precede and provoke them. The substance of such response is not simply sustained in the thin air of subjectivity itself by the collective ability of subjects to suspend their disbelief in a fictive "as if," in the midair of their subjective presuppositions. That is a distressingly subjective, even comic, view to strike. As Žižek himself often points out, it is like those cartoon characters that have walked off a cliff but do not fall until they look down and realize that nothing is holding them up.

On this point I think Milbank is right to criticize Žižek's excessive subjectivism. From Hegel's point of view, Žižek's view of virtuality is one-sided.

It fails to do justice to the claims of the virtualities on the "substance" side—I have translated Hegel's substance or subsistence into "insistence"—for the event is no less instantiated in things (substance) than it is expressed by the names that galvanize the beliefs of the subject. That is why I said above that the insistence of God is aimed like a projectile at our head. The name (of) "God" arises as a response to events; it gives words and image (*Vorstellungen*) to powers that overtake the subject and lay claim to it. If the "Spirit" is the name of a *subjective presupposition,* that is only because it is first of all the name of something that *substantively prepossesses* the subject, something *sachlich* that *poses or puts itself to* the subject and calls it forth, or as I would say, something insistent by which the subject is solicited and hence constituted in the first place. There is no big Other, but neither are there merely human agents.[9] There are events that take us by surprise, specters that spook our settled tranquility. So in my view, the focus falls not on the subjective presupposition, but on the subjective responsibility to what has been put to the subject, *pre-posed* or *pro-posed* to it, what has been proposed as a *problema,* gotten insistently in its face, put it in the accusative, all the while requiring both hermeneutical scrutiny about what is being called for which is crucial to responsible action.

Otherwise the decisive event is reduced to pure decisionism. The virtuality of the event is felt in both the "beliefs" of "subjects"—an inadequate way to describe "responsibility"—and the insistent energies of things, and it shows up in both names and things. The event includes not only what is named by our names but also what is worlding in the world, the thinging-of-the-thing in Heidegger's play on *Be-ding-ung,* which is aimed at nudging the Kantian "condition" from the subjective side to the side of the *Sache.* Speaking Hegelianese, events require both substance and subject; events transpire between substances and subjects—that is the chiasm. Events are both realized in things and named by subjects, but they are named in response to the call events pay upon subjects, called forth in response to events by subjects of responsibility, not in a double kenosis but a double call, which I have been calling the chiasm of insistence and existence.

My theopoetic (per)version of Hegel, my way of rereading Hegel, is to conceive a world in which the absolute would be *neither substance nor subject* but *specter,* in which "substance" and "subject" would only be provisional stand-in nomenclature we draw from the history of metaphysics for more nameless and boundless events, for events still unnamed, where Spirit has been weakened into the insistence of the event, into the specter of the *peut-être.* By the same token, history would be a radically immanent movement without the steadying hand of teleology at its wheel. That is

what it means to say that there is no big Other. Hegel relocated the absolute but he himself left in place its classical attributes drawn from the reservoir of strong theology. But in my view history is really history, really has
the teeth and eventiveness of history, only as a radically a-telic and contingent process, that is, as an *eventive* and spectral process. The outcome of
the coming of the event, its *Resultat*, is radically unforeseeable, and there
is no one identifiable and overarching result but only so many fortuitous
effects.

So instead of a teleological movement I see history marked by the vaga-
ries of change and chance, the fortuitousness of little gifts and graces, by
fortunes variously good or bad, by all the fortuitousness of the "perhaps."
The "Spirit" is one more mystified or mystifying name for insistence, for
the spectral event, for the play of events, multiple, unruly, and "chaosmic."
Events are not contained by a *telos* guaranteeing their direction and good
outcome. The event is but a promise that provokes us and stirs our heart,
or a memory of the dead which haunts us. Instead of teleology there is
only or at most the promise still unkept, lodged in events still unsaid, while
substance and subject are nothing more than a certain abstract shorthand
devised by metaphysics for the play of events. Instead of the absolute
steering all, we are thrown back on our own responsibility, made radically
responsible for responding to the address that comes to us from events,
without being delivered over to sustaining our fantasies. If it is events
which call, it is we who are made responsible. Hegel argued that nothing
in the realm of ideas, of the concept, or meaning, nothing even about God,
can be a real and effective actuality unless it becomes what it is in space and
time, that is, unless insistence came to exist. But the becoming effective of
the absolute, its actual existence, is our responsibility, just as deutero-Paul
said that it is we who are expected to fill up what is lacking in the body of
Christ (Col. 1:24).

I think that dialectics in any of its flavors—from orthodox high Hegelian through moderate Malabouian plasticity to eccentric Žižekian—is
a distortion of the dynamics of the event, an attempt to repress, rule, or
monitor the event by means of a dialectical logic, and hence a fear of one
small word. Thinking the event is not a matter of negation, or of the negation of a negation, either in the orthodox Hegelian sense or Žižek's revisionist Lacanian sense, but of negotiating amid ambiguous and spectral
shadows. Dialectic is but one kind of difference and it lacks the authority
to monitor the totality of events. Dialectic is a particular kind of difference
inscribed in *différance* whose anarchic energy precedes it, makes it possible
and displaces it. The deconstructive break or interruption, what we called

above a breaking in aimed at freeing up what is breaking out, can never be condensed into a single operation, a particular logical form, a limited and determinate differentiation like "negation." Of course, this forces me to admit that the same thing holds of "affirmation," so that any privileging of affirmation must have in mind a kind of archi-affirmation, which precedes both affirming subjects and the particular logical form of affirmative propositions.

Responsibility means to respond to an event, to enter the register of life, of free play, of the gift, of the grace of the event, whose spectral force is contracted in orthodox theology into an actual being (*primum ens*), or in Tillich into the ground or Being of beings, or in mystical theology into a Hyper-being beyond being. To respond to the event means to give the event a chance, to take a chance on the event, to engage in an archi-affirmation of an archi-energy, an archi-promise that stirs ambiguously within names and things. I endorse Žižek's insistence that with "Christianity" nothing is finished, that nothing more than a transition will have been marked. But that is not because we manage to persuade ourselves to sustain a fiction; it is because the future stretches before us as a *problema*, a task to be achieved, in which we bear the responsibility to fill up what is lacking in the insistence of God.[10]

RESPONDING TO ŽIŽEK

While I think that my own account of insistence gives a more sensitive and less subjectivistic rendering of the event, I have tried to point out a number of underlying sympathies between my work and Žižek's. But Žižek has criticized my work in a way that reflects his underlying and, in my view, unjustified polemic against postmodernism generally. I think his reading of what I have said about the event is too quick, based not on reading the book in which I said it, but on reading another book intended for a popular audience, along with an interview, and a short version of it in my dialogue with Vattimo. The latter is gone through so hastily as to be criticizing "Caputo" while actually citing Vattimo (MC, 259nn22–23). By failing to consult *The Weakness of God* in which my views are set forth in some detail, these pages of *The Monstrosity of Christ* represent not merely a misrepresentation but a missed opportunity. So despite my sympathy for his work, we have differences both conceptual and rhetorical.

The conceptual difference is that Žižek mistakenly attributes to me the view that the relationship between the name and the event which insists in that name is like the relationship of body and soul (MC, 257), as if the name is a material container of an immaterial event, or as if the event is an essential plenitude assuming transient embodiment in historical names. But my materialism, to use a word for which I have no truck, goes all the way down. I have held from the start that events are promises not plenitudes, and that events are not souls getting embodied in historical names. I think, as he does, that material names in fact engender spectral events, that events are an effect of an effect, which Hegel calls reflexivity. Žižek would have only reached the third page of *The Weakness of God* before he found himself reading:

> It is especially important to see that a name does not house an event the way the body houses the soul in Platonism. On the contrary, it would be better to say that the event is the offspring of the body of the name and that without names there would be no events. The event is conceived and born within the body of the name. But names outstrip themselves and come undone just in virtue of their capacity to link up with other names, which gives rise to the event they themselves nurture. Names set off chains of promise and aspiration or chains of memories that outstrip themselves, in the face of which the name itself collapses and soon gives out, being unable to sustain the memory/ promise it itself engenders. A name is a promissory note that it cannot itself keep. In the "democracy to come," for example, "democracy" is a name that may someday collapse under the strain of the "to come," which is the force of the event that will force the name beyond itself. In the "democracy to come," the "to come" is more important than the "democracy." A name is conditioned, coded, and finite, whereas the event it shelters is unconditional and infinite in the sense of being capable of endless linkings and endlessly productive dissemination. One is a nominalist about names because of one's respect for the event.[11]

Žižek grants my post-theism, that I have taken my leave of God as the big Other, and to that extent have my moments as a death-of-God theologian, but this I am said to have done "in name only," as Katharine Moody puts it, with the result that I allow the Good Old God of metaphysics in through the back door. If I deconstruct the name of God in favor of the event of a Call, that Call, in Žižek's estimation, turns out to be the Good Old God all over again, now appearing under the name of the event, thus representing the return of an immaterial exception to the material realm.

But as the above citation shows, Žižek is mistaken about this point, which is the conceptual root of his misreading. I have said repeatedly that

God is not the hyperousiological mystery cultivated in negative theology, but a call from I know not where, and that the call is not the work of a Prime Caller but of a calling that gets itself called in the middle voice, in a mundane and this-worldly way, which bears an interesting comparison to his own idea of the auto-formative collective. There is no Caller calling, no entity or agency behind it, and certainly no immaterial being or region of ideality as Žižek claims. The only names and the only agents we know of are human and altogether material things. That is why I say not that God exists but that God insists, that God does not do, undo, or fail to do anything. The call "gets itself called" on the plane of materiality in which the play of names takes place. I think that a "promise" is a chain of events set off by the disseminative potential "inscribed" in names, that promises "get themselves named" in the process of the play of differences. Promises are a function of dissemination, a work of graphic and phonic, semantic, syntactic, and pragmatic multiplication.

Names are precisely not the material garb of immaterial events. Names are themselves provisional and historical effects of the play of differences and events are effects of these effects, arising from the gaps, the holes, the spacing, the disseminative potential for new nominations that no name can close down, that names contain without being able to contain. If names are "material," so are "events," but "matter" is more than atoms in a void. I think the language of "materialism" is clumsy and worse than useless, but in saying that, I do not mean to embrace a two-worlds Augustinianism. If the event in the sense in which I mean it is denied, the result would be that there are names that name everything they mean to name and speakers who can exercise effective authorial control over what they do and do not want to name, and names would confine us to actuality instead of extending us beyond what lies under our nose. I think, on the contrary, that events are the lines of force that lead out from names and belong to the disseminative fecundity of names, which works behind the backs of authors. My view is that the name (of) "God" plays a paradigmatic role in this regard, at least in the monotheistic traditions, as a name that promises the possibility of the impossible, that it stands in for (or as Žižek would say, "contracts") what we desire with a desire beyond desire, where desire is not one more Lacanian lamentation over some lost something or other.

I take the event as a "spectral" effect—names are haunted by events—in a hauntological not ontological, that is, a completely non-metaphysical sense. I have nothing to do with two-worlds metaphysics, if that still needs to be said. My "materialism" is that there is no other "place" for *différance* to take place than "matter," that is, in spacing and timing, but I regard "materialism" as a particularly inept and ham-fisted way to put that point. As my materialism is inspired by Martha, I would rather say that the scriptures are about land and children, peace and justice, mercy and forgiveness, and cups of cold water extended to wayfarers—which is also why they also lead to so much violence and war—which Levinas calls the materialism of the other person,[12] and that events describe a praxis not a metaphysics.

I really don't think there is much difference between Žižek and me on this point. My own weak theology, my notion that the Crucifixion does not pay off any debt but puts us in debt, that is, makes us responsible to make the "promise" of the "kingdom of God" come true, and that this is all a matter of "spectrality," is pretty much what Žižek's death of God comes down to, as he points out. But when I speak of the way in which we respond to the event that is harbored in the name of God, I much prefer the language of the "desire" for God, or with Meister Eckhart, the language of the birth of God, not of God's death. I use "life" and "birth," not "death," as a way to speak of the response we make to the event contained in the name of God, the moment of the event of grace, the moment "God" has become a force in the world. I also don't want to call it pure life, since I think that life is life/death, *survivre*. I agree with Katharine Moody, who has carefully compared *The Weakness of God* and Žižek and rightly found that the differences between us are not nearly as great as Žižek construes them.[13]

The "conceptual" root of our difference is fairly easily dispatched. But there is another and deeper disagreement, which has its roots in Žižek's rhetoric. Žižek's criticism of me is part of a general effort on his part to discredit "postmodernism" as an anemic pluralism, as aseptic and lifeless, with no taste for blood and revolution (260). He criticizes me for reducing religion to an empty, desubstantialized form of the "to come" (MC, 256–57), deprived of ontological positivity, unable to see the "truth" of Christianity, that eternity must always appear in time, events must be actualized in the concrete. That, as I have just pointed out, is a misunderstanding, sweeping up serious philosophical points under a polemic against political correctness, which I venture to say is what really annoys him. I do not know how often this will need to be said, but allow me to be repeat it one more time—*à venir* is not a dreamy, distant future present in which things promise to be better. It is the infinite pressure exerted on the immediate present by the promise, so that nothing that at present has the audacity to call itself "democracy," for example, is equal to the call. The *à venir* is an infinite, infinitival exaction that galvanizes subjects in the moment of decision, not a future happy day; it is the powerless power of the call of the event, not a coming parousia. It is not the future present. It is the unclosable distance between insistence and existence. This point, I think, is perfectly clear if Derrida is read with care.

Žižek criticizes me for neglecting the Incarnation as the materialization of God. Might I respectfully suggest another neglect instead: that Žižek has simply neglected to read or at least to take into account *The Weakness of God*, a phrase I borrowed from St. Paul to use as the title of my book about Jesus (not "Christ"). In the present work the entire force of my use of "Martha" is to marshal an argument for a religious "materialism," if we insist on using that word. (I think that insisting on this word is blackmail.) Of course, I do agree, a shift takes place between Judaism and Christianity, as Žižek insists, but this is not a shift *to* but a shift *within* messianic "materialisms." It is a shift within messianic postures, a shift between different configurations of the messianic figure, which is a figure inscribed in space and time. In Judaism, we are called upon to expect and make ready for the Messianic age. In the Christian narrative, the Messiah has already come, but that means that we ourselves are called upon to carry out the messianic event, to bring it to completion, to occupy the messianic position, as a way to make ready a *second* coming, where—once again!—everything turns on what is coming. Christians and Jews both live in the time of the "to-come," for even if Christians believe that the Messiah has already come once, they want the Messiah to come *again*.

Indeed, the first followers of the "Way" never expected anything called Christianity. "Christianity" was an event, an unforeseeable surprise visited on the followers of the Way (and you can imagine how much more of a surprise it would have been to Jesus). Christianity only opened its doors for business, began writing down its stories and organizing itself, when it realized this coming *again* was going to be deferred; the coming was going to be a long time coming. The "Christian" event lies in a *voir re-venir,* a watchful not-seeing Jesus come *again*. We keep watch for Jesus coming again—let's see if he comes. "Christianity" means, let's see if *we* can *be* his coming. What the Christian and the Jewish version of the messianic event have in common has been marked off by Benjamin's reversal of the messianic age—where *we* are the ones in the messianic position, the ones the dead have been waiting for to remedy the evil that has been done to them. The messianic structure is a structure of making us responsible to the rigors and demands of the *à venir*. It has nothing to do with an indecisive pluralism or an anemic dreaming of a distant day. The messianic is but another form assumed by the insistence of God.

In other words, Judaism and Christianity are messianic cousins, two different *Vorstellungen*, each in its own way responding to the insistent promise of the event, each in its own way translating the *à venir* of the *événement* into words and deeds. I do see one difference between them, however, which is the built-in structural supersessionism of Christianity, a trap into which I think both Vattimo and Žižek fall. Such supersessionism is nowhere to be found in *The Weakness of God*, which is more interested in Jesus than in Christ. If one emphasizes "subjective beliefs" as seriously as Žižek does, it is impossible to be Christian and *not* supersessionist. That is because supersessionism is what Christian belief *is*, namely, the belief that the Christ whom the Jews were waiting for has arrived and fulfilled the "Old Law" and the Jews missed their chance. A "Christian" believes that the "Old" Testament is superseded by the "New" one. Of course, much as you might be tempted, you should not feel free to persecute Jews or anyone else on that account and you should always be tolerant of people who disagree with you. But if you believe in subjective beliefs, and if you don't *believe* in supersession, then you're not a "Christian" believer.

That is why I have displaced "belief" in the name of an underlying *faith* in the event and treated "belief" as strictly a matter of *Vorstellungen*. Supersessionism is so endemic to *Christianity*—it would, of course, have dumbfounded "Yeshua," a committed Jew from Nazareth—that it even shows up in its atheistic versions (Žižek, Vattimo), in which not only is Jesus not a God-Man (a strict monotheist like Jesus would not have been surprised at that part), but there is no God for Jesus to be, which would have absolutely floored Jesus. Supersessionism is so deeply inscribed in Hegelian approaches to Christianity that the word actually serves as a fair translation of *Aufhebung*, the moment in which the opposition of the preceding positions is superseded in the complete or consummate composition, the true religion, just the way "Christ" is the "*pleroma*" of the Law, not its destruction. Unlike Žižek, I do not think it is just political correctness when postmodern theorists warn about the supersessionist implications for Jews (and everyone else) embedded in "Christ."

Of course, in the end, truth to tell, both Jesus and Christianity are contingent figures for Žižek, something like a Hitchcock movie or Stephen King. The core argument stands quite free of any of them and runs entirely on Lacanian steam. As Milbank says, Žižek is just taking every opportunity to "mime" Christianity, which is nothing more than a large tent under which the camel of Žižek can push his Lacanian nose. If Žižek were a materialist, a historical materialist, he would show more interest in the material Jesus and less interest in the opportunity "Christology" provides him to make his argument. But Žižek show little interest in the earthly Jesus, in the man of flesh and blood who actually lived in time and space, whom he practically never mentions by name. What interest is it, for example, that the "seven last words" on the Cross, including the "Eli, Eli" saying, on which so much of his interpretation depends, are literary devices, the creation of narratives written by Christian storytellers a half century later who were likely not even born at the time of the Crucifixion.

When Žižek says "Christ" is a name in which we contract the void, I respectfully submit that he is saying the name of Christ is a nickname he uses for Lacan. He means we can use the Christian story the way an analyst might deal with a patient, by going along with his fantasies until the man comes to see for himself that it's all a fantasy. You agree with the patient that there's a snake under his bed and you do not argue with him. But the question is, how do we deal with this snake? How large is it? Is it venomous? How might we entice the snake outdoors? The analyst has a serious conversation with the man about the snake until the man himself realizes, seriously, there is no snake (and until the snake realizes this, too—I know the joke).

I myself think "Jesus"—I didn't say "Christ"—is a placeholder, not for the void, but rather for the face of promise in the facelessness of the void, the promise that the narratives in which the memory of this man lost in the fog of history has been constructed and constituted, *vorgestellt*, set forth by and for the "Christian" imagination, constitute a spectral and theopoetic configuration of forgiveness, love, compassion, and non-violence, in the name of which quite a great deal of blood has been spilled by his followers, *in hoc signo vinco*. I think there are other placeholders in other traditions and languages in which other, equally important events take place. But this one is mine—we are all accidental Christians, Jews, all accidental cosmic tourists of one sort or another—because I happen to have been formed by the cultural world in which it took root. I think being Christian means being conscious of the contingency of this situation, living in the distance between association and dissociation with one's historical legacy, being Christian as if not, "uncoupled" from an accident of birth while also appreciative of one's legacy.

If Žižek's materialism means he is interested in the concrete, the earthly, the embodied, then that would require him to show a little more interest in the earthly-material Jesus of Nazareth. More generally, it would require he show some interest in the actual history of actual religions. But he shows little interest in the concrete, historical work of construction that led from a devout but sharp-tongued monotheistic Jewish troublemaker up to the

Council of Nicea, which would have left Jesus dumbfounded. Jesus would not have known what, "in God's name," they were talking about. It would be all Greek to him. And I don't think that such mundane or material matters matter a whit to Žižek.[14]

GIGANTOMACHIA: MILBANK AND ŽIŽEK

That brings me back to the fear of one small word. My differences with Žižek are rooted in his distrust of the chaosmic and unwieldy *peut-être* to which Derrida and I have recourse. He shares this distrust with Milbank. The two of them oppose my *peut-être* with their competing absolutes of Absolute Peace and Absolute Conflict, suggesting something of the mythological scene of Gigantomachy, the combat between Heracles and Alcyoneus, Olympian Cosmos and a dark Chaos. The war is between two overarching cosmic narratives, which are pitted against each other quite nicely by Gareth Woods, speaking in summary of Milbank: "In the beginning was the Word . . . and everything will be fine"—enticing Katharine Moody to add, speaking in summary of Žižek, "In the beginning was the Void . . . and nothing will be 'fine.'"[15]

It is worth noticing, I should add, that the very fact that their debate is not cast as a war between theology and anti-theology is a good example of their common debt to postmodern discourse. The "theological turn" among European intellectuals, even of the most hardened neo-Marxist sort, is to turn to theology for help in addressing basic questions in ontology and political theory, going back to the fascinating interpretation of St. Paul by Alain Badiou, which drew Giorgio Agamben and Žižek into the debate. Although it would make Žižek and (less so) Milbank uncomfortable to say so, there is nothing else to call this turn but "postmodern," if postmodernism means a recognition of hybridity, a weakening of rigid modernist binarities like matter and spirit, faith and reason, objective and subjective, philosophy and theology. Their debate concerns whether this hybrid theological monster is to be interpreted dialectically or analogically. Žižek's willingness to play the Christian role is a strictly postmodern ploy; it would previously have been off-limits to a secular leftist intellectual fifty years ago.

Of course, for the most part Žižek and Milbank cannot think of things mean enough to say about postmodernism, which they both regard as a spineless and indecisive compromise with late capitalism, pluralism, and liberal individualism. On their telling, postmodernism means that Platonic truth collapses into relativistic "conversation," decision dissolves into a pool of undecidability, genuine political action into political correctness, and love into sexual libertinism. In this regard, whatever their differences, both authors ride a high theological horse. Both love G. K. Chesterton's old chestnuts about orthodoxy offering the most radical revolution, or about past papal censures of scientific research providing reason its best protection. That produces more and more dreadful monsters: Milbank (an Anglican) is happy to invoke the pope to counter the Reformation and Žižek happily calls himself a Stalinist to counter democracy. Milbank defends "Red Toryism" and pleads that paternalism has its bright side and Žižek wants us to see the rose in the cross of an "austere socialist dictatorship" (MC, 292). That leaves their readers to decide just how much they actually mean these things, and just how much we should love the monsters of Milbank and Žižek.

There are times when Žižek is very close to the spectral logic of the *peut-être* that I am defending. For example, Žižek provocatively suggests an odd kind of "positive" unbelief in an undead God, like the "undead" in the novels of Stephen King, a "spectral" belief that is never simple disbelief along with a God who is never simply dead (MC, 101).[16] God is dead but we continue to (un)believe in the ghost of god, in a living dead god. If atheism ("I don't believe in God") is the negation of belief ("I believe in God"), what is the negation of that negation? It is not a higher living spirit of faith that reconciles belief and unbelief but a negation deeper than a simple naturalistic and reactionary atheism (like Hitchins and Dawkins). Belief is not *aufgehoben* but rather not quite killed off, even though it is dead. That could produce a completely deconstructive result: *sous rature.* Belief is muted, erased but surviving under erasure, like seeing Marley's ghost even though Scrooge knows he is dead these twenty years; like a crossed-out letter we can still read, oddly living on in a kind of spectral condition. Things are neither black nor white but shifting, spectral, ambiguous, incomplete, virtual. We have bid farewell to God, adieu to the good old God (*à Dieu*), farewell to the big Other, Who Makes Everything Turn Out Right, Who Writes Straight with Crooked Lines, who maketh me to lie down in green pastures. Still, that negation of negation does not spell the simple death of belief but its positive mode in which belief, while dead, lives on (*sur/vivre*). This unbelief would be the "pure form" of belief, and if belief is the substance of the things that appear not, Žižek proposes a belief deprived of substance as well as of appearance. When all is said and done, one has to ask, exactly how far is Žižek's view from Derrida's "spectral messianic"? Sometimes the difference seems, as Milbank says, merely one of tone (MC, 118). If this spectral logic were pursued to the end, we would find a spectral *foi* that displaces subjective *croyance*. But Žižek is too much dedicated to the monstrous battle of absolutes to settle for the spooky spectrality of the "perhaps."

I cannot resist saying that the opposing forces in this war march under faux flags, like ships pretending they are friendly vessels. So if Žižek mimes Christianity, Milbank mimes materialism. But Milbank is no more interested in the "materialism" he salutes than Žižek is in the "Christianity" he thinks worth saving. Both are used as fronts to cover the absolutes they are really defending. Both positions are sustained throughout by an unmistakable irony. Milbank makes no bones about the fact that the goal of his argument is to lie down in green pastures with his friends on the other side, that the whole point of the theory of analogical participation and theological materialism is to break the bite of matter where matter matters most, death and corruption in the grave. Milbank may be a critic of dialectics but it seems to me that his tripartite movement of affirmation, negation, and eminence is dialectics at an even higher velocity. The irreducible heart of Milbank's Augustinian-Thomistic analogy is to insure that matter does not have the last word, that there is room in matter to triumph over death, to enter a domain where the bite of space and time and corruptible flesh has been bridled. Then we will live on with imperishable bodies made of who knows what, of matter of some sort or other, matter *eminentiore modo,* but certainly not matter in any sense that matters.

That is also why, when Chesterton speaks of "a matter more dark and awful," we know to take this matter with a grain of salt, that Chesterton is only willing to go so far with these dark matters. We all know that this is all part of a Chestertonian rhetoric of reversals, an apologetic of Christian faith in which things are continually stood on their head (which is the part that Žižek admires) in order to make sure that we all end up anastatic, upright, and resurrected, not flat on our backs in the grave. For Chesterton there is *nothing* really dark and awful at all, not *in the end,* not at the *eschaton,* when things are not dark but light, not awful but glorious, not dead but resurrected. Chesterton is like a predictable formula novelist whose stories always have a happy ending, and whose art is to try to persuade the reader that this time the hero is really done for and will not survive. What we admire is not the heroism of the hero, whose fate was never really at risk, but the art of Chesterton the detective novelist in throwing a phony scare into us, as if something dark and awful really were about to happen, which of course it does not, not in the end. We simply check the page number to see how many pages he has given himself to extricate his hero. The one thing we know when we read Chesterton, if we do not tire too quickly of the topsy-turvy logic, is that he is speaking of the Incarnation and the divine economy of salvation, of bright and glorious salvation, and that the very last thing he thinks, the very last thing he would ever subscribe to, is the matter more dark and awful of the abyss of real and absolute loss that Žižek is speaking about.

What Žižek does with Chesterton is brilliant—namely, he believes him; he actually takes him at his word. That would have completely dumb-founded Chesterton, leaving the famous polemicist blustering, lost for words, totally unprepared. Chesterton never imagined that some rogue like Žižek would sneak up on him from behind and take him completely by surprise—by actually believing him. How could Chesterton have seen a Žižek coming, someone who really does think that human existence is broken from the start by a dark, awful, irreparable trauma and that all there is left to do is come to grips with it? Of course, Žižek has no real need of his Chesterton, no more than Chesterton does of his matter more dark and awful, no more than Milbank does of his materialism; it is after all a bit difficult to countenance the idea that someone who thinks we reach the heights of life in death, in rotting in the grave, is the true materialist in the room. The problem posed in reading *The Monstrosity of Christ* is that nobody in this book believes what they are saying. They are all saying the opposite of what they believe because they think that this has a strategic advantage in the war they are waging with each other. The exchange is great theatre, full of warring knights of one dogma or another, each disguised as his opposite. Milbank's "materialism" means he wants to go to heaven and live forever. Chesterton's "matter more dark and awful" is his way of saying everything will work out quite well in the end. Žižek's "Christ" means we are all lost; it is the mask he wears in this play, his nickname for a way to contract the void, to make a grim philosophico-psychoanalytic point he can make in any number of ways, where anything from Stephen King to the Nicene Creed will do.

WHY MUST WE LOVE MONSTERS?

What, then, exactly is the compelling need we are under to agree with either Milbank or Žižek or to choose between them? Why do we have to love either one of these monsters? Why do we need to suppose that at the metaphysical base of things there lies either a Primordial Peace or a Primordial Violence—or a primordial anything, at least one that we could ever get our hands on? Why do we need to love this exaggeration of Lacanian psychoanalysis, which includes the suggestion that human emancipation is somehow going to depend upon the formation of a psychoanalytic community? Who could afford to be a member? This suggestion rivals Milbank's garden of Eden on the fantasy register. Why, on the one hand, must we love this dangerous exaggeration of the One Holy Catholic and Apostolic Church, a specter straight out of the darkest Middle Ages and a strong candidate itself for a matter more dark and awful? The real monster here is metaphysics, the metaphysical impulse, seeking to be a theory of everything, as if the world were so much plankton for its gaping all-consuming jaws, where everything is peace or everything is war, on the monstrous assumption that everything must be *something* and we must *know* what that is. That is the end of the event, whether it is snuffed out by the white light of Glory or by the absolute dark of unnamable trauma. In Milbank and Žižek, the event is eaten by a monster and the entire exchange is driven by the fear of one small word.

In a theopoetics of the "perhaps," on the other hand, our lives are woven in and by multiple repetitions that proceed without the need to treat this forward repetition either as a downbeat and futile search that will be always frustrated or as underwritten by an uplifting metaphysics of participation. For what need do we have to choose between a metaphysics of misery or a metaphysics of glory? Why inscribe either absolute contradiction or absolute peace at the heart of things instead of ambience and ambiguity? Why either cosmos or chaos instead of the unsteady chaosmotic process of unprogrammed becoming that is the matrix of novelty and invention? In a modest theopoetics of "perhaps," life is a joyful but risky business that may turn out well or badly, a repetition forward in which I produce what I am repeating, in which I invent what I am discovering, but in which I am divested of any assurances about what lies up ahead—or deep down at the metaphysical base of things where Monsters wage a giant, gigantic war.

I very much admire what Žižek says about the "contingency of necessity" and his rereading of the death drive, which are very close to my use of the Kierkegaardian notion of a forward repetition. But I resist his idea of some sort of Deep Trauma which strikes like some Metaphysical Meteor that cratered downtown Ljubljana. Is this not just the search for a transcendental signifier all over again? Why do we have to believe that something deep is out there but alas it is lost and life is hopeless search for it? That is repetition as reproduction. Why not rather say that by searching for it, it is there, produced by the repetition? In a deconstructive theory of repetition we produce what we repeat. The repetition is generative, engendering, positing something not merely as a dream but by the dream, *by the* impossible. The active dreaming of the dream, the dreaming up, gathers momentum as we dream, repeat, desire, pray, and weep, over the coming of something whose coming we are engendering, or is being engendered, as the very structure of desire. Dreaming is the *pharmakon,* a risky supplement, a joy that flows through our veins that is liable to poison us if we are not careful. Nothing primordial is lost from which we have been traumatically cut off. Why do we need such a story? Does it give us a perverse pleasure to wallow in such dark myths? I follow Zarathustra and his animals, who warned us against animals who want to make themselves sick. Forward repetition is just desire desiring, what desire does, how it works, and if desire is a fault, it is a happy fault. Why invent a myth of lamentation and loss, whether of a lost phallus or a lost garden of delight?

We who practice a theopoetics of "perhaps" adopt the post-metaphysical idea that gives up searching for any such primordial underlying something or other, be it a primordial loss or a primordial victory. Is there some reason we get only two choices, either God as an illusion spun by the *objet petit a* or God as the Alpha and Omega, the really real and really Big Alpha (male)? This is just metaphysics spinning its wheels all over again. The irony is that both Milbank and Žižek actually acknowledge the stalemate. It is a point supported by Milbank, when he says neither of these views can be proven (MC, 153), and by Žižek, when he says each of them can continually reframe the other's position without end and that the argument has now spun itself out (MC, 247). The real difference between them, as Žižek points out, is not a primordial reality but a primal hermeneutic ur-decision: Žižek thinks the world has been disenchanted and Milbank still sings hymns to the old enchantment—and neither of them is going to budge about that. That's the bottom line in this debate. Well, then, why continue it? Why play this game? Why subject the rest of us to it? Why not leave these monsters to themselves? Why not leave monsters to summer action films and video games? What better reason for the two of them to swear off metaphysics and reconsider the poverty of poor *peut-être,* quiet as a dove, savvy as a snake, like a sheep amid these violent wolves!

In any reasonably faithful account of what passes for human experience, all that can be truly said to be "given" is something not quite given, a promise/risk, a "perhaps," that is not reducible to one or the other, to absolute peace or absolute trauma. Why must we believe that underneath it all is something profoundly productive or destructive? Why not simply confess that the "matter" that really matters is the risky matter of life, life marked by an unknowable and fundamental undecidability, an ineradicable secret or mystery which reminds us that we do not know who we are, that we do not know what is (deeply) what, or what we truly want, yet to make this confession without nostalgia, without despair, without theological triumphalism but with a joyful sense of discovery and a faith that cannot be contracted into a belief? I readily agree that something important is strategically contracted in the name of Jesus, but for me this means neither the One Holy and (Very) Roman (Monarchical) Catholic Church nor a Monstrous Trauma. It is rather an event that is constituted in a perplexing *poetics*, in the reversals that mark the kingdom of God, where the first are last, the outsiders are in and the insiders are out, where the one who preaches this poetics of the outsider ends up getting himself killed for his trouble. But I do not see that this marvel must amount to either Žižek's void or Milbank's metaphysics of plenitudinous participation, which seem to me metaphysical leaps into the abyss, be it the abyss of nothingness or of the excess of being beyond being, which are the recto and the verso of each other. What could be plainer than that we are instead dealing with the marvel of the promise/risk—the chance of mercy and love, the grace of compassion and forgiveness, and that is all we get to know on earth and all we need to know? Does anyone really think the Sermon on the Mount has anything to do with all this metaphysical tilting and jousting? With a battle between competing Monsters?

I recommend neither the imaginary nor the real, neither the hallucinatory, imaginary pacifying Neoplatonic illusion of Milbankian analogy, nor negative dialectics, the grim lamentations of Lacanian trauma. I endorse the *viens, oui, oui* of the post-metaphysics of *peut-être*, the hope against hope that the future will be better, the hope that is not a stranger to despair. I would rework the idea of the *objet petit a* as the buzz things have—little things, like rain in our face or Mallarmé's cake and cup of tea—in a joyful repetition forwards as we forge a life for ourselves. If there is a failure here it is a happy failure, a *felix culpa* without the Lacanian lament over the long-lost phallus, and more like the joyous failure of great musicians who happily conclude that no matter how many times they go back to Mozart they never cease to be amazed at how many things they missed. I recommend the riskiness of the venture, of the adventure, which I think is metonymically, metaphorically, paradigmatically inscribed in the name of God, who is, on my accounting, no small measure of trouble. One might even say God is infinite trouble, that than which nothing is more troubling, in which is inscribed all the passion of life. But trouble is no more the marker of the fatality of Absolute Trauma than a guarantor of Absolute Peace. Trouble is spooky but it is not a Monster. It the risk of the perhaps, the specter of *peut-être*, the occasion of the prayer of the precarious.

GIGANTOMACHEAN ETHICS

The irony that should be lost on no one is that this lack of the "perhaps" actually can lead to violence. This is not a passing observation. Milbank practices the vintage violence of theological imperialism—is there any other?—a disturbing and dogmatic theological dismissiveness of anyone who disagrees with the medieval metaphysics of Thomas Aquinas. The more time that goes by, the more Radical Orthodoxy is becoming a Tommy-come-lately, well after this cycle has been played out in the twentieth century Catholic renewal of Thomism.[17] This Milbank offers in the name of peace. As Derrida said in another context, if this were not so serious, it would be extremely funny. Radical Orthodoxy reminds us, in case we might have forgotten, why no one outside closed confessional conclaves trusts confessional theology and how terrifying it would be if such theology ever regained real political power, as it is trying mightily to do and with some success in the American Christian Right today. There is truly a matter more dark and awful.

The best advice Žižek has to offer is the perplexing conclusion to *The Parallax View*: Bartleby.[18] To be sure, any theory of the *perhaps* can appreciate the important role played by Bartleby, as Derrida has nicely shown. It is also a crucial ingredient in a theology of the "perhaps not," of the *hos me* sayings, where one prefers not to be identical with oneself, not to consolidate one's position in the contingency of an accident of birth. I should always prefer not to say "I *am*" this or that. In a weak theology, "preferring not to" can provide a powerful example of the power of powerlessness. What is forgiveness if not to prefer not to retaliate? To prefer not to can mean strategic civil disobedience to an unjust law, or boycotting goods produced by polluters and corporations with unfair labor practices as part of a larger plan of non-violent intervention. It can mean to go on strike, hoping to strike a spark by sparking a strike, the way Rosa Parks sparked a revolution because she preferred not to sit in the back of the bus. But Žižek hardly has Gandhi's non-violent resistance in mind, or Martin Luther King's.

Then what does he mean? Do not come to the aid of an ailing system, let it collapse, then one day, off in the future, maybe centuries from now this Monster called Capitalism will collapse. Do not collaborate with the enemy. So his "materialism" amounts to the worst anti-materialism, the worst idealism: forget the wretched of the earth, forget the concrete, embodied, historical, incarnate material beings who are materially suffering, and keep uppermost in your mind an abstract, long-term Dialectical

Principle, the actual misery of concrete people in the meantime be damned. Their suffering flesh is what We Who Know the Principle call the "short term." Is that what he means? Is that not the worst "scarecrow" Hegel, the dead bodies accumulated by the Spirit's march through history, the worst Monster of all? The worst ideology? Is this just a certain Marx advising us to let Capital rush to its own self-destruction, watching it collapse under its own crises?

We have been through this before, in the debate between Camus and Sartre, when Sartre was prepared to write off the worst horrors of Stalinism in the name of the revolution and Camus was rightly horrified. As first-century Christians learned long ago, waiting for the Messiah to show up can be a drawn-out affair. When they complained to Paul that some of them were dying and the Messiah had still not returned, the ever-resourceful Paul came up with his Jesus-coming-on-a-cloud story in *I Thessalonians*, which is no option for Žižek, who thinks that Paul is dealing in fabulation. Besides, what is to guarantee that whatever replaces Capitalism after it capitulates will not be an even worse ultra-capitalism? When I read philosophers saying such things, I think there is more good advice about the political order in any randomly chosen edition of the editorial pages of the *New York Times* than is dreamt of by the philosophers. They howl at the moon of the Revolution while in the meantime the right wing takes over everything.

I think that Jesus—who it should be noted does not even make the index in *The Monstrosity of Christ*—would have been dumbfounded by this debate about the metaphysics of Christ. If one thinks, as I do, that the Nicene Creed would have left him speechless (after somebody translated the Greek for him), what about associating him with withholding mercy to the least among us? So that's materialism? I think we should prefer not to follow Žižek's advice.

THE CHIASM, THE DOUBLE KENOSIS, AND ANOTHER PARALLAX

God can happen anywhere, but God needs us. God is not above being but within, neither a first being (a Big Being who "does" things) nor the Being of beings (a Deep Being which guarantees that things get done). That is why God needs our help. God insists, we exist, and together that constitutes the chiasm, the intertwining, which is my subject. God needs our response to be God; we need God's prompting to be human. This is not only Christian heresy but even a heretical Hegel, heresy all the way down.

God depends on the response. It all depends, including God. Whether or not an event will have occurred, whether or not there will have been grace, will be determined by us, by our response, by the decision of the other in us. After the fact, we will see whether there will have been a response. We will just see how things turn out, without contriving a retroactive herme-neutics that predicts after the fact, that sees an event coming but only after it has happened.

A theopoetics with its eye on Martha's world can provide for a salu-tary "materialism" that avoids the monsters of metaphysics. (As everybody wants to be a "materialist" these days, even the theologians, my requisite materialism will be of the theopoetic flavor.) God is an insistence whose existence can only be found in matter, space, and time. *Where else* could God be God? Exactly what *other* choices are there? What is called Hege-lian "Idealism" I redescribe as the power of an idea, and I redescribe an idea as an event that calls, which is the power of powerlessness, which is the insistence of the event, all of which I am contracting into a theology of *peut-être*. The idea is neither a pure form nor an ideal object, neither an immaterial being nor an effective force, but a wispy *souffleur*, a prompting coming from offstage, which is what Derrida calls an "unconditional with-out sovereignty."[19] The responsibility of the response is ours—that is what I call the "materialism" of Martha, which means making ourselves worthy of the events that happen to us, turning the virtual event into material actu-ality. Idealism solicits, materialism answers. Materialism means that we are the hearers of the call, the ones laid claim to, solicited, spooked, visited, invited, enjoined to materialize events, to make them happen materially, which is why Levinas says that the true materialism is found in offering a cup of cold water to the wayfarer. Faced with the hunger of the other, he says, "there is no bad materialism other than our own."[20]

If I have assured the infidels of my materialism, I have also been assur-ing the faithful from the start that I am praying, that this theology of the event is a theology or theopoetics of prayers prayed by the precarious. Materialism is the answer not to our prayers but to God's, the answer we make to God's entreaties. By this I mean that God calls and we are the ones called upon, that God solicits and entreats us and the rest is up to us to make matter(s) better or worse. That is the chiasmic intertwining of God's insistence and our existence. So it is God whose situation is precarious, who thus prays to us and seeks our aid and succor. The precariousness of God is the inevitable companion of the weakness of God. God needs us and God prays to us, petitioning us to please, I pray you, do my work as I cannot do it myself. That is the precariousness of God and prayer is for the precarious. But insofar as we also pray, for we are woven of prayers and tears, we in turn pray for the heart to respond, to make ourselves worthy of the event. We pray for peace, long for justice, dream of the messianic age, call for the democracy to come, pray and weep over what is missing in the body of God. These are God's dreams and ours, God's prayers and ours, with the result that we and God are in this together, and together form a common bond or *religio*, both praying for the messianic age, for the coming of the Messiah. That is the chiasm.

God calls, we answer. God is the problem, we are the solution. That is the chiasm. So to Malabou's double kenosis I say yes, and add a second yes, a double prayer, a double precariousness, even as I add another parallax to Žižek's pot: our prayers to God are but God's prayers to us, from another point of view. Our tears for God are God's tears for us. Yes, yes. *Viens, oui, oui.* Yes, I said yes. Is that not God praying? Are these not God's tears? Are we not all siblings in the same sea of tears, God's included? God is at the heart of our religion and we are at the heart of God's. That is the chiasm of God's insistence and our existence.

We are always praying for grace, praying and weeping over the chance of the event, which is a chance for grace. To pray is to say "perhaps," to expose ourselves to the abyss of "perhaps," to meditate the grace of a chance, the chance of a grace. Theopoetics enters upon a place that was first opened up by Hegel, even if it is a place Hegel himself did not see coming. That would make it Hegel's event, perhaps.

Fuck off, Caputo

PART THREE

Cosmopoetics
THE INSISTENCE OF THE WORLD

THE INSISTENCE OF THE WORLD
From Chiasm to Cosmos

Where were you when I laid the foundations of the earth?
—JOB 38:4

INTRODUCTION TO PART 3

We promised at the start to honor the animals of Jesus, and now we must make good on that promise, this time by honoring the animal that Jesus is, the animal that I am following (*je suis*),[1] whose animal needs were recognized by Martha. Indeed it is time to honor the history of the animals that we all are and are following, which I have emblematically called Martha's world, the world to which we all belong in the most deeply material sense. Yet, despite our pledge to follow the animals of Jesus, we have in truth been focused almost exclusively on human beings and God, on the chiasmic intertwining of God's insistence and the need God has for human existence to fill up what is lacking in the body of God. So the time has come to shed the anthropocentrism and humanism of the first two parts of this study. Now we must ask, what about everything else? Does God need anything else? Does anything else need God? More unnervingly still, does insistence have a wider reach than the name (of) "God"? What about non-human animals and non-living things? What about Nietzsche weeping over that horse? What about the stars and the distant origins of the universe? Is not the "little town" of Bethany in the story to be found on planet Earth? Does it not have a planetary and ultimately a cosmic setting and is its fate not bound up with the fate of the planet and the solar system? Does not any possible theopoetics have a wider cosmic context?

These are not the kinds of question we are used to asking, not in the humanities generally and not in continental philosophy in particular, which today finds itself under fire for having kept nature and the physical sciences at arm's length. I have been arguing in the present study that I have found it necessary to delimit Kant in order to make room for Hegel, and then to delimit Hegel in order to make room for the event. But now I must take care that what I have been calling theopoetics not succumb to the Kantian move I criticized in the second part of this book, which is to delimit what the scientists are telling us in order to make room for what we are doing back in the "humanities center," in "philosophy" and "theology" and "literature." So, in the final part of this book I wish to press the case still harder against the Kantian tilt of postmodernism that I criticized in part 2. In doing so I take the occasion to examine a contemporary critique of the continental tradition from Kant to the present that is particularly frustrated by the so-called theological turn in which this tradition seems to have culminated, a critique that would certainly include the present undertaking.

It is a sign of the times that nowadays everyone wants to be a "materialist," even the theologians. My idea, on the other hand, has been to treat the name (of) "God" as a response to the deepest promptings of our life and in so doing to undermine the binarities of "theism" and of "atheism," of the "religious" and the "secular," and also of "materialism" and "idealism," on the grounds that these categories block our access to the event. A theopoetics of the events ought to be in principle post-theist and post-atheist, post-materialist and post-idealist, and even post-religious and post-secular, on the grounds that I am feeling about in a more elementary space which gives place to events. But beyond the philosophical inadequacy of these binary schemas, they are a trap, a kind of blackmail, forcing a bad choice on us under pain of incurring the deep "odium" each harbors for the other. The *odium theologiae* is deep indeed and it cuts both ways: not only the odium of evolutionary biologists for Bible thumpers, but also the no less odious demonization of "atheism" by people who really do believe in demons! With my event-driven theopoetics I am trying to burrow beneath this binarity and to defuse the mutual animosity by meditating upon the event that insists in the name (of) "God." This, I propose, has to do with something we all share in common—the solemnities and levities, the tragedies and comedies, the laughter and the tears, the promise and the risk of mortal life (*vita mortalis*), which is, I propose, the selfsame boat in which we all find ourselves afloat (or sometimes sinking). The name (of) "God" is one of the names we have constructed—or rather, one of the names that has gotten itself constructed—in our lives in order to name what Derrida calls "the promise of the world,"[2] a promise and a threat in which we are all commonly caught up.

The point I want to pursue in the third and final phase of this study is that the promise/threat is made in the midst of a cosmic roll of the dice.

In "Circumfession" Derrida tells us of his mother's love of poker and that she stayed up late playing poker the night before he was born. He used this game to signal the fortuitousness of his life, like the chance congruence between his circumstances and Augustine's. The game is a figure of chance itself, of the chance of life, which shows up not only in Derrida, who rightly passes for an atheist, but even in Augustine, in the Providential importance that Augustine himself attached to the game of *tolle, lege* that he could hear some children playing, which Augustine considered the occasion of a great gift of grace. Chance or grace, grace or chance, the gift of chance or the gift of grace? These are categories of the "event" and they signal our common circumstance, theist, atheist, or something yet unnamed. That is what I here frame against a cosmic background and situate within a cosmic dice game. Here I will advance the proposition that the new species of theologians for whom I call—more theopoetician than theologian, of course, and more Hegelian than Kantian—will be practitioners of what I designate here a "cosmo-theopoetics," a willingness to say "come" to a cosmic "perhaps," where it is the world itself that insists, that comes knocking at our door.

This will entail giving the model of Martha's world a cosmic import. Mary, let us recall, is content to luxuriate in the divine insistence, to linger in the still inexistent, while Martha makes the transition to existence and reality. Martha thus enjoys a double gift, both of insistence and existence, both of inner union with Jesus and of taking action in the outer world. Mary loves the voice of Jesus and lingers over the sweetness of the call. Martha hears the call but, realizing that the call calls for a response, she swings into action. In Mary, the call abides in a worldless and immaterial beauty while Martha appreciates the materiality and worldly reality of the call. Martha knows that Jesus needs a place to sleep and eat, and takes care of his bodily necessities. She knows, to put it baldly, that Jesus has animal needs. Martha is much more of a "materialist" than Mary, meaning more appreciative of the press of material needs. She knows that Jesus is a human animal, as are we all. That is the blending of divinity and human animality that Hegel called the "monstrous compound," that Derrida called "divinanimality," and that Kierkegaard regarded as the real "scandal"—this miserable human being with dirty hands and feet and having unmentionable needs is not just this miserable thing but the God! Jesus is both an animal and a god, suggesting the possibility of what Derrida calls a possible "zootheology."[3] For Kierkegaard this moral shock—a God assuming the most embarrassing animal needs—exceeded the classical logical paradox of two natures in one person. On Eckhart's telling, the divine "birth" takes place more perfectly and completely in Martha, which means in the present polemical context that Jesus favors the "materialist" over the idealist or immaterialist. God is born in her soul in cooking and cleaning the house and in providing for material needs of Jesus we dare not mention. Martha means the most material preparation for the arrival of the divine guest and her attention to these needs does not divert her from her unity with Jesus; it is the basis of it.

My intention now, in the third part, is to make the case for a Martha-like religious "realism" and "materialism," if I must use these helpless categories, for the press of animality and materiality upon our humanity and upon the chiasm. I will examine my conscience about whether my account thus far has not been inadvertently privileging Mary and so, contrary to the command of (Eckhart's) Jesus, ignoring that Martha has chosen the better part. Is there not a residual privileging of the figure of Mary in the account thus far of the chiasmic intertwining of God and human being? Is this chiasm not too narrow, too closed, too intimate, too "immaterial" a relation? What about everything else, everything non-human?

Thus in loyalty to Jesus and his animals, to the human animal that Jesus is, we must venture into the wider world, expand our parameters and pry open the perspective of our "perhaps" to the solicitation of the "world" as a whole, indeed of the vast cosmos that stretches well beyond us and subsists without us. Perhaps the chiasm reaches farther and wider than the insistence of God. Perhaps it extends to the insistence of the world itself and is caught up in the promise of the world—the promise of a cosmic dice game, which means the promise/risk, the chance of grace, the grace of chance.

I will argue that this cosmo-theopoetics could be formulated in terms of a "religious materialism." This is an expression that I dislike for all the reasons that I have given. But it has the double advantage both of drawing a contemporary crowd and of being more or less bullet-proof when the critics of "religion" start shooting. I am, to my utter consternation, from time to time taken to be a right-wing, two-worlds Augustinian, largely, as far I can tell, because I use words like "God" and "theology" and cite Augustine's *Confessions* lovingly, which seems to move some readers to stop reading. In this way I hope to silence such baseless criticism while also assuring my religious friends that I am not recommending a leap into the abyss.

Such a "religious materialism," I might add, is surprising only to critics of religion who have managed to immunize themselves against any actual knowledge of religion and theology, who are tone-deaf to the minor chords and discordant notes in the history of theology, and who speak of "religion" and "theology" in the singular, as if there were one, as if there were but one. They have managed mightily to ignore the fact that the heroes of "religion" wherever we find them, from Mahatma Gandhi to the Reverend Martin Luther King Jr. and Mother Teresa, are regularly dedicated to material needs, to feeding the hungry, caring for the ill, freeing the imprisoned and emancipating the oppressed. Such materialism should certainly not be surprising in an "Incarnational" religion, which officially professes to be all about "flesh"—*caro, sarx, chair, Fleisch*—even if it sometimes does not behave that way.

Let us pose the cosmo-theopoetic question of insistence as follows. The event is what is calling, but the caller of the call in constitutively unavailable, which is why we leave it in the middle voice and we say that something is getting itself called in and under the name (of) "God." That leaves us puzzled about the reach and the dimensions of the call. Is it God who calls? Might it not be the world? Is it God calling from beyond the world—or is it the world calling under the name of God? Does God call through the world—or does the world call through God, through the name (of) "God"? Is the insistence of the world the insistence of God—or is the insistence of God the insistence of the world, of something happening in the world under the name of God, under the name (of) "God"? Is God the "ancient of days" or is there something older than God?

Of course, however this may be decided, or not decided, the call calls; the call stands. Jesus calls and Martha responds. It is a question of response, not of answering a questionnaire.

THE HUMAN AND NON-HUMAN

We in the humanities have swallowed a bit too easily Heidegger's famous dictum, "science does not think." We humanists think, we are proud to say, but science does not. If we believe that, then we need to use the thinking on which we pride ourselves to rethink that line. I suggest we start by disabusing ourselves of the way we humanists think about the "non-human." So I here call upon the resources of our "perhaps" to weaken our built-up resistances to thinking that, perhaps, the human and the non-human are not opposites but intertwined. Perhaps the chiasm obtains not only between God and human beings, but between the human and the non-human.

The war that broke out between the "humanities" and science, the "science wars," the war of the "two cultures," is a function of the hostilities that irrupted in "modernity," at the birth of the *via moderna*. The first *causes célèbres* of that war were the torching of Giordano Bruno and the trial of Galileo by the Church, which were, to say the least, "public relations" disasters for the Church from which it has not, to this day, recovered. After that, nobody trusted theology. That set the stage for the subsequent battle: theology on this side, science on the other; human subjects on this side, material objects on the other; mythic enchantment on this side, scientific disenchantment on the other. Remarkably enough that battle is actually still being engaged today—by the Christian Right's crusade against evolution, where the mutual odium I referred to above rages unabated and is cynically manipulated by conservative politicians with virtually unlimited financial resources to get poor people to vote against their own economic interests.

The debate between the natural sciences and the humanities is flawed at its roots because it is framed in terms of the opposition between "subject" and "object." The scare quotes signify that we are dealing with the historical construction of the *concepts* of "subject" and "object." That means that when we pound the table and say that such and such—be it the structure of the DNA molecule or the story of Adam and Eve—is "objective" and not a "construction," we must admit that, as a matter of historical objectivity, "objectivity" is a modern construction. That does not mean either that nobody was ever objective before modernity or that objectivity is an illusion; it just means that the historical specificity of the category of "objectivity" needs to be recognized and properly described. Just as I am not trying to rid the world of "transcendence" but simply to redescribe it, neither do I want to get rid of "objectivity" but simply to redescribe it in such a way that it is not the enemy of humanity. The redescription of such modernist categories is the main use of the admittedly overused word "postmodern."

The work of Michel Serres goes a long way toward disabusing us of the prejudices embedded in this opposition. Serres argues that we must recognize that tools and objects generally are not merely inert things but agencies with a life of their own, so to speak—where everything turns on the "so to speak," on recognizing the common patterns that run back and forth between the human and the non-human. Rather than call non-human things "objects," Serres suggests, perhaps we should call them "technical quasi-subjects," because of their "native wit." They are not simply slaves or tools we use. In that sense, human beings have always had "artificial" intelligence:

> We've always been artificial for nine-tenths of our intelligence. Certain objects in this world write and think; we take them and make others

so that they can think for us, with us, among us, and by means of which, or even within which, we think. The artificial intelligence revolution dates from at least as far back as Neolithic times.[4]

We have always been "hybrids," just like the paintings of angels who are all at once birds, humans, and divine emissaries. Those who know Serres, in particular, will hear *La Legende des anges* playing quietly in the background of this final phase of my plea for "perhaps."[5]

A great deal of the postmodern shift toward the integration of the human and non-human is captured in Donna Haraway's groundbreaking essay "A Manifesto for Cyborgs"—the very word "cyborg" sends humanists heading for the exits—where she says that instead of fearing the contamination of the human by the non-human, we should take pleasure in establishing their connections while also assuming responsibility for the connections we make. So I am here following her advice. Hitherto I have linked human beings with what I have been calling the insistence of God, but now I venture to intertwine human beings with materiality, animality, and even with the machine, with what "insists" there, a miscegenation found in Derrida himself and beautifully emblematized in the saucy title of Michael Naas's superb study of Derrida and religion titled "Miracle and Machine."[6] We are experiencing today what Haraway calls "three crucial boundary breakdowns," the breakdown of the human/animal border, of the border between the living organism and the machine, and even of the border between the physical and the non-physical.[7] Boundary breakdowns spell the breakdown of modernist boundaries; that is as good a way as any to use the word "postmodern" and to drive the Kantians mad.

The result is that today all creatures great and small, natural and technological, "subject" or "object," everyone and everything no matter who or what, are said to have their "rights," something that Derrida condensed into his felicitous post-Levinasian quip, *tout autre est tout autre*, every other is wholly other, even (especially) his cat staring at him as he steps out of the shower naked.[8] The "cultural" and "ethico-political" momentum of postmodern thinking is constituted by a gradually diffusive, disseminative, de-colonializing, and democratizing movement from men to women and children, from west to east, from north to south, from strong to weak—these are all genial figures of "weakness" for me—extending to everyone in any way marginalized in the old order, to "the least among you" (Matt. 25:45). Thinkers like Serres and Haraway and Derrida (following a certain "Martha") are urging us to keep the momentum going, to embrace a still-wider ambit of the animals that we all are, of all the animals and of all

living things, weakening the rigid lines we have drawn between them in
the past. And then to go further, to extend the reach of the insistence of
the *tout autre* to the non-living, to the "material," up to and including the
weakening of the binarity of material and immaterial. That is an unnerving project. In postmodernity, the rigid lines of demarcation in modernist border-disputes are displaced by models of hybridity and contamination, of migration and illegal immigrants, of dissemination, dangerous
supplements, and undecidability. All this is demanding something of us. It
requires that this theology of the "perhaps," which I have been describing
as a "theopoetics" of the "chiasm," undergo a further shock, not by jetti-
soning our idea of "insistence" but extending it to every thing (*tout autre*),
in such a way that each thing lays claim upon us in a genuinely demanding
way (*tout autre*), which is, after all, what we mean by "insistence." A cosmo-
theopoetics embraces an ever-wider intertwining of the human and non-
human, recognizes the broader reach of "insistence," meaning that we are
called upon or laid claim to by forces of a wider scope and that we must
brace ourselves for a wider and more welcoming hospitality, one worthy of
our model, Martha. Cosmo-theopoetics nudges us into close contact with
thinkers like Michel Serres and Bruno Latour, figures who unfortunately
have not been given prime time in continental philosophy in America. But
I can hardly imagine a more perfect example of cosmo-theopoetics than
the writings of Michel Serres, where we come upon a magnificent constellation of arguments, tropes, and figures of a new way of being. I include
here by reference but can only make a passing salute to the work of eco-
theo-feminism and to the wider definitions of the divine found there. I
have in mind, especially, the work of Luce Irigaray, where the event that
is harbored in the name (of) "God" is tied up with the buzz sent sizzling
through our bodies by Eros,[9] and who in her more recent work recommends thinking about Mary, Jesus, and the Buddha in terms of air and the
elements, a suggestive point to which I will return in the final chapter.

FROM THEOPOETIC TO CHAOSMIC THOUGHT

Under the pressure of such questioning, what I have been calling theopoetics turns out to be a "regional" discourse inside a larger cosmic setting. To some extent, I have already been speaking of the cosmic setting,
have all along invoked an implicit cosmology, in my ongoing taunting of
two-worlds theory. I have been using in a provisional and strategic way the
Deleuzean expression "plane of immanence" while trying not so much to
scuttle "transcendence" as to redescribe it, to redistribute transcendence

over an ever-widening plane, so that "transcendence" and "immanence" end up being redescribed in such a way as not to re-enkindle the war of two worlds set off by Plato and Augustine. The cosmos opened up by Copernicus collapses the distinction between "heaven" and "earth," one of the most cherished distinctions religion knows. The earth *is* itself a heavenly body, one more heavenly body made up of stardust, as are our own bodies. We are already heavenly bodies, which means that "heaven" and "hell" must report back at once to headquarters for reassignment, where they turn out to be ways of describing our terrestrial lives here "below." Every body—everybody, everything—is a heavenly body. Heaven is overtaken by the heavens.[10] Dust to dust, indeed, but it is all stellar dust. Our bodily flesh is woven of the flesh of the earth, even as the earth itself is the debris of stars, the outcome of innumerable cyclings and recyclings of stellar stuff, all so many rolls of the cosmic dice. We are not "subjects" over and against "objects," but bits and pieces of the universe itself, ways the world is wound up into little intensities producing special effects of a particular sort in our bodies in our little corner of the universe.

Rather than "subjects" and "objects," think of our life and intelligence as something like the inside of the outside of the same thing, where the universe opens up a window on itself in order to peer within or engage in a moment of reflection. Our promptings are the promptings of the universe in us. That means whatever calls, whatever addresses and solicits us, whatever is getting itself called in us, is a calling of the universe in us, a way the universe has found of making its feelings felt, making its wishes known locally, in us. We are like a place where the universe takes a kind of qualitative leap or crosses a threshold and the stars start talking to themselves. But my point is that we should not be unduly vainglorious about all this. For all we know, such leaps into intelligent life have perhaps—"perhaps" is of the utmost importance in speculative cosmology—already happened, and are happening elsewhere, and will continue to happen in innumerable places throughout the universe, before, after, and otherwise than us! Furthermore, the traces of our "intelligence" are spread across the kingdom of non-human animals in very unnerving ways. It was this figure of the "place where" that Heidegger was exploiting (for the purposes of a "higher" humanism) when he spoke of the *da* of *Sein,* while the figure of inside/outside was being deployed in Merleau-Ponty's chiasm of the visible and the invisible, the inside/outside of the flesh of the world, which we can see here has cosmic proportions.[11] Merleau-Ponty, of course, is the source of our use of the word "chiasm" and his later work, cut short by an early death, is one of the souffleurs prompting me from offstage in this book.[12]

The point of insisting upon the intertwining of the human and the non-human, of our bodies with the cosmos, can be illustrated with the example of human sight. Our power of vision, as well as the particular structure of the color spectrum available to sight, is a direct and precise effect of the astronomical composition of our sun, which has set the parameters of vision which we and other animal forms have evolved. To ask whether what we see, as if it were inside our head, "corresponds" to what is out there, "outside our head," is to ask a question not only without an answer but without a meaning. We have the right to ask any question, but not every question deserves an answer; some questions are phony and need to be questioned. Asking that question is like asking how the tree knows, and whether it is certain, that it is raining or that the sun is shining. We, too, are trees and plants.[13] We *are* the relation between our bodies and our world, already in the world as a particular configuration of the world.

The problem of "epistemological correspondence" that goes back to Descartes—while serving the salutary historical purpose of getting the Enlightenment up and running and getting the Church and the King off our backs—is finally resolved by being dissolved. It cannot in principle ever arise in any adequate account of the chiasm because "we" are the very *issue* of this relationship. We *are* already this "natural" chiasm or, as Michel Serres says, a "natural contract."[14] We do not need to negotiate and enter into one. As Heidegger (there is no "worldless subject") and Wittgenstein (there is no "private language") and Levinas (the other is "older" than us) well realized in strictly philosophical terms, we do not have to "build a bridge" to the world. We are the bridge. If the bridge were not already there, we would not be there in order to worry about how to build it or to do anything else. We are neither obliged nor able to construct a relationship to the world because the relation constructs us and anything we do construct presupposes the relationship. We are plants, sprouts shooting up from the local conditions in which we have been produced, in just the way that vegetation started to shoot up when the ozone layer grew thick enough to shield the earth from the ultraviolet rays of the sun, and in just the way the terms of our vision have been fixed by the composition of the sun. We *are* already "out there" because we *are* that relationship. "*Immer schon*" as Heidegger liked to say.

COSMO-THEOPOETICS

Think of a poetics as a song of appreciation, like a hymn or a prayer, in the spirit of Merleau-Ponty saying that a given language is a particular way to "sing" the world. Think of a cosmo-poetics as a song sung in response to a cosmic call, to a summons coming from cosmic forces that are themselves being discharged in our bodies. That means that the name of "God"—just like a painting by Picasso and not unlike a chimpanzee stunned by the power of a waterfall—is one of the ways the world comes to words in verbal bipeds such as us, one of the ways the world "worlds" (Heidegger), one of the ways the insistence of the world finds an outlet in existence. We along with what Haraway calls our "companion species" (and by "companions" she does not mean "pets"), all of us living things along with the so-called inert things, contribute in ways wondrous to behold to the worlding of the world.[15]

The deepest Hegelian point I am making against the residual Kantianism I am trying to burn away is this: the *tout autre* character of the call we are describing does not imply a call from "beyond" the world, or from "another" world to this world, which is the mythic supernaturalist form it takes in the literalization of a religious *Vorstellung*. It represents instead another worlding of the world, one we did not see coming, which I encapsulate in Derrida's phrase "the promise of the world." The call always calls in and as the world, in and as the calling of the world, where the world is always capable of taking us by surprise, of visiting itself upon us in an utterly unforeseeable way (*tout autre*). Every religious "ecstasy," every life "reborn," every encounter with a personal Jesus, every Buddhist "enlightenment," is another worlding of the world, a new and grace-filled event in the field of the grace of the world. The cosmic counterpart to the call that is being called in the name of God (theopoetics) is the call of the world (cosmopoetics). That call is the "promise of the world," the promise that is being made in and by the world, within which the name of "God" assumes its place as but one of several calls. The name of God is a first name, but only one of many first names, albeit one of paradigmatic significance in theo-poetics. But theopoetics belongs within cosmopoetics in just the way the promise/threat that is held out under the name (of) "God" belongs to the promise/threat of the world. That means religion is a form of mundane life, of the only life and the only world we know anything about.

If that Hegelian point holds up against the Kantians, and I am arguing that it does, then the name (of) "God," or "religion," will be "material" to the core, by which I mean that it will have to do eating and sleeping, cleaning the house and cooking, with all of the highs and lows of material life, all of the multiple rhythms of our bodies. What *else* would it have to do with? Much as we all love Mary, Martha is the model. It is in this context that, in the remaining chapters of this book, I will address more directly the challenge that is posed to continental philosophy and to religious think-ing generally by a new and quarrelsome wave of "materialism" and "real-ism." But I hope to show that we followers of Martha have no quarrel with materiality or reality—indeed we consider it our strong point—but we do quarrel with what has become of God, of the name (of) "God" in these debates. If truth be told, these debates seem to me reactionary, reacting against the way the name of God has come back into play even among very secular philosophers like Derrida. They greet the so-called return of reli-gion with the return of anti-religion.

But religion, on my account, is all about deeds and bodies, about "car-nal" life, about the elemental conditions of carnality—about food and nourishment, about sickness and health, about birth and death, about children and old age. Religion is about the flow of life in our bodies, about celebrating and blessing life, riding its waves of elation and exhilaration, of exuberance and joy, even as it rides out the depths of depression and sor-row and lifts life up when life is laid low. Religious practice is light with lev-ity and heavy with gravity, constantly going over and going under. Its songs and ritual dances sway in the winds of joy and bow down under the drafts of sorrow. It mourns and it pipes. It celebrates with the joyful and gives succor to the sorrowful. Life is how the elements of the universe ebb and flow through our bodies; life is the course the universe cuts in our bodies, the wounds it leaves, the elation it brings. In all this religion is heterono-mous, not autonomous. "Religion" is response, a response to life; it gives existence to an insistence. "Postmodernity" means we recognize that it is one (but only one) among the several responses we make to the elemental powers of the universe, to the events that take place in life, in which every-thing that we hope for and dream of is concentrated, in which the name (of) "God" plays a paradigmatic role.

Contrary to the stereotypes, postmodern paradigms are designed for "truth." We are all for truth. But the point is to focus on the sort of "truth" that religion has, which Bruno Latour has crisply formulated as a matter of transformation not information, a point first made by Eckhart's Mar-tha. The name (of) "God" arises as a way of assuming responsibility and thus giving body to the trace of a call, making way for an event to even-tuate in life. In short, the name (of) "God" is not the subject of a set of representational truths about facts of the matter, which is what became of it in modernity. It comes in the form of stories and fables, sayings and parables, greetings and farewell. It is not verified but witnessed. The name (of) "God" is the name of a deed, not of an entity. It does not offer infor-mation about the universe otherwise unavailable to scientific research. It speaks about the heart of our experience of the event. While it cultivates the ancient memories of the community, it is not historiography. The truth of the name (of) "God" takes the form of something to be done, not of a proposition to be debated, which is the peculiarly modernist distortion of religious truth that postmodern critique helps to dispel. Otherwise the name (of) "God" is a tinkling cymbal, even if I speak all the languages in the world and with the very tongues of the angels (1 Cor. 13:1). In short, religion is what the sociologists and anthropologists call a "material practice" or what Heidegger called, with a bit more brio, a mode of "being in the world."

The body of Jesus whose animal needs Martha appreciates beats with the pulse of the earth, as much with the pleasure of a meal with his friends and the joy of a wedding celebration as with the pain of a cruel execution. When we remember him, we remember him by a meal in common among companions, meaning those with whom we share bread (*panis*). His is a gospel of bread—of the bread of commensality, of bread for the hungry, of working for our daily bread. Jesus is inseparable from the bread of the earth, and the earth is inseparable from the world. The world and the promise/threat of the world are brilliantly contracted in the figure of Jesus as he circulates among the poor and the powers that be, among the paralyzed and the tormented, "teaching and healing," making straight the channels through which life and health and well-being flow, even unto death. The energies of the elements converge in his body. We remember him sacramentally, with bread and wine, in harmony with the fruits of the earth and the sky, with mustard seeds and olive trees, the rhythms of the cosmos pulsating through his body.

NINE

AS IF I WERE DEAD
Radical Theology and the Real

To perceive the object as such
implies that you perceive the object as it is
or as it is supposed to be when you are not there . . .
So to relate to an object as such means to relate to it
as if you were dead.
That's the condition of truth . . . the condition of objectivity.
—JACQUES DERRIDA

I object to the blackmail, to the bad choice—theism or atheism!—and to the violence of double genitive in the *odium theologiae*—the total contempt for religion on the part of secularists, the demonization of atheism by the theologians, which leads to outright violence by religious extremists. The whole thing is a perfect recipe for war. The current form this blackmail has taken in recent years is a new wave of "materialism," "realism," and "atheism" that has arisen in reaction to the so-called theological turn. These terms are used more or less interchangeably, as if theology is allergic to reality and materiality, which is the point where we radical theologians sigh in despair, as if we had to choose. The (not so) new blackmail is: Reality or fiction! Materiality or spirit-seeing! Science or fideism! These not-so-new materialists seek to rekindle the old science wars and to wage a new version of the old battle over what is really real, pitting tough-minded scientists against tender-minded types who lack the heart to face reality and so take flight to the fancies of poetry and the fantasies of religion. The new breed of scientific realists, what I will call warrior realists, are merciless iconoclasts, out to destroy all the graven images of the scientific real in order to let the real itself be itself in all its unvarnished reality.

As we more deconstructively minded types could have predicted, this massive assault on theology is massively theological, finding its theological counterpart in the neo-Orthodoxy of Karl Barth: they want to pave the way for absolute transcendence by clearing away every relativity and immanence. To be sure, the difference is that Barth was protecting the transcendence of God, not of gluons. But the analogies between these two apologists of the absolutely absolute and really real and truly transcendent—let us say their common theological assumptions or what Derrida calls their "implicit theologemes"[1]—are unmistakable, not the least of which is their common contempt of images and mediations (*Vorstellungen*). These friends of the absolute want to relativize every human construction (be it the "church" or "social constructions"), degrade every mediating image of the real, and devalue every man-made mediation (it usually is men!). Of course I do not object to the presence of an implicit theology, which I could have predicted, but to the absolutist nature of the theology. As always, I steer around such gigantomachean debates and number myself among the friends of interpretation, whose counterpart in theology is Paul Tillich and his theology of the cultural mediation and the concretization of transcendence and the divine. For us post-Tillichians, if you want transcendence, you will have to construct it yourself and not sit back and wait for it to fall from the sky, which does not mean there is anything phony about such transcendence. It is real enough, and indeed a more realistic transcendence. All we radical theologians are doing is trying to append to it a more sensible explanation of its provenance.

My new species of theologians, the ones who say "perhaps," are thus not *anti*-realists, who do not "believe in reality," as if reality were a matter of personal belief, with opinions to be found on both sides of the issue. As soon as we open our mouths, we affirm a profound faith in reality, wittingly or not, so profound we have never even thought to say it out loud or write it down. Skepticism, Heidegger said, is refuted not by any argument but by the very being of Dasein.[2] Reality does not wait for our consent; our relation to reality is the whole momentum of our being. We have a "natural contract" with nature, as Serres said, which was signed in advance for us without our consultation. Our relation to the "other"—please note, this is the way we continental philosophers tend to speak of the "real"—to other persons, to other living things, to anything and everything, is older than we are. *Tout autre est tout autre.* It has us before we have it, and it does not await our notarized signature.

My new species of theologians is not against science. It has never even occurred to us to doubt that science discovers new things every day. Indeed, if we worry at all about science, it is because science does discover new things every day, and this has social, political, ethical, economic, and environmental consequences that require our close attention. My theologians of the "perhaps" are not the enemies of science but among its best friends. In saying "perhaps," we are saying nothing more or less than any practicing scientist will say. If you interrupt scientists in their labs or find one who has retired and has the time to philosophize, they will be happy to tell you that the current "scientific explanation" means where the weight of the evidence points today, that at the present time this is our best explanation, but there is a great deal more that we do not know. They explore an infinite universe with an acute sense of their own finitude and that of science. Tomorrow, perhaps, we will be forced to conclude something slightly different or, who can say, perhaps something fundamentally different. We never know what some obscure fellow we have never heard of, working in a patent office somewhere, will come up with next week.

"Perhaps" plays a precious role not only in radical theology but no less in science because it protects the *revisability* of scientific explanations, the open-endedness of the scientific future, the right to ask any question even when things seem quite settled, the right to insist that the present explanation is the best construction available, but with the proviso that whatever has been constructed is deconstructible.[3] Scientists are deconstructionists, to the last man or woman, and the point behind training graduate students in science is to get them to stop worshiping science as a demigod and to start thinking deconstructively. That is why scientists, who are skeptical without being skeptics, tend to be modest in speaking about scientific "truth." They are all for truth but they are less inclined to say that *p* is "true" than to say that the weight of the current evidence favors *p*. Scientific explanations are *structurally* revisable, meaning that every explanation science gives, however carefully constructed, is after all constructed by human hands, so to speak, and hence is deconstructible. That is the only way, for example, to keep science safe in Kansas and to protect it from the creationists, for whom creationism is held a priori and is not revisable at all. What we say in common sense, "it's only a theory," is the last thing we would say in science. Evolution is not *merely* a theory; it rises triumphantly to the heady level of a theory, and an amazingly successful one at that, while an alternative like "creationism" fails to get as far as a theory— because it is not testable and revisable. "Creationism" is not an alternative theory or construction deserving equal time because it is not a scientific theory at all. Thus far from relativizing science, such revisability or deconstructibility is the condition of possibility of scientific theory and of free and genuine scientific inquiry. Deconstructibility is the very heart of science. Every "law," scientific or ethico-juridical, is deconstructible (revisable and repealable, appealable and amendable) just in virtue of the fact that it has been constructed in the first place. Otherwise the history of science is the history of dogma.

So my new species of theologians, members of the society of friends of the "perhaps" to the last, are opposed to neither reality nor materiality. If somehow we were deprived of reality and materiality as subject matters, we would walk off the job. We would have nothing left to do or talk about. Nor are we trying to lock ourselves inside a prison house of simulacra, whatever that could possibly mean (beyond criticizing a culture held captive by the media, I doubt it means anything at all!). When it comes to science, my theologians of the "perhaps" are all brave hearts, having the heart both to concede the contingency and revisability of our understanding of the real and to hold science open to the dream of a science to come. Having adopted Martha as our model, our whole idea is to come to grips with the "real world," the one we have to deal with at this very moment, even as we cultivate a heart for a real beyond the real, for an ultra- or hyperreal.[4] Indeed, we are more realist than the realists, never satisfied with what is merely real, hyper-realists in love with the real, by which we mean the "promise of the world," the events harbored in the bowels of the real.

So, following the lead of Martha, let us expose our poor theology of "perhaps" to the mercilessness of the warrior realists and see if there is any mercy in this cold world.

GRÂCE

Me voici. Here I am. *Merci, grâce.*

If prayer is for the precarious, what is more precarious than the cosmic dice game of which we are the outcome? What is more precarious than the cosmic situation contemporary cosmologists describe? What is more a matter of pure chance or pure contingency, pure perhaps or pure serendipity, than the fact that I am here? I serve at the pleasure of cosmic elements, hanging on by a prayer, an archi-prayer in which nobody asked anybody for anything, which is how deconstruction defines the pure gift, pure gratuity, and pure grace. As Kierkegaard's Constantine Constantius asked about the fact of being born, "why was I not consulted?"[5] (Remember, my new species of theologians are all theologians of grace.)

Here I am, in this time and place, in this body. That the precise genealogical history leading up to me in particular has unfolded, that there is this land, this continent, this geological formation, this earth with this satellite moon, that there is this sun, this solar system, this galaxy, as they exist at this very cosmic moment—all of this is a fortuitous event of literally astronomical proportions, part of a history of events against all odds, a contingent constellation (literally) of chance occurrences, a precarious mix of happenstance that happened to combine in a singular way so as to land me here, to land us all here and now, even to land the Earth here, not too far and not too close to the sun, basking in its "Goldilocks" place. Here we all are. *Nous voici.* Were it possible to roll the dice one more time, to set off that massive explosion one more time it would, perhaps, all turn out differently. The ruleless rule, the principle without principle of "perhaps," proves to be of cosmic scope. It requires a sequence of events of unthinkable complexity and fortuitousness, of vast cosmic cyclings and recyclings of stellar materials, and it would, perhaps, produce different combinations every single time the cosmic dice were rolled again.

Our being here is shot through with stellar precariousness "thanks to," *merci,* a singular intersection of forces, at the "mercy" (*à la merci*) of the merciless elements, of untold stellar sequences. We are the beneficiaries of the blind beneficence of khoral forces, *grâce,* which are not beneficent agents intending to do us good, which do not even know we are here. As our bodies result from a rare roll of the stellar dice, we are in our bones precarious, meaning beings of prayer (*precor, precari*), dependent upon forces whose good favor we entreat. As the foggy outlines of this immense cosmic story begin to emerge in the latest advances in astrophysics, shrouded in "perhaps," we detect no little wisdom in the so-called "primitive" religions which had the grace to thank the forces of "nature" for their good fortune. The nature-religions make perfect geological, cosmological, astronomical, and theological sense. Our lives are a function of fortuitous forces. We are here thanks to a great cosmic stupidity—chance combinations, fortuitous sequences—for which we have to be grateful even if we are not sure whom to thank. Here we are, thanks to *khora,* or no thanks. The stupidity of a grace. An event, a sequence of events, all thanks to one small word, "perhaps." Our perhaps is our per-happening, mercifully, mercilessly. *Merci.*

And that's the good news. The bad news is that the new cosmology provides a breathtaking account not only of cosmic birth but also of a cosmic death. Just as death will overtake us personally, our generation, and future generations, it will also befall the species, the planet, the moon, the sun, the galaxy, the universe. The new cosmology proposes a "death of God" for which even the strongest alliance of Hegelians and classical theologians is not prepared, which they did not see coming—the death of the universe in universal entropic dissipation, in cold dark dispersal. If God's life is inscribed in space and time, then on this accounting God's death cannot—short of resurrecting from the dead the old two-worlds cosmology—be inscribed in a larger, longer dialectic of deathless life. The world ends with a whimper because it began with a bang, the Big Bang, which makes our life possible while also destining us all to an increasingly accelerating (relatively speaking, of course) death. The entire history of the universe *is* an explosion of which we are the stellar debris. In this theory, the only possible sense of Malabou's "plasticity" that can "survive," if we may say so, is "explosive," the utter destruction of any possible form of anything and everything. The universe is not unfolding but unraveling. It is not on a long Ulyssean journey because it is never coming home. Its adieu is not *au revoir* but good-bye forever. It is a *kenosis,* an *Entäußerung,* an infinitely accelerating alienation and externalization, an emptying out, an explosive expansion into oblivion. Its end is not a completion but a termination. Its *telos* is not an entelechy, an ontological fulfillment, but an extinction. The universe is rushing headlong into cosmic death.

Perhaps.

It might be more complicated. It might also be the case that the course of this universe is but a single case of a string of universes before and after this one. In such a "multi-verse" the sequence that unfolds from the Big Bang to a final thermal equilibrium is itself a local phenomenon, but one of many, one in an infinite series of such sequences, not to mention that this universe might be but one of many alternate universes in which every road not taken here is taken elsewhere. We never rule out what some presently obscure and anti-social graduate student may come up with next week.

CONTINENTAL PHILOSOPHY AND THE NEW REALISM

To be sure, "existential" theologians and philosophers ever since Kierkegaard have been deeply interested in "limit" phenomena like "facticity," "thrownness," and "being-unto-death." As we have seen Paul's *hos mē* texts were interpreted by Heidegger in terms of Dasein's factical life. But for fear of the specter of "scientism" they have largely ignored science. They have paid no mind to the biology, cosmology, and astrophysics behind life and death, which is part and parcel of the general neglect of the mathematical-natural sciences on the part of its dominant figures, although as the examples of Michel Serres and Bruno Latour show today, there is a "minor" tradition of French philosophers that has been paying attention to the natural sciences all along.[6] When mainstream continentalists talk of "science," they tend to mean psychoanalysis or the social sciences, although the Deleuzeans venture as far as the biological sciences. For all the talk about welcoming the "other" of philosophy, continentalists mostly welcome the other "humanities," like history, literature, and painting (but *not* theology), which really means more of the "same," which is how hospitality often turns out. If someone mentions the mathematical sciences, the dominant continental tradition will cup its ears, warn of "scientism," and chant the Heideggerian mantra that "science does not think," which provides an alibi for not thinking about science. Poets think, we are told, but mathematical scientists do not, and all the heads in the Humanities Center nod piously. Lately continental thought has taken a "theological" turn, which in light of this history, its realist-materialist critics say, we should have seen coming, the way an endodontist can predict an abscess will eventually swell and fester. It is rigged, *a priori*, in virtue of its inveterate Kantianism, to end up in theology. Of course, the history of continental thought has included some famous, brilliant, best-selling, and eloquent atheists like Nietzsche, Camus, and Sartre, all of whom made headlines by lamenting the cosmic mercilessness. But ever since Kierkegaard's pseudonyms took out after Hegel it has also provided a safe haven for religion, which has come to a head in the recent theological enthusiasm.

The "return of religion" has, in turn, set off panic selling in the market for continental philosophy among a younger generation of philosophers in the first decades of the twenty-first century, after the death of Derrida in 2004, the last of the *soixante-huitaires*. For these critics, the "theological turn" amounts to the *reductio ad absurdum* of continental philosophy—if that is where continental philosophy leads us, then continental philosophy is dead, or if it is not, it should be the first order of business to kill it off. The new generation wants to hold the feet of continental philosophy to the fire of Nietzsche's bravado about the death of God, for which it will turn out even Nietzsche himself lacked the nerve. What good is a death of God if we still have to deal with religion? They want to ensure that all this continentalist bombast about the death of God really amounts to something. For were God truly dead and buried, these critics think, continental philosophy should have perished along with it, instead of providing religion with its last refuge or outpost—a final place to hide before the "singularity" arrives, not Derrida's singularity, of course, but Ray Kurzweil's.[7] This critique is focused on what Quentin Meillassoux calls "fideism." By this he means delimiting the reach of speculative and scientific reason in order to leave the barn door open for religious faith, allowing religion to insinuate itself into the fabric of the very rationality which philosophy was entrusted by the Enlightenment with keeping safe (AF, 46–49).[8] This critique is aimed above all at Kant, whom Meillassoux charges with sabotaging the Enlightenment by turning the "Copernican Revolution" upside down, perversely reversing it into a pre-Copernican humanism or anthropocentrism.

The current critique of the continental tradition from Kant to the present is not the familiar attack on continental philosophy coming from analytic philosophy but a more radical critique that includes analytic philosophy in its sweep. It implicates Wittgenstein no less than Heidegger, attacking both "unconcealment" and "language games" by means of a more ruthless realism, a more materialist materialism, a more uncompromising objectivism and reductionism meant to cut off the death-deferring tactics European philosophers have deployed for more than two centuries now. "Continental philosophy" has nothing to say about what is really real. It simply undertakes an inventory of human subjectivity and confines itself to a buzzing, blooming world of subjective experience, taking no mind of the fact that on a cosmic scale the bloom on the world is fading fast. The return of religion is the last straw, the turning point, the spark that touches off a fire that engulfs continental philosophy as we know it. When I say "as we know it" I mean the heritage of Kant, the fateful—fatal?—program announced by Kant when he says, "I have found it necessary to deny knowledge in order to make room for faith." Continental philosophy suffers from something like a genetic flaw inherited from Kant, which has aided and abetted the current outbreak of religion, resulting in a generation of continentalists who wear thick glasses and feel their way with a stick, moving about in the shadows where religion carries out its dark business.

Meillassoux is if nothing else bold, and given how much circling around the same is involved in the constant talk in continental circles about the "other," his work is something new and interesting. It will help break the log jam of contemporary continental philosophy, which is running out of new things to say about the "other," and needs to change the subject. Given its interest in the *tout autre,* continental philosophy ought to greet Meillassoux as a surprise, an unforeseeable, *tout autre,* quite. His position from my point of view is all wrong but it is oddly close to being all right, almost alright, with a tweak or twist or two that would change quite a lot. I agree with his critique of Kant's fideism and I am impressed at just how close he is to Hegel, as he himself protests, and so he has my sympathies from right out of the gate. He cannot understand that people do not see he is a Hegelian.[9] Like Malabou and even more so Žižek, he is another of the contemporary contrarian and heretical Hegelians, which means that he is at least a distant cousin of my new species of theologians. So I dare to number him among the post-Hegelian continental philosophers of religion, albeit in the most idiosyncratic way imaginable, although this may gain him his walking papers among the new realists. But I would try to bring his heretical Hegel closer to mine, to get him on board with my Derridean "perhaps," and talk him off the ledge of his notion of "absolute contingency," which I think needs to be reconsidered. I would see if I could get him to redescribe the "inexistence of God," which goes hand in hand with a call for justice—with all of which I agree—in terms of the "insistence" of God.[10] The two notions are oddly close to each other yet separated by an abyss.[11]

Meillassoux makes a legitimate complaint about continental philosophy and the trouble it buys for itself, which we both think is always traceable to taking its lead from Kant instead of Hegel. Like him, I want to burn off the lingering Kantianism of continental philosophy. In my faux-Tillichian two types of continental philosophy of religion, I am critical of an abridged postmodernism that reduces postmodern theory to apologetics and a theory of appearances. I have made a bit of friendly fun of the fideism that Meillassoux is attacking by calling it "postmodernism light."[12] Of course, while I have taken a stand with Hegel, I also warned the Hegelians that I cannot be trusted to stand by my post. I am critical of the deeper alliance of Hegel with the classical theologians who think they are criticizing Hegel but who are allied with Hegel on the ineradicable life of God, on the depths of divine providence and of God's everlasting being. That, I have complained, would shield the divine names from our "perhaps," whereas my whole idea is that "perhaps" burns through everything and indeed heads the list of divine names. In the long run, what is called the death of God by Hegel, unnerving though it may be to classical theology, is but a moment in the larger inexhaustible life of God, a stage in the unfolding of the infinite being of God, of which classical theology cannot but approve. It is not by chance that the phrase is taken from a Lutheran hymn. Hegel and the theologians are agreed: God cannot explode. God's plasticity, *pace* Malabou, cannot possibly include explosion, annihilation. But the astrophysicists do not have Hegel on their reading list; they think the "absolute" is an explosion, and Meillassoux thinks the only absolute is contingency itself.

I think Meillassoux and the new critics have a point about the flight from science in continental philosophy and about the weak knees of fideism. But they are so given to a kind of ruthless realism, what I will call below, adapting a phrase from Bruno Latour, a "warrior realism," that it blinds them from what they have stumbled upon. It's like they found a hitherto unknown Picasso in the attic but they don't know anything about painting. They have found the makings of a religion without religion but they either oddly distort it (Meillassoux) or take flight from it. When Ray Brassier champions the cause of nihilism, I think he does not see (or at least has not yet explained) that this nihilism is not without value, and that it is not for nothing—but they seem to be know-nothings about that nothing. My own idea, which I have picked up from meditating upon the story of Mary and Martha, is to stick with the hermeneutics of trouble, to proceed on the assumption that we get the best results by staying on the trail of trouble, by facing up to the difficulty of life, by swallowing the pills of a ruthless problematizing, however bitter, even if this "perhaps" seems like poison. Brassier identifies our being-nothing, our cosmic precarious-ness, but he is a know-nothing about the value of nothing, about its cos-mopoetics, and hence about what I will call here the grace of nihilism or the nihilism of grace. As I said at the beginning, the most radical point in radical theology, the pill that orthodox theology finds the hardest to swallow, is that radical theology turns out to be in the end, and this is its most pharmacological moment, the dangerous drug of a theology of "per-haps," a theology of the chance of grace, the grace of chance. That is what I am going to call in the final chapter being-for-nothing, where the story of Mary and Martha will come back one more to time to be our guide. I will situate grace against the prospect of a cold cosmic death in a merciless universe, which I have no intention of evading. But in the present chapter I want to deal with the fear of two small words that continental philos-ophers have shown, of "science" and "objectivity," which have proven to be specters that have haunted continental philosophers from Kant to the present and have rightly occasioned the charge of fideism.

AS IF I WERE DEAD: A CIRCUMFESSION

The line of criticism of continental philosophy opened up by the war-rior realists cannot be answered simply by letting our old Kantian instincts kick in, by cupping our ears and shouting "reductionism," like cardiac patients reaching for their nitroglycerin every time they feel tightness in their chest. I say this for two reasons, which I will formulate in such a way as to give a certain amount of scandal to my continental friends, with the hope that it will get their attention. But I am also asking, praying really, not to be misunderstood: my abiding interest is in God, perhaps, and I pass my nights praying and weeping.

Physics Is All the Metaphysics We Are Going to Get

The mathematical sciences are said to be the "hard" sciences, meaning the coldest, meanest, most dispassionate, and most "objective" sciences, the least given to fantasy and feelings, and among these physics holds pride of place. In saying a thing like that, a lot will come down to what we mean by "objectivity." In what follows I follow the felicitous definition of objectivity advanced by Derrida, that it is the study of things as if we were dead (or never born). So even the coldest and most "objective" science depends upon the structure of an "as if." My advice, therefore, is to replace false distinctions like Kant's distinction between phenomena and noumena, or high-flying distinctions like Climacus's between how the world is known by God and how it is known by us, and misleading ones like the modernist distinction between subjective and objective, with a more phenomenological distinction between how things look now, while we are alive, and looking at things then, as if we were dead or never born. That, I propose, supplies the phenomenological content of "objectivity" and constitutes all the objectivity we need. In the terms I have been using here, objectivity is the approach to things before, after, or outside the chiasm, as if there were no chiasm, no intertwining of the insistence of the event and our existence. That is my version of the Pauline *hos me* counsels. As if we were dead or had never been born. While this sounds like a very eerie and alien way of thinking, it served as the point of departure of my *Against Ethics*.[13] The way that I described it there was to say that ethics takes place in a world where the stars do not know we are here and they, like khora, could care less.

Of course, that is hardly my own idea. It is a way of looking at things that goes back at least as far as Pascal, who also had an ear for cosmopoetics, who sees humanity as a bit of cosmic dust, that is, cosmically speaking, insignificant, in which he observed a considerable religious point that allows humankind to garner a certain grandeur. In this view we are disasters, having been literally, astronomically dis-astered by the Copernican Revolution, deprived of a star (*astrum*) that looks over us with loving care, deprived of our beloved Platonic "sun," with results that are cosmically colossal and phenomenologically cata-strophic, throwing all of our instinctive assumptions into reverse. Much as Copernicus loved Plato, his theory ended up delivering a bit of blow to Plato's allegory. The sun, we have since learned, differs from the flittering shadows on the wall only because its coming to be and passing away are so drawn out that we do not notice that it too is a cosmic moment, flaring up and dying off over the course of several billion years or so. As the only difference between the sun and the shadows on the cave is the speed with which they pass away, the distinction between time and eternity in Plato turns out to be a matter of a difference in velocity. What Meillassoux wants to force Kant to swallow, what the Copernican Revolution really means, applies no less to Plato's allegory.

If metaphysics is the study of the really real, and if by "the really real" we mean what is or would be there with or without us, then physics is all the metaphysics we're ever going to get. Notice I do not say physics *is* metaphysics, unlike Badiou, who pronounces "axiomatically," like a Vatican encyclical, "ontology *is* mathematics." That is because I don't think *anything* ever gets to be "metaphysics" in the classical sense. "Metaphysics" in that sense is the Power that would drive out my poor "perhaps," whereas my whole point is to say we are permanently haunted by "perhaps." I do not embrace a naturalist metaphysics, no more than I embrace a supernaturalist metaphysics. I resist every embrace of metaphysics. When it comes to embraces, I vastly prefer flesh and blood (which is my materialism). Whenever anyone tries to get as far as metaphysics in the classical sense, they end up arguing in circles, just as Kant predicted, and such circles are to be greeted with "incredulity," just as Lyotard said. So I say that physics, which is restricted by its methodological limits, and is never going to get to be metaphysics in the classical sense, is all the metaphysics we are going to get, meaning, it's the best vocabulary for us (the living) to speak now of how it would be if we were not here (dead or never born). I hasten to add, again lest I be misunderstood, that this implies that physics is hardly enough for us to get along with now, while we are still living, but I will say more about that below. In that sense, any so-called theory of everything would not be everything. I do not mean to sound greedy, but the theory of everything is not enough.

All I am saying at this point is that if physics is the study of a real that we have no reason to presume has any real care for us, or takes any mind of us, or has any need for us to be there to think about it, then physics is all the metaphysics we can expect to get. That is because mathematics is the only vocabulary we have at our disposal with which to imagine the way things would "look" if we were not there to "look" at things (if we were dead or never born). I venture this assertion on strictly phenomenological grounds. The idea of a nature that is a book written in the language of mathematics[14] according to Galileo is nature taken as if we were dead. That in turn implies that the "life-world," the world of the living, is a book that cannot be restricted to the language of mathematics. The life-world is the world in which we are still alive, while mathematics is the language of the dead, a point that I make in the circumscribed terms of the present discussion and without offense to mathematicians, living or dead, the vitality of whose work I greatly admire.

Continental philosophy has made a profitable living out of the critique of metaphysics, and I have shared in the profits. My present way of putting this critique is to say that physics is more and more doing the heaving lifting in what was called metaphysics in the past. Metaphysics in the classical sense is never going to get any further than physics in the present, and physics is never going to get as far as what we used to call metaphysics. When contemporary theoretical physicists speculate that, perhaps, at bottom what we call the physical universe is composed of vibrating filaments called superstrings, I very much doubt that the traditional metaphysicians, unequipped with either mathematics or experimental evidence, have anything to add. In my view, if you are interested in metaphysics, I recommend you brush up on your "superstring field theory" or whatever will supersede superstrings next week. As any physicist would tell you, this theory is itself far from confirmed and in no way insulated from the "perhaps." That does not diminish scientific theory but makes it exciting. What we philosophers used to call "metaphysics" is fast giving way to the macrophysics of the imaginably large scope of the universe (if there is but one) and the microphysics of the unimaginably small. What we used to call "metaphysics" in philosophy, theories of being as such in terms of the forms, substance, essence and existence, monads, Spirit, and so on, amounts to highly imaginative and impressionistic accounts—and hence a kind of "poetics"—of the main features of the medium-sized things we meet up with in ordinary experience. These theories inevitably run into the antinomies Kant predicts because there is no way to resolve the fascinating but sweeping and conflicting claims made on behalf of monads, absolute Spirits, the world as will and representation, or other such impressions.

Badiou is a good example these days. He wants to leave no place for reality to hide from mathematics, so he announces that "ontology *is* mathematics." That is an enormous promissory note that swells the hearts of the realists. The bad news is that he is unable to justify that axiom, so he simply declares it "axiomatic," something he very highly values (*axio*), meaning that he is done arguing on its behalf, which is pretty much the pope's stand on ordaining women. The axiom gets a pass. He just thinks that this is what any "modern" person should think. So Badiou is doing no more than "stipulating" that this is the way he is using the word "ontology." Badiou is certainly free to make a decision like that but this tells us nothing about what ontology "is" when Badiou is not around. Meillassoux, on the other hand, understands that mathematical physics is limited by its methodological presuppositions and that this plays into the hands of the fideists. So he declares that he is engaged in "speculative" thinking, not mathematics. The "speculative" move avoids Badiou's stipulative axiomatization, but then this speculation rushes headlong into the very antinomies about which

[handwritten marginalia:] This all seems terribly misinformed

[handwritten marginalia:] Uh... yes it does

[handwritten marginalia:] As if they were different! Mathematics is speculative thinking!

Kant warns us when "speculative" reason is detached from experimental confirmation. I am saying that the work of theoretical physics is about as far as I can see us ever getting with what we used to call "metaphysics," and I have Lyotardian incredulity that any possible theory of everything is everything we need. I am saying that as long as we are alive, we need a theopoetics, which needs in turn to be reinscribed within a cosmopoetics that stays up to date with what is going on in speculative physics.

The cosmic schema to which contemporary physics at present subscribes is fascinating—philosophically. It is not just a curiosity for philosophers while they are off the clock. It seems in many respects not all that far from Nietzsche's famous fable at the beginning of "On the Truth and Lies in the Nonmoral Sense," about that distant corner of the universe in which humble little animals invented proud words like "truth," with which I launched my *Against Ethics*.[15] I will call the fantastic voyage from the Big Bang to entropic dissipation the "basic schema." By "schema" I mean a revisable theoretical projection and by "basic" I mean the most cogent account we have at present of the largest overarching context or setting of human life. François Laruelle, one of the fellow travelers of the new realists, using an expression he picked up from Marx and Engels, speaks of the context "in the last determination" of human life. This of course needs to be qualified in two ways. First, it is not really the last, but the latest, as these are far from settled matters, but at least there are available in principle scientific ways of actually settling debates about theories like the Big Bang, instead of being set adrift on the endless seas of the interminable debates about monads or getting lost in the black hole of the ontological argument in traditional speculative metaphysics and never being heard from again. Secondly, it is far from enough, far from sufficient, to have a big idea of how things look if we were dead; it remains of pressing and irreducible importance, I would say of vital importance, to also come up with some account of what things look like now that we are alive and for the while that we are alive, which is what I mean by a poetics and where I am going with all of this.

According to the best—but again hardly the last—word from the physicists right now, the universe is headed for total destruction, when a "trillion trillion trillion years from now," in a nicely written bit of rhetoric from Roy Brassier's *Nihil Unbound,* the "implacable gravitational expansion" will have pushed the universe "into an eternal and unfathomable blackness."[16] A trillion trillion trillion years from now there will be real trouble, even if it is not exactly imminent—whereas Milbank and the Radically Orthodox think that a trillion trillion trillion years from now we will still

---

Handwritten marginalia:

Top: For so much attack on metaphysics, I don't know of → LOL!

Right top: Caputo producing anything in the field → You. Caputo projects a lot.

Left margin: Very dubious

Left margin: for ses ha ha.

Left margin: A theory based on calculus.

Right margin: ha! HA! What a fool! Your "basic schema" is also "just a theory"— though I agree, philosophy is used to lean more about physics.

Right margin: Instead of romantically appropriating lay-conceptions of science—why doesn't he go into the philosophy of science?

Bottom: What does this even mean & what is his claim regarding the function of this context?

be belting out our hosannas on high. Brassier is a master of such trouble, even a bit smitten by it, one thinks. He seems to get a bit of a buzz when he gets off lines like this about our cosmic death. So I do not think he is immune from cosmopoetics; it's just that he prefers the darker, brooding variety, which also gives pleasure to us back here in the life-world. In the cold light—or the dark—of the basic schema, life will have proven to be a local phenomenon, a temporary, futile negentropic resistance thrown up against the irresistible force of entropy which extinguishes both word and world. The lights will have gone out in Heidegger's *Welt* even as Wittgenstein's languages games will prove to have been played with dead languages, and all of Levinas's infinite others will be stone dead. The chiasm will close down and go out of business. The dynamics of *insistence* will be stilled. Insistence will be trumped by *desistence,* having been deprived of our existence. That is the latest bulletin from the science departments to the Humanities Center.

The Copernican Revolution (the real one) demands we think about the earth and sun as if we were dead, when there will be no lovers watching the "rising" and "setting" of the sun, a view that springs from "following the math," which is the only way we can "conceive" such a thing. What I am trying to do is to stick with the idea of the Copernican Revolution (by which Meillassoux says we continental philosophers have been stampeded into a kind of relativistic subjectivism), which has set off a chain of ever wider, deeper, and more radical de-centerings and recontextualizations of our lives. That possibility is, by the way, I would argue, already inscribed in Heidegger's hammer, which could be decontextualized and analyzed in terms of its weight and chemical composition, quite apart from its place as a tool in Dasein's "world." That would result in a purely mathematical analysis.

Physics Has Philosophy on the Run

The good news is that "There are more things in heaven and earth than are dreamt of in your philosophy, Horatio." The bad news is that we philosophers and theologians are playing the role of Horatio and that physics keeps discovering more things. The crisis that confronts philosophy today is that contemporary cosmology is stealing philosophy's thunder because, as we have seen in the previous chapter, it is stealing philosophy's wonder.[17] Theoretical physics is the new "wonder." It has taken possession of the very ground in which philosophy is supposed to plant its roots—wonder and the imagination. We do not need to be swept up in the Tao or the "wow" of physics to concede that contemporary physicists are out-imagining, out-wondering, and out-wowing the philosophers.[18] It's not just that they know more mathematics than the philosophers but that they have more imagination, which is why they get more invitations to appear on the "Science" and "Discovery" channels on TV. Their mathematical imaginations are more stunning, more breathtaking, and make for fantastic animations. If you are looking around for signs of the ancient and venerable vocation of the philosophers, which is wonder, check out the contemporary speculative cosmologists, whose speculations on the nature of things, *de rerum natura*, really are more wondrous than anything dreamt of in philosophy today.

The philosophers talk about the *tout autre*, the radical surprise, the unprecedented singularity, the "impossible," but the speculative physicists deliver on it, do it, and come up with it almost every week. It is the speculations of the physicists that "soar," not of the philosophers. If we seek to speculate on the "mind of God" we are more likely to learn something of its workings from the minds of physicists who are making their way back to the creation. Will the physicists end up having the final word on God, that is, on the name (of) "God"? Furthermore, if there is no such thing as the final word on God, if the name of God is the name of a question not an answer, of a problem not a resolution, if having the final word on God makes no sense, will that, too, end up being established by the physicists? Obviously, I think not, but I also think that Kantian fideism does not solve anything. In fact, it plays right into the hands of scientific reductionism.

Continental philosophers have largely earned their stripes by following a Kantian tack, undertaking a transcendental delimitation of science, trying to contain it critically, not by trying to learn something from it. For the most part they try to deny knowledge (science) in order to make room for existential phenomenology or cultural analysis or gender studies or whatever we are doing at the Society for Phenomenology and Existential Philosophy that year, in short, behaving like post-Kantians. That is one of Žižek's complaints about "postmodernists" and it is legitimate. That I think has positioned them badly to deal with the current crisis, which the so-called "return" of religion has brought to a head.

So what now? As any good stockbroker can tell you, when there is panic selling, that is a good time to buy. You need to have faith that the market is oversold and that there is value out there to which we have been blinded by sheer panic. To begin with, the point of the chiasmic thinking I have adopted is to cut a wide swath around both scientific reductionism and transcendental epistemology. The scandal I am trying to give my continental friends does *not* amount to signing on to the "scientism" that we all rightly worry about (lots of scientists do, too; not just philosophers). Make no mistake, I hold the dogmatic frame of mind (no "perhaps") of the new atheists—Dennett, Dawkins, and Hitchens—in disdain. I am trying to avoid driving either way on the two-way street of the *odium theologiae*. I do not think natural science is or should be descried as reductionistic, which I take to be a kind of reactionary anti-modernism. I am describing science in terms of its contribution to a cosmopoetics, to an explosion of wonder and imagination, of the possibility of the impossible, of the most extraordinary leaps of creativity, vision, inspiration, and originality, what Derrida likes to call the "invention of the other." When I associate the scientific imagination with the theological imagination, I am not trying to reduce theology to science or science to theology. I am trying to follow the animals of Jesus, the animal that Jesus is. I am not trying to reduce anything but to adduce the work of imagination in the collaboration between the theological and the scientific. Events can happen anywhere. It is a question of faith—but not of fideism. That is my next point, which I take up in chapter 10.

TEN

FACTS, FICTIONS, AND FAITH
What Is Really Real after All?

Thus to request the idol-breakers to smash the many mediators of science, in order to reach the real world out there, better and faster, would be a call for barbarism, not for enlightenment. Do we really have to spend another century alternating violently between constructivism and realism, between artificiality and authenticity? Science deserves better than naive worship and naive contempt. Its regime of invisibility is as uplifting as that of religion and art. The subtlety of its traces requires a form of care and attention, a form of spirituality. —BRUNO LATOUR

Having thus redescribed "objectivity" as a way to think about the world in which we live as if we were dead or never born, let us now take a careful look at the words that have sparked the current critique of continental philosophy—Meillassoux's critique of "correlation" and "fideism," in that order. This criticism has been set in motion by the theological turn, or the return of religion, which is taken to be a regrettable consequence of continental anti-realism. I think there is something to this critique of fideism but it should be put to better purpose. It should be used to get beyond fideism and to come up with a more worthy idea of "faith," which I characterize in terms of our desire beyond desire, constituting the heart of a heartless world—and the lesson we learn less from a heartfelt Mary than from a hearty Martha.[1]

WARRIOR REALISM

As interesting as Meillassoux's work is—he helps break something of a log jam in continental philosophy conferences—he has also muddied the contemporary waters with an ill-advised attack on "correlationism." I have never been an enthusiast of the term "correlation," but it is not a bad word and given the present assault on its good name I may perhaps be excused if I feel that the muse of continental philosophy has laid her hands upon me to rise to its defense. While the word has its limitations, as I will show below, it simply refers to any bilateral relation. The word was used by Husserl, who spoke of noetic-noematic "correlations" and "correlational analyses" in *Ideas I,* to refer to the perfectly sensible idea that to every "object" of thought, perception, imagination, and so forth there corresponds an "act" of thinking, perceiving, and imagining, and vice versa, so that a change on one side occasions a correlative change on the other side.[2] To the house before my nose at this moment there corresponds a perceptual act. To the house on this lot ten years ago but no longer here today there corresponds an act of memory. The Copernican Revolution is as good an example as any. To the movement of sun around the Earth there corresponds one set of assumptions on the part of the astronomer; to the movement of the Earth around the sun there corresponds a shift in the astronomer's assumptions. The lack of some theory of correlation reduces thinking, perceiving, and the like to magic, in which objects simply drop from the sky, a point that holds for everything from quantum physics to remembering where we left our umbrella. The law of correlation is a law of direct proportions: the more changing, shifting, and reconfiguring that takes place on the "object" side, the more corresponding activity is required on the subject side—and vice versa (if we shift from perceiving to imagining, or shift locations, etc.), as in any correlative pairing or bilateral relation. Variations of perspective and modality on the object side are met with by corresponding variations on the subject side, and vice versa. The idea is a thoroughly realist one, going back (via Franz Brentano, an ex–Catholic priest) to the medieval Aristotelian realists, who spoke of "intentionality," the act by which the soul "tends toward" or "aims at" (*modus significandi*) being, while being or the real for its part (*modus essendi*) is what is aimed at, like the archer aiming at a target.

What troubles Meillassoux about the idea is that, in its strongest version, it takes the form of a metaphysics of subjective idealism, of the sort we find in Berkeley's *esse est percipi,* and in its weaker version it results in Kant's transcendental idealism, in which Kant concedes that the world in itself is there but argues that we cannot know it as it is in itself. But from the medieval point of view, Berkeley and Kant represent a breakdown in the theory of intentionality, a failure to maintain the tandem between the soul and being, falling too much to the one side of the soul and failing to balance the realist equation in which the notion is originally framed. Instead of serving as its correlate, the subject side ends up creating (Berkeley) or at least forming (Kant) the object side, which is pretty much the fate of the idea in "modernity." The question Meillassoux raises is, is the "absolute" reality of the real compromised when it is brought into "relation" with thought? Once we begin to describe the way that our knowledge of the world is "constituted," have we relativized the world to our knowledge and locked ourselves inside our own representations (how the world is for us), cut off from reality (as it is in itself)? Have we contaminated objectivity with subjectivity and locked ourselves in a cage or prison house of human language (the linguistic turn), of subjective experiences (phenomenology), of endless interpretations (hermeneutics)? Meillassoux criticizes both analytic and continental philosophers from Kant to the present for having done exactly that and he calls for a return to the pre-Kantian early modern scientific objectivism and mathematicism of Galileo and to the real Copernican Revolution, not the phony one cooked up by Kant by which it was subverted.

It is well known that Husserl's language was unguarded enough in this regard that his most distinguished successors also thought Husserl had indeed overstepped his own methodological precautions and slipped into some kind of metaphysical idealism. That is no longer the received opinion today.[3] Husserl has his limits, but he is not a metaphysical idealist. His theory of "constitution" had to do with the epistemological genesis of our knowledge of the world, not with the metaphysical creation of the world. It is especially important to remember that the often misleading formulations of *Ideas I* were not Husserl's last word about phenomenology or about the genesis of the natural sciences in particular. But even were this charge true, the first and most fundamental thing that Husserl's major successors—Heidegger and Levinas, Sartre and Merleau-Ponty—flagged in Husserl was his seeming flirtation with some version of idealism. It is obvious that they did not accept any such implication, whether or not it is actually there, and that they themselves steered well clear of it.

Everything that happened in phenomenology after Husserl was framed by Heidegger. Heidegger came to Husserlian phenomenology from the same medieval Aristotelian realism as Brentano—the association of Brentano with Husserl is what first drew his attention to Husserl—to which Heidegger was first exposed as a student in German Catholic neo-Scholasticism. He would later say that Aristotle was the greatest "phenomenologist" of antiquity, while for Husserl it was Descartes who provides the historical prototype of phenomenology. That is why a generation of Catholic philosophers, brought up on Aristotelian realism, migrated to phenomenology through Heidegger. Heidegger reinvented phenomenology in terms of Aristotle and reinvented Aristotle in terms of phenomenology, and after that everything in phenomenology was decisively different just because it was being framed not in Cartesian-Kantian terms but in

Aristotelian realist ones. John Wild, the leading figure in the emergence of phenomenology in the United States, made exactly the same migration: from Aristotelian realism to an Aristotelian version of phenomenology.[4] When Merleau-Ponty redescribed being-in-the-world in incarnationalist terms, Aristotle's critique of Plato on the senses and the body was in the background. As for Husserl himself, I regard the strictly epistemic correlation he was describing as an abstract and thinned-out feature and function of the chiasm I have been describing, of the intimate interweaving of our bodily being with the world that engendered it. But correlation itself is simply a law of direct proportions about knowing and the known; it is not, and it certainly need not be, a form of idealism, metaphysical or transcendental, to which it is reduced by Meillassoux, who is frankly as "fundamentalist" about "objectivism" as any Bible-thumper from Kansas is about creationism (of which, by the way, he actually goes so far as to accuse the likes of Foucault and Derrida). While Meillassoux goes on to say a number of fascinating things, I regard the formal argument he makes against what he is calling correlation as the fruit of a poisoned tree, which depends upon utterly botching the meaning of this idea. Virtually every characterization of "correlation" in his book is demonstrably wrong.[5]

The best way to see what is wrong with Meillassoux's view[6] is to turn to the work of Bruno Latour, the distinguished French practitioner of "science studies," that is, the study of the historical, social, and experimental conditions under which scientific theory is produced, widely known as the "social construction" of science. Not surprisingly, Latour has been accused precisely of subjectivizing the sciences, but since he is also, interestingly, a figure who enjoys a hearing among the speculative realists, his response to this criticism is particularly apt at this juncture. Allow me to repeat that given the dismissiveness shown by so many continentalists toward the natural sciences, Meillassoux and these young realists have a point. But their point has been overrun by their "warrior realism" (Latour refers to the "culture wars" between humanists and natural scientists), by reinstituting with a fury the tired wars of realism and relativism, of fact and fiction, of "social construction" and "reality," that have already been fully played out in the twentieth century. Is that the renewal that the speculative realists are promising? Do we really have go through that again? Is there anybody out there who does not "believe" in "reality?" If there is, they need a psychiatrist not a philosopher. The "cold-war" realism of the new realists has been deftly dressed down in advance by Latour who was wounded one day when asked this very thing, whether he believed in reality, which occasioned a wise and witty book in response titled *Pandora's Hope* (PH, 1–3).[7]

The problem is this: Once we point out the role that is played by practicing scientists in constructing a scientific account of things, have we relativized science, absorbed the real into the mind of the scientist and destroyed the objectivity of science? Does not the "real" (objectivity) demand the absolute disappearance of the human intervention (subjectivity)? Are not objectivity or reality and subjectivity or the human investigator *inversely and unilaterally* related instead of being *directly and bilaterally* related, as demanded by the notion of correlation? Latour's thesis is that if you asked practicing scientists that question (in a way they could understand) you would be greeted with dumbfounded and uncomprehending silence. The very opposite is true. The more complex the scientific community, the more sophisticated the scientific instruments at its disposal, and the more elaborate the mathematics, then the *more real* the result, not the more "subjectivistic." In short, the more construction, the more reality, and conversely, precisely in accord with the law of direct proportions observed in Husserlian "correlation." The absence of this law of direct proportions, the absence of any correlation, would mean that scientific objects have simply dropped from the sky, like a divine miracle, whence the implicit theology, where reality is being treated like the God of Barth's neo-Orthodoxy.

Latour supports his thesis by way of several fascinating "case studies," a novel idea for a philosopher of science! "Embedded" (like a war correspondent with an army) with a team studying the transition between a savanna and a forest in the Amazon rain forest, Latour shows that there is no gap between "subjects" (words) and "objects" (things) that needs to be spanned by a theory of "correspondence." Rather, things get gradually and successively packed into words by way of a series of charts, satellite images, photographs, diagrams, and finally (a) paper, words in a report, each phase fitted together with the next, each nested in the next, each of which is a sign for the next, like a series of translations or transformations (or "correlations"), by crossing which scientific "reference" is carried out (PH, 56–57). These gradual transformations make the world knowable, each one recycling the other in ever more precise ways. The truth circulates through the series, which can be traversed in either direction—from the soil to the "paper" or from the "paper" to the soil, whence the bilateral correlativity stressed by Husserl. The question of how to span the "gap" between a pure subject and a pure object, between mind and reality, comes up only if (perhaps having never met an actual scientist) you erase all the intervals and intermediaries and force a choice—more blackmail—between "subjectivity" and "objectivity, "idealism" and "realism" (PH, 73).[8]

Louis Pasteur discovered that the yeast peculiar to lactic acid is a living microorganism, upsetting the prevailing idea that it was a purely chemical degradation of a non-living substance, which he did by a series of devious experimental plots and ingenious stagings. It is fair to say that Pasteur tricked this new actant into making an appearance on the stage, and as a result two new actants make their appearance, a new yeast and "Pasteur" (the name of a thinker is the name of a matter to be thought, said Heidegger). The facts are made up (by the experimental contrivance); nonetheless, the ferment is invented not by Pasteur but by the ferment. The facts are both made up and not made up; both/and, not either/or, direct proportion not inverse proportion. So there is a contradiction only if we persist in seeing "construction" and "reality" as an either/or, a zero-sum game, related by a unilateral inverse proportion, instead of seeing that an experiment is an "event," the emergence of a novel result from the convergence of the several elements of the experiment, the yeast, the laboratory equipment, the French academy, all of which "gain" (plus–plus) from their mutual association (PH, 125–27). Whatever other criticisms we might have of Kant, this is the completely legitimate point that Kant got right when he came up with his version of the Copernican Revolution, a point that Meillassoux suppresses. Kant was arguing that modern natural scientists do not simply gaze open-mouthed at the world and take good notes. They are artful actors, deviously devising experiments and deploying mathematical equations that trick nature into yielding her secrets; furthermore, their instruments are not inert things but actants themselves who play all kinds of tricks on them and have a life of their own, like "quasi-subjects," Serres says. Finally, the microbes themselves really do have a life of their own and the trick of the experimentalist is to get them all on the same stage (or page). But Kant should have left it at that instead of putting his epistemological pedal to the metal and driving off the cliff of a priori forms and the phenomena/noumena distinction.

As Gaston Bachelard said in French: *un fait est fait,* a fact is made. Since we cannot say in English "a fact is facted" the best we can do with the play on words is to say that "a fact is an artifact," or "a fact is manu*fact*ured," meaning both made up and not made up. I also like the English "forged," which can mean producing either a real or a counterfeit product. It is not in spite of but because of their artful fabrication that facts are autonomous, even as Pasteur is not an impartial observer but passionately partial to his theory. Constructivism and realism are part of the same equation, directly proportionate to each other. Warrior realism wants to erase Pasteur. Pasteur sprinkles, boils, filters, heats, adds, and extracts, and he needs to be really skillful at doing that; then he steps back and the lactic acid yeast appears "before his eyes." "Naive realism" tries to erase Pasteur from this scene, Latour says. "Pasteur authorizes the yeast to authorize him to speak in its name." The two exchange credentials. Why should Pasteur erase the trace of his own work? (PH, 131–32). The more human intervention by Louis Pasteur, the more reality. The pertinent distinction is not between construction and reality, but between successful and unsuccessful constructions, experiments, theories. When constructions succeed, they are a triumph and the result is accessed reality, like the successful construction of a road that gets us where we want to go. The opposite is a failed experiment or theory, or even worse, something that parades itself as an alternative scientific theory, like "creationism," which fails not by being falsified but by never getting as far as a falsifiable theory or a testable construction. Creationism is not a "mere construction" but an impostor masquerading as a construction.

In a passage that nicely parallels a point made by Heidegger about the laws of Newton,[9] Latour will even go so far as to say that Pasteur's microbes were not "there" before Pasteur, which is why nobody saw them. It is only after they meet Pasteur that they appear. Pasteur happened to them—even as they made him famous in return. It is not the case either that they are purely active and Pasteur their passive observer, or that he is purely active and they are passive products. Rather, both are actants, co-actants, in a collaborative process (PH, 145–47). When Latour talks like that, when he speaks of "history," when he tries to talk his way around the old game of cat and mouse played by "epistemology" and "ontology," it is as plain as the nose on Husserl's face that Latour is doing "phenomenology," that is, he is speaking of the *known as such.* The known precisely insofar as it is known is the central subject matter of phenomenology and its principle of correlation, and it has nothing whatsoever to do with saying that what is known of the real is not real, as if the real becomes less real by being known. Every time Latour says "history," read the phenomena of phenomenology, particularly of the post-Husserlian flavor. His "pragmagony," the genesis of the things themselves (PH, 193–94), is a genetic phenomenology, whose "phenomena" are not "mere" appearances but the real appearance of the things themselves, as when we say "the president made an appearance the day we toured the White House." Warrior realists like Meillassoux lead us to believe that science makes "progress" by inverse proportion, by progressively learning to shed subjectivity (human biases and our barbaric obscure past) in order to reach objectivity (things in themselves, the radiant future), which is simply false. Latour replaces that mythic schema of pure subjects and pure objects with the hybrids of actual history, and he redescribes the arrow of progress in time as the ever-increasing imbroglio of human and non-human actants, which is a feature of both the past and the future, since it is the hallmark of human civilization generally. Because we were never modern, neither were we ever primitive (PH, 198–99).

Up to now I have been defending what a genuine theory of "correlation" would look like. But I said above that while "correlation" is not a bad word, it is not perfect and not my word of choice. When Latour speaks of "the collective in which humans are entangled with [non-humans]" (PH, 175), of "assemblies of connections" and of "negotiations" and "collaborations," Latour is describing is what is meant by a correlation, but with an important correction. Latour is describing a series of correlations in the plural, not a single correlation of scientific "acts" and scientific "objects," as in Husserl's transcendentalist formulations. Latour means the more complicated "imbroglio" of everything human and non-human (which swap properties with one another), including all the experimental equipment, professional societies, and other elements in scientific labor that go to make up what post-Husserlians like Don Ihde like to call a "post-phenomenology."[10] In other words, what's wrong with "correlation" is not the relationality but the binariness, what Husserl called the "two-sidedness" of the correlatives,[11] the failure to recognize that the relation is more than two (PH, 148). The limitation of the word is to suggest a merely two-sided (and implicitly dualistic) relation between "consciousness" and "reality," which is testimony not to metaphysical idealism but to Husserl's excessive cognitivism and his residual privileging of the paradigm of thinking as "looking at" (*an-schauen*), which Latour calls the pure "gaze." That is why, following Derrida, I like to emphasize the middle voice, something that is "getting itself done" by means of what Latour would call a multiplicity of agencies (actants) difficult to identify, with no clearly discernible doer. In contemporary phenomenology, the genesis of scientific objectivity is described not by way of a philosophy of "consciousness" but by way of a phenomenology of embodied scientific researchers working both in the field and in laboratories, using complicated equipment, housed in institutions belonging to social networks. The interesting thing, of course, is that this is the position taken by Husserl in the 1930s, although the position was weakened by a transcendental dualism, the rigid distinction between the transcendental and empirical. So instead of seeing a zero-sum war between "science studies" and contemporary "phenomenology," instead of "freeze-framing" phenomenology into Husserl, as Don Ihde quips, and indeed into one reading of one phase of Husserl's thought, Latour would do well to recognize a kindred spirit when he sees one.[12] He needs all the "friends" he can get.

Latour helps us see that we have been blackmailed by modernity, and that we are being blackmailed by Meillassoux, into making a false choice between construction and reality, either an omnipotent human creator (Feuerbach on religion) or an omnipotent transcendent reality (Barth on God). Like witnesses on a stand being grilled for a yes or no answer by a lawyer, we are forced to choose: either we made it or it is real; it is either fact or fetish, a true God or an idol. This puts us in an impossible "double bind" (FG, 83), because the mediations, the means, are both necessary and declared impossible. Accordingly, Latour says, we can also see that the modernist prohibition on the "fetish" (bestowing autonomy on what we have made ourselves) turns out to be a prohibition on understanding how one passes from our actions to "the autonomous entities that are welcomed by that action and revealed through it" (FG, 35). So the work of scientific "construction" is a work of "welcoming" the scientific real, "welcoming the other," as they say back in Paris, a practice of hospitality to the other, like Martha making ready the house for the arrival of Jesus. It belongs to a practice of letting the real reveal itself, a classic and rather Heideggerian definition of phenomenology—and that goes for divinities as well as for lactic acids, Latour adds. We construct, but we do not create *ex nihilo* (not even God does, he adds, with a tip of the hat to Whitehead, not to mention the actual text of Genesis). Creators regularly experience that they are not the masters of what they create, that they are overtaken by their creations, like novelists who come to love or despise their own characters and who are surprised at what their characters are capable of, or like thinkers who experience themselves being guided through their text by autonomous forces inherent in their own creation. We write the preface last, Derrida says, in order to create the "illusion of mastery." We are of course neither master nor slave but co-actants, imbricated in our own effects, or as Derrida says, situated at an unstable point between what we can control and what we cannot control in a text.

The mediations we construct are passages and images while the warrior realists are like the iconoclasts, Byzantine or Protestant fanatics out to destroy images, the fanaticism of "nihilism," which Latour very interestingly defines as the denial of all mediators (FG, 96). How much better it would be, they delude themselves in thinking, were we able to access reality without mediation. The interesting thing is that there is an implicit theologeme in the warrior realists of an ominous and ultraconservative type. They want science—in the old theology "God" inspires exactly this sort of desire, too—to trade in the *acheiropoieton*, what is not made by human hands, on the premise that if a human hand has intervened, it is sullied, weakened, desecrated (FG, 70–71). The world revealed in physics must be like the image of Jesus on the Mandylion (Image of Edessa), which the faithful regard as a painting not made by human hands—free at last, let us say, from the poison of any human poiesis, theopoetic in the sense of being made directly by God, as opposed to a discourse produced by us about God.[13] Mathematics replaces Hebrew as the language God speaks. The warrior realists do not appreciate that in science as in religion without the human hand the transcendence—the truth and objectivity and the divinity—would never come into view. The more mediation, Latour argues, the more transcendence, which is of course the law of direct proportions. It is not a question of choosing between reality and our means of access to reality; the one increases directly in proportion to the other, resulting in an accessed reality.

The self-destructive axiom of the warrior realists is that they find it necessary to deny our access to reality in order to preserve the reality of the real. Like Meister Eckhart praying God to rid them of God, they pray the real to rid them of their access to the real, so that the real may be a miracle, dropped from the sky. We are asked by them to purify our relation to the real so that the real is all real and there is no relation, for having a relationship to the real compromises the real and contaminates an absolute with a relation—a problematic that is not unlike Levinas's notion of the *tout autre*, a comparison which, to their credit, they themselves recognize. They seek a real without relation, mediation, image, contact, sign, inscription, or picture—in short, a real without access. They want to make everything accessible to the sciences but they deny the character of science as an access. Their sacred mission is to destroy every graven image of the real, to be the iconoclast of the images of the absolute, which is "the highest piety in intellectual circles" (FG, 68–69). It is as if the moon becomes something less when lovers moon over its nighttime glow or the Big Bang dissipates the moment it is theorized. So the warrior realists are still pious. Against this Latour proposes an alternate piety, a version of the story of Abraham where Isaac is an image of the image, so that when God stays the hand of the Patriarch by sending his angel (a mediating "messenger") God is sparing the life of images. By the very arrival of the angel, we are instructed about the necessity of angels, of images, messages, and mediators; every parable is a parable of the necessity of parables. The angel is the "dangerous supplement" (Derrida) of/from God, which is the point being elaborated so brilliantly in Michel Serres's *La legende des anges*, which I discussed above.[14] Against this fanatical realism, Latour recommends an alternate realism, the more sensible, realistic realism practiced by those who are "friends of interpretable objects" (FG, 70).

Words like "interpretation" and "access" produce allergic results in the warrior realists. But the opposite of accessible objects is inaccessible objects, objects about which we know nothing. The opposite of interpretable objects is not reality-in-itself, bared and unsheathed, unconditionally present in itself, but a blank slate, sheer confusion or utter meaninglessness. To lack an interpretation is to be at a loss, to fail to make contact with anything real, contemporary or ancestral, ranging all the way from sheer perceptual confusion to the inability of someone untrained to read an X ray or the results that came in on advanced astronomical instruments. The question is not how to make unconditioned contact with reality but how to find the right conditions under which it is possible to make contact with reality at all. Without the right conditions, the result is not unconditioned reality but a total lack of contact with reality. Without interpretation, the result is not pure uninterpreted facts of the matter but a void. The more complex and sensitive the conditions, the longer and deeper our reach into reality, like the ability of trained interpreters to use highly sophisticated instruments to gain a glimpse into the nature of things quite unavailable to the ancients. But such insight is clearly a function of the state-of-the-art technology of the time, which gives results as different as the first results Galileo achieved with his telescopes and the instruments of the Galileo space probe which extend our vision and knowledge into the far reaches of space. The more refined the conditions of construction and interpretation, the deeper the grasp of the real.

A condition is not an obstacle to reality but an angle of entry into the real, and the pertinent point is that such angles of entry are constructions that are structurally deconstructible, revisable and reinterpretable. The relevant distinction, then, is not between construction and reality, which is a completely specious opposition, but between effective constructions and ineffective ones, gross constructions and more refined ones, appropriate and inappropriate ones. Unconditional access to reality is an illusion, like the illusion of Kant's dove that thinks it would be able to soar all the more freely but for the resistance offered it by the wind. It is the illusion of shedding all interpretation, instrumentality, and mediation, the sort of knowledge theology has always attributed to God and on occasion has extended to the angels and to mystics who think they have already been granted it while here on earth. But for those of us embodied beings, who pull our pants on one leg at a time, the opposition of interpretation and reality is blackmail, a sophistical confusion and an unfortunate means of indefinitely perpetuating the science wars. As always, I am not objecting to the fact that there are implicit theologemes embedded in the warrior realist schema—I think that is true for us all—but rather to the bad theology, the high theology of omnipotence and omniscience, instead of the much more realistic weak theology of the "perhaps."

The friends of interpretable objects are the friends of "perhaps" and consequently the truest and best friends of scientific inquiry. To say "perhaps" is to say science proceeds with caution, following the shifting tendencies of the evidence, understanding full well there is much that we do not know, that we do not know what is coming next, always reserving the right to revise whatever we say today in the light of what will turn up tomorrow. Reality is reality but our access to reality is tempered by time and circumstance and we are always laboring under contingent presuppositions which change with time. "The best proof of this," Latour says, "was given when, in the 1880s, to Pasteur's great surprise, enzymology took over," and Pasteur's results were reinscribed ("articulated" he says) in a new context (PH, 151). The life of scientific research and inquiry depends upon constructions which are structurally deconstructible and revisable or recontextualizable, correctible and perfectible, and lacking which science would turn into the worst dogmatic violence.

Science gives us access to reality and reality is what is accessed, and this accessed reality is through and through a work of the most delicate, difficult, and tentative construction and structural deconstructibility. The *history* of science, which is the history of what science knows, of the known as known in science, of its interpretable objects, of their constant renovation and occasional revolution, of their structural revisability, is the best evidence that scientists too are friends of interpretation. Reality is always already interpreted, welcomed, or disclosed under determinate conditions and presuppositions. It is a ridiculous blackmail, actually very funny, to insist that reality is compromised when it is disclosed. Knowledge would then be reduced to a malicious computer virus: the moment you open the document of reality, you wipe out all the data! The tandem of construction and reality shows up every time a scientific explanation is retested, revised, revisited, jettisoned, or reinscribed in a new framework. Otherwise the history of science would be the history of divine deliveries descending from on high into the open laps of the scientists who have merited such special graces. But scientists depend not upon their laps but upon their laptops and labs. The history of science is a history of construction and deconstruction. The moment the church, or the state, or the local full professor says that the current explanation is not deconstructible, the science is over, the heresiology is launched, and the war has begun.

No wonder, then, the warrior realists are worried by the things Latour says. No wonder they wonder whether he has fallen like a bad angel into the sin of correlation. Have no fear, Harman and Meillassoux ultimately conclude; Latour is without sin. Huddled like Vatican diplomats over the dangerous words of an outspoken priest—actually it is the nuns who are under attack, since the priests have mostly been cowed into silence—trying to detect the odor of heresy, they decide that although he says dangerous things, he is not a heretic in their self-styled "school."[15] I would suggest that the reason that is so is that no one is what they are calling a correlationist, and that those who are would benefit more from therapy than speculative realism. Latour has already diagnosed this diagnosis under the name of "belief." It turns out that the warrior realists themselves are the only ones who nourish a naive belief in the naive belief that they attribute to the name of "correlation."

Their victory over a straw "correlationism" is a conquest of a non-existent country, or at most of an unoccupied one (here at last we have found a philosophical use for Badiou's empty set!). The moment you actually supply a proper name for a world-denying, so-called correlationist, let's say Derrida, it takes very little effort to show that the claim is ridiculous. In this connection, I regret to say that the remarks Latour himself makes about "deconstruction" and "Derrida" betray a stupefying innocence of both, on a par with Meillassoux's equally stupefying claim that philosophers like Derrida and Foucault are "dangerously close to creationists" (AF, 18).[16] Evidently, the only way this critique can be sustained is never to mention an existing figure but to sustain instead the unrelenting bombardment of the unoccupied fields of something called "correlation" (or, in Latour's case, of "postmodernism" or "deconstruction") dropping the explosives of "reality" or "science," while never studying an actual scientific experiment (or in Latour's case, never carefully analyzing an actual "postmodern" text). Rhetorically, the way to sustain it, as Latour shows about Plato, is to create a ridiculous straw Callicles ("correlation," "postmodernism"), deprive him of his genuine argument, and let him be outsmarted by a Socrates who, as Nietzsche showed and Latour agrees, is behind all this rationalist excess. What Bruno Latour does is immensely valuable and demands a wider hearing. But I will hazard the hypothesis that, on the level of theory, Latour has nothing to add to Derrida.[17]

In the end, this critique of a naive belief called correlationism is without end, caught in an infinite regress, perpetually deferring the question of who is actually a correlationist—Latour? No, the Lord Cardinal Inquisitors of the new church have conferred on this and found the accused innocent. Latour himself points the finger at other unnamed "bad" practitioners of science studies. Then, surely Husserl? No—not if we ignore Meillassoux's caricature of the position and read Husserl carefully; Husserl advises we look to the nineteenth-century sense-data empiricists. Then certainly Heidegger? No—Heidegger in turn suggests Husserl. Then Derrida and Foucault? Obviously they are creationists? No, no, that is silly—then . . . ?

I think the best defense against the charges filed by the warrior realists of murder most foul, of slaying the real—shall we say "rei-cide" since we can't say homicide?—is simply to wait for the prosecution to produce a body. I myself have lived for years among the tropes of these postmodern tropic islands, spent my professional life working among the natives, living on what must be considered by the warrior realists the Molokai of Postmodernism, but I have never encountered the disease. I have never met such "correlationists" as these, but I await with no little curiosity their appearance. Meillassoux owes it to himself and to us to take a field trip among the postmoderns and to send back a report, filled with photographs, I would hope, about this native population he claims he has discovered. Such amazing people, odder than the man who mistook his wife for a hat, they do not believe in reality. We have so many questions. Do they feed themselves? Do they reproduce? Do they apply for tenure? Do they bother even to get up in the morning? We would all love to meet them, to catch at least a fleeting glimpse, even a trace or fossil they have left behind, or maybe an image like those fuzzy pictures of the Loch Ness monster. We are overcome with curiosity. Perhaps they are all dead now—we hear stories the last one died in 2004—and we have only archival evidence of these strange ancestors. Still, I am certain that National Geographic could produce an award-winning documentary about them, which would credit Meillassoux at the start for having discovered an exotic race and earn him everlasting fame in the annals of anthropology.

THE BIG TOE

What Meillassoux wants to know, what we radical theologians want to know, what we all want to know, is what is really real?—an old question we cannot shake, an old question that keeps on shaking us, and either way does not admit of a one-word answer. The world described by physics is real in the sense that it is there even if we are not there to point that out. Then there is the real that is there when we are also there, and for the while that we are there. The reality of the real suffers not a loss from our presence but a gain. The real has not been absorbed into us, whatever on earth and under heaven that would even mean, and I doubt it means anything at all, but has for precisely that while acquired another stratum of reality with a texture and complexity all its own. After all, our relation to reality is as real as the reality to which we are related. This we are describing here in terms of the chiasm, while Latour describes it in terms of chains of actants, of longer, richer, and more complex concatenations of connections. Either way, *nous voici,* here we are, *in medias res,* in the middle of the real. To speak of things as if we are not here (no chiasm) still requires construction (the chiasm) to be pointed out.[18] If human beings had never happened, we would have no problems at all. We would have neither Meillassoux nor Kant, neither realists nor idealists, materialists nor spirit-seers, theists nor atheists, to duke it out with each other about what is really real. That actually would not be an altogether bad outcome, since there are, as we learn from Martha, other, more urgent matters awaiting us.

So let the word go forth: we theologians of the "perhaps" affirm without hesitation that physics is the study of the real, and it is even a theory of everything that is real. If the speculation about superstrings is ever experimentally confirmed, that will be the much sought-after "theory of everything" (TOE), uniting relativity and quantum theory. But, our small theopoetic point is this: even the big theory of everything is not big enough. The theory of everything is not all in all and it will always remain in an important way incomplete. We must be exceedingly careful about how we formulate its incompleteness and not fall into the egregious mistake made by either Kant or Meillassoux, by transcendentalism or warrior realism. The reality disclosed by physics is related to our knowledge of it *neither* as an "appearance" constituted by knowledge (Kant) nor as an "objective being" such that the role of knowledge is to get out of its way lest we end up with some supposedly subjective "correlation" (Meillassoux), but as the physical basis of things is related to everything that is built up on that basis, as the founding stratum is related to the strata that are founded upon it. Physics provides the basic schema; it addresses the *basic* stratum of the real, of everything built up from that base and upon that bottom. Physics is the theory of everything that is real, of what everything is *at bottom,* but not of everything on top, not of every *modality* of everything that is real. It is the theory of everything material but not of everything that matters. Mathematics is the language of the basic schema but it is not the only language we need. The basic schema deals in principle with everything but not from every point of view. Physics is or seeks the theory of everything, but it does not supply every theory we need; it is not the theory of everything about which we need a theory. There is not anything that is not governed by physics, but physics does not have an account of every way in which things are governed or behave. It is a theory of everything but not of every way.

The big TOE would be the foundation upon which everything is built, but it is not big enough to cover everything that has been built on the foundation (or stands on its feet, as it were). Even if the basic reason the roof leaks when it rains would ultimately go back to string theory, by the time you got from string theory back to the roof, the house would be inundated. Life and human life are no less real than the subject matter of physics, even if it be true that they are not part of the permanent furniture of the cosmos. Even if human and animal bodies are not as old as the universe, and even if they are in the cosmic scheme of things fortuitous short-timers, they are places in which the universe is curled up in curiously inventive and intense concentrations, altogether fascinating moments in which the universe shows what it is capable of, what it is made of, while at the same time showing "us" what "we" are made of (as if we were not parts of the universe, too!). Thinking and feeling are cosmic, chaosmic, and chiasmic events and require their own appropriate discursive forms, in which the role of the poetics whose cause I am advancing here is irreducible.

That means we tip our hat to physics and agree that physics is as much metaphysics as we are going to come up with. But we need something more than any such metaphysics. We need more vocabularies, more discursive and pragmatic resources, more modalities, which is why I am working late into the night on a "poetics." Even if we agree that metaphysics covers what is real, we still need to talk about the real inter-relations of the real, of the chiasmic intertwining of human reality with reality at large, the curling up of reality that takes place in human reality. So when we say "here we are," what is really real is not some one-sided real but the chiasm in the sense of the intertwining of the human with the non-human, the complex of actants described by Latour, the border breakdowns described by Haraway, the kingdom of all our animal companions, and the kingdom of God announced by Jesus and other comparable poets of the impossible. We need them all. We love them all, all creatures great and small, all theories big and not so big. We do not want to squander the resources granted us by the name (of) "God" in the name of preserving an ill-advised version of realism. That is why in addition to a metaphysics of the real we really need a poetics of the chiasm, that is, a descriptive discourse of the relationship to the real, of a theopoetics that finally makes contact with a majestic cosmopoetics.

So let us be clear. When I say that physics is all the metaphysics we can expect, my position can be described in terms of current debates as a form of "materialism"—although my grammatological instincts make me fiercely opposed to "ism" words—not a reductionistic materialism but an open-ended one in which the constituent components of the universe are not atomic units and larger compounds but virtualities and actualities. Žižek thinks that matter is all, but the all is a non-all,[19] and Malabou describes a "reasonable materialism" that does not turn life into a cybernetic or neurological program.[20] Derrida, Žižek, Malabou, Meillassoux, and I are all "materialists" in the sense that we are not *City of God* Augustinians; we do not think there are two worlds, one in space and time, the other transcending space and time.[21] It is in order to "supplement" physics that Malabou emphasizes a transformational "plastics," Žižek introduces "parallax shifts," Meillassoux produces a rather extraordinary account of contingency and a coming God, and I speak of a "poetics" of the event.

The real is the "absolute" in the sense that it is the world that is there while being "absolved" of taking mind of us, or the world that is there whether we mind it or not. It is nonetheless not now a world without "minds" (remembering that I speak of the chiasm in order to avoid the unnecessary dilemmas created by speaking of minds and bodies or subjects and objects). If physics opens its doors for business by means of a radical decontextualization (removing us from the picture), it is also true that decontextualization was preceded by a context and is inevitably followed (whether we like it or not) by recontextualization (since we are the ones taking the picture, thereby having been always already installed in the chiasm). Of course the universe does not need us—we are gratuitous, an effect of cosmic dice—but it has us nonetheless, need us or not. The interesting thing—the irreducibly theological thing, the theology that insinuates itself into our conversations when our guard is down, the thing that merits our attention—is that we cosmically insignificant beings in a distant corner of the universe have to live with that facticity or contingency, having recognized it to begin with. We are the ones who point it out or, to give this a different twist, we are the place where the universe points that out about itself. We are the place in the universe where—that is the locationary twist of the Heideggerian locution *da*—the universe takes note of its own gratuitousness. We are the place in the history of evolution where "evolution" get itself named, where living beings evolve who can point out that living beings evolve, the place where the universe does its thinking and jots down a few notes about itself. The mistake is to think that this recenters everything around us instead of seeing that our eccentric, marginal, and fortuitous condition is part of what is being pointed out.

This means that while the "absolute" is absolute it is also drawn into a "relation" from which it is continually withdrawing. That is a perplexing situation that torments Laruelle and in turn has led him to torment the rest of us with what is perhaps the most tortured and tortuous prose in contemporary philosophy. The curious thing is that this situation has been well described—as the warrior realists much to their credit recognize[22]— by a phenomenologist of sorts, by Levinas (of all people!) when he speaks of a relation of absolutes, of absolutes continually absolving themselves from the relation. Levinas's point of departure was Husserl's idea of the alter ego as *ganz anders,* as an absolute other (*tout autre*) whose experiences were in principle inaccessible to us, where the impossibility in principle of intuitive fulfillment is not a shortfall of this experience but the really interesting feature that is *constitutive* of it.[23] But Levinas thought that Husserl had made a category mistake by treating the absolutely other as an epistemic phenomenon. Levinas thinks this compromises its alterity— one of continental philosophy's terms of art for the "real"—which can only be protected in Levinas's view if it is respected as an ethical event. Levinas worked this out by way of a conundrum familiar to any Jewish theologian—ever since Yahweh told Moses to mind his own business when Moses got excessively nosy about the proper name of God (Exod. 3:14). The problem Moses was posing was how the Israelites were supposed to have a relation with an Absolute that insists on withdrawing from or absolving itself from that relation. For Levinas the God of the Hebrew scriptures supplies the model for the genuine reality behind what Husserl was after, an "absolute" whose entire point is blunted if it does not find some way of entering a relationship from which it is also necessarily withdrawing. People like Laruelle and Levinas, and Heidegger and Merleau-Ponty before them (and some unknown authors of this part of Genesis, before them), are working on a poetics, an imaginative description, working from within the chiasm, where the relationships of absolutes withdrawing from that relationship shows up, and they find variously imaginative and ingenious ways to mark off the way it shows up. If it didn't show up, none of us would be talking about it. That remarkable showing is what has kept philosophers and theologians talking and gainfully employed from the start.

So we need not be anxious that the world will have slipped away when we wake up in the morning or have any anxiety that the universe is going to surrender its autonomy and be swallowed up by our knowledge (again, I have no idea what that could even mean). All that happens is that the ever-expanding universe becomes the ever-widening "world" of which we are an irreducible (so long as we are not dead) if increasingly miniscule part, a point first noticed by Pascal and Cusanus, who first noticed its religious value. The chiasm (of which "correlation" is an abstract, pale, and thinned-out feature) does not mean the universe belongs to us but that we belong to it, just as speaking of "my parents" does not reduce them to me but refers me to an absolute past with which I can never be contemporaneous. Our relation to the world does not "reduce" the world to us, but releases us from our contraction to ourselves, so that the more we learn about the universe, the less contracted we are. A robust Aristotelian realist like Aquinas—who had at least as much invested in preserving the absoluteness of God as materialists have in protecting matter—said that a knowing being differs from a non-knowing being because the latter is contracted to itself and the former is expanded into and "becomes all things." Becoming all things is an Aristotelianism that Meillassoux reads backwards, as if Aristotle has said all things become us. The most moving, ironic, iconic, and spectacular example of this point nowadays is Stephen Hawking, whose ALS (amyotrophic lateral sclerosis) disease has contracted his body to itself, restricting him to twitching a muscle in his right cheek, even as his thought soars across the cosmos.

As a terminological matter, I should add, it is useful to distinguish the "cosmos" or "universe" studied in cosmology from the "life-world" that is described in a cosmopoetics. The "life-world"—Latour calls it "history"—does not mean that the world is alive or that it is a part of our living bodies, but that the world is the place where we live, so that the more the sciences tell us about the universe as it is without, before, and after us, the wider our world becomes. The universe is the ultimate or widest sphere of decontextualization (taking us out of the picture, thinking as if we were dead), while the life-world is the widest context. The life-world is the wide, wide world, the world-wide web of the whole wide world in which we live. The universe is the determination in the last instance in its order, just as the life-world is the determination in the last instance in its order, and these two orders, cosmology and cosmopoetics, are not adversaries but correlates, meaning that if you start with one, you can cross over to the other. Hegel saw this, but as the young Hegelians complained, in an upside-down way.

So if we humans are, in the cosmic scheme of things, disasters, or headed for disaster, we also have—at least for the while—a lucky star. I say a lucky star, not an eternal-Platonic sun, just a local sun around which we revolve in a rhythmic spin that has engendered, over a series of random cosmic events, what we call the lucky chance of life, including human life.

The kind of trouble Meillassoux is trying to start by resurrecting from the dead the old problem of epistemological "correspondence" cannot in principle ever arise in any adequate account of the chiasm because, as I said in the last chapter, "we" are the very *issue* of the chiasm. We are plants and the forms of our experience are no more "subjective" than the heliotropic movements of a tree or a plant. We are forms of life emergent on the surface of a little planet in an obscure corner of the universe kept warm and well-lit for the moment by a little star we call our own on a planet enjoying a Goldilocks location. Until it does not. That makes it all a temporary arrangement. We have here no lasting city. But that does not make it an unreal city or confine the real within our city limits.

Accordingly, physics needs to be supplemented by biology, and biology by the study of theopoetics (to make a long story short), not in cleanly separated and militantly maintained strata but in a continuum of complexity that allows for gaps when thresholds are surpassed, following along the lines described by Žižek's notion of parallax gaps. Matter—a word that is mainly useful to common sense where it is used with too much confidence—is all. That is what it means to say that physics is as much metaphysics as can be expected, in search of a theory of everything. But (this) all is not enough; this everything is not everything we need. This everything is a non-everything; this all is a "non-all," admitting of countless complexifications and unforeseeable intensifications, unfoldings, in-foldings, invaginations, curlings-up, all the way from supposedly "inert" bodies—which is an intolerable notion if matter and energy are simply different expressions of the same thing—to what we too neatly call living bodies, to animal bodies, to human-animal bodies, in which, if not the "life" at least the "energy" of so-called inert bodies is "intensified," as Deleuze would put it.

THE "HUMANITIES" BETWEEN LIFE AND DEATH

Now we can say something on behalf of what we call in English the "humanities" (the Germans say *Geisteswissenschaften*), which will consist in something more than simply building up a defense against science. The humanities, too, belong to the study of the real, of human reality, and their subject matter is as real as real can be. So what I am calling for here under the name of a poetics, of theopoetics and cosmo-theopoetics, constitutes a call for what Derrida calls a "new" humanities. The humanities at large cultivate the disciplinary eyes and ears to follow the tracks of life's finer, more complex chiasmic "correlations," these more deeply contextualized strata of reality, in its finer lacings and interlacings—as when Husserl spoke of a need for a vocabulary describing things that are "notched, scalloped, and lens-shaped."[24] Human experience is a delicate latticework of things that are precisely not formalizable or mathematicizable, even though they will always have a basis and a correlate in the basic schema in accordance with the "materialism" that we announced when we said that physics is all the metaphysics we are likely to get.

The starting point of the new humanities is to recognize the border breakdown between the human and non-human. The humanities have always had to do with the chiasm, the intertwining of the insistence of the event and our existence, but this must include the intertwining of human and non-human, the correlations between the anthropological and the ethological, the biological and the physical, which are as real as real can be. We are required to understand the delicate and non-formal features of the relationships that emerge among human beings, and between human beings and the non-human animals, and finally with the non-human universe that precedes, engenders, and will finally succeed all of us animals. We find exemplary cases of such work in Michel Serres and in the collaboration of neuroscience and continental philosophy of the sort we see in Catherine Malabou. Art, religion, and philosophy—an antiquated list, compiled by Hegel, too short, too simple, and misleadingly labeled as the "Absolute Spirit"—are privileged places of humane inquiry, of liminal reflection and interrogation at the limits. Each of them provides a particular kind of poetics of the human condition and it is in this connection that I have drawn particular attention to the study of "religion," particularly in a Hegelian vein, which describes the intertwining of God with us, of Emmanuel.

The humanities have for their special task the study of the human chiasm, of the intertwined realities or the real relations of human reality with the real world in which we live, in all of its unformalizable multiplicity and unprogrammable complexity. The divide that exists between analytic philosophy and "continental" philosophy is, beyond the very real meanness of the exclusionary politics, a division of labor. Simplifying to an extreme, analytic philosophers have to their credit paid proper attention to the logic of the natural sciences and the makeup of formal systems, to the study of all those features of human life that admit of formal and mathematical inquiry, so that the interest of the later Wittgenstein in the non-formalizable constitutes a continentalist opening in analytic philosophy. The attention of "continental" philosophers, on the other hand, has been drawn to the non-formal and non-mathematical features of reality, to describe not so much its "logic" as its "phenomeno-logic," meaning the texture and structure of experience in the broadest sense, while its early but now faded interest in the foundations of mathematics and the natural sciences constitutes an analytic opening in continental philosophy. That is why continental philosophy has developed such a close affinity to literature and the arts and why, when it thinks about science at all, it is likely to be drawn to the social sciences or, at most, as with Deleuze, to biology and the life sciences. What is causing panic on the part of the current critics of continental philosophy, on my accounting, is the slippery slope that leads from continentalist commerce with art and literature to what its critics consider its outright "contamination" by religion, and that has led to a market sell-off.

One might say, to employ a typical bit of continentalist conceit, that the continentalists are interested in life and analytic philosophy in death. But by this, I hasten to add, I mean that continental philosophy is a study of the very texture of life while the formal and mathematical structures studied in analytic philosophy are neuter or neutral, non-living, "anonymous," a "what" rather than a "who." In saying this, I do not mean to describe an opposition but a composition. In raising the question of the rumored death of continental philosophy, I proceed from a suspicion that the lines that separate life from death are not so clean. In my spectral way of thinking, it is difficult to say that the dead are completely dead or that the living are completely alive. On the view that I take, the lived experience of life is at every point exposed to these life-less formal structures even though these formal structures do not completely yield the lived experience of life.

In this respect Derrida holds a special place of importance *between* analytic and continental philosophy, between life and death, between physics and *anthropos,* between nature and culture, between formal languages and informal ones (which explains his interest in John Austin and the tradition of ordinary language analytic philosophy). It is of telling, indeed decisive importance, that one of the most consistent points made over the years by Derrida—superficially the most "literary" of the continentalists, to the point of being popularly portrayed as a capricious aestheticist—is that life is structurally inhabited by death. By death I do not only have in mind the "Existentialist" notion of being-unto-death that is not to be outstripped, of inescapable mortality, as if that were not enough for one lifetime!— but of being "already dead." By this he means that human life is already marked and inscribed by structures neuter and neutral, anonymous and automatic, technical and mechanical—of which the most famous is *différance,* which spells (or misspells) the anonymity of *khora,* of spacing, of the space of play of time (*Zeitspielraum*), as Heidegger called it. As soon as

I speak my name in the first person, *viva voce,* I am marked by death. The name I was given at birth is the name that can be used in my absence, that survives me, and will be inscribed on my tomb.

What Derrida described under the name of the logic of the supplement, which undermines the distinction between nature and culture, is presently being realized with a vengeance in the info-technologizing supplement of the human body, with genetic codes and prostheses of every sort, up to and including the prospect of human faculties supplemented by computerized implants. Derrida made his debut as a philosopher by arguing against the "purity" of the "living present" of Husserl's phenomenology of *Erlebnis* and the *Lebenswelt,* meaning that when we speak of life we are really speaking of life/death, which explains Latour's interest in "hybrids"[25] and Haraway's in cyborgs. Derrida insisted precisely upon the specters of death in all this life—his grammatology is already a "hauntology"—that is, of the impersonal-anonymous structures of "spacing" that inhabit the life of living speech, the living present, and its life-world.

Of Grammatology is a deconstruction of the nature/culture divide in Rousseau and his modern anthropological followers. In it *différance* is shown to be the "dead" element in the "living present," that is, the formal, neutral, or differential spacing of a technology embedded in the heart of living speech. That means—to speak a little Franco-Greek—that if the very *physis* of the human *zoon* is *logos,* and if *logos* presupposes *différance,* and if *différance* is *techne,* then human "nature" is from the inside out always already technological, that life is always already marked at birth by death. We have never been purely human;[26] we have never been purely alive; there has never been any pure human life. In support of this, Derrida very early on adduced a "materialist" point in Husserl against Husserl, the most "idealist" of philosophers, when Husserl made the "Origin of Geometry" dependent upon the material technology of writing.[27] The materialism of writing is the process of constituting objects through generations of materially transmitted signifiers. Signifiers are defined, on the one hand, by their capacity to function in the absence of the signified, so that every fossil and archive is an element of reading ancient scripts, and on the other hand by the death of the author, who has left them behind. That makes a mockery, one that strictly speaking is really very funny, of Meillassoux's attempt to refute Derrida by digging up the phenomena of "ancestrality" and the "arche-fossil," as if Derrida stood in need of being instructed about the logic of archives, fossils, and traces left behind by the dead, and about the ability of a signifier (like a fossil) to function in the absence of the signified (the past).

Let us listen to Derrida one more time:

> To perceive the object *as such* implies that you perceive the object as it is or as it is supposed to be when you are not there . . . So to relate to an object *as such* means to relate to it as if you were dead. That's the condition of truth . . . the condition of objectivity.[28]

To which we need only add, "dead or not yet born." But there are countless other examples of life/death, beginning with the very definition of humans as tool users. *Différance* is a technical, non-human, a-human principle in living speech, in life itself, so that—to put it in the form of one of those aporias which Derrida loved to savor—the "principle" of life in living things is not the *anima*, the soul, but death, that is, a structure of anonymity. That also means that there is nothing about *différance* that restricts it to language or even to the human, and that as a structure of spacing and timing it provides a way of thinking not only about human-animal experience, but also non-human-animal experience, as well as the non-living, so-called "merely" physical universe. It is especially handy when we reach a point with mathematical equations for which we cannot in principle have intuitive or lived fulfillment, which is a much better example than the one Meillassoux managed to come up with (ancestrality).[29] Derrida's criticisms of Husserl's intuitionism is confirmed by contemporary quantum physics, where the plasticity of our imagination reaches a breaking point. It is instructive fun to listen to quantum theorists say that they themselves do not know what they are talking about, meaning that they can "do the math" but they cannot imaginatively fulfill the point to which they are being led by their mathematics. First with Einstein and then with quantum physics, science is increasingly breaking its bondage to imaginative fulfillment, and hence to what Derrida called early on the "metaphysics of presence."

FROM FIDEISM TO FAITH

It has taken me a long time to get to this point, but my point is this. While I think the specter of what the warrior realists call "correlation" is a red herring, I think the more interesting side of Meillassoux's argument is the specter of "fideism" that has spooked the investors in continental philosophy and sparked a sell-off. If you want to clear a room full of philosophers, you need do no more than shout "faith," "religion," "theology."[30] That will cause a panic run in these seekers of wisdom and send them rushing headlong for the exits. If Meillassoux is tilting at windmills in his critique of correlation, I agree with his critique of Kant's famous dictum about denying knowledge to make room for faith. I count myself among those who practice a "philosophy of religion" that descends from Hegel (through Tillich), not from Kant (through Barth), and I would add Meillassoux to my list of Hegelians. Kant I think was engaged in a kind of philosophical damage control, a retrenchment that staves off knowledge in order to keep ethics safe (ethics being as much religion as Kant could abide). Kant I think does indeed open the door to a kind of half-hearted, fingers-crossed epistemological postmodernism, an "apologetic" use of continental philosophy. As I argued above (ch. 5), the Kantian approach uses postmodernism to provide a skepticism that in turn provides a cover for fideism.[31] The apologetic appropriation of postmodern criticism is a way to keep the powders of faith dry when the waters of modernist critique begin to rise. My idea is not to keep faith safe but to expose it in all its insecurity and unsafety. Religion, in my view, is a *Vorstellung*, not of the Concept of course but of the "event." Religion gives narratival form and flesh to underlying events—like the promise, forgiveness, hospitality, justice, hope, expectation—and faith. I treat religious beliefs and practices as a theo-poetics, a poetics of the *theos*, or the *theios*, in human life, a way of describing what is going on in our lives under the name of "God" and the "gods" and the "divine." As opposed to the Kantians and Barthians, I prefer the approach advanced by Laruelle, one of the writers favored by the new realists, who wants to *use* theology and to give it a human meaning.[32]

So I rise to the defense of faith, but not of fideism, and this in the name of the event. Fideism is a negative and apologetic strategy, a way of saying "you cannot prove me wrong so I am free to believe . . . ," whereas faith is an affirmation. Fideism is trying to protect belief and to delimit its exposure to a more searching analysis. But what I am calling faith, *foi,* is not a confessional belief (*croyance*). Faith is more deeply circum-fessional than a confessional belief. Beliefs belong to the circled wagons of the denominational traditions, of creedal assertions, including both theistic assertions and atheistic assertions. What I am calling faith has nothing to do with belief in a world behind the scenes that will be the eternal reward for muddling our way through this vale of tears, even as it has nothing to do with turning human life into atoms migrating in a void. My first, last, and final confession is to confess a circumfessional and primal prayerful faith in the insistence of the event. If philosophy is a philosophical explication of the event, "theology," the insistence of radical theology (as a variant form of "radical hermeneutics"), is a theology of the insistence of the event. It treats the various confessional and historical religious traditions as so many ways that events take place, so many ways to make conditional historical response to the unconditional solicitations, invitations, injunctions, promises, and recollections, which take place as so many events. When people speak of "losing their faith" they usually mean that they are switching *croyances* and life goes on. But to lose your *foi* would be to lose your innermost makeup and let life sink into despair. So my confessions about physics as the next-best thing to metaphysics or all the metaphysics we can expect to get is not meant to use "science" to drive "theology" off the premises, but to redescribe theology as radical theology, as a theopoetics of the event, as a perspicacious optics of the scene of life, of the chiasm, not as a metaphysics of beings, Being, or the beyond-being. Once theology clears its head of metaphysics, it can see a good deal better what its calling is, what it is called to do, which of course involves the clearheaded circumfession that it cannot see what is coming. That is the hallmark of the faith of a new species of theologians to come, whose prototype I have for reasons of economy of exposition condensed into the figure of Martha.

Having thus dispelled the confusion created by the panic of the warrior realists over correlation and having distinguished faith from fideism, let us now turn to the question of a certain religion without religion, sustained by a faith filled with unfaith, in what is God, perhaps.

ELEVEN

A NIHILISM OF GRACE
Life, Death, and Resurrection

Martha said to Jesus, "Lord if you had been here,
my brother would not have died.
But even now I know that God will give you whatever you ask of him."
Jesus said to her, "Your brother will rise again."
Martha said to him,
"I know that he will rise again in the resurrection on the last day."

—JOHN 11:21-24

I return now to the hard hypothesis, that life is a passing feature of the universe, an interim phenomenon, not an ultimate or permanent part of the cosmic furnishings. An ineluctable fate lies in store for us—terrestrial, solar, galactic, and universal death in entropic disintegration, that point when there is no chiasm or poetics, no life or religion. What then of God, perhaps?

WE'RE STILL HERE: COSMIC OR COMIC?

To this end we can do no better than to return to the cold, disenchanted, demythologized, disappointing, reductionistic, realistic, rationalistic world view of one of the critics of continental philosophy, best encapsulated in all of its apocalyptic fury in the brassy materialistic brio and bravado of Brassier's *Nihil Unbound*. Let us unbind nihilism and let it all hang out. Let us expose ourselves to the terrible trauma of the real, our heads bloodied but unbowed by the degree zero of being-nothing, which boils away both substance and subject, art, religion, and philosophy, *bios* and *zoë*, *physis* and *techne*, dissipating everything fideistic and correlational. Let us leave behind the luxurious plenitude and lush planes of the *Lebenswelt* for the thermal equilibrium of entropy unbound, where being-in-itself is nothing-for-us, nothing to us, and we nothing to it. What is being degree zero to me or I to it that I should weep for being-nothing?[1]

Now what?

Here we are. We are still here. Does death make a mockery of our lives? Does cosmic death matter? What exactly does it mean or matter for us, here and now, to take this entropic dissipation into account? Or is this cosmic matter ultimately a comic one? Johannes Climacus lampooned Hegelian speculation on world history while neglecting personal existence by referring to his hero Socrates. As a young man, Socrates studied astronomy and followed the early physicists but he gave all that up and turned to ethics. Socrates decided that, for fear of "being mocked by existence," there was already plenty to do by staying at home and grieving over his own existence before he could get around to worrying about world history (let alone a trillion trillion trillion years hence). "But he had plenty of time and enough eccentricity to be concerned about the merely *human,* a concern that, strangely enough, is considered an eccentricity among *human beings.*"[2]

So is it indeed an eccentricity to be concerned with human beings? If so, what are we humans supposed to do in the meantime?

What does the "meantime" mean? We have heard this question before, not only from the wicked wit of Johannes Climacus but from St. Paul. It was the same end-of-the-world question put by the Corinthians to Paul, which provided the occasion for Paul's *hos mē* (*quasi non*) instructions in 1 Corinthians 7:25–31, to which we referred in our discussion of Žižek above. There is an odd parallel here which I was hinting at when in the previous chapter I described physics as an inquiry into reality "as if we were dead." Physics gives a whole new meaning to Paul's proclamation that the world in its present form is passing away and that we are living in a *kairos,* a pressing but opportune moment. Contemporary cosmology provides us with a corresponding cosmopoetic axiom for a provisional time. The difference, of course, is that Paul thought the time was quite short and that we were headed for the *Parousia,* whereas the cosmologists think the universe is headed for oblivion (perhaps, that matter is far from settled) and the time is immense and long, so long as to seem irrelevant. But either way, the fullness of time or the emptiness of entropy, long or short, it raises the matter of finding the meaning of the meantime. On either scale, the time is relatively short, even if only cosmically short, and time is exposed in its structural facticity, be it existential or cosmic facticity. Either way, we need a set of instructions keyed not to eternal truths but to provisional ones, interim truths tuned to what to do in the meantime. For we seem always to live in the meantime, which today means a vast cosmic meantime between the Big Bang and entropic death, which is the time of life itself, terrestrial and for all we know—perhaps—extra-terrestrial life, which does not seem unlikely.

Can we not imagine a parallel set of *hos mē* counsels keyed to a cosmic scale? We should live as if we are but a contingent result of the equations of physics. We should live as if we live not. We should live as if we were no longer here, which means to live with an appreciation of the opportune moment that has been granted to us by the cosmos here and now. We should savor and appreciate the moment. We should live in such a way that what we buy and accumulate should not prove to be a distraction to life itself, which is here today and gone tomorrow. We all have been assigned roles to play but we are not identical with these roles and they should not be allowed to obstruct the larger gift of life itself. We should live without allowing such contingent roles and finite goals to substitute themselves for life itself. Do not lace the garments of contingency too tightly. We should not confuse the call of the event with any mundane vocation, for these vocations belong to the passing form of the world. Every such call is subject to recall, every vocation to revocation. We should, to borrow a phrase from Deleuze, make ourselves worthy of the event that has happened to us,[3] which is, if we feel an irresistible need to have an "ethics," the ethics of the event, an interim or eventive ethics—as opposed to a noisy Gigantomachean ethics.

For Paul, the exceptional moment is the time of a transition from one form of life to a new life, from this world to a new being instituted by the return of Jesus. Therefore, while we have the time, while the opportune moment (*kairos*) is still available to us, let us do good (Gal. 6:10). For us, the exceptional moment is the time of life as a whole, the time while there is still life at all, and the interim ethics, or better still, the interim poetics, it imposes is the poetics of life itself, the insistent call of life itself. So while the opportune moment is still available to us, let us say yes to life, *viens, oui, oui.* Let us strike while the *kairos* is still available. Let us make ourselves worthy of the events that happen to us, which are always events of life. For us, it is the time of life, of the whole of life, that is the *kairos*, the opportune time. The difference between *chronos* and *kairos* is not necessarily a difference in content (*Gehalt*), as the young Heidegger said, not necessarily what we do but *how* we do it, by making ourselves worthy of the events that happen to us. In the cosmic view, it is not a specific time *in* life that is passing away in favor of a coming new time, but the entire time *of* life. Life itself is passing away. It is not only the form of this world (*to skema tou kosmou toutou*) that is passing away, but the form of the world itself, *die Welt*, the world we live in, the world of all life.

LIFE IS WITHOUT WHY

In the view I adopt here, once again invoking Meister Eckhart, the master of letters and of life, life is "without why." The issue of the insistence of the world in our bodies is that life is without why. We live because (*weil*) we live, for the "while" that we live, and that is what calls upon us, what insists itself into our sinews and bones, and issues in Meister Eckhart's famous saying.

> If a man asked life for a thousand years, "*Why* do you live?" if it could answer it would only say, "I live because I live." That is because life lives from its own ground, and gushes forth from its own. Therefore it lives without *Why*, because it lives for itself. And if you asked a genuine man who acted from his own ground, "Why do you act?" if he were to answer properly he would simply say, "I act because I act."[4]

Life is more important than any "why" we inherit or construct for life. The journey of life is more important than its ultimate term, which is "terminal," which is the last thing we want to hear from our doctor. The movement of life itself is more important than the defining finish, the *finis* or *causa finalis*. In short, life is more important than death, even as life is co-constituted by death, so therefore we should live as if we did not live, live without reifying, substantializing, or fetishizing any of the passing forms of life, and without subordinating life to a goal external to life. We should live without allowing any of the beliefs and practices (*croyances*) that are the accidents of birth to block the deeper movement of faith (*foi*) in life, to prevent the event whose salience presses in or insists upon us in this in-between time.

Brassier is trying very hard to become an all-out atheist, an anti-theologian of the disaster, but atheism is a difficult business. For in so doing he has worked himself into a very theological posture and one that is much too Augustinian for my tastes, a *City of God* Augustinian, I hasten to add, not a praying-weeping circumfessional *Confessions* Augustinian, which is the hybrid species that I am trying to cultivate in this poetics and the prototype of my new species of theologians. By this I mean that Brassier shares with Augustine the belief that if a thing does not last forever, it has no true reality, and if it perishes it has no true value. These are first principles of two-worlds theology, the twin bases of classical metaphysics that go back to Plato and achieve their most dramatic formulations in the Christian Neoplatonism of the *City of God* and the apophatic theology of Christian Neoplatonists, who had little time for time and were not quite sure what to do with their bodies beyond disciplining them. Milbank thinks that a trillion, trillion, trillion years from now we will still be here, participating in God's eternal being, singing eternal hymns from on high. By such a standard, the only thing that could seal the bond of being is the God of classical metaphysical theology. Brassier shares this theoretical assumption with John Milbank, for whom anyone who denies the existence of the God of the Augustinian-Thomistic metaphysical brand is a nihilist. Brassier and Milbank are in perfect agreement on this point, and they differ not in drawing the implication of nihilism but only in their assessment of the nihilism thus drawn. They differ in their contrasting desire to bind or unbind nihilism, to bind nihilism with the bond of being or to unbind the nihil from being's bonds.

I think that the truth of nihilism lies neither in binding it (with onto-theology) nor unbinding it (with thermal equilibrium), but in celebrating it as a grace, what I am calling the nihilism of grace. I think the very opposite of Milbank and Brassier: the only things that can be valued or treasured are things that are mortal, finite, transient, and temporal, their very impermanence being the condition under which we hold them dear.[5] Mortality, as I like to say, is vital. We hold things dear by holding them fast, and we hold them fast because we know that we cannot hold on to them forever. Lovers hold each other fast because they know their love will not last forever. Until death do us part. Instead of wanting to live as if we did not die, as in two-worlds theology, I think we should live as if we did not live, as if we have life only for a while. If die we must, we want to die of love, to die in love. The intensity of life is a function of its transiency, which is the issue of "perhaps." Impermanence intensifies existence. The very precariousness of things makes them precious. The precariousness of things, which means that we are all hanging on by a prayer, increases their worth, which is why we are praying. The fact that things have come about by the most extraordinary strings of cosmic luck and singular sequences of cosmic cycling and are vulnerable to the slightest shift in cosmic circumstance does not lessen but only magnifies their preciousness. The impermanence of things gives them a special singularity, a haunting bittersweetness, and casts a patina of mortality over what is held closest to our heart.

Rather than dashing our theopoetics and cosmopoetics to pieces, death is in fact a major player in them, constituting their condition of (im)-possibility. For if something lasted forever, if it endured forever, it would soon enough lose its fragrance, be drained of meaning and emptied of value, and we would be exposed to something worse than a sickness unto death, namely, a sickness unto *undeath*, what Blanchot and Levinas call the impossibility of dying.[6] If mortality is vital, immortality is lethal. The beauty of the songs we sing to love, and love itself, depend upon the fact that the lovers know they will die. Without death we would be incapable of any virtue, from courage to hospitality, for we would have nothing to risk. Without death, there is no risk, and without risk, there is no promise, and without promise there is no life. Where the youthful Nietzsche concludes his sketch of cosmic nihilism by saying "and nothing will have happened," the Zarathustra of the mature Nietzsche responds, "Was that life? Well then, once more!" Eternal recurrence for Nietzsche is the attempt to unite "being" as it was understood in Platonism, namely as permanence, which is a Nietzschean "lie," with becoming as it is understood on the plane of immanence, which elicits the joyful affirmation of Nietzschean *Ja-sagen*, a Franco-German *oui, oui, ja, ja,* a joyful Joycean yes I said yes.

That throws an interesting light on "materialism," and the brief I have been making for something of a religious materialism. I propose that the best working or pragmatic definition of materialism is provided by mortality: the bottom line of "materialism" is measured by the inescapable finality of death. The program that is running in the background whenever the opposing sides line up to debate "religion versus materialism" (which occludes the possibility of a religious materialism and radical theology) inevitably turns out to be some version of personal survival, reincarnation,[7] immortality, or bodily resurrection (what I like to call bodies without flesh), some version of St. Paul's taunt, "O death, where is thy victory"— after which St. Paul died and to the best of our knowledge was never heard from again, not in the flesh. Of course, thanks to the material technology of writing, Paul became one of the West's most famous ghosts, haunting everyone from Peter, to whom he gave a lot of trouble in the flesh, to the present, which he continues to disturb. Death, it seems, got the last word in the debate that Paul had with it in the flesh, but he lived on in the way all writers do, in their words and works (but not, which is what Woody Allen rightly wanted, in his apartment). So the question of materialism comes down to resurrections.[8] Materialism means to live as if we live not; religious supernaturalism means to live as if we die not.

The investors in a certain religion expect eternal returns; they concentrate their entire portfolio in one fund, betting that death pays off in perpetuity, in a truly "perpetual annuity." A materialist, on the other hand, thinks that when you die, you rot, and the best you can hope for is to become a ghost (for which the technology of writing is of inestimable value). I treat every other version of "materialism" as derivative. The objection that each side makes to the position of the other is exactly the same: nihilism, which is we might say the "nuclear option" in disputes like this. The believers in immortality think that the materialists are nihilists because they reduce life to a dying life, a *vita mortalis,* to nothing but a fleeting moment in this vale of tears, that is, to nothing. The materialists, on the other hand, think that religious people hold that the very summit of life is reached only after death, when we are rotting in the grave. While making light of the only life that is real, here on earth, they put all their hopes in a life that does not exist, so that the best thing that could happen to them is death, that is, nothingness. The positions (*croyances*) are perfectly symmetric.

Now the interesting thing is that Brassier agrees with the supernatural-ist view, that death makes a mockery of our lives, reducing them to noth-ing, which is nihil unbound. I follow Meister Eckhart and recommend we suspend these polemics and embrace a cosmo-theopoetic faith in life. The faith whose cause I take up is neither the fideism that rankles Meillassoux, nor the ethical faith that Kant tried to make safe, nor the confessional belief (*croyance*) that the orthodox believe will allow them to lie down in green pastures on the other side (Psalms 23:2), but rather the unsafe faith, the *foi* that animates or rather, I should say, that haunts what, following Derrida, I call a religion without religion.[9] (The "soul" for me is not the *anima* that ani-mates life but the spectral effect of living-on.) This faith, which cannot insu-late or immunize itself against un-faith, is a faith in life that does not know how to keep life safe from death. This is faith in the promise/threat. It fails to be either safe or saving, and in fact maintains our exposure to the worst. It begins and ends in the confession, in the circum-fession, that nothing keeps us safe, that the stars do not know we're here. It does not claim to circum-vent the law of entropy and it makes no pretense of knowing the secret word that wins the prize of an all-expenses-paid trip to the "otherworld" outside space and time in bodies without flesh. It struggles against death but it does not taunt death and ask where its victory is, which is all too clear.

This is the faith that confesses that, given the best of what we know about our universe at the moment, we are all disasters, dis-astered, that this little star of ours we call "the" sun is a figure not of the "One" but one of the innumerably more than one, not the One above the many but one among many, only one of innumerable suns in countless galaxies, in a universe that may be but one of countless universes, perhaps. Solar and stellar death were unthinkable for the Greeks, who defined the gods and the divine in terms of imperishability, who took the soul to be akin to the divine. They took the heavenly bodies to be made of incorruptible mat-ter, and they never imagined a universe without life, a time before or after life. They made the mistake of thinking motion was a defect and identified divinity with the motionlessness of death, of resting in peace in the grave. I love the Greeks as much as the next fellow, but I thoroughly reject the idea that the Greeks did "philosophy" while we, alas, have succumbed to science. The Greeks did philosophy with an obsolete science in their heads while we do philosophy in clearer, colder post-Copernican and even post-Einsteinian times.

Time, like the times, has changed. The astrophysicists have propounded a new history of time. They tell us of the precariousness of our situation, that we are cosmic accidents, that if we went back to the Big Bang and started all over again, we might not get the same results, might not get this solar system or this bluish spaceship Earth, or any of its inhabitants. We friends of the "perhaps" place our faith neither in the becoming essential of the accidental nor the becoming accidental of the essential, but in accidental becoming, in the accidental itself, in what happens, in what is going on in what happens. We are here at the mercy of the elements, thanks be to the Big Bang, which did not mean to do us any favors, which is not asking for thanks, but whose expenditure (explosion) without return has made it all possible (and impossible). Nobody asked anybody for anything. We answer a call we never heard. It's just a pure gift in which what is given is given without good intentions, without any intentions at all, without why. A pure gift, a pure gratuity, a pure grace, a pure chance, pure contingency, or pure serendipity, a pure "perhaps." *Me voici, merci.*

Unlike Brassier I take this very final setting *of* the sun, its going under once and for all, to be at the same time the setting *for* a certain faith, the condition of a chance of grace, of the grace of a chance. I take this impossible thought that the earth and sun, the galaxy and the universe, are hurtling to entropic death to be the condition of (im)possibility of faith. To be sure, we should not forget that this very theory is itself a certain form of faith, motivated by the present evidence, founded on good reasons that are stronger than the alternatives, but recognizing that there is nothing to say that everything will not be transformed by some hypothesis presently unsuspected by the scientists. If prayer is for the precarious, faith functions not in opposition to un-faith but in utter dependence upon it. There would be no reason for faith if we were not so deeply unbelieving, in just the way that there would no reason for hope if things were not so hopeless. But faith and hope in what? In the grace of life, which is never simply life, but life/death, and in resurrection.

RESURRECTION, PERHAPS, POSTMODERN STYLE

When faced with death, resurrection is always the issue. But what is resurrection? How can we who dare to say that mortality is vital, that immortality is lethal, have anything to say of "resurrection?" In a theopoetics of "perhaps," which turns on the reduction to the event, that question takes the form of asking what event stirs within the many resurrection stories, tales of life reborn, and the various versions of reincarnation scattered around philosophy and religion in so many different cultures. What are we to make, for example, of the resuscitation of Lazarus and even of the resurrection of Jesus in the New Testament? Such stories are taken in theopoetics as so many *Vorstellungen,* narratives in which we set forth our desire for life even as life realizes or sets forth its own impulse in us. Remember that for Hegel a *Vorstellung* is not simply a subjective image or fantasy but is always two-sided, always both substance and subject. This we have translated into the chiasm of the event that comes calling and our response. That we said takes place in the middle voice. In a *Vorstellung* there is an event, something that is getting itself promised or recalled or desired in us; something addresses us and we respond. Here the event is life and "resurrection" is the response.

What is resurrection? Resurrection means more life, perhaps. As Cixous says, speaking of Derrida after his "death sentence," the diagnosis of his pancreatic cancer, resurrection means a reprieve, a temporary leave from death, being given more life, perhaps, more time, being reborn when all was lost, where such temporary being, however temporary, even just a week or two, is precisely what is so precious.[10] I will mention here three resurrected bodies, three ways in which the event of life desiring and being desired in us is set forth, an analysis that belongs to what we might call a radical resurrection theology, where theology means theopoetics, following the traces of the insistence of the event.

(1) We start, as is our custom, with Martha, whose mind is always fixed on existence, on the real world, on being worthy of the events that happen to her. Consider the exchange between Martha and Jesus when Jesus arrives in Bethany and the way it tends to work against the intentions of the framer of this story.[11] I do not merely mean that the author has Jesus intentionally wait until Lazarus dies so as to provide Jesus with an occasion for a display of divine power, which makes Jesus's weeping at the scene a bit of divine crocodile tears (aside from being a fine way to treat a friend!). I have in mind rather Martha's complaint that had he been here Lazarus would not have died. When Jesus assures her that all will be well in the end, that her brother will rise again, Martha makes it clear that is not what she means. I know that our brother Lazarus will be raised on the last day, she says, but that is not what I am talking about (John 11: 23–24). That is not what she desires. She seeks the possibility of the impossible here and now, in the world, not in another one. A woman of consummate good

sense, she is talking about existence, time, matter, and the world. What she obviously wants, and what she gets, is to have Lazarus back now, in time, back here in Bethany, back in his mortal body, in the flesh where of course Lazarus will have to die again. Martha asks Jesus for a reprieve, for more time, for more life, for a life that both she and Jesus know very well will not be without death. They all knew that this victory over death is strictly temporary, strictly temporal, just for a while, that it means that Lazarus was going to have to go through this all over again. But that was good enough for them. Like Derrida and Cixous, Martha was asking Jesus for a "leave" of death, an "instant of grace," for a temporary remission of the irremissible mortality of Lazarus, like the remission from Derrida's pancreatic cancer for which Derrida and Cixous were praying. Life, our mortal life, is not finally a sign of anything else, not in the end something we would exchange for something else, *quid pro quo*, this for that, not even here, in the most famous story in the New Testament about the power of God over death. We live in order to live; we live life for life, not for something else. The life of grace is the grace of life.

(2) Deleuze's "A Life" offers still a second version of what might be called a postmodern resurrection story, another way that resurrection is resuscitated in a theology of "perhaps," as opposed to the resurrection of "bodies without flesh" in the high-flying theology, the soft Gnosticism, of strong theology.[12] Deleuze explores still another limit state, not of a remission from a terminal disease, but the chance of waking from a comatose state, where affective life is dimmed down into a neutral almost undetectable flow, an uncanny deathly life, a barely living remnant of life, "bare life," neither human nor animal, male nor female, good nor evil, *vita tantum*. In Dickens's *Our Mutual Friend*, the rogue Mr. Riderhood, having nearly drowned in a boating accident, lies in a coma on the table, surrounded by the doctor and the four townsmen who pulled him out of the river:

> No one has the least regard for the man . . . but the spark of life within him is curiously inseparable from him now, and they have a deep interest in it, probably because it IS life, and they are living and must die.[13]

The scene before us, the man lying there, who is nothing but "a flabby lump of mortality," an all but inanimate bit of mortal flesh at the brink of death, is "solemn":

> If you are gone for good, Rogue, it is very solemn, and if you are coming back, it is hardly less so. Nay in the suspense and mystery of the

latter question, involving that of where you may be now, there is a solemnity even added to that of death, making us who are in attendance alike afraid to look at you and to look off you.

It is neither life alone, which we take for granted, nor death alone, in which we concede that death comes to us all, but precisely the suspension between life and death, the fluctuation between two worlds, that is truly "solemn." That is the solemnity of life/death, the solemnity of the ur-ethical and ur-religious event of life/death, I would say. These men are all fellow mortals, all equally exposed to fire or to stormy winds or, as here befell Riderhood, the rush of river waters. Where is "he" now, the bit of living flesh which while living in the world bears the name "Riderhood?" They are reduced to hushed voices, even to tears, to prayers and tears, when they think they see a spark of life:

> The four rough fellows, seeing, shed tears. Neither Riderhood in this world, nor Riderhood in the other, could draw tears from them; but a striving human soul between the two can do it easily.

When the rogue's daughter, Pleasant Riderhood, enters the room she is surprised to see her most unpleasant and curmudgeonly father the object of so much sympathy and interest, which occasions in her the thought that here, in this solemn scene, lies the possibility of a new man:

> Also some vague idea that the old evil is drowned out of him, and that if he should happily come back to resume his occupation of the empty form that lies upon the bed, his spirit will be altered.

Soon enough he shows signs of winning this fight with death, begins to revive, returned from that "inexplicable journey," and the daughter and four rough fellows rejoice. But then:

> The low, bad unimpressible face is coming up from the depths of the river, or what other depths, to the surface again. As he grows warm, the doctor and the four men cool.

A better man, they all think, would not have had this luck. "The spark of life was deeply interesting while it was in abeyance" but no longer, now that the same surly Mr. Riderhood is back, "the old father, unimproved." Ungrateful to the men who saved him, unaltered, undeconstructed, he "takes his departure out of the ring in which he has had that little turn-up with death." Riderhood squandered a chance for resurrection, for a new life, a new being, a genuine repetition. What the world got instead was a repetition of the same, a lost chance. Fate had unexpectedly given Mr. Riderhood another role of the dice, another chance to reenter the world an altered spirit, reborn, resurrected, like Lazarus. This, unhappily, he failed.

Deleuze describes "a life" as "complete bliss," alluding (with Spinoza in mind) to what in theology is called the "blessed life," *beata vita,* an expression that Agamben makes much of in a valuable commentary, and one that Augustine famously pondered long and hard.[14] For Deleuze the blessed life *is* life, and life itself is the occasion of a solemnity—"because it IS life," Dickens says. The blessed life flows on the plane of immanence; theology and life converge, not in an ominous worldly theological bio-power over life but in an auto-theo-cosmo-poetics of life, of "a life." Riderhood is an unhappy man who refuses to be saved, declining the invitation that the cosmos, in its infinite if unintentional generosity, had extended to him, refusing the invitation to be reborn, to come out of that tomb still wrapped in the burial sheets a new man, a new being, living a new life. He refused grace. Dickens thus has staged for us a new version of the Lazarus story, one in which Lazarus, invited by the Lord to come forth, declines the invitation and insists he would rather stay put in his tomb. Or a new version of the Easter story, where Riderhood's comatose state is like Holy Saturday, hovering between death and life.

The key to what Deleuze himself is after lies in the "a" of "a life," which refers not to "the" life of someone in particular but to pure immanence, to the immanence of life in itself, which is not life in or of anything other than itself. This Deleuze says is a self-sufficient "bliss" (*beatitudo*). In Deleuze's metaphysics, "a" life means a "transcendental" flow of life beneath the level of "empirical" individuality—beyond good and evil because beneath good and evil. As the reference to Husserl in Deleuze's text suggests, this is brought out by a kind of transcendental "reduction," not to a transcendental subject but to an anonymous field of life, to the plane of immanence, of which empirical individuals are passing inflections. Accordingly, the reduction to pure life is effected not by transcendental consciousness but by way of a literary narrative about a boating accident, which isolates a pure life with whom everyone empathizes, regardless of the empirical virtues or vices of the rogue Mr. Riderhood.[15]

I am adapting Deleuze's text to my own theopoetic purposes while being disloyal to his metaphysics, which I always resist as ill-advised. I am using his analysis of beatitude to throw light on what I am calling life "without why," identifying "bliss" (*beaititudo*) with life as its own "because."[16] By "mere life" I am not saying that we should cling to life no matter what, however deprived of quality or in however cravenly a manner. Nor am I gainsaying risking one's life. I am saying that wherever there is life, even mere life, there is hope for more life, for a new being, a new life. Indeed, far from clinging cravenly to my own life, it is in the name of more life that I would be moved to surrender my own life for the life of others. What I mean by mere life is that the chance for more life is still alive, and that the future is always better, not because it is, of course, but because it might be, which is the "might" of life in a weak theology of "perhaps."

The thing that separates this theopoetics from Deleuze is that the suspense of the scene, the suspension of "a life" between life and death, is not the token of a metaphysical vital flow but of the undecidable fluctuation of the "perhaps," of the chance for a new life, of the insistence of life, of the maybe / maybe not of more life. The scene takes place not on a metaphysical plane of immanence but on what we might call the quasi-phenomenological plane of the event, the other order of the insistence of the event. I am not distinguishing a bottomless sea of metaphysical virtuality and transient actualities, as is Deleuze. I am distinguishing insistence and existence, a call and a response, an opening and a chance to reopen life anew. So for me the idea of returning to a plane of immanence or virtualities means a chance for renewal and repetition. "A life" belongs to the plane of "perhaps," to the other order of "perhaps" where the "beatitude" of life lies in the grace of the event, in a chance for life, for more life, perhaps. Deleuze himself is more interested in the transcendental or metaphysical flow of life, a rather infinite deathless flow of pure life, than in the empirical actualities that are born and die. He overindulges the transitoriness of empirical individuals in favor of the transcendental flow, which for me is too close to the comic situation pointed out by Climacus of forgetting that I exist. I, on the other hand, am more interested in the chiasmic intertwining of the call and the response of life. I am more insistent that the insistence of God requires our existence, more insistent that the insistence of life requires our response, and so I am more interested in the way the "existing individuals" exist, in the response they make in existence to insistence, to an insistent call, which also in the end finally pays a call upon them to desist. I do not want this cosmic situation to issue in the comic one warned against by Johannes Climacus, of forgetting that I exist. I want it to issue in the intensification of existence.

(3) Finally, I take up the most famous resurrected body of all, the body of Jesus. As Deleuze's analysis implies, it is clear that the body of Jesus on the cross undergoes a similar reduction to bare life, one where his crucified

body is made equal with the bodies of the good and bad thieves on his either side. Before death, we are all equal. The empirical qualities of the Son of God and the two thieves are neutralized in a scene of bare life hanging on a cross, of bodies barely hanging on to life, a scene of utter solemnity for all three and for all who witness this unhappy scene, as its countless depictions in the history of art bear witness. It is at this point that the scene is set for resurrection in the New Testament, the glorious resurrection of Jesus literally added on to the story later on in Mark in a bit of last-minute editing before the gospel hits the press. This famous supplement became the cornerstone of "Christianity" and its councils, which for me is a glorious *Vorstellung*, by which I mean a *Vorstellung* of the glory of more life. In a theopoetics of the event, the real resurrection is already found on the cross itself, in the story of the forgiveness Jesus extends on the cross to his executioners, with lips barely able to move. There Jesus stands up, ana-static, tall and erect above the economy of violence and retaliation, since according to the protocols of the story, the "Son of God" of this fabulous narrative, or his Father, could easily have commanded his angels come to his physical rescue. Such forgiveness is the way that "Jesus" lives forever, because it instantiates an unforgettable giving, an impossible forgiveness, an event. Then this same chance of resurrection is extended to the two thieves on his either side, where it is seized upon by the good thief. Moved by the innocence of Jesus, he responds to the insistence of the event that takes place in the crucified Jesus, to ask Jesus to negotiate forgiveness for him when Jesus arrives in his kingdom. The good thief resembles a Mr. Riderhood come back to life a new man, while the bad thief goes to his grave unresurrected, unreconstructed, just like Mr. Riderhood, as if Lazarus would refuse to come out of the tomb, all so many figures of the either/or of responding to the insistence of the event.

At the point Deleuze, following Dickens, has isolated—the point of the extreme reduction of life to bare life and the "solemn" moment of the fluctuation between life and death—the scene is set for resurrection, a chance for renewal and repetition, perhaps. What we call in Christian Latin "religion" always has to do with the grace and solemnity of life/death. There is a hope (against hope) that the rogue will come back from that deep river of "perhaps" to the world of transcendencies a new man. Here is resurrection, perhaps, repetition, renewal, at least the chance of it. It is a long shot, a roll of the dice, but there is a chance of a grace, the grace of a chance. Notice where "God" is located in such scenes in a weak theology: not on the plane of transcendence, as a sovereign power, an Über-agent, the most supremely actual of all actualities, who can awaken the comatose or raise the dead from their graves or dash the Roman soldiers against the rocks. Nor is God the pure flow of subsistent life in a metaphysical vitalism, no more than God is either a necessary being (rationalist theology) or a dubious hypothesis (empirical skepticism). God is instead located in the chance for grace, in the insistence of a chance for existence, in the grace of a chance for life, for more life, perhaps. God does indeed play dice, a game of chance with grace.

Faith thus means faith in more life, in life/death, in the grace of the moment, of the hour, of the day, of the life-time, which is not only menaced by the prospect that time is running out but constituted by it, so that the very thing that makes faith in life possible also makes it impossible. This faith is "believing in life," bearing in mind that the English word "belief" comes from love, *lieben*, which shows up in the archaic English *lief*—"I would as lief stay home as travel"—so that belief means what we love to think. To believe is to be-love, to love what we believe, to believe what we love, and what we love is life, more life, and a chance for a new being. I do not mean we do not love non-living things but that we need to be alive to love them. I am not saying "life" is an ultimate, irreducible, metaphysical absolute, a strong category. It is not ultimate; it is just the last one we can come up with in this interim moment, where we cannot see what is coming. If it were a metaphysical absolute, it would be destroyed, having made itself safe from death and destroyed the "perhaps," the might-be of a new being.

But why do we love life? That is like trying to answer the question, "why is there 'truth'?" in Heidegger, where any "why" we would come up with already belongs to the sphere of truth. Truth happens and we find ourselves within it. So, too, life happens and we find ourselves within it, and any why we would come up with would itself be already contained within the sphere of life, would just be more life. We love life because we love the rain on our faces even as we also love sunny days and the difference between sun and rain, but what is that except life itself? We love life because life is life, because we love life, and this tautology, by saying the same, says everything. Loving life is our best theory of everything. We love life not despite but under the very condition of its mortality, of being a transient gift, a lily that lasts but a day, a lily of the field that cares not for itself, that neither sows nor reaps but is adorned with the very glory of God. The beauty of the songs lovers sing is intensified by the fact that the lovers know they will die. The great aporia faced by love is whether surviving the beloved is a blessing or a curse, whether the beloved should be blessed with the longer life or spared the pain of surviving, of having to live through the pain of separation death brings. We believe in life because life is precious beyond belief, and life is made more precious by the realization that life lasts but a moment, not only personally but cosmically, that there are long stretches in the universe devoid of life, long eons before life existed, and there will be even longer eons when life will be no more. That means that to be alive, here and now, is a gift, like a miracle, which is the lived truth of geo-centrism.

I live in order that I live. I live "without why," without an end or telos, "unbound" from the need of an end or telos. Unbound nihilism lies in the unbinding of life from the telos of a something (else) and allowing life to be for nothing (but itself). The result of such unbinding is "religion" in another mode, bound back, according to the old etymology (*re + ligare*), only to life unbound, religion as a binding to the unbound, where life is unbound from anything other than or transcendent to life. Life is not telic because life is cyclical and circles have no end, and it is not teleological because any possible *causa finalis* is finished off by a final terminal blow. Life is and can only be its own "because." Life is lived for itself not for an end. The promise of life is not a distant goal but the immediacy of the moment, of eating and drinking, of making friends and making love, of giving and forgiving, of joy and sorrow. Of course we eat in order to live (*uti*), as Augustine said, but enjoying (*frui*) an evening meal by sharing it with friends or family is a reason to be alive. When we remember Jesus, we remember a common meal. We eat in order to live but we live in order to enjoy a life of commensality. The same thing can be said of sight and sexuality and all the other "means" of life that Augustine condemned if you took them as ends. *Pace* Augustine, I live because I live, I have life in order to have more life, and if I die for others it is in order that they may live, something we see reproduced in self-sacrificial behavior in other animal species as well as in our own. More life does not necessarily mean more for me. I am describing a poetics, not a stock portfolio. Life is "headed" nowhere other than more life, and life seeks nothing more than more life, mine or the others. The flower that flourishes unseen in the desert blossoms for itself, has its own *arête* and ebullient quality. The question of the meaning of life is displaced by the question of its art, where the art of life is to learn to live gracefully, savoring the grace or gift of the day, the gift of time. Behold the lilies of the field.

COSMIC GRACE: BEING-FOR-NOTHING

As Heidegger points out, the formulation of Eckhart's saying by Angelus Silesius is quite precise: we live because (*weil*) we live.[17] The mystical poet does not say that life has *no* "because" but that it is its *own* "because," that it has no "because" outside itself—in some transcendent origin or destination. We are not trying to get through the day for the sake of getting to the *end*, which is what is known as "wishing your life away." We are not in a rush to get to the end of our days, like daily commuters trying to get to the end of the line in order to get home after work. When we come to the end of the line on this trip, we will wish we had not, unless we really have become weary of life, which I think is the cardinal sin, meaning the one that unhinges life and undermines faith. If life is a journey, it is a journey in which we are in no rush to get to the journey's end, in which the journey is its own end. When we get to the end of our days, even the bad days will look good, each of them a grace, and at that point the art of life will be to learn how to die gracefully while not going gentle into that good night, raging gracefully against the fading of the light.[18] The meaning *in* life, not the meaning *of* it, is found at the point that each day is found to be a grace, an event of grace, the grace of the event. The grace of life is not a gift bestowed upon the world by a Superbeing, but is an emergent effect *on* the plane of the world. It is not a gift from outside the world but an inflection *of* the world, the intensity of an event transpiring in the world, which visits upon the world an unforeseen opening. The space of the world is bent and inflected by a religious genius like Jesus, by his words and deeds, by the event that takes place in and through his life and death, which ripples across the world in the memory and the promise of his name. The intensity of this event is the insistence and the persistence with which it insists. Grace is the pulsation of the event on the plane of the world. The grace of life is the very grace of the world, what Heidegger calls the "worlding" of the world, the way the world "worlds" from day to day, which is another very instructive tautology. That is the daily grace—what I have previously called the "quotidianism" of life—that is embedded in the everyday exchanges of life, what Richard Kearney so felicitously calls the "micro-eschatologies" of life.[19] The life of grace is the grace of life, of day-to-day life, of everyday life. The day of grace is the grace of the day, the grace of one more day.

One is reminded of Agamben's amusing gloss on "glorious bodies" in *Nudities*, which culminates in a serious point. Of course, the blessed in heaven cannot actually use their sexual organs, or have a real need of a digestive tract, with all of the heavenly plumbing problems attendant to digestion, unless one follows the suggestion of a French theologian whom Agamben cites that defecation too will be glorified, which is a place I will not go. Agamben seizes upon the solution that Aquinas poses to these conundrums, that these organs will remain as glorious testimony to the several human potencies, something like a general wearing stars on the shoulders of his uniform that testify to his past valorous deeds. The "glory" of the risen body is centered in the "inoperativity" of the then no longer operative organs, which actually is a tip-off to their mortal meaning. When Jesus shares a meal with the disciples without a need for nourishment we catch glimpse of an inoperative function wrested free from the functioning organic and operative body. This glory does not result in a purely useless body but in bodily activities emancipated from their functional ends, in which the *uti* is absorbed into *frui*. Without trying to deny their function, eating, seeing, hearing, and sexual activity are all transformed into glorious bodies, savored for themselves, just the way walking or leaping becomes the glorious bodies of the dancer.[20] In this inoperativity lies their meaning. My idea is to translate this inoperativity from heaven to earth, to take the Thomistic solution as a token of an earthly bliss, giving glory not to the afterlife of bodies without flesh but to more life, here and now, in the flesh.

There isn't anything you would want life "for," nothing that would not simply be more life. There isn't anything for which you would exchange life, which is confirmed not contradicted when someone gives up their life for others, for the *life* of others. When people like Martin Luther King Jr. give their life for their cause, their cause is more life, not for themselves but for others. That in fact is the chain of life, as parents pass on life to children and then pass away. Contrary to Brassier, the atelic structure of life does not mean it is being-nothing, but that it is "being-*for*-nothing," for nothing other than itself. Notice all these crucial prepositional interventions in this grammatology—involving "in" and "of" and "for"—all examples of what Michel Serres calls the angelic deflections of prepositions, saving angels whose genuflections inflect nouns and verbs in saving ways, or almost, since we are never saved without also being lost. In my heretical Hegelianism, I take my stand neither with being in itself nor being for itself nor being in and for itself, but with being-for-nothing. The exposure to nothingness imposed by entropy upon being exposes not a simple nihilism but the nihilism of grace, being-for-nothing, being for nothing other than itself. I propose a kind of joyous and gratuitous nihilism, a celebratory nihilism of grace, where life is lived for nothing other than itself. Life is without why, without purpose, external to itself. Life is for free, not because it is without cost but because it is free from any "for," because it is "for" nothing, for nothing *else*. It is an excess, a gratuity, a graciousness, a grace. This grace of its "being-for-nothing" has to do with the "event."

So the view struck in theopoetics is quite the opposite of classical ortho-dox or supernaturalistic theology. For the saints of theopoetics, life is not only not "justified" or "explained" by the afterlife; it is *refuted* by it. The only possible way to love God is if there is no such thing (existent) and if the stories of such things are stories about life/death. That is all because life is a gift, a grace, not an economy. Life is undermined from the moment it is subjected to the economy of a "why" beyond life. If we assert an "afterlife," a life beyond this life, it would be impossible to avoid turning this life into the coin of the realm in an eternal economy. The body of Jesus becomes a ticket to the great beyond. The kingdom of God is reduced to the rule of spiritual consumerism and capital accumulation. It would be impossible to be generous and gift-giving because everyone would know that generosity has its payoff in long-term returns. Worse still, the lack of generosity will be punished, so that the Good Samaritan better be good—or else he will be made to pay for it! In an economy of salvation we are forced to think the Good Samaritan is just trying to avoid something even worse! But if that is why you come to my aid, I would perhaps rather you not bother.

Literalized, heaven and hell ruin everything. It was in order to escape such traps as this that the saints were driven to say they would prefer hell to heaven if that is what love demanded, and beyond that to say that they would prefer solidarity with the damned to a God who would condemn anyone to such a place as hell.[21] The name of God is meant to be the name of love, and the saints were in love with love, so if ever "God" auto-immu-nized himself against the demands of love, then the saints loved love more than God. As the saints of theopoetics bid adieu to virtue, if virtue is a ticket redeemable for an award in the afterlife,[22] they also bid adieu to God. Once we say "*this* life," *in hoc statu vitae*, once we delimit "life" from some superlife (instead of from death), then we inevitably have something else up our sleeve. We are inevitably thinking of making a trade-in. We are put-ting "this life" on the table, making it a negotiable item and cutting the best deal we can get with the celestial broker, which is what a "covenant" is, be it new or old. That is the end of faith. Life is then conducted on the plane of beliefs treated like coupons with a cash value instead of having a faith in or covenant with the impossible. We have here no lasting city—but the lat-ter is what orthodox theology really wants. Whatever happiness "this life" affords is but a taste of what is coming, which tempts us to tolerate a good deal of misery in "this life."

Back to the secret agreement made between Hegel and the classical theologians: in the end, in the long run, in the *telos* or the *eschaton*, it all turns out well. Even atheists like Sartre and the Marxists had a theological confidence that the hell of Stalinism was just the dialectic of the Revolution writing straight with crooked lines to earn us all an earthly heaven. The only thing more paralyzing than "heaven" is "hell," a pathological fantasy of absolutely sovereign and imperial punishment by the "God of love" who, unlike Jesus on the cross speaking to the good thief, would remain infinitely uncompassionate, unmoved throughout all eternity by the cries of the damned and their infinite suffering. The theologians of "hell"—like the mythical correlationists who do not "believe in reality"—are more in need of therapy than refutation. If on the other hand the theorists of eternal damnation declare hell empty and announce a universal salvation, then in the resulting economy, it really doesn't matter what you do on earth, or how you invest, as you get the same eternal returns, meaning the hypothesis is meaningless for life. Life is demeaned the moment it is made a means, the subject matter of a covenant or contract, instead of recognizing that we already belong to a contract with life that was signed in advance for us by being born and does not require our countersignature.

Once again, in a theopoetics of the event, the idea is not to get rid of *Vorstellungen* like "heaven" and "hell" but to interpret them properly, in terms of events, and return them to the hell we produce on earth for ourselves and even more so for others, and to the heavenly graces of life which is beatitude enough. In a theopoetics, we are always talking about the grace of life, which is exactly why life can be hell. Let us not forget even for a moment—and this goes to the heart of a theology of "perhaps"—it is precisely because life is a grace that life can be a curse, that there is no hell worse than a ruined life. Hell means ruined time, for which there can be no compensation. If life is priceless, there is no possible payment that can compensate for ruined life, whether it has been ruined by the ravages of injustice, or by the ravages that time inflicts on the body, or by a perfectly innocent shift of a chromosome in prenatal life or of the earth's crustal plates, or by natural disasters brought on by climatological conditions, which belong to what Nietzsche called with cruel precision the "innocence of becoming." That is also why it makes sense for individuals to have the right to end their lives if their life has become hell, which means, if their life has fallen beneath an indefinable threshold of dignity. So if I sound like I am saying that our troubles are healed by grace, or if I am repeating the structures of a religious soteriology, I hasten to add that I do so without religion in the garden-variety sense. I locate religion entirely on the plane of the event, extricated from all commercial exchange with divine beings about an after-life, forced to face the fateful fact that the chance of grace comes down to the grace of chance.

To speak of life as a "grace," a "gift," a "miracle" in which we have "faith and hope and love" is to unapologetically adopt a "religious" discourse, but of a more radical sort than is afforded by the old two-worlds theology. Religious discourse is a liminal or a limit-discourse, a discourse that finds itself pushed up against a limit-situation that has run up against the limit of all limits, the limit of life/death, the extreme situation par excellence.[23] Life, or rather life/death, is an "ultimate" category only in this sense, that it is the *ne plus ultra* beyond which we cannot see, from beyond which no one returns, where we have no reliable reports sent back by reporters on the scene. As to whether it is some ultimate *in rerum natura* we have no idea, a point I will revisit in the next chapter. But in the meantime we can safely say that, with life/death, we reach that point where our faculties have been drawn or been driven to the limit, where we gasp for air, seeking to represent the unrepresentable horizon and presupposition of everything we think and posit, desire and do. We are pressed to think the unthinkable, to account for the unaccountable, to assess the value of what is invaluable, to put a price on what is priceless, asking what life is for when there is nothing for which we would exchange life.

We turn to a religious discourse *faute de mieux,* out of desperation, all other categories having collapsed under the pressure of the limit, where religious categories wax poetic, and poetic categories wax religious, where the boundaries between poets and prophets and philosophers, always porous, simply give way, waiting for some discourse to come that will, perhaps, do better. In the meantime only as a poetics is religion possible. Religious discourse arises at that precise point when the legs of sense give way beneath us, when we run up against the limits of sense and non-sense, the point that divides sense from non-sense, when we lack the categories that we need in order to make sense and the categories we come up with represent all the sense we can make. Then we set out in search of a vocabulary of excess, of the limit and the excess of the limit, of words to describe the slash between the limit and what lies beyond the limit. Religion is one of our slash words, one of the most venerable vocabularies of excess (but certainly not the only one), its most ancient office being to supply us with narratives about limit states: life and death, birth and old age, marriage and children, sickness and health, joy and sorrow, love and enmity, poverty and abundance, all the miseries and the glories, all the marks and scars that form along the seams of the human condition, which is also why it has correlates among non-human animals. While these are the categories of the limit they permeate everyday life. They do not carry us off to another world but illuminate the iridescence and luminescence and darkness of this world, of *the* world, of life/death. The categories of radical religion are ultimately categories of grace, of the gift, of the gratuitousness of life, of the "for nothing else," the "for nothing more" of life, and life is this life. Life is only a gift, and a gift is only a gift if it is "without why."

Brassier is a bracing venturer and bold adventurer on the seas of trouble, a limit-thinker and thus far, for all his anti-religion, a religious thinker (almost) who will not stand for religion, not even without religion, atheological and almost a/theological, almost thinking on the slash, but not quite. Brassier leads us up to the limits of nihil unbound, of being degree zero, of being nothing, not only to our personal being-nothing but to terrestrial, solar, and cosmic being-nothing, provided of course that two weeks from now theoretical physics is not revolutionized by a new breakthrough. By describing the cosmic limits of our situation, by sketching the outlines of being-nothing, he is but one short step away from the intuition of being-*for*-nothing, which is what we mean by the grace of life. Life is living-for-nothing, for nothing else than life, about which the proper discourse is both a logos and a poetics, for it presupposes a logos—the "natural" sciences—which provides the "basic schema," which draws the lines of the limits while remaining mute about the chiasmic dynamics of thus enclosed space. Speculative cosmology theorizes a majestic cosmic sweep in which we are but a bit of stardust, a thought which discharges a very considerable cosmopoetic effect. The pre-Copernican distinction between "heaven" and "earth" is dissipated once we realize the Earth *is* a heavenly body, as are our own bodies, the bodies that we ourselves are. We already are a heavenly body, soaring through the heavens on spaceship Earth, which is, perhaps, what lies behind the dreamy *Vorstellung* of "heaven," in the singular.

The new cosmology requires, elicits, or provokes a new cosmopoetics, which has an ear for the voices that call from the limits, and an eye for its non-formalizable features. The very thing that would seem to make life impossible—a gratuitous and temporary episode in a vast and pointless narrative, a short story in a cosmic epic without purpose, a tale told by the idiot of entropy—that is what makes life possible. The very thing that destines life to impermanence and extinction makes life a precious event. The very thing that makes life meaningless gives it meaning. Life is an "accident" all the way down, neither the becoming accidental of the essential nor the becoming essential of the accidental, which renders the category of "accident" obsolete and means that we must abolish the distinction between the accidental and the essential. Life is a totally fortuitous event. If the cosmic dice were rolled again, they might never again have produced life, and certainly not the life which we ourselves have here, at this moment, in this moonlight, with this spider, as Nietzsche's Zarathustra puts it so perfectly. But what seems to Brassier the gratuitousness of a great cosmic stupidity seems to me the stupidity and gratuitousness of a grace, of a gift, a piece of luck, made all the more precious by its episodic, accidental, impermanent, precarious, and mortal destiny, by the never becoming essential of the accidental, by its *destinerrance.*

THE GRACE OF THE WORLD

What is going to come, perhaps, *is not only this or that;*
it is at last the thought of the perhaps, *the* perhaps *itself . . .*
the arrivant could also be the perhaps *itself,*
the unheard of, totally new experience of the perhaps.
—JACQUES DERRIDA

THE PROMISE OF THE WORLD

So we come to stand on the ground of a certain materialism but of
an odd sort, the groundless ground of a certain religious materialism. Like-
wise we stand on the ground of a certain religion, but it too is an odd sort
of religion, a religion without religion,[1] with a weak theology not a strong,
a theology of insistence not existence, of "perhaps" not of an *ens necessa-*
rium. There is grace, grace happens, but it is the grace of the world. There
is salvation, but we are "saved" only for an instant, in the instant, saved
without salvation by a faith that does not keep us safe. This insistence upon
time and mortality is poorly described as a form of radical atheism because
it is a way we have come upon to reconfigure what we mean by God and to
break the grip not only of a strong theology but no less of a violent atheism
and above all of the tiresome wars between the two. There is salvation, but
being saved is a matter of time, of saving time, of a time that saves. There is
faith, but we have reconfigured faith to be a faith in time, in love, in life, a
way of standing up for life, a passion for life, having faith in what Heidegger
called the worlding of the world. There is resurrection, but it is only for
a moment, granting more mortal life not eternal life, for which Martha,
the sister of Lazarus, pressed a tardy Jesus. There is transcendence but it is
the transcendence that happens on "this side" because after all there only
is one side. In the terms of the classical distinction, which I am trying to
redescribe, transcendence happens as the immanence of transcendence in
immanence, on this side, this life, this mortal life.

My entire idea is to reclaim religion as an event of this world, to reclaim religion for the world and the world for religion. I have not annulled the religious character of our life but identified its content and extended its reach, by treating it as a name for the event by which life is nourished. In so doing we have redescribed and marked off religion within the boundaries of the world. Religion emerges in response to the promise of the world, to the promise/threat that threads its way through the goods and evils, the joys and sorrows, the loves and enmities of everyday life and knits them together into an inextricable weave. The promise of the world is not extinguished by evil, not suffocated by suffering and setbacks, not abolished by the cosmic forces, but grows like a root that makes its way through rocks to find a nourishing soil. It is the hope, the chance, the faith that the future is always better, not because it is, but because that is what we hope and that is what hope means.

This religion, which finds a voice in theopoetics, this religion without the diversion of otherworldly religion is a religion of a mundane grace, of the grace of this world. A grace is a gift, and life is a gift of time and death, the grace of an instant, a mortal grace, not an otherworldly one, a grace that finds words in a weak theology of the world. This world does not want for miracles. In the "graced" (*graciée*) world what we take for granted, the givenness of the world, emerges as a gift given, and the otherwise uneventful sequence of settled possibilities is exposed to the possibility of transformation. The world becomes something miraculous, something impossible, the way the world was opened up for Proust by a little cake and a cup of tea. If we assume that with God nothing is impossible, that God is the possibility of the impossible, which is the meaning of the name (of) "God" set by the terms of strong theology, then this theopoetics does not want for God, for gods, who are all around us. Time and death permit the impossible in things to break through, where the impossible is what we hail in a risky world that is no less full of grace. Grace belongs to the poetics of the gift, to its theopoetics, to its cosmo-theopoetics, as its living mortal heart.

In a theopoetics of grace, the name of God emerges from the vocabulary of the gift, where God and death are the givers of all good gifts, where all the lines of force in things are lines of giving. God and death, where death is the blue black night which intensifies the light of life. If we think in terms of "grace" the name of God is not far off. Theopoetics thus comes equipped with a theogony which traces the origins of the gods back to the graciousness of the gift, to the gift of grace—as opposed to the theogony of strong theology, where the god arises from a war with death and chaos, or from the triumph of an immense omnipotence over pure nothingness, and a warrior theology makes a vainglorious boast, "death, where is your victory?" In a theopoetics, the name of God arises as a way to sing the gift-edness of the world. The grace of the world runs softly in the background, drowned out by the routines of everydayness until it is made audible by the occasional silences of the soul—by the soul I mean the body, animal spirits—which has been brought up short, given pause, by the heartbeat of the world, by the suspension between life and death. Was that the holy face of God—or the ghastly ghostly facelessness of death—that slipped through the cracks, greeting us with an uncanny smile? In theopoetics, God and death are companion spectral poets, each serving to intensify to the limit the insistence of the event.

What in strong theology bears the name of "God" is in a theopoetics of "perhaps" the grace of the world, its rhythms and pulsations, its invisible intensities, in a movement that Joyce called quite brilliantly the chaosmic, the chaos/cosmos, the disorderly order, the open-ended order that gives life a chance. The world is graced and fortuitous, according to both physics and theopoetics, which is the basis of speaking of the promise of the world and of a cosmo-theopoetics. In the framework of strong classical theology, God is some sort of sovereign heavenbeing who governs from on high the sublunary things down below and who intimidates the poor things (like Job) if they raise any questions about the fairness of it all. But in what I am calling a theopoetics of the world, the world itself is already miraculous and already full of grace—which has nothing to do with denying its pain, its rift, its nightmare, which also belongs to the chaosmic play of the world, to a play of cosmopoetic chance, to the promise/threat.

To invoke the name of God is not to call upon some otherworldly agent for relief and assistance here down below. It is to be called upon by some-thing embedded within the world, and so also embedded within ourselves, which is the possibility of grace, the hope for grace, the promise of the world. We are surpassed, brought up short by something that comes over us, not from some heavenworld behind the scenes, or by some heavenman whom we will join on the clouds, but from the very spacing and timing of the world, from the invisibility folded within the visible, from the time-lessness deeply inscribed in time, from the super-sensible that fires and charges the sensible and touches the lush corporeality and carnality of our souls. The name of God is entangled with the world, or rather, it is a way to name the world's own auto-entanglement, the jointed and out-of-joint chaosmic points in the world that allow the chance, the play, the promise, the "perhaps" in things to break through, to break in, to break out, which means to come. What is described as arching over or beyond the world in strong theology is redescribed in a theology of "perhaps" as a modality of the world, as a way the world sweeps over us and takes our breath away, makes itself felt in all its intensity, or slips subtly in between the cracks of the world, not existing from on high but insisting from below.

In the chaosmic play of the world, which optimizes chance, promise, and perhaps, the mighty being of the God of classical omnipotence theology becomes the subjunctive might of might-be in a weak theology. The promise of the world is the promise of the "perhaps." The being of the world is its "maybe-ing"; its *être* is its *peut-être*. That promise is the promise of an instant of grace, of the grace of an instant, of the possibilities that simmer in the world, emerging here and there, above all in the possibility of the impossible, which exceeds our dreams and awakens a desire beyond desire:

Do you think we will still be around in ten years, he asks her?[2]
Perhaps. We might.

This "might" commands all the quiet power of the possible. God and death, death and God, are the end of the world, life at the outer limits of the world, the lines of demarcation by which our mortal lives are etched. These ghostly companions accompany us along our mortal paths, inciting in us an impossible desire, a desire for the impossible, filling us with the promise of being saved in a world where nothing can be safe, the promise of a world where everything is under threat, which it turns out is ingredient in the grace of the world.

COSMIC GRACE AND A COSMO-THEOPOETIC JESUS

In the meantime (and it is always the meantime), in the time of life, we should live as if we live not. In the meantime, we should live while and because (*weil*) there is still life. To that end, allow me to offer an example of the real and material religion I am talking about, which I have condensed into the figure of Martha.

In Terrence Malick's fascinating film, *The Tree of Life* (2011), Malick sets the story of the heartrending death of a son against a cosmic background, reframing the ancient problem of the book of Job in the updated context of the Big Bang and the history of evolution on earth. The old tale holds up quite well, at least in terms of posing the problem. The film leaves some of its critics complaining that it also poses the same old solution, the old story of the cosmic majesty of the universe and the mystery of evil resolved by the same old schoolyard bully God trying to shout Job down—"where were you when I laid the foundations of the earth?"—instead of giving Job an honest answer. (Omnipotence has a way of going to your head.) That will not do any more. Nowadays, as science gets further and further back to the beginning, the tables of that question have been turned on God and we are more and more asking, "Where were *you*?" Nonetheless, despite all the Heideggerian "whooshing"[3] of cosmic forces in that film, Malick succeeds in bringing the cosmic shock and awe into contact with the travails of a tiny little family on the surface of a little planet in a remote corner of the universe, thereby setting the family drama on a vast cosmic stage.

Malick's film is a vivid illustration of the lines of force in what I am calling cosmo-theopoetics, in which the great gush of cosmic powers revealed to us by the new cosmologies do not crush our short and sometimes brutal lives here on our little blue planet Earth but accentuate them. The cosmic does not reduce us to a comic absurdity; it does not abolish the personal, or make a mockery of it, or expose the utter senselessness of our short and mortal lives. Socrates had no need to drop his studies of the early physicists in order to turn to ethics—on the contrary! There is no nihilistic clash. Nothing on *Earth*, if I may say so as pointedly as possible, would ever make us say such a thing—other than having overdosed on *The City of God*. So I speak not of a cosmic clash but of a chiasmic intertwining, like the intertwining of sun and eye. Our vision has evolved in tandem with the light of the sun—it is not humiliated by its vastness! The very existence of the eye is a function of its sensitivity (response) to light (insistence), and the particular makeup of our sun fixes the spectrum of the colors we see. The two are not at war with each other but work hand in hand, or rather, see eye to eye. Our bodies are the issue of solar, galactic, and cosmic stuff, the offspring of the elements. We are all stardust, made of ancient particles. The chiasm means that the cosmic stuff gives birth to us and we in turn allow it to come to birth in us (we are both substance and subject, Hegel said), in all of us, the best and the worst, the strongest and the weakest. Terrestrial life does not clash with the cosmic powers but constitutes their realization, their miniaturization, their localization.

I referred above to the recent work of Luce Irigaray in which she undertakes to think of Mary, Jesus, and Buddha in connection with her lifelong meditation upon the four elements.[4] I take Irigaray's work to be another arrow pointing in the direction of my coming species of theologians but no less a reminder of the ancient theopoetics of the so-called nature religions, whose supposedly "primitive" intuitions and institutions were overwhelmed by the "revealed truth" borne by the Christian-European-colonial invaders. The nature-religions were all but killed by this revelation, of which they had no need in the first place. They understood far better than their violent visitors from afar the attunement of the cosmopoetic and the theopoetic, the tandem of sun and eye, air and breath, wind and spirit, sea and life, rock and god. The coupling of the ancient mythic "elements"—earth and water, fire and air—with the "gods" is what makes up the divine. These "religions" honor the spark of life that pulses through our bodies, the wind that makes the limbs bow down, and the spirits coursing through "the animals," our fellow travelers here on earth. They help us see that a theopoetics is but a local cosmopoetics, brought home to us here and now, realized in this moment, on this tiny little planet, in one solar system among millions, in one galaxy among millions, in how many universes we cannot as yet say.

I am not advocating a return to nature religions and an overturning of the biblical traditions of Judaism and Christianity. I am not a party to the war Levinas wants to make between the sacred and the holy. I want to hold the two in creative tension with each other like a Socrates who would not think it necessary to give up physics in order to study ethics. I am advocating, as I have throughout, that we bear in mind the animals of Jesus. "See, I am sending you out like sheep into the midst of wolves; so be as wise as serpents and innocent as doves" (Matt. 10:16). At the beginning of the Gospel of Mark, where Mark is describing the mission of Jesus, he tells us that Jesus was sent out into the desert for forty days on the winds of the Spirit (*pneuma*) where he was fed by the angels (as was Elijah, hence a messianic sign; 1 Kings 17–19) and enjoyed the companionship of the wild animals.[5] The latter is a reference to the peace between the wild animals and human beings that will be enjoyed in the day of the Messiah that the prophets foresaw, when the lamb would lie down with the lion (Isa. 11:1–5). While this peace requires that the lions all become vegetarians, and is questionable on strictly biological grounds, it is an excellent piece of theopoetics, which honors the "companionship" of the species described by Donna Haraway in a time when the "wild" and the "wild animals" have to be protected from us. Jesus is a man of flesh and blood with animal companions and with animal needs, which are ministered to by angels and fully appreciated by Martha. This fantastic divinanimal story stages a magnificent theopoetic or cosmo-theopoetic scene with which I conclude.

To support this point I offer here a final sketch of a cosmic Jesus and a cosmic grace, a little experiment in reading Jesus in cosmo-theopoetic terms. I treat Jesus as a Judeo-pagan prophet and healer, in tune with the animals and the elements, in whose body the elements dance their cosmic dance, supplying as it does a conduit through which the elements flow, and I treat the elements as a cosmic grace which is channeled by the body of Jesus. I say "Judeo-pagan" as a way to give a further twist to James Joyce's play "jewgreek." I say "pagan" strategically, as a way of underlining that there is a powerful thematic of nature and the natural world in the Jewish scriptures of which we tend to lose sight, particularly in the aftermath of Levinas's allergic reaction against the "paganism" of Heidegger. I read the grace that emanated from the body of Jesus—grace you could feel if you could but touch his garment—as cosmic grace which he circulated and dispersed throughout the field of grace he called the "kingdom of God." I do not mean a return to the mytho-cosmic "body of Christ" of the early Christologies, whose ascension into heaven clears the skies of demons so that human souls may ascend to heaven unobstructed.[6] I do not mean the mystical body of Christ favored by Paul or the theological speculations of the early Church fathers, or the celestial body of a heavenly Church found nowhere on earth favored by Milbank. I mean an earthly body and a very earthy Jesus. I do not mean the heavenman of the old two-worlds theology but the earthman of a cosmo-theopoetics.

In order not to confuse the two I call him here, as I have in the past, what he was called in Aramaic when once he walked the dusty roads of Galilee—Yeshua, the earthman; Yeshua, a man of earth![7] "Yeshua" defamiliarizes the power-packed name "Jesus," which carries a massive and unmanageable amount of semantic baggage and strong theology. It aids our return to the earthly memory of a figure mostly lost in the fog of history, who left a lasting mark on those who knew him in the flesh, and whom we try to discern in and through and behind the Christian enhancements and heavenly adornments of a later Christology (*Vorstellung*). The formation of that Christology immediately launched a corresponding heresiology that ended up putting Yeshua on the side of the very powers that be that murdered him. It turned him into a heavenly money changer in the "economy of salvation," and made his body a mystical ticket that buys us passage to another world, rising with him on a cloud at the end of days. That Christology banished his animals and abolished his animality and ours, against the good advice of Martha, and all but annulled the event— but for a trace, the retracing of which is a project of "radical theology."

The "kingdom of God" in the New Testament is an exceptionally ironic "kingdom," a most anarchic monarchy, upside down and turning on topsy-turvy reversals. It is made up of a striking assembly of very unroyal rogues, of very earthy bodies, of bodies woven from the elements, and of bodies unraveling under the press of elemental breakdown. The bodies of epileptics and paralytics, hungry bodies, the bodies of the poor, of lepers, the feverish mother-in-law of Peter, people possessed by demons, a dead girl and the dead Lazarus, the blind and the mute, and of course the bodies of the sinners, of prostitutes, tax collectors, and the two thieves hanging on the cross—such is the makeup of the singular "court" of what the New Testament calls the "kingdom of God." Truth to tell, as a kingdom of bodies with elemental animal needs, it is nothing short of an animal kingdom. At the center of this amazing space, circulating among these bodies, is the body of the king, but a most unroyal king in a most uncourtly court, the body of Yeshua, to which they are all magnetically drawn. They brought all these people to him, Matthew says, "and he cured them." The earthman moves among them dispensing the grace that emanates from him. He moves their hearts with his words, touches them with his fingers, and even with his spittle, curing diseased bodies, straightening bodies twisted by paralysis even as he releases hearts bound up by sin. Twice the earthman heals by spitting, once by spitting into the earth and rubbing the spittle into the eyes of the blind man (John 9:6), and another time, by spitting on his hand and touching the tongue of a man with a speech impediment. He is no less a man of fish and bread and wine. He celebrates with the guests at the wedding feast of Cana and makes sure the wine flows, and feeds the hungry crowds with fish and bread. His critics accuse him of being a libertine who ignores the food laws and who would dine with anyone, however unclean. But Yeshua said it is not what goes into our mouths that matters but what comes out. He came to bring good news to the poor and the hungry and the imprisoned, to bring about a day of jubilee, of forgiveness and release from debt, and eventually the outraged powers that be made him pay for that with his life.

When we remember him, we do so with a meal of bread and wine, the fruits of a delicate complex of earth and sun and rain. His "good news" is sacramental to the core, the good news of a salutary cosmo-sacramental "materialism" of good food, of bodies fed, limbs straightened, the blind made to see, the deaf made to hear, demons expelled, leprous bodies cured. If those to whom he preached and with whom he dealt in daily commerce were "sinners," as his hypocritical critics charged, they were first of all sinned against. They led short, desperate, and destitute lives that have been well compared by Craig Keen to the "slumdogs" portrayed in a very graphic film.[8] The four "elements" circulate through the body of the earthman, in his fiery anger at hypocrisy, in the *pneuma* by which he is filled, in the earth and water of his spittle. The kingdom of God is an animal kingdom, a kingdom of animal needs to which Yeshua's divinanimal ministry responds. The kingdom of God is a field of flesh, of flesh laid low and flesh raised up. The cosmic powers come to birth (*physis*), come alive, in "flesh," in bodies of flesh, and the body of Jesus is the channel through which cosmic graces rush.[9] The graces of the world are concentrated in his body and through him they pass into those he touches or who are touched by him. He is the mediator between this grace and them, and those who come in contact with him are transformed.

This portrait allows me to return to Martha and to the story of the raising of Lazarus one final time. Given such a cosmo-carno-theopoetics of grace, and given Yeshua's preference for Martha's "materialism" to Mary's beautiful but idealist soul, it is fitting that the storyteller in the Fourth Gospel chose Martha to say that she wants her brother back. She wants the impossible, not in eternity, but back here, on earth, in space and time. While it is dubious that there is an authentic tradition behind that story, I can imagine one. Yeshua was the sort of man whose *pneuma* filled any room that he entered. Kierkegaard objects that it is paganism to think of Jesus like that. But paganism is not an objection in theopoetics; it is one of its constituent principles. I imagine that he would have gotten to Bethany as quickly as was humanly possible (*pace* the cynical author of this story, who has him wait two days to be sure Lazarus was good and dead so that he could put on a display of his supernatural powers!). But by the time he got there, Lazarus was dead. So Yeshua did all that he could do, which was to sit up with the sisters through the night, dividing their grief in half with him, talking them through their loss, as the unheeding stars danced overhead. They would sip some wine together, and break a bit of bread their neighbors had given them to see them through this terrible time, occasionally interrupting their weeping with a laugh or two about the endearing quirks of their friend and brother. The stars are unmindful of the sadness down below but Yeshua is not. He had come to mediate between the sisters and the stars, to let the cosmic graces of the earth and sky, the cosmic gifts of bread and wine, of airy laughter and moist tears, pass back and forth between his grieving flesh and theirs. When the morning light flooded their eyes sore from tears, they too would rise, obedient as always to the solicitation of the rising sun. They would somehow have found the strength to begin again, to start their lives over again, now without their brother, whom they could not forget and could not have back, in accordance with the aporia of an impossible mourning.

Yeshua gave them back their lives. He gave them more life. Yeshua fulfills the promise of the world. When people meet him, they are reborn.

Placing ourselves there, overhearing a conversation we can only imagine, we ask ourselves, what is sounding in the resonant voice and soothing words of Yeshua, words that echo through the night and disperse into the dark expanse, off in a distant little corner of the heavens we call planet Earth? Is it God? Is it the world? Is it life? My modest proposal is that we have to do here with the event that insists in the name (of) "God," which I could as well describe as the promise of the world, as the grace of the world. In either case, I am trying to follow the trace of an event, to pick up its tracks, to hear the echoes of a distant call, of an insistence that insists from afar and from of old across cosmic skies. That call reverberates in the rhythms of our flesh, in the shifting tides of mortal life, which is as Dickens says, and there is no improving upon his formulation, a "solemn matter."

LIFE, PERHAPS

As the promise of the world is also a threat, I cannot conclude without a warning.

I am not giving the category of "life" a pass. I am not trying to insulate it from my "perhaps." I am not trying to turn it into a strong metaphysical category, as in metaphysical vitalism, or a *primum ens* or even a *primum inter pares*. I am not saying it is beyond question, that it cannot be surpassed. "Life" is no more safe than "God." Life, like God, is trouble. As my task as a friend of a dangerous "perhaps" is not to find a safe shelter but to make things difficult, to expose our exposure, I conclude with a difficulty, which is always the difficulty of "perhaps." Agamben is mistaken to think that life is the fundamental category of the coming philosophy.[10] It seems to have been the fundamental category of the present philosophy but in the coming philosophy it may very well be the next frontier to fall—perhaps. "Life" might be the last arrow we have in our quiver at the moment as we struggle to come up with an interim poetics, but nothing guarantees that it is "ultimate," last, the final unsurpassable framework. On the contrary, it grows more highly provisional with each passing day. When we say "ultimate" we are usually confessing the limits of our imagination, meaning the last thing we have thought of, or else we simply mean that we are getting weary and running out of other ideas. Ultimate just means we have reached our limits, the outer reaches of our present horizon, the last outpost in our domain.

What we today in the West call in Christian Latin "religion" has always had to do with the "ultimacy" of life. When Brassier says in effect that Nietzsche's philosophy is just more religion, that *Lebensphilosophie* is just religion all over again, another way to re-enchant the world, and when Peter Hallward says that Deleuze's philosophy is just more theophany,[11] my only quarrel with them is that I do not regard that as a criticism of Nietzsche and Deleuze but the reason they are interesting, which means, contributors to an anthology of theopoetics. But we now have good reasons to believe that, on a cosmic scale, life is a local and interim phenomenon, something found here or there and that comes and goes, which means that "religion" is as well. Religion is part of the bloom on the rose that blossoms for the *while* that the rose blossoms, until it does not, until the rose dies. Religion is for the time of the chiasm, for the while, for the while we are here, for the meanwhile of an interim eschatology. The universe does not need us but God, the name (of) "God," does need us. Religion is a form of life meant to address the interim which is life, to provide the interim of life with an interim poetics, with a way to sing a song to the world and life, to celebrate the outbreak of life in the midst of a cosmic play. When we say in Christian Latin "religion" we are looking for a way to nominate the event, the grace of the event, the event of life, of more life. Religion is precisely the vocabulary of excess we have come up with in the face of carnal, mortal, bodily life.

But we never know, in virtue of the very idea of the event, what is insisting, what is persisting, what wants to exist, in the insistence of the event. When we say or pray "come"—and come is not one prayer among many but the very form of prayer—we cannot see what is coming, and we do not know what we are asking for. Be careful what you pray for. That is why we have centered everything on the decentering category of "perhaps," the imperative I dare not call categorical, the call I dare not call an imperative—to remember to always say "perhaps." "Life," like "God," is a way to nominate the insistence of the event, but the weak force of our "perhaps" is to concede that every such nomination is precarious, a nominal and hence provisional state of affairs, a confession that insistence is exposed to desistence. So the question to come, the coming challenge, the question whose measure it is difficult to take, even to imagine, is what happens when the *perhaps* that animates life becomes the *perhaps* that overtakes life, overtakes the carnality, mortality, and corporeal embodiment of life. What happens when these categories, which seem ultimate to us, undergo a transmutation, when these limits, the very limits of what we mean by limit situations, are put under pressure, pressed to the limit, put into question? Any possible "philosophy" of "religion"—in a hauntology, everything would eventually end up in scare quotes—will be put in question and shaken to its roots precisely insofar as life itself is questioned and transformed. What happens when the theopoetics and cosmopoetics of the event, of the limit situation, are forced to expand their horizons beyond the limits of bio-life, beyond any strictly biologically based and therefore biodegradable life, beyond any notion of life that still entertains the illusion that it is absolutely distinct from *techne*? Ironically, such an expansion would resemble the ancient dream of the "afterlife" in the religion of the two-worlds theology, but it would resemble it the way iPhones resemble angels, and it would be realized in a way religion did not see coming—by techno-science. Instead of becoming saints, we became Cylons.

We have argued at some length that it is futile to try to wave this kind of trouble off with Kant's transcendental delimitation of science or by objecting that science does not think. Alas, *pace* Kant, science is not dealing with phenomenal appearances, and *pace* Heidegger, science thinks. Science thinks because it too is liminal thinking, thinking up to and against the limits of space and time. The old saw that philosophy deals with ultimate causes while science deals with proximate ones is, beyond obsolete, simply ridiculous. Science is dealing with ultimates, with what is happening at the extreme limits of space and time, of life and death. Science is not reductionistic but expansionistic, humbling our imagination with the unimaginably large and small, the unthinkably old and distant, which is as ultimate as ultimate gets (remembering that "ultimate" simply means the last thing we have thought of so far). Science is not mechanistic; the vibrating filaments of superstring theory are not exactly atoms-in-a-void. Physics is not a captive of an atomistic-mechanistic-deterministic way of thinking. Physicists think unthinkable thoughts about the bizarre behavior of quanta of energy, alternate universes, and other dimensions. They are not dealing with proximate nuts-and-bolts problems but ultimate mysteries, raising questions about the origin and destiny of the universe and of the deepest makeup of space and time, of life and of the history of living bodies. When I said that even the theory of everything is not everything, I was not saying it is a theory of mere appearances. But I was saying, as everyone from Thomas Kuhn to Ian Hacking and Bruno Latour has shown us, science moves under the impulse of deeply historical forces, the fits and starts of happenstance, intuition, imagination, and leaps of faith, in an effort to stay in play with profoundly playful phenomena. Philosophy can no longer protect itself with old chestnuts like "science deals with problems, philosophy deals with mysteries," "science asks what time is it, philosophy asks what time is," Cardinal Bellarmine's caution that Galileo asks how the heavens go and religion asks how we go to heaven, which is of a kind with Heidegger hidden in his *Hütte* proudly pronouncing that "science does not think." Those are reactionary slogans, sound bites good for church billboards, talking points for the humanities departments faced with a cutback in the liberal arts curriculum, ways that the humanities seek to retrench in the face of the relentless advance and encroachment of science upon the domain of classical philosophy.

The specter of "perhaps" hangs heavily over the heads of philosophy and religion. Contemporary techno-science has begun to close the distance between science and philosophy, between science and religion, between technology and miracles, between heaven and earth, between life and non-life, between life and death. If the task of philosophical thought is to think against the unthinkable boundaries of thought, today that limit is being redefined, reimagined, and reconceived *not* by religion or philosophy but by speculative physics and contemporary bio-technologies. The philosophers and theologians, on the other hand, must beware of simply reacting, retrenching, retreating in order to protect at least some turf they can still call their own and justify tenure and have their own department in the college. Science thinks the very boundaries or limits of our most fundamental categories, of the universe itself, pushing those ancient limits back, questioning to what extent these traditional limits are fixed and immovable, wondering whether and how death itself may be deferred or even in principle eliminated and thereby challenging *everything* that philosophy and religion have hitherto presupposed.[12]

The great phenomenologies of life, of the living body, of lived experience and of the flesh, or the current debate about the distinction between *zoe* and *bios,* will be gradually rendered obsolete directly in proportion to the power we acquire to relieve life of one biological limit after another and, perhaps, in principle, at the furthest limits of our imagination, for better or worse, to detach it altogether from its biological basis, which is the distant dream or nightmare of contemporary robotologists.[13] The great feminist philosophies will be gradually transformed by the advancing technologies of reproduction which will relieve the bodies of the women who so choose of pregnancy and giving birth, not to mention what would happen to feminism if sexual difference and sexual reproduction were, at the outer limits, perhaps, superseded by pushing replication beyond biology altogether. The horizons of natality and of mortality itself are being relentlessly pushed back, subjected more and more to the subversive pressure of "perhaps," even as questions are raised more regularly about the earth as our permanent home, which is what so frightened Heidegger. As relativity theory transformed our notions of space and time and gravity, the bizarre world of quantum theory and string field theory are gradually making the category of matter itself more dubious. The next frontier is life whose borders are more and more being blurred.

Natality, mortality, carnality, terrestriality, materiality—hitherto "ultimates," the outer limits, unquestioned necessary horizons of thinking—
come into question as contingent limits, surpassable horizons, inscribed
within the horizon without horizon of "perhaps." Perhaps, what lies
ahead are bodies without flesh, the eerie undead, the common project of
both robotic technology and classical resurrection theology, of Cylons
and saints. Perhaps, everything we mean by body, life, and being-in-the-
world may be transformed, "in the twinkling of an eye" (1 Cor. 15:52), at a
moment when the boundaries between science and philosophy, science
and religion, technology and theology, life and *techne* simply give out,
which is part of the pressure applied by the word "perhaps" upon traditional disciplinary boundaries, which is the residual substance still clinging to the buzzword "postmodernism." The *tout autre*, the singularity, the
unforeseeable, the impossible—the very stock-in-trade of continental philosophy—threaten to turn continental philosophy inside out by exposing
it to a future it did not see coming, to an event that does it in. I am not
proposing such a future. I am exposing it, pointing out our exposure to it.

GOD, PERHAPS

What then of God, perhaps?

"Perhaps" is older than God. It insists as the immemorial in an ancient
memory of an uninhabitable desert.[14] What exists is inscribed in the primal scene of a desert within the desert, more deserted than any historical
or geographical desert. "Perhaps" is a place more elemental than anything
that takes place within it. Older than everything cosmological, theological, zoological, anthropological, "perhaps" is not chaos or radical evil.
It is a spacing that is neither good nor evil, and this because it provides
the distance between the two, between any two or more than two existents. "Perhaps" is not mere indifference but more radically neutral—*ne
uter*—although it constantly verges on becoming uterine—*ne-uterine*, like
a womb, a primal place in which, from which existents emerge. In a commentary on Angelus Silesius, referring to what he calls "the test of *khora*,"
Derrida asks:

> Is this place created by God? Is it part of the play? Or else is it God
> himself? Or even what precedes, in order to make them possible,
> both God and his Play? It remains to be known . . . if it is "older" than
> the time of creation, than time itself, than narrative, word, etc. . . . if it
> remains impassively foreign, like Khora, to everything that takes its

place and replaces itself and plays within this place, including what is named God.[15]

What—or who—is "perhaps"? It is the very taking place of place, a kind of kin of the *il y a* (Levinas), the *es gibt* (Heidegger), of the *tohu wa-bohu*, a *cousin/cousine* of the *tehom* of Genesis. What exists is always already inscribed in "perhaps," caught up in the insistent condition of an ancient archi-spacing, in an ancient non-originary condition that is as old as time, an archi-space from time out of mind. Existents—the distinct and particular things that make up our world—take place in a medium or milieu or desert place that is older than the world or life, older than nature or history, that is older than time and eternity, much older than Europe or philosophy or science, or Islam and Judaism and Christianity, older than religion.

What does "perhaps" do? "Perhaps" does not *do* anything. It does not pray or weep; it does not desire anything, or give anything. It doesn't give a damn.[16] "Perhaps" does not take place but it is what makes it possible for what exists to take place—or to lose its place. Older and more withdrawn even than the God of the most negative of negative theologies, it does not make these things possible in an active sense, like Elohim, by calling them out of the abyss by the word of its mouth. It is more like the elements that are already there, as old as Elohim, that make up the condition or container to which and in which Elohim speaks, like the receptacle or the receiver of the divine action, like those empty and desolate places that Elohim fills with light and life. "Perhaps" is not a terrible tragic fate, although it has a kind of "necessity," not the upper, eternal necessity of Elohim, but the lower necessity of the inescapable condition that "perhaps" ineluctably imposes on what exists.

"Perhaps" is not somebody who does things but an aboriginal modifier of what exists, coming as it does "before creation." It is an anteriority always already imposed upon what exists, an inoriginate medium or milieu, without truth or falsity, without good or evil. "Perhaps" is a kind of non-originary origin, a groundless ground that is an almost mocking counterpart to its more prestigious paternal partners—the *agathon* or Elohim or the One, the imposing and erect fathers with which "perhaps" is juxtaposed, with which it contends like a lamb among lions. "Perhaps" is a kind of inescapable anarchivable *anarche*, almost forgotten, below the level of truth, below both being and the good, subtending the visible existents up above. "Perhaps" exposes the fundamental contingency of what exists, the risk, the chance, the shakiness, the *ébranler*, the flux, that sees to it that creation, contra Einstein, is indeed a dicey business, a *beau risque*, a poker game played well into the early hours of the morning. "Perhaps" describes a dangerous world, without extinguishing the world's promise. "Perhaps" does not mean we should lose our faith that the world is worth the risk or that we should descend into tragic complaint. On the contrary, it calls for what is coming, strange and unforeseen though it be. I have ended up in my old age in a desert, like a certain an-khora-ite, praying and weeping for the coming of *the* impossible, for the coming of what I cannot see coming.

"Perhaps" is a certain *anarche* that issues not in a street-corner anarchism or violent lawlessness, but in a radical, creative, and even sacred anarchy. Our lives are inscribed within a bottomlessness that no theoretical eye can fathom, in virtue of which we are ever exposed to time and tide and chance. What exists is neither protected from on high nor consigned to evil or violence or to a monstrous abyss that will swallow us whole like a tragic fate. What exists is inscribed within an aleatory element, exposed to an unavoidable chance and contingency which keeps the future open and unfinished. As a spacing, which is necessarily a disjointedness, "perhaps" is a way to confess that what is built up can in principle always be unbuilt, which is why things contain their own auto-deconstructibility. That is not nihilism but the condition of our lives, the condition of being created, and the chance of future creativity. That is the chance for grace.

Nor should such thinking be mistaken as quietism. In the spirit of a certain Martha, the insistence of "perhaps" provides the makings of a politics of "perhaps," of a certain democracy to come, reminding us of the fragility of our institutions and our doctrines, reminding us to proceed with caution, both with a certain faith in what is coming and a salutary skepticism about what is currently passing itself off as good or true. For we are forged from fragile stuff, from earth and wind and water, all with a will of their own, all liable at any moment to leak through our mortal frame or throw us to the wind or expose our feet of clay.

"Perhaps" depicts a loosely joined and fragile condition. It describes the play within the joints that join us, which makes for maximum flexibility and reinventability, even as it exposes us to the worst. "Perhaps" enables the chance of the gift and the gift of chance; it clears the space for the grace of a gift and the gift of a grace. Like a certain spectral spirit, the insistence of "perhaps" hovers over things, pronouncing an ancient but ever-wary benediction, like an Elohim who pronounces things "good" all the while keeping his fingers crossed. Good, perhaps. *Merci, grâce.* Maybe.

Is it God who calls? Is it the world? Is it life? The point is that this is not a query requiring an answer but a call calling for a response. That is the lesson of Martha, who embodies the transition from insistence to existence, doing the truth. Martha utters a double yes. Yes, yes to the earth, to life, to God, to the event that visits her under the name of God, making herself worthy of the event that happens to her under the name of God. We learn from her that the name (of) "God" is the name of a deed, a mundane work of love and hospitality to a divine guest, by tending to the affairs of the quotidian world. But why respond at all? Because our works and days are because they are, because they are what they are, which means that they are not for the sake of a "why" of which they are the coin in trade, life springing from the gratuity of a grace. Martha, Martha, Jesus said, meaning that in her what insists in the name of God is also translated into existence, into a response, where the notion of a "correct belief" that can be cashed in for eternal rewards is a cynical ruse, a thinly veiled threat, more blackmail, the work of long robes, the money changers in the Temple. For Martha, truth means *facere veritatem,* and it is a distortion, worse than an idle distraction, to try to fit the name (of) "God" into some theo-cosmological economy, as if it picks out an Über-being in the sky who dispenses rewards and punishments.

What, then, of God? Perhaps, God, the name of God, the insistence of the event that persists in the name of God, the possibility of the impossible, harbored in and by the name (of) "God," will be transformed. God perhaps, in virtue of everything *tout autre* that stirs within this name, will be reinvented, reconceived, and reimagined, unless perhaps this name is simply dropped in favor of a presently unheard-of successor form, which is another way that the impossible is made possible.

Is it God that insists? Is it life? Is it the world?

Perhaps the coming life will be no "life" at all, none that we today can recognize; the coming God will be no "God" at all, the coming theology no "theology" at all, and the coming "religion" no religion at all, not as we know any of these things. Then we shall require an entirely new vocabulary of excess, one for which we today are unprepared, when art and religion and philosophy, when life itself as we know it will be transformed, perhaps beyond recognition, when the only God and the only religion that still survive will hang by the thread of this "perhaps." Perhaps, what we mean by God, the event that insists in the name of God, is the "perhaps" itself:

What is going to come, *perhaps,* is not only this or that; it is at last the thought of the *perhaps,* the *perhaps* itself . . . the arrivant could also be the *perhaps* itself, the unheard-of, totally new experience of the *perhaps.* Unheard-of, totally new, that very experience which no metaphysician might yet have dared to think.[17]

Perhaps all that will remain of God will be the chance of an unforeseeable future, and the name (of) "God" will have meant clinging to the grace of "perhaps," which will perhaps turn out to have been the very subject matter of theology and of a new species of theologians, unheard-of, totally new.

Who cares? This book is little more than the speculations of a witless old man.

NOTES

---

1. GOD, PERHAPS

1. Jacques Derrida, "Force de loi: Le 'Fondement mystique de l'autorité'" (Paris: Galilée, 1994), 60–61; "Force of Law: 'The Mystical Foundation of Authority,'" trans. Mary Quantaince, in *Acts of Religion,* ed. Gil Anidjar (New York: Routledge, 2002), 257. ("Perhaps—one must always say *perhaps* for . . .")

2. Jacques Derrida, *Politics of Friendship,* trans. George Collins (New York: Verso, 1997), 34, 41, 43.

3. The expression "the fear of one small word" is a riff on the use that Žižek makes of a line from G. K. Chesterton, who is speaking of our fear of "four words: He was made Man." See Slavoj Žižek and John Milbank, *The Monstrosity of Christ: Paradox or Dialectic,* ed. Creston Davis (Cambridge, Mass.: MIT Press, 2009), 25. Chesterton meant the Incarnation, and he really meant it. Žižek says these four words really mean the death of God. I am saying that they are really both too strong-minded, too orthodox, both afraid of just one small word. I will come back to this in chapter 7.

4. "The Rotation of Crops," in *Kierkegaard's Writings,* trans. and ed. Howard Hong and Edna Hong, vol. 3, *Either/Or, Part I* (Princeton, N.J.: Princeton University Press, 1987), 281–300.

5. Jacques Derrida, *Paper Machine,* trans. Rachel Bowlby (Stanford, Calif.: Stanford University Press, 2005), 74.

6. For an excellent introduction to the workings of this other order of the "perhaps," see Rodolphe Gasché, "Perhaps—A Modality," in *Of Minimal Things: Studies on the Notion of Relation* (Stanford, Calif.: Stanford University Press, 1999), 173–91. Gasché explores the logic, or grammatologic, of "perhaps" in connection with its use by Heidegger as a way to stay on the way to the Way, the *Tao,* which for Heidegger means staying *unterwegs,* on the way to the secret reserve of language. See also Colby Dickinson, "The Logic of the 'As If' and the Non-existence of God: An Inquiry into the Nature of Belief in the Work of Jacques Derrida," *Derrida Today* 4, no. 1 (2011): 86–106 (although we should remember the distance Derrida preserves between deconstruction and a "regulative ideal").

7. Derrida, *Politics of Friendship,* 43.

8. Derrida, *Politics of Friendship,* 29.

9. On the thematics of the animal in Derrida, see Jacques Derrida, *The Animal That Therefore I Am,* ed. Marie-Louise Mallet, trans. David Wills (New York:

Fordham University Press, 2008) and *The Beast and the Sovereign,* vol. 1, trans. Geoffrey Bennington (Chicago: University of Chicago Press, 2009) and vol. 2, trans. Geoffrey Bennington (Chicago: University of Chicago Press, 2011). On the assessment by the Jesus Seminar, see *The Five Gospels: The Search for the Authentic Words of Jesus,* trans. and commentary Robert W. Funk, Roy W. Hoover, and the Jesus Seminar (New York: Macmillan, 1993), 169–70.

10. Derrida, *Paper Machine,* 90.

11. In my articulation of the figure of "insistence," I will draw throughout upon the motif of "specter" and "hauntology" found in Jacques Derrida, *Specters of Marx: The State of the Debt, the Work of Mourning, and the New International,* trans. Peggy Kamuf (New York: Routledge, 1994).

12. Derrida, *Paper Machine,* 89–90.

13. See Jacques Derrida, "Faith and Knowledge," no. 21, in *Acts of Religion,* ed. Gil Anidjar (New York: Routledge, 2002), 56.

14. Derrida, *Paper Machine,* 74.

15. Jacques Derrida, *Given Time, I: Counterfeit Money,* trans. Peggy Kamuf (Chicago: University of Chicago Press, 1991), 30.

16. If in logic "impossible" means the logical contradiction of the possible, then *the* impossible is more than impossible. If the possible is merely the logically possible, then "perhaps" is more than possible. See Jacques Derrida, *On the Name,* ed. Thomas Detroit (Stanford, Calif: Stanford University Press, 1995), 43.

17. Jacques Derrida, *Of Grammatology,* corrected ed., trans. Gayatri Spivak (Baltimore: Johns Hopkins University Press, 1997), 18.

18. I will rely upon and elaborate throughout Derrida's distinction between *foi* and *croyance,* found in "Faith and Knowledge," no. 11, p. 47 and in many other later texts.

19. Derrida, *Paper Machine,* 96.

20. Derrida, *On the Name,* 64.

21. Derrida, *Politics of Friendship,* 35, 42–43.

22. John Keats, *The Complete Poetical Works and Letters of John Keats—Cambridge Edition* (repr., Whitefish, Mont.: Kessinger, 2010), 277.

23. Jacques Derrida, *Memoirs d'aveugle: L'autoportrait et autres ruines* (Paris: Éditions de la Réunion des musées nationaux, 1990), 129; *Memoirs of the Blind: The Self-Portrait and Other Ruins,* trans. Pascale-Anne Brault and Michael Naas (Chicago: University of Chicago Press, 1993), 130.

24. Jacques Derrida, "The Force of Law," in *Acts of Religion,* 257 (translation modified).

25. As a matter of terminological usage, Derrida himself prefers the English "perhaps" to "maybe." That is because "perhaps" suggests happenstance and chance, and hence is closer to what he means by the "event," while "maybe" is more closely linked to the being and potentiality of metaphysics. But I have not given up entirely on "maybe" and I especially appreciate the ambiance of "might" (strong) and "might be" (weak, subjunctive). See Jacques Derrida, "Perhaps or Maybe," *Pli: Warwick Journal of Philosophy* 6 (1997): 1–18.

26. This is the question I raise with Richard Kearney about what he calls the "God Who May Be" versus what I am calling "God, perhaps." See John D. Caputo, "God, Perhaps: The Diacritical Hermeneutics of God in the Work of Richard Kearney," in "Philosophical Thresholds: Crossings of Life and World," ed. Cynthia Willett and Leonard Lawlor, SPEP supplement, *Philosophy Today* 55 (2011): 56–65, and Kearney's reply, "Eros, Diacritical Hermeneutics and the 'Maybe,'" also in the SPEP supplement. Some of the present discussion is borrowed from these pages.

27. What is the difference between "perhaps" and khora? Almost nothing. I will come back to the question of "perhaps" and *khora* in ch. 12.

28. See the exchange I have with James Olthuis about the makeup of *khora* in Neal Deroo and Marko Zlomsic, eds., *Cross and Khora: Deconstruction and Christianity in the Work of John D. Caputo* (Eugene, Oreg.: Pickwick, 2010), 174–96; and with Richard Kearney in Mark Dooley, ed., *A Passion for the Impossible: John D. Caputo in Focus* (Albany: SUNY Press, 2003), 107–28.

29. As Derrida points out, the trace of such an idea is already inscribed in the old theology, in the dangerous tradition of Bruno, Cusanus, and Böhme. "They define God as 'perhaps.' God is the perhaps." Jacques Derrida, "Deconstructions: The Impossible," in *French Theory in America*, ed. Slyvère Lotringer and Sande Cohen (New York: Routledge, 2001), 31.

30. The chiasmic intertwining of Cixous and Derrida that constitutes their life-long friendship is described by them as their mutual "insistence," she in him, he in her, his texts in hers, her texts in his. See Hélène Cixous, *Insister of Jacques Derrida*, trans. Peggy Kamuf (Stanford, Calif.: Stanford University Press, 2007), 52.

31. This goes back to Heidegger, *Being and Time,* trans. John Macquarrie and Edward Robinson (New York: Harper & Row, 1962), 319 (§57): the caller refuses to make itself known, to identify itself, and this indefiniteness is not a defect but belongs to its positive constitution.

32. The first time I find him doing so is also one of the best: Jacques Derrida, "Psyche: Invention of the Other," *Psyche: Inventions of the Other,* vol. 1, trans. Peggy Kamuf and Elizabeth Rottenberg (Stanford, Calif.: Stanford University Press, 2007), 1–47.

33. For one thing, as Johannes Climacus says, prayer as the infinite pathos of existence is incommensurate with any outward expression and always has something comic about it. I always think of the paintings of saints with an unctuous look on their face, their eyes cast heavenward, by which I was surrounded while growing up. *Kierkegaard's Writings,* trans. and ed. Howard Hong and Edna Hong, vol. 7.1, *Concluding Unscientific Postscript to* Philosophical Fragments (Princeton, N.J.: Princeton University Press, 1992), 90–91.

34. Remaining loyal to the difficulty of life is the motif of *Radical Hermeneutics: Repetition, Deconstruction and the Hermeneutic Project* (Bloomington: Indiana University Press, 1987). The radical theology of the present book may be thought of as the outcome of this radical hermeneutics, although it is of course

one that I did not see coming. I am always feeling around for a non-foundational sense of "radical," for a radical risk or groundlessness as opposed to a single absolute ground or foundation. I will say a bit more about the difficulty with God in the next chapter.

35. Jacques Derrida, *Dissemination*, trans. Barbara Johnson (Chicago: University of Chicago Press, 1981), 61–173.

2. THE INSISTENCE OF GOD

1. Jacques Lacan, *Le Triomphe de la Religion précédé de Discours aux Catholiques* (Paris: Seuil, 2005), 79–80; cited by Slavoj Žižek in Slavoj Žižek and John Milbank, *The Monstrosity of Christ: Paradox or Dialectic*, ed. Creston Davis (Cambridge, Mass.: MIT Press, 2009), 241.

2. *Kierkegaard's Writings*, trans. and ed. Howard Hong and Edna Hong, vol. 6, *Fear and Trembling* and *Repetition* (Princeton, N.J.: Princeton University Press, 1983), 32.

3. I make use of the good English word "trouble," so much so that this book could be said to be about the trouble with God. I use the English "trouble" while keeping in mind Heidegger's use of *Bekümmerung*, which he used to translate *cura, curare*, in his 1921 lectures on Augustine's *Confessions*. These lectures, along with the 1920–21 lectures on St. Paul, document how a phenomenology of religion anticipates the later fundamental ontology of *Being and Time*. They were part of the first Freiburg lectures on the "hermeneutics of facticity," which deal with the "difficulty" of factical life. Later on, of course, he famously settled on *Sorge*, translated as "concern" or "care." The entire problematic of "difficulty" goes back to Kierkegaard, which was my point of departure in *Radical Hermeneutics* (Bloomington: Indiana University Press, 1987), but as usual Heidegger does not credit Kierkegaard. See Martin Heidegger, *The Phenomenology of Religious Life*, trans. Matthias Fritsch and Jennifer Anna Gosetti-Ferencei (Bloomington: Indiana University Press, 2004), 151–55 (§12).

4. John L. Allen Jr., "Bishops' Staffer on Doctrine Rips Theologians as 'Curse,'" *National Catholic Reporter* (August 19, 2011), 6. My subscription to the NCR is one of the remaining vestiges of my Catholicism, the spectacle of which today reduces me to tears.

5. See Charles Sheldon, *In His Steps: What Would Jesus Do?* (New York: Grosset & Dunlop, n.d.). This book, which we know was published in 1896, was one of the sources of the "social Gospel" movement. Its subtitle ironically fell into the hands of the Christian Right, where today it has become a completely reactionary slogan for an anti-social gospel and an anti-gospel politics, for keeping the taxes on the rich low and for depriving the poor of needed help. This book was the point of departure for my *What Would Jesus Deconstruct? The Good News of Postmodernism for the Church* (Grand Rapids, Mich.: Baker, 2007), an expression of my exasperation with a Church that has made the name of Jesus into a watchword for an attack on the poor.

6. I use the defamiliarizing name "Yeshua," instead of the canonical name "Jesus," in order to point to the figure lost in the fog of history, the event behind what is happening in the New Testament, the imagination of which lies behind my approach to "God," which shows up again and again in the images employed in this text and is worked out more explicitly in part 2 of *The Weakness of God*. I will return to Yeshua in chapter 12, below.

7. For a creative use of trauma in theology, see Shelly Rambo, *Spirit and Trauma: A Theology of Remaining* (Louisville: Westminster John Knox Press, 2010).

8. This is the starting point of my *Against Ethics: Contributions to a Poetics of Obligation with Constant Reference to Deconstruction* (Bloomington: Indiana University Press, 1993).

9. I am clearly borrowing this word, and this structure, from Merleau-Ponty. I will return to the sense it has for Merleau-Ponty in my discussion of "cosmopoetics" in part 3, below.

10. On the role of "come" in opening up the plane of the "event," and as a kind of prayer, see Jacques Derrida, "An Apocalyptic Tone That Has Recently Been Adopted in Philosophy," in *Raising the Tone of Philosophy*, ed. Peter Fenves (Baltimore: Johns Hopkins Press, 1993), 164–65.

11. Angelus Silesius, *Der Cherubinische Wandersmann*, ed. C. Waldemar (Munich: Goldmanns, 1960), bk. 1, no. 8. *Cherubinic Wanderer*, ed. Josef Schmidt and Maria Shrady (London: SPCK, 1986). "Angelus Silesius" is the pen name for Johannes Scheffler (1624–1677), who among other things put Meister Eckhart into verse. Heidegger introduced the philosophers to Angelus Silesius in Martin Heidegger, *The Principle of Reason*, trans. Reginald Lilly (Bloomington: Indiana University Press, 1991), 35ff. For a commentary, see John D. Caputo, *The Mystical Element in Heidegger's Thought* (New York: Fordham University Press, 1986), 124–27.

12. "Omne Datum Optimum," in *The Complete Mystical Works of Meister Eckhart*, trans. and ed. Maurice O'C Walshe (New York: Crossroad, 2009), 227.

13. See my exchange with Gianni Vattimo in *After the Death of God*, ed. Jeffrey Robbins (New York: Columbia University Press, 2007).

14. The documents relating to Eckhart's condemnation along with a perspicacious commentary can be found in *Meister Eckhart: The Essential Sermons, Commentaries, Treatises and Defense*, ed. Edmund Colledge and Bernard McGinn (New York: Paulist Press, 1981).

3. INSISTENCE AND HOSPITALITY

1. Jacques Derrida, "Hostipitality," in *Acts of Religion*, ed. Gil Anidjar (New York: Routledge, 2002), 360–62.

2. See the Greek versus the Christian posing of the "thought project" in *Kierkegaard's Writings*, trans. and ed. Howard Hong and Edna Hong, vol. 7, *Philosophical Fragments; or, A Fragment of Philosophy and Johannes Climacus; or, De*

Omnibus dubitandum est (Princeton, N.J.: Princeton University Press, 1985), 9–22.

3. Hostipitality extends beyond other humans to the other within me, to the "self" which is a question to itself (*quaestio mihi magna factus sum*). Today we understand that it is also demanded by the other than human. "God" and "animals" have a great deal in common, which is also why in the history of religion the one is often figured as the other, and why angels are depicted with the wings of birds. When Jesus goes out in the desert to pray, he is attended by angels and accompanied by the beasts of the field (Mark 1:13), which provide Jesus with hospitality in the desert/*Khora*. Both God and animals are "strangers" that an excessive and inhospitable humanism would like to master and assimilate. Instead of respecting the alterity of animals, "animals" are treated en masse, in a word, the *animot*, Derrida says, which we conclude is obtained by subtraction, "humanity" minus the logos that makes us their master. God, Feuerbach thought, is just us all over again, humanity doubled, projected in idealized alienated form. Nothing strange about either one, humanism thinks. Everywhere humanism sees only the human, Heidegger says, which it always sees coming, Derrida adds, seeing everywhere its own projection. Everything about prayer resists the operation of projection, which shows up in Derrida's "divinanimality," which is a strange construction if ever there were one. See Jacques Derrida, *The Animal that Therefore I Am*, ed. Marie-Louise Mallet, trans. David Wills (New York: Fordham University Press, 2008), 132. I will come back to Jesus and his animals in ch. 12, below.

4. Jacques Derrida, *Given Time, I: Counterfeit Money*, trans. Peggy Kamuf (Chicago: University of Chicago Press, 1991), 6.

5. "One can imagine the objection. Someone might say to you: 'Sometimes it is better for this or that not to arrive. Justice demands that one prevent certain events (certain '*arrivants*') from arriving. The event is not good in itself, and the future is not unconditionally preferable.' Certainly, but one can always show that what one is opposing, when one conditionally prefers that this or that not happen, is something one takes, rightly or wrongly, as blocking the horizon or simply forming the horizon (the word that means *limit*) for the absolute coming of the altogether other, for the future." Jacques Derrida, *Negotiations: Interventions and Interviews: 1971–2001*, trans. Elizabeth Rottenberg (Stanford, Calif.: Stanford University Press, 2002), 105; cf. 94, 182. The event is the singularity of the unprogrammable. To demand that we always open the door, no matter what, is just another rule or program.

6. See the interesting study of Philipp Rosemann, *Omne ens est aliquid: Introduction à la lecture du "système" philosophique de saint Thomas d'Aquin* (Louvain/Paris: Peeters, 1996). Rosemann is a gifted interpreter of the dialogue between the medieval and postmodern.

7. "Therefore let us pray to God that we may be free of God . . ." "Beati Pauperes Spiritu," in *The Complete Mystical Works of Meister Eckhart*, trans. and ed. Maurice O'C Walshe (New York: Crossroad, 2009), 422.

8. Meister Eckhart, *Meister Eckhart: The Essential Sermons, Commentaries, Treatises, and Defense,* trans. Edmund Colledge and Bernard McGinn (New York: Paulist Press, 1981), 200.

9. *Meister Eckhart: The Essential Sermons,* 177.

10. Sharon Betcher, *Spirit and the Politics of Disablement* (Minneapolis: Fortress Press, 2007), 1.

11. Amy Hollywood, *The Soul as Virgin Wife: Mechthild of Magdeburg, Marguerite Porete, and Meister Eckhart* (Notre Dame, Ind.: University of Notre Dame Press, 2001).

12. *Meister Eckhart: Essential Sermons,* 180.

13. Gilles Deleuze, *The Logic of Sense,* ed. Constantin V. Boundas, trans. Mark Lester with Charles Stivale (New York: Columbia University Press, 1969), 149. For an interesting study of the event in Deleuze, see Ole Fogh Kirkeby, "*Eventum tantum:* To Make the World Worthy of What Could Happen to It," *Ephemera* 4, no. 3 (2004): 290–308.

14. The limits of this collaboration between Derrida and Deleuze lie in keeping the sense of the virtual weak enough to allow it to be taken by surprise. The collaboration collapses at that point when the event is nothing more than the actualization of a potency, a part of its program. The crucial point is that the "virtuality" here means a purely open-ended promise but not a programmable predictable process of potentiality passing into actuality.

15. John D. Caputo, *The Weakness of God: A Theology of the Event* (Bloomington: Indiana University Press, 2006), 155–81; and Richard Kearney, "Epiphanies of the Everyday: Toward a Micro-eschatology" in *After God: Richard Kearney and the Religious Turn in Continental Philosophy,* ed. John Panteleimon Manoussakis (New York: Fordham University Press, 2006), 3–20.

16. Jacques Derrida, "Avances," in *Le Tombeau du Dieu Artisan: sur Platon,* by Serge Margel (Paris: Minuit, 1995), 38–39. See also John D. Caputo, "The Promise of the World," *Transfiguration: Nordic Journal of Christianity and the Arts* 10 (2010): 13–33. I will return to the promise of the world in the last chapter.

17. This is a Heideggerian point defended ably in David Wood, "Topologies of Transcendence," in *Transcendence and Beyond,* ed. John D. Caputo and Michael Scanlon (Bloomington: Indiana University Press, 2007), 169–87.

18. Jacques Derrida, *Specters of Marx: The State of the Debt, the Work of Mourning, and the New International,* trans. Peggy Kamuf (New York: Routledge, 1994), 23–25.

19. This saying is included in the OED entry for "adverb."

20. Michel Serres, *Angels: A Modern Myth,* trans. Francis Cowper (Paris: Flammarion, 1995), 129.

21. In Greek, the middle voice signifies a reflexive action that begins and ends in the subject, as when I say in English "I give myself time to deliberate." I am using it in an impersonal sense to say things are getting themselves said and done without an identifiable agency under the name of God, instead of saying that an agent God does things.

22. Jacques Derrida, *H. C. For Life, That Is to Say . . .*, trans. Laurent Melesi and Stefan Herbrechter (Stanford, Calif.: Stanford University Press, 2006), 2–4.

23. "Epoche and Faith: An Interview with Jacques Derrida" (with John D. Caputo, Yvonne Sherwood, and Kevin Hart), in *Derrida and Religion: Other Testaments*, ed. Yvonne Sherwood and Kevin Hart (New York: Routledge, 2005), 28–31.

24. Hélène Cixous, *Le prénom de dieu* (Paris: Edition Bernard Grasset, 1967). See Hélène Cixous, "Promised Belief," in *Feminism, Sexuality, and the Return of Religion*, ed. Linda Alcoff and John D. Caputo (Bloomington: Indiana University Press, 2011), 131.

4. THEOPOETICS AS THE INSISTENCE OF A RADICAL THEOLOGY

1. Martin Heidegger, *The Phenomenology of Religious Life*, trans. Matthias Fritsch and Jennifer Anna Gosetti-Ferencei (Bloomington: Indiana University Press, 2004), 89.

2. That means the radical theologian too can be haunted—by the lost comfort of life in the confessional theologies.

3. Giorgio Agamben, *The Open: Man and Animal*, trans. Kevin Attell (Stanford, Calif.: Stanford University Press, 2004), 17–19; Giorgio Agamben, *Nudities*, trans. David Kishik and Stefan Pedatella (Stanford, Calif.: Stanford University Press, 2011), 91–103; Andrea Nightingale, *Once Out of Nature: Augustine on Time and the Body* (Chicago: University of Chicago Press, 2011).

4. This notion of theopoetics is not "theopoetry," as David Miller contends, because these discursive resources are not deployed as a way to poetically ornament an established confessional faith and prior theological knowledge. On the contrary, it begins by delimiting and displacing the latter; then it produces a discourse cut to fit the events that take place *in* confessional faith and theological knowledge. I make a distinction that parallels Miller's, between a faith (*foi*) in an event that takes its leave of any confessional *croyance* and its *credo*. Miller is right that I put myself at a distance from the theopoetics attributed to Altizer's death of God, but that is not because I reject Altizer's radical theology *tout court* but because his radical theology is up to its ears in Hegelian metaphysics. Altizer's Hegel is orthodox whereas my theopoetics of the event represents a heretical and post-metaphysical Hegelianism. Having said that, I quite agree with Miller that theopoetics displaces the "-ology" in theology, and that a theopoetics evokes events that are without author, events that do not mean but be, that are chaosmic and open-ended. That is very much my argument in *The Weakness of God: A Theology of the Event* (Bloomington: Indiana University Press, 2006). See David L. Miller, "Theopoetry or Theopoetics," *Cross Currents* 60, no. 1 (March, 2010): 6–23.

5. In my *Against Ethics: Contributions to a Poetics of Obligation with Constant Reference to Deconstruction* (Bloomington: Indiana University Press, 1993), the "against" meant standing against the various metaphysical backups of ethics, the meta-ethical theories of the foundations of ethics, where the "ethics" meant rules, and the "poetics" meant sticking to the event of obligation.

6. There are excellent examples in both Christian antiquity and contemporary thought of theological truth as fundamentally a matter of practices, of what Augustine calls *facere veritatem*. See T. Wilson Dickinson, *Specters of Truth: Exercising Philosophy and Theology* (PhD diss., Syracuse University, 2011).

7. *Lectures on the Philosophy of Religion: The Lectures of 1827*, One-Volume Edition, ed. Peter Hodgson (Berkeley: University of California Press, 1988), 190–91.

8. Hans-Georg Gadamer, *Truth and Method*, 2nd rev. ed., trans. Joel Weinsheimer and Donald G. Marshall (New York: Crossroad, 1991), 388.

9. This does not imply that any answer, or any question for that matter, is a good one.

10. Jacques Derrida, "The University without Conditions," in *Without Alibi*, ed. and trans. Peggy Kamuf (Stanford, Calif.: Stanford University Press, 2002), 202–37.

11. My thanks to Prof. Peg Birmingham of DePaul University for the question.

12. *Kierkegaard's Writings*, trans. and ed. Howard Hong and Edna Hong, vol. 22, *The Moment and Late Writings* (Princeton, N.J.: Princeton University Press, 1998), 35.

13. The American Academy of Religion.

14. Gilles Deleuze, *The Logic of Sense*, ed. Constantin V. Boundas, trans. Mark Lester with Charles Stivale (New York: Columbia University Press, 1969), 149.

15. John L. Allen Jr., "Bishops' Staffer on Doctrine Rips Theologians as 'Curse,'" *National Catholic Reporter* (August 19, 2011): 6. Cited above, ch. 2, n. 4. The cases of Elizabeth Johnson and Margaret Farley, not by accident Roman Catholic nuns, are good examples of this phenomenon.

16. Slavoj Žižek, *The Puppet and Dwarf: The Perverse Core of Christianity* (Cambridge, Mass.: MIT Press, 2003), 112–13.

17. Giorgio Agamben, *The Time That Remains: A Commentary on the Letter to the Romans,* trans. Patricia Dailey (Stanford, Calif.: Stanford University Press, 2011), 23–43, 67; Martin Heidegger, *Phenomenology of Religious Life*, 83–89.

18. Heidegger, *The Phenomenology of Religious Life*, 86.

19. Martin Heidegger, *Being and Time*, trans. John Macquarrie and Edward Robinson (New York: Harper & Row, 1962), 224 (§38), cited by Agamben, *The Time that Remains*, 34.

20. I am elaborating and expanding Derrida's distinction between *foi* and *croyance* in "Faith and Knowledge: The Two Sources of Faith and Knowledge at the Limits of Reason Alone," trans. Samuel Weber, in *Religion*, ed. Jacques Derrida and Gianni Vattimo (Stanford, Calif.: Stanford University Press, 1998), 1–78.

21. See Jacques Derrida, *Given Time, I: Counterfeit Money*, trans. Peggy Kamuf (Chicago: University of Chicago Press, 1991), 30.

22. See Jacques Derrida, *Rogues: Two Essays on Reason*, trans. Pascale-Anne Brault and Michael Naas (Stanford, Calif.: Stanford University Press, 2005).

23. Getting straight what Derrida means by *à venir* is crucial. Allow me to refer to my "Temporal Transcendence: The Very Idea of *à venir* in Derrida," in *Transcendence and Beyond*, ed. John D. Caputo and Michael Scanlon (Bloomington: Indiana University Press, 2007), 188–203.

24. I refer to the famous argument in Jacques Derrida, "The Force of Law: 'The Mystical Foundation of Authority,'" trans. Mary Quantaince, in *Acts of Religion,* ed. Gil Anidjar (New York: Routledge, 2002), 242–58.

5. TWO TYPES OF CONTINENTAL PHILOSOPHY OF RELIGION

1. *Kierkegaard's Writings,* trans. and ed. Howard Hong and Edna Hong, vol. 12.1, *Concluding Unscientific Postscript to "Philosophical Fragments,"* (Princeton, N.J.: Princeton University Press, 1992), 184. I have too often in the past been content with criticizing the part of Hegel that I reject. Here I work out the part of Hegel I accept and that I now realize is central to my project and to all radical theological work, a point visited upon us all by T. J. J. Altizer, who is something of the uncle of radical theologians like myself. My thanks to Jeffrey Robbins and Clayton Crockett for forcing me to face up to this question. My Hegelianism has to do with my journey to Syracuse, which turned out better than Plato's.

2. I am saying "two types," not "*the* two types." My newfound Hegelianism does not include becoming an encyclopedist who puts everything in its place. I do not claim everything belongs in one or the other of my two types. I merely claim this is an interesting distinction and invite you to watch out for it.

3. *Lectures on the Philosophy of Religion: The Lectures of 1827,* One-Volume Edition, ed. Peter Hodgson (Berkeley: University of California Press, 1988), 84–85, 92, 402–404. Hereafter "LPR."

4. LPR, 422–25.

5. LPR, 425–26n93.

6. Jacques Derrida, "Avances," in Serge Margel, *Le Tombeau du Dieu Artisan* (Paris: Edition de Minuit, 1995), 38–39.

7. That is the criticism I have always had of Hegel. That I do not retract. I am simply saying now that this is not the whole story when it comes to Hegel.

8. I think this broadly fits together with what Jonathan Z. Smith is arguing in *Imagining Religion: From Babylon to Jonestown* (Chicago: University of Chicago Press, 1982).

9. Heidegger, *The Principle of Reason,* trans. Reginald Lilly (Bloomington: Indiana University Press, 1991), 38–39.

10. See above, ch. 4, n. 4.

11. Friedrich Nietzsche, *Truth and Philosophy,* ed., trans. Daniel Brazeale (Atlantic Highlands, N.J.: Humanities Press, 1979), 84.

12. Jacques Derrida, *Psyche: Inventions of the Other,* trans. Peggy Kamuf and Elizabeth Rottenberg (Stanford, Calif.: Stanford University Press, 2007), 1:23–47.

13. The double sense of *Vorstellung* can be put in the Derridean terms of the trace, where the trace is not a faint copy or imperfect image of a pure and prior presence, but a trace that traces, that is tracing out or producing, constituting, or imaging forth; that is the first sense of *Vorstellung* that Hegel called the subject. But the trace that traces always comes in response to the event that is visited upon us, by which we are moved; that is the second side, which Hegel called the substance.

14. The structure of the "with/out" is the motif of *Religion With/out Religion: The Prayers and Tears of John D. Caputo,* ed. James H. Olthuis (New York: Routledge, 2001).

15. While my poetics has much to learn from Paul Ricoeur and his analysis of narrativity and the necessity to think through what myth gives us to think, the contemporary source of the abridged version of the postmodern philosophy of religion is Paul Ricoeur and the school that formed around him. Its most distinguished contemporary proponent is Merold Westphal in whose debt I stand for a long and productive dialogue on this point and whom I wish to thank for his astute comments on this manuscript. If Westphal were to think my insistent God is thin soup, I would maintain the culinary discourse by speaking of his postmodernism "light." See my "What Is Merold Westphal's Critique of Onto-theology Criticizing?" in *Gazing through a Prism Darkly: Reflections on Merold Westphal's Hermeneutical Epistemology,* ed. B. Keith Putt (New York: Fordham University Press, 2009), 100–15; and "Methodological Postmodernism: On Merold Westphal's *Overcoming Onto-theology,*" *Faith and Philosophy* 22, no. 3 (July 2005): 284–96. The most recent and thorough discussion of this difference is found in my "On Not Settling for an Abridged Edition of Postmodernism: Radical Hermeneutics as Radical Theology," in *Reexamining Deconstruction and Determinate Religion: Toward a Religion with Religion,* ed. J. Aaron Simmons and Stephen Minister (Pittsburgh: Duquesne University Press, 2012), 271–353. This collection spends a lot of time on the dialogue between me and Westphal, in the background of which is the dialogue between Hegel and Kant, Tillich and Barth, and finally between Derrida and Ricoeur.

16. Kierkegaard, *Concluding Unscientific Postscript,* 118.

17. See Quentin Meillassoux, "Excerpts from *L'Inexistence Divine,*" in *Quentin Meillassoux: Philosophy in the Making,* by Graham Harman (Edinburgh: Edinburgh University Press, 2011), 231–32.

18. Paul Tillich, *Theology of Culture,* ed. Robert Kimball (London: Oxford University Press, 1959), 25.

19. Bruno Latour, *Pandora's Hope: Essays on the Reality of Science Studies* (Cambridge, Mass.: Harvard University Press, 1999), 298.

20. John D. Caputo, *The Weakness of God: A Theology of the Event* (Bloomington: Indiana University Press, 2006), 113–24.

21. For example, if St. Francis of Assisi says, "God is good," and Gordon Gekko says, "Greed is good," this should not be interpreted to mean that St. Francis is a man of God (no scare quotes) and Gekko is a man of money (no scare quotes). St. Francis has no more privileged or unmediated access to God (no scare quotes) than the greediest Wall Street stockbroker. The difference is that St. Francis responded to events of love and compassion that cluster under the name (of) "God" against which Gekko took every precaution to protect himself lest it cost him money. It is not God and mammon that divides them, but events and their response to events. We thank God, so to speak (meaning we thank "God") for St. Francis, while we pray for Gekko, asking God (meaning "God") to make him see

the light. The reduction to the insistence of the event also explains why a good many people who believe in "God" behave like Gekko, while a good many people who do not believe in "God" behave more like St. Francis. It is by the fruits of the event, not their names, that you will know them.

22. Francis Thompson, *The Hound of Heaven* (New York: Dodd, Mead and Company, 1922; reprint: Classic Reprint Series, Forgotten Books, 2012). This poem is in the public domain and is available online at multiple sites.

23. John D. Caputo, *More Radical Hermeneutics: On Not Knowing Who We Are* (Bloomington: Indiana University Press, 2000), 249–64.

24. This is a saying of unidentifiable origin circulating around the internet.

25. Jacques Derrida, *Rogues: Two Essays on Reason,* trans. Pascale-Anne Brault and Michael Naas (Stanford, Calif.: Stanford University Press, 2005), 110.

26. See ch. 10, below. Latour, *Pandora's Hope;* Don Ihde, "ANT Meets Postphenomenology," *4/S* (2008), http://www.4sonline.org.

27. See Vic Mansfield, *Tibetan Buddhism and Modern Physics: Toward a Union of Love and Knowledge* (West Conshohocken, Pa.: Templeton Foundation Press, 2008), with an introduction by the Dalai Lama. My thanks to Patty Giles for the reference.

28. Jacques Derrida, "*As If* I were Dead: An Interview with Jacques Derrida," in *Applying: To Derrida,* ed. John Branningan, Ruth Robbins, and Julian Wolfreys (London: Macmillan, 1996): 216. See Steven Shakespeare, "The Persistence of the Trace: Interrogating the Gods of Speculative Realism" (unpublished manuscript).

29. Jacques Derrida, *Of Grammatology,* corrected ed., trans. Gayatri Spivak (Baltimore: Johns Hopkins University Press, 1997), 18.

6. IS THERE AN EVENT IN HEGEL?

1. The links between Hegel and Aristotle have long been recognized. See an old but very good book, G. R. G. Mure, *Introduction to Hegel* (London: Oxford University Press, 1940); and more recently, Alfredo Ferrarin, *Hegel and Aristotle* (Cambridge: Cambridge University Press, 2007).

2. The following paragraph is a gloss upon Jacques Derrida, *Given Time, I: Counterfeit Money,* trans. Peggy Kamuf (Chicago: University of Chicago Press, 1991), 122–23.

3. *Kierkegaard's Writings,* trans. and ed. Howard Hong and Edna Hong, vol. 6, *Fear and Trembling* and *Repetition* (Princeton: Princeton University Press, 1983), 200–201.

4. I am invoking the paradigm of life as irruptive upsurge (*ebullitio*) in Meister Eckhart where life is "without why." We love life because (*weil*) life is life, for the "while" of irruptive life. There is plenty of time for peace, but in the meantime there is the time of life. There is plenty of space for peace, six feet under, but in the meantime there is the span of life. The time of life, the space of a lifetime, is the time of the *peut-être,* which gives the event a chance. On Eckhart's notion of

ebullitio (*exitus, Ausflüssen*), see the sermon "Beati Pauperes spiritu," in *The Complete Mystical Works of Meister Eckhart*, trans. and ed. Maurice O'C Walshe (New York: Crossroad, 2009), 420ff.; and *Meister Eckhart: The Essential Sermons, Commentaries, Treatises, and Defense*, trans. Edmund Colledge and Bernard McGinn (New York: Paulist Press, 1981), 199ff. For a commentary, see John D. Caputo, *The Mystical Element in Heidegger's Thought* (New York: Fordham University Press, 1982), 127–34. I revisit this in part 3.

5. Catherine Malabou, *The Future of Hegel: Plasticity, Temporality, and Dialectic*, trans. Lisabeth During (New York: Routledge, 2005). All page numbers enclosed in parentheses in this chapter are to this work, including Derrida's preface.

6. The seminal figure in process theology is Alfred North Whitehead. Whitehead's work was first developed as a process theology by Charles Hartshorne and continues today in distinguished thinkers like John Cobb, David Ray Griffin, Philip Clayton, Roland Faber, Ingolf Dalferth, and, for me in particular, for anyone interested in the back and forth between process thought and postmodernism, the important work of Catherine Keller. Over the years, the Metaphysical Society of America has entertained an ongoing debate between process theologians and Thomistic philosophical theologians.

7. In my parlance, Malabou is referring to the chiasmic intertwining of the insistence of God and existence.

8. For the relevant texts and a discussion, see John D. Caputo, *The Mystical Element in Heidegger's Thought*, 126–27.

9. G. W. F. Hegel, *Lectures on the Philosophy of Religion: The Lectures of 1827*, One-Volume Edition, ed. Peter C. Hodgson (Oxford: Clarendon Press, 2006), 457. That phrase in particular serves as the touchstone text in the debate between Žižek and Milbank about whether the Christian Incarnation or negative dialectics represents the true materialism, which I will discuss in the next chapter.

10. Martin Heidegger, *Being and Time*, trans. John Macquarrie and Edward Robinson (New York: Harper & Row, 1962), 435 (§74).

11. Martin Heidegger, *The Principle of Reason*, trans. Reginald Lilly (Bloomington: Indiana University Press, 1991), 112–13. I think the history of the spirit in Hegel is assimilated by Malabou to the play of the epochs in Heidegger's *Seinsgeschichte*. Heidegger's *The Principle of Reason* seems to be playing in the background of her reading of Hegel.

12. Here we can see how and why Meillassoux is close to Hegel and Tillich.

13. With Derrida, I hold that "*Différance* is therefore the formation of form." See Jacques Derrida, *Of Grammatology*, corrected ed., trans. Gayatri Spivak (Baltimore: Johns Hopkins University Press, 1997), 63. I would argue that "form" is a constituted effect of *différance* and therefore that the notion of "plasticity" as transformability is a function of *différance*, especially if the series of transformations is non-programmable, since non-programmability presupposes *différance*. All of the arguments Derrida made in *Of Grammatology*, 57–65, against the notion of linguistic form in Hjelmslev and the Copenhagen School can be brought to

bear on "plasticity," not in order to oppose it but to show that it is dependent upon *différance*.

14. There is some doubt about this: in the expression "plastic explosive" it is not that the plastic is the explosive but rather that the explosive has been plasticized. As Pete Mandik says, "I must confess that I find a bit hard to swallow the suggestion that neuroscientific discourse is infected by a poetic association between 'brain plasticity' and 'plastic explosives.' The 'plastic' in 'brain plasticity' doesn't mean 'explosive.' Not even the 'plastic' in 'plastic explosive' means 'explosive.' It's the 'explosive' in 'plastic explosive' that means 'explosive.'" See Mandik's review of Malabou's *What Should We Do with Our Brain?* in *Notre Dame Philosophical Reviews*, 2009.04.27. But if the plastic need not be explosive, an "event" must certainly be capable of being explosive, of being the end of everything. You can hear this in English, when a bomb is described in military parlance as an "in-coming," which literally translates Derrida's *invention*.

15. See the important essay, "The End of Philosophy and the Task of Thinking," Martin Heidegger, *Time and Being*, trans. Joan Stambaugh (New York: Harper & Row, 1972), 60.

16. Jacques Derrida, *Politics of Friendship*, trans. George Collins (New York: Verso, 1997), 29.

17. Jacques Derrida, *Negotiations: Interventions and Interviews: 1971–2001*, trans. Elizabeth Rottenberg (Stanford, Calif.: Stanford University Press, 2002), 182, where Derrida says that in the expression "democracy to come" the "to come" is more important than the "democracy."

18. In *Ontology of the Accident: An Essay on Destructive Plasticity*, trans. Carolyn Shread (London: Polity Press, 2011), Malabou explores a radically negative plasticity—catastrophe, mental breakdown, dementia, trauma—an adieu to life while still being alive, a purely negative possibility inscribed within being and form, producing a new deformed form. This essay is an admirable work of phenomenology, of a certain kind of radical phenomenology, not a discussion of Hegel, Heidegger, or Derrida. Malabou is speaking for herself and it is clear that she is making room for the risk, for what I am calling "perhaps." The only thing one continues to wonder about is whether the word "plasticity" can be stretched that far.

7. GIGANTOMACHEAN ETHICS

1. MC = Slavoj Žižek and John Milbank, edited by Creston Davis, *The Monstrosity of Christ: Paradox or Dialectic* (Cambridge, Mass.: MIT Press, 2009). Some sections of the present chapter have previously appeared in a review of this book in *Notre Dame Philosophical Reviews*, 2009.09.33. See http://ndpr.nd.edu.

2. Slavoj Žižek, *The Puppet and the Dwarf: The Perverse Core of Christianity* (Cambridge, Mass.: MIT Press, 2003), 169–70.

3. Žižek, *The Puppet and the Dwarf*, 171.

4. G. W. F. Hegel, *Lectures on the Philosophy of Religion: The Lectures of 1827*,

One-Volume Edition, ed. Peter C. Hodgson (Oxford: Clarendon Press, 2006), 457.

5. Whatever sallies Žižek directs at postmodernism, his notion that Hegelian "death of God" theology requires a more radically negative *consummatum est* that avoids relapsing into an affirmative humanism was made some quarter of a century ago in Mark C. Taylor's *Erring: An A/theology,* where Taylor argued that "*deconstruction is the 'hermeneutic' of the death of God.*" So if Žižek thinks that he has a friend in Jesus it is not really the Jesus of T. J. J. Altizer but of Taylor's deconstructive a/theology. In Taylor, the deconstruction of the "transcendental signified" dismantles not only the good old transcendent God but any big contenders for the place vacated by the demise of the old God—Subject or Object, History or the Book, Structuralism or Humanism or Science. The death of God in Nietzsche, Taylor, and Derrida is the death of anything that pretends to have the last word, which goes for psychoanalysis, too. Even if Derrida respects psychoanalysis, Derrida keeps a safe distance from the monstrous exaggeration of its importance in Žižek. Taylor's book is a landmark and it cuts off in advance the erection of psychoanalysis (into a new idol, that is). I myself am not convinced that Taylor respected the spectrality of the slash in his a/theology—the upshot of a "death," of God or of anything else, in deconstruction should always be a specter, not a simple extinction. In deconstruction, nothing can be simply dead. The death of God, I am arguing, ought to mean the birth of *peut-être,* which is why I speak instead of the birth of God. Nevertheless, in both deconstruction and psychoanalysis (à la Žižek), "Man" is not the secret of God. The secret is, to paraphrase Derrida, there is no Secret, no big Other who has the Secret. Deconstruction is the deconstruction of the theological "place," the very place of the big Other, therefore of the very taking place of theology as we know it while calling "come" to a new species of theologians, to a new theology insisting in the old one. See Mark Taylor, *Erring: A Postmodern A/Theology* (Chicago: University of Chicago Press, 1885), 6. For a superb statement of the significance of this movement which properly situates my work in relation to it, see Jeffrey Robbins, "Introduction: After the Death of God," in *After the Death of God* (New York: Columbia University Press, 2007), 1–24. On the secret, see Jacques Derrida, *On the Name,* ed. Thomas Dutoit (Stanford, Calif.: Stanford University Press, 1995), 29–30.

6. See Slavoj Žižek, "From Job to Christ: A Paulinian Reading of Chesterton," in *St. Paul among the Philosophers,* ed. John D. Caputo and Linda Martín Alcoff (Bloomington: Indiana University Press, 2009), 56–57; MC, 60, where this paper was reproduced.

7. Gillian Rose, *Dialectic of Nihilism: Post-Structuralism and Nihilism* (Oxford: Wiley-Blackwell, 1991).

8. Žižek put his point in terms of the dialectic of necessity and contingency. If the unity of necessity and contingency is posited in necessity, then the necessity was just lying there waiting to be discovered by us and we regress to a pre-critical idea of truth as something in itself to which consciousness conforms, instead of the idea that our way to truth is part of the truth itself. So it has to be posited

in contingency, where the subjective discovery is the subjective constitution of necessity, and our discovery of eternal truth generates eternal truth. The outcome of a contingent process is the retroactive appearance or constitution of necessity. If a future contingency occurs, it afterward looks like a necessary chain led up to it. After an election is over, it retroactively looks like a trend. So not only is there a "necessity of contingency" (necessity using the contingent) but also a "contingency of necessity," constructing what is discovered, producing what it returns to, which is formed out of contingency and grasped only retroactively (MC, 77–78).

9. In theology, I strike a position between supernaturalism, which annuls human activity, and a pure anthopologism, which makes everything a human doing. See Phil Snider, *Preaching After God: Derrida, Caputo and the Language of Postmodern Homiletics* (Eugene, Oreg.: Cascade Books, 2012), which brings this point to bear upon homiletics.

10. That is the basis of a productive theo-politics, in my view. See my "Beyond Sovereignty: Many Nations Under the Weakness of God," *Soundings: An Interdisciplinary Journal* 89, nos. 1–2 (2006): 21–35. For an excellent exploration of a political theology that also insists upon a theological impulse in politics, see Daniel Miller, *Political Theory After the "Return of Religion": Radical Democracy as Religious Affirmation* (PhD diss., Syracuse University, 2011).

11. John D. Caputo, *The Weakness of God* (Bloomington: Indiana University Press, 2006), 3. The text of Derrida cited here is found in Jacques Derrida, *Negotiations: Interventions and Interviews: 1971–2001*, trans. Elizabeth Rottenberg (Stanford, Calif.: Stanford University Press, 2002), 182.

12. Emmanuel Levinas, *Difficult Freedom: Essays on Judaism*, trans. Sean Hand (Baltimore: Johns Hopkins Press, 1990), xiv.

13. Katharine Moody, "Between Deconstruction and Speculation: John D. Caputo and A/Theological Materialism," forthcoming in *The Future of Continental Philosophy of Religion*, ed. Clayton Crockett, Jeffrey Robbins, and B. Keith Putt. Moody regards Žižek's hasty reading as foreclosing a dialogue with what she calls my "a/theological materialism." Žižek, she argues, is blind to our similar views on subjectivity, freedom, revolutionary decision, the non-all, and the weakening/death of God. She is rightly critical of the meta-narratival privilege both Milbank and Žižek accord to their own narratives. See also Clayton Crockett, "Monstrosity Exhibition," *Expositions: Interdisciplinary Studies in the Humanities* 4, nos. 1–2 (2010): 114–122 for another excellent account of my relationship to Žižek properly thought through.

14. In the third part of the present work I will take up once again the figure of "Yeshua," the concrete, enfleshed, and earthly Jesus, returning to the animals of Jesus, to the (human) animal that Jesus is, and to my guiding figure of Martha. The "Incarnation" is a theologeme in a strong theology about a heavenly being that comes "into (*in-*) flesh (*caro*)" in order to save it, which is the centerpiece of a cosmic metanarrative which provides us with a way to escape the flesh and live on and on in bodies without flesh. O, death, where is thy sting?

15. See Gareth Jones, "Editor's Choice," *Reviews in Religion and Theology* 2 (1997): 6, and Katharine Moody, "Between Deconstruction and Speculation," where she has just cited Jones.

16. See also Joshua Delpech-Ramey, "An Interview with Slavoj Žižek: 'On Divine Self-Limitation and Revolutionary Love,'" *Journal of Philosophy and Scripture* 1, no. 2 (2004): 32–38, http://www.philosophyandscripture.org/Issue1-2/Slavoj_Žižek/slavoj_Žižek.html.

17. It is disappointing that the prodigious erudition of Milbank has culminated in the repetition of arguments every mid-twentieth-century Catholic seminarian was taught to memorize, right down to the demonization of Duns Scotus. Milbank and the authors who swim around him in the "school" of "Radical Orthodoxy" flatter themselves that the entire world may be divided into either medieval Thomistic metaphysicians (themselves)—or nihilists (everyone else). This conceit was standard fare in isolationist Catholic universities in the first half of the twentieth century that railed against modernity and was dislodged, at least for a short time, by the Second Vatican Council and the theology of Yves Congar. The letter and the spirit of Vatican II were crushed by John Paul II, who saw to it that if a cleric so much as used the words *populus Dei* his ecclesiastical career was over and that, if you are a woman, it will never even begin.

18. Slavoj Žižek, *The Parallax View* (Cambridge: MIT Press, 2006), 375–85.

19. See Jacques Derrida, "The University without Condition," in *Without Alibi,* ed. and trans. Peggy Kamuf (Stanford, Calif.: Stanford University Press, 2002), 202–37.

20. Emmanuel Levinas, *Difficult Freedom: Essays on Judaism,* trans. Sean Hand (Baltimore: Johns Hopkins University Press, 1997), xiv.

8. THE INSISTENCE OF THE WORLD

1. Jacques Derrida, *The Animal That Therefore I Am,* ed. Marie-Louise Mallet, trans. David Wills (New York: Fordham University Press, 2008), 3–4. Derrida is playing with the French *je suis,* which can mean both "I am" and "I follow." Derrida's thesis is that there is no simple binarity between human and animal, no simple binarity between the defining characteristics the canonical tradition has invoked to separate the two—like the logos, laughter, dying, ethics, art, etc. Such characteristics run a differential course both within human practices, so that there is no one thing called "human," and between human animals and non-human animals, so that there is no such thing as their simple absence from non-human animals. Human practices cannot be purely human, pure or purely within humanity, as there are all sorts of ways that humans are not human; just so, such practices cannot be purely excluded from animals, as there are interestingly human things about animals. It's not that there are no differences but that the differences are differential, not binary.

2. Jacques Derrida, *"Avances,"* in Serge Margel, *Le Tombeau du Dieu Artisan* (Paris: Edition de Minuit, 1995), 38–39.

3. Derrida, *The Animal That Therefore I Am*, 6.

4. Michel Serres, *Angels: A Modern Myth*, ed. Philippa Hurd, trans. Francis Cowper (Paris: Flammarion, 1995), 50. The translation of the title is very misleading. The French reads: *La Légende des Anges* (Paris: Flammarion, 1993), meaning both "story" and *legendum*, as in a key to reading.

5. Seeking a parable of contemporary information technology, Serres first adopted the Greek god Hermes, and then later on switched to the angel (*angelos*, a messenger), the world's first IT system. Serres's work, a brilliant example of the tandem between the scientific and the theological imagination, provides a hint of a new species of theologian. Information technology is a "repetition" of angelology—smart phones repeat angels—a point where two distant points in linear time can be folded together like the opposing corners of a handkerchief, in which whatever it is we are dreaming of when we dream of angels is increasingly being realized by the new technologies. *La Légende des Anges* contains a number of photos on opposing pages of angels and airplanes in strikingly similar poses. Angels guard us, provide us with guidance, a function now being assumed by the GPS systems. Serres also knows that angels are also avenging angels and he is wary of the politics of angels. They announce peace on earth but a "heavenly host," a "host of angels" is a "hostile" force, an army that knows how to visit violence on the "enemies of God." The angel thus embodies instant movement through space; instant messaging; a guidance system; the problem of evil. Finally, by reason of their ethereal immaterial makeup, angels foreshadow a body neither earthly nor heavenly but virtual or electronic, which makes the very idea of "matter" look a little old-fashioned, which is Haraway's third "border breakdown." See John D. Caputo, "On the Wings of Angels: Post-humanism and Info-technotheology," in *The Twenty-Sixth Annual Symposium of The Simon Silverman Phenomenology Center*, ed. Jeffrey McCurry (Pittsburgh: Simon Silverman Phenomenology Center, Duquesne University, 2011), 8–28. For an alternate take on angels as the first bureaucrats, see Giorgio Agamben, *The Kingdom and the Glory: For a Theological Genealogy of Economy and Government* (Meridian: Crossing Aesthetics, 2011), 144–64 (§6, "Angelology and Bureaucracy").

6. Michael Naas, *Miracle and Machine: Jacques Derrida and the Two Sources of Religion, Science and the Media* (New York: Fordham University Press, 2012).

7. Donna Haraway, "A Manifesto for Cyborgs," in *The Haraway Reader* (New York: Routledge, 2004), 8, 10–13. This well-known essay is very much in the animal spirit(s) of the new cosmopoetics I am describing, especially since the "cyborg" introduces the ominous element of the machine that threatens the "living body."

8. Derrida, *The Animal That Therefore I Am*, 3–11.

9. See Luce Irigaray, "Belief Itself" and "Divine Women," in *Sexes and Genealogies*, trans. Gilliam C. Gill (New York: Columbia University Press, 1993), 23–72.

10. For a charming bit on the difference between "heaven," in the singular, and "the heavens," in the plural, see Jean-Luc Nancy, "In Heaven and on Earth," in *Noli me tangere*, trans. Sarah Cliff, Pascale-Anne Brault, and Michael Naas (New York: Fordham University Press, 2008), 69–99.

11. Maurice Merleau-Ponty, *The Visible and the Invisible*, trans. Alphonso Lingis (Evanston, Ill.: Northwestern University Press, 1969).

12. While still a student, the young Heidegger had an early interest in mathematics and the foundations of logic, and a special interest in differentiating the concepts of time in physics and in the study of history. But unfortunately this went nowhere after *Being and Time*, as he became instead increasingly wary of and antagonistic toward science and especially technology as his work evolved. See John D. Caputo, "Heidegger's Philosophy of Science: The Two Essences of Science," in *Heidegger on Science*, ed. Trish Glazebrook (Albany: SUNY Press, 2012), 261–80. Merleau-Ponty on the other hand was steeped in the emerging science of empirical psychology, but even he never got around to investigating the new world that was being explored in physics.

13. Heidegger cites this line by Johann Peter Hebel: "We are plants, which—whether we like to admit it to ourselves or not—must with our roots rise out of the earth in order to bloom in the ether and to bear fruit." Martin Heidegger, *Discourse on Thinking*, trans. John Anderson and E. Hans Freund (New York: Harper & Row, 1966), 16.

14. In addition to the "natural contract" we should negotiate with the Earth in order to avoid environmental destruction, there is a natural contract that we need not and could not negotiate since it is the very one we ourselves *are*. See Michel Serres, *The Natural Contract*, trans. Elizabeth MacArthur and William Paulson (Ann Arbor: University of Michigan Press, 1995).

15. There is even, I would say, a "natural religion," not in the usual sense of the religions of nature, where humans worship natural forces but in the sense of a non-human practice of religion. "Human religion" has its counterpart in an "animal religion," as Donovan Schaefer says, and is found among other species, like the well-known studies of elephants attending to their dead and chimpanzees struck with wonder at a waterfall, wonder having been also very wisely identified as where "philosophy" begins. See Donovan Schaefer, *Animal Religion: Evolution, Affect, and Radical Embodiment* (PhD diss., Syracuse University, 2011).

9. AS IF I WERE DEAD

1. Jacques Derrida, *Rogues: Two Essays on Reason*, trans. Pascale-Anne Brault and Michael Naas (Stanford, Calif.: Stanford University Press, 2005), 110.

2. Martin Heidegger, *Being and Time*, trans. John Macquarrie and Edward Robinson (New York: Harper & Row, 1962), 271 (§44c).

3. I first made a series of arguments like this about science in *Radical Hermeneutics: Repetition, Deconstruction, and the Hermeneutic Project* (Bloomington: Indiana University Press, 1987), ch. 8, where I referred to science as the "hard case." See Robert Crease, "The Hard Case: Science and Hermeneutics," in *The Very Idea of Radical Hermeneutics*, ed. Roy Martinez (Atlantic Highlands, N.J.: Humanities Press, 1997), 96–105. I also think there are resources in Heidegger's *Being and Time* for approaching science sensibly. See John D. Caputo, "Heidegger's Philosophy of

Science: The Two Essences of Science," in *Heidegger on Science,* ed. Trish Glaze-brook (Albany: SUNY Press, 2012), 261–80.

4. John D. Caputo, "For the Love of the Things Themselves: Derrida's Phe-nomenology of the Hyper-Real," *Journal of Cultural and Religious Theory* 1, no. 3 (July 2000), http://www.jcrt.org/archives/01.3/caputo.shtml.

5. *Kierkegaard's Writings,* trans. and ed. Howard Hong and Edna Hong, vol. 6, *Fear and Trembling and Repetition* (Princeton, N.J.: Princeton University Press, 1983), 200–201.

6. There is a valuable tradition of continental philosophy of science going back to Alexandre Koyré, Gaston Bachelard, and Georges Canguilhem and leading up to Michel Serres and Bruno Latour, which demonstrates the historical side of sci-entific theory making and theory change. Unfortunately, this tradition has always been a minor chord among continentalists. See Gary Gutting, ed., *Continental Philosophy of Science,* Blackwell Readings in Continental Philosophy (Oxford: Wiley-Blackwell, 2005).

7. See Terry Grossman and Ray Kurzweil, *Fantastic Voyage: Live Long Enough to Live Forever* (Easton, Pa.: Rodale Press, 2004); and Ray Kurzweil, *The Singular-ity Is Near: When Humans Transcend Biology* (Baltimore: Penguin Books, 2005).

8. AF = Quentin Meillassoux, *After Finitude: An Essay on the Necessity of Con-tingency,* trans. Ray Brassier (London: Continuum, 2008).

9. Graham Harman, *Quentin Meillassoux: Philosophy in the Making* (Edin-burgh: Edinburgh University Press, 2011), 168–69.

10. As I will argue in the next chapter, I think what Meillassoux says about "cor-relation" is misbegotten and the weakest part of his argument, and since every-thing follows from this misconception, the argument is the fruit of a poisoned tree. Nonetheless, the overall position he strikes is interesting. The position is so anti-Kantian as to be peculiarly Hegelian: to limit faith in order to give philoso-phy unlimited authority over God and hence to rationalize revelation, not unlike Spinoza or Hegel. Philosophy denies both the transcendent God of theism and the God-less immanence of atheism, and in its place it produces a new God of its own construction, a coming but "inexistent" God who someday may show up. That means philosophy cannot be reduced to experimental science, for the latter is restricted by its methodological limits (finitude) and so plays into the hands of religious faith and insures the persistence of the God of the gaps. But neither can it be metaphysical in the old sense, which turns on the ontological proof of the existence of a necessary being, to which Meillasoux opposes the postmodernists, who say that everything is contingent. Metaphysicians and postmodernists alike share a common assumption that there is a clear distinction between necessity of the One (God) and the contingency of the many. In saying this, Meillassoux has in mind throughout the more "voluntarist" or "divine will" versions of meta-physical theology, according to which God is absolutely necessary, transcendent, and inscrutably free to alter the laws of nature and morality "at will." That is not the only or even the dominant opinion of theologians; it is rejected by Aquinas

and the "intellectualist" traditions. But Meillassoux has a philosophical point to make; he is not actually reading the history of theology. The third, or "speculative," position is to assert the necessity of contingency, the necessity *that* everything is contingent, which Meillassoux calls the principle of the "factial" (*le factual*). The contingency of the world leads not to a transcendent necessary ground in which we can only have faith (God), as in religion, but to the perfectly intelligible necessity that contingency itself is necessary. It cannot be that the contingency of things is itself contingent.

This is argued for by an odd sort of tables-turning method, which takes its point of departure from the critique of correlation: the "strong correlationists" maintain that reality could always be otherwise than the way we have constructed it in language or consciousness, to which knowledge is limited. But that position cannot stay put in the skeptical relativism it wants to be; it is an intuition of the necessity of contingency, that it is inescapably necessary that things could always be otherwise, and thereby gains access to the speculative insight into the non-necessity inscribed in things. So the unknowability of the transcendent God is converted from a minus into a plus. The minus: every argument for a necessary being falls into infinite regress, explaining one contingent thing by another. The plus: this is not a failure to reach a necessary being but a direct insight into the non-necessity of any one being. The necessity of the contingency of every being eliminates the possibility of fideism and the need for faith. Being unable to come up with a sufficient reason is not an inability but an insight into the impossibility that any particular being could be necessary. What's ultimately wrong with the idea of "God" for Meillassoux is that when we get to God, we are forbidden to ask where God came from. That, I would add, bears a strong resemblance to Tillich complaining that to treat God as an existent being, a first entity, makes God finite (contingent) because particular beings come and go whereas God is the infinite (necessary) matrix of all such comings and goings. Faced with the God of theism, Tillich says, the only appropriate response is atheism. Meillassoux also supports this with an amazing reading of Hume: the inability to see the necessary relationship between the antecedent and the consequent is actually an intellectual insight into the real lack of causal necessity, thereby switching the "non-reason" from us (skepticism) to the things themselves (realism).

Meillassoux is not saying that the natural world is chaotic but that it is subject to a non-observable (speculative) contingency. There are laws and regularities and even causal connections in nature, but they are all contingent. Gravity is a law, but it is not necessary. It is thinkable that tomorrow there will be no gravity. Chaos is disorder, but radical contingency is a "hyperchaos," meaning that disorder may be—"perhaps," not as a realistic "possibility" but as a "virtuality" or absolute possibility—destroyed by order just as easily as order may be destroyed by disorder. The (divine will) theologians maintain order by importing the will of a transcendent unknowable God to regulate the chaos, whereas Meillassoux says contingency is necessity enough and it does not need a necessary being somewhere in the sky to maintain order. The principle of "insufficient reason" is that there is no necessary and sufficient reason for any particular thing but we do know the necessity of contingency. The principle of the factual also implies the principle of non-contradiction, for if a thing were both itself and its contradiction it would already be any "other" that it could become; it would then be an unchanging, unchangeable, and necessary being. But no being is contingent.

None of this means that Meillassoux is done with God. Far from it—he is the most theological of the speculative realists and the most Hegelian. It only means that after dispensing with the God of the ontological argument, God as an *ens necessarium*, it would remain possible that God might someday happen to come about, even if God happens not to exist now. God's current inexistence does not exclude a possible future existence. Indeed it is absolutely necessary that God (like everything else currently inexistent) might possibly exist later on. Why Meillassoux would ever be led to say such a thing—as I said, he is nothing if not bold—brings us to his idea of justice and to the age-old problem of evil. Justice demands we supersede both classical theism (because it affirms a God who permits the worst injustices) and classical atheism (because it allows the injustice done to the dead to go unrepaired). That demand is met by positing the hope for the possible emergence in the future of a God who will raise the dead and reward them for their hitherto unrequited suffering by way of a Christ-like figure called the "Child of Man" (more shades of Hegel's Christianity). This yields a God, religion, and resurrection in which we may hope and believe strictly within the limits of reason alone, that is, of the principle of necessary contingency of everything, God included.

I am oddly sympathetic with Meillassoux's extremely eccentric views, but I think what he is getting at is much more sensibly presented in Derrida, in whom we find notions of the "perhaps" (contingency), a coming God which is not conflated with a future actuality, a spectrality, hope and justice, and a critique of the insufficiency of the principle of sufficient reason which, if I may say so, are a good deal more reasonable. I recommend Christopher Watkin, *Difficult Atheism: Post-Theological Thinking in Alain Badiou, Jean-Luc Nancy, and Quentin Meillassoux* (Edinburgh: Edinburgh University Press, 2011) for a superb discussion of Meillassoux. This note is in part excerpted from my review of Watkin in *Notre Dame Philosophical Reviews*, June 10, 2012, http://ndpr.nd.edu/news/31269-difficult-atheism-post-theological-thinking-in-alain-badiou-jean-luc-nancy-and-quentin-meillassoux.

11. The coming God means a call not a future actuality. The dead "call" to us for justice but that call has to do with changing the present and the future; the injustice done to them cannot be undone, and where is it guaranteed that everyone will receive justice? Why should that be necessary if nothing is necessary? Resurrection means more life, not resuscitation.

12. See ch. 5, n. 15. I am not saying such faith is irrational, which is the historical meaning of the word "fideism," but that it lacks the heart for a harder look.

13. John D. Caputo, *Against Ethics: Contributions to a Poetics of Obligation with Constant Reference to Deconstruction* (Bloomington: Indiana University Press, 1993).

14. I am not saying that mathematics is the one true language. I am saying it is the language of the dead, that is, it is the only one fit to describe how things would be were we all dead. In the meantime, there are all the other true languages, the languages of the living, and they are innumerable, needed for when we are still alive.

15. Friedrich Nietzsche, "On the Truth and Lies in the Nonmoral Sense," in *Philosophy and Truth: Selections from Nietzsche's Notebooks of the Early 1870's,* trans. Dan Breazeale (Atlantic Highlands, N.J.: Humanities Press, 1979), 79.

16. Ray Brassier, *Nihil Unbound* (London: Palgrave Macmillan, 2007), 228.

17. See Fabio Gironi, "Science-Laden Theory: Outlines of an Unsettled Alliance," *Speculations* 10 (2010): 9–45.

18. Fritjof Capra, *The Tao of Physics* (Boston: Shambhala, 1999).

10. FACTS, FICTIONS, AND FAITH

1. A reader eager to see the point of what follows in this chapter will skip to chs. 11 and 12. I do not advise it. It is never a good idea to skip the arguments that lead up to the punch line.

2. Edmund Husserl, *Ideas I,* trans. Fred Kersten (The Hague: Kluwer, 1998), 258 (§88).

3. Dan Zahavi, *Husserl's Phenomenology* (Stanford, Calif.: Stanford University Press, 2003).

4. John D. Caputo, "Continental Philosophy of Religion Then, Now, and Tomorrow," *Journal of Speculative Philosophy* (Proceedings of the Society for Phenomenology and Existential Philosophy, 50th anniversary sessions) 26, no. 2 (2012): 347–60.

5. Correlation does not mean "we only ever have access to the correlation between thinking and being" (AF = Quentin Meillassoux, *After Finitude: An Essay on the Necessity of Contingency,* trans. Ray Brassier [London: Continuum, 2008], 5) but that we only ever have access to being through thinking (try "not thinking!" and see how that works for you). The "co-" in "correlation" is not a "vicious circle" reducing being and thinking to each other (AF, 5–6); it signifies that the path from thinking to being is the same as the path from being to thinking, that the path is reversible, as Bruno Latour shows in another context (see below). To describe language or consciousness as intentionally related to the world does not mean that the world is "entirely relative" or "relative to us" (AF, 7) but that we are related to the world through language and consciousness. Correlation is a species of relation, not a species of relativism. Correlation does not mean "there is a world only insofar as a consciousness transcends itself towards it" or that the real thing "exists only as a correlate of our own existence" (AF, 7) but that we have a relationship to the existing world only because language and consciousness are structurally

self-transcendent, that they are "rei-tropic" in just the way that plants are heliotro-pic. Try being related to the world without language and while unconscious! The result would be a rock or stone or, in our case, being stone dead. Correlation does not mean the loss of "the great outdoors"—as if Heidegger and Merleau-Ponty needed instruction from Meillassoux about the outdoors! Correlation means that "the great outdoors" is a great bit of language, a great way to speak of the world (AF, 7), apart from the misleading implication that we are not also a bit of the outdoors, being a bit of the world ourselves, however small a bite. That we humans are able to identify the age of the universe and a time before humans were around to identify anything is amazing, but it is entirely without "self-contradiction" for a theory of correlation (AF, 14). It is inexplicable without correlation, which is why this fascinating notion was never noted by stones or rocks. Meillassoux pins his opening argument on "ancestral" realities, posited on the basis of an "archi-fossil" that "designates the material support on the basis of which the experiments that yield estimates of ancestral phenomena proceed" (the rate of radioactive decay of an isotope; AF, 10). But the only reason Meillassoux knows anything about ancestral realities is that he read about the results that have been reached by com-munities of scientists, making use of sophisticated experimental equipment, and following the rules of evidence, who have agreed on this point; if they had not, Meillassoux would not have read about it. Correlation explains how science both relates us to the ancestral world and relates the ancestral world to us, in a way beyond all imagining to the ancients; but it does not render the world "relative to us" in any subjectivistic sense. It is not the case that ancestrality contradicts the principle of givenness (= scientific rules of evidence!) by indicating a time before givenness (= human experience) took place, that is, a world without us, except by equivocating on the word "givenness." It is the case that the discovery (= given-ness) of fossils by us in the present is the basis for speaking of a time without us, prior to human experience (= givenness). The last of Meillassoux's six "tissues of absurdities" is in fact an accurate account of the whole point of correlation so long as one observes an elementary distinction between the givenness of the sign (fos-sil) and the givenness of what is signified (the past) and so long as one does not, as does Meillassoux, attempt to suppress the differences among varying types of givenness or manifestation (AF, 14), which is a logic textbook case of amphiboly. As Meillassoux himself concludes this discussion, the question "how can a being manifest being's anteriority to manifestation?" is only an apparent paradox (AF, 26–27). If it were a contradiction, Meillassoux would never have read about it. The answer in this case is the logic of signifiers explained by Derrida's theory of the trace, when he argues against Husserl that the true value of signifiers is their capac-ity to operate in the absence of intuitive fulfillment (see note 38 below). Moreover, Meillassoux's futile deployment of "ancestrality" was refuted pointedly and quite precisely by Heidegger in *Being and Time* (= BT), §§44–45. Phenomenology is a theory of "truth," of the relationship in this case between science and reality. Of course, Heidegger says, "Entities *are,* quite independently of the experience by which they are disclosed, the acquaintance in which they are discovered, and the grasping in which their nature is ascertained" (BT, 228). But phenomenology supplies an account of "truth," which means, of how we gain access to such entities. The sort of thing that stampedes Meillassoux is when Heidegger says that before Newton his "laws" were not "true," but Heidegger is being technical and precise; he is speaking of the object precisely insofar as it is *known*. Since before Newton these laws were un*known*, they were neither "true" nor "false" but not yet uncovered. With Newton, they were discovered, un-covered, and so became "true" (known, disclosed as such) and Newton became "Newton." "Once entities have been uncovered, they show themselves precisely as entities which beforehand already were" (BT, 269; cf. 255, 272–73). They make a kind of retroactive appearance. Bruno Latour says exactly the same thing about Pasteur's microbes (see below). Ancestrality means that we know and can say *now* what existed *then*. Without a sensible version of correlation (not Meillassoux's caricature), there is no way to explain revisability, since the alternative is that ideas would simply have dropped from the sky, full-blown and unrevisable, as if from God on high. Meillassoux has conflated science and reality the way a fundamentalist confuses the Bible and God. Reality is reality and it does not need us or science, but science is how we are related to reality, and that does need us. Reality is reality but "truth" is a relationship, and relations require relata. Our relationship to reality is structural; it is what we are. Reality's relationship to us is contingent; it lasts only as long as we do. That is really not very confusing: we need the sun to be warm, but the sun does not need us to warm. That is not solar relativism! The correlation does not turn reality into a phantom that disappears at midnight when we fall fast asleep. I myself find it hard to avoid concluding that it is a rather willful misunderstanding to insist that it does, a willful attempt to obfuscate what a generation of philosophers have with considerable effort made perfectly clear, that it is trying to simply make them look foolish, the way Plato makes Callicles look foolish.

6. For detailed, robust, and decisive critiques of Meillassoux's argument as a whole, see Adrian Johnston, "Hume's Revenge: À Dieu, Meillassoux" in *The Speculative Turn: Continental Materialism and Realism,* ed. Levi Bryant, Nick Srnicek, and Graham Harman (Melbourne: re.press, 2011), 92–113, and Martin Hägglund, "Radical Atheist Materialism: A Critique of Meillassoux," in *The Speculative Turn,* 114–29. See also Christopher Watkin, *Difficult Atheism: Post-Theological Thinking in Alain Badiou, Jean-Luc Nancy and Quentin Meillassoux* (Edinburgh: Edinburgh University Press, 2011). My focus here is on his "brief exposition" (AF, 7) of correlation, which might better be described as his "summary execution" or "drive-by shooting" of the idea, failing which the entire subsequent argument fails (whence "the fruit of a poisoned tree.")

7. PH = Bruno Latour, *Pandora's Hope: Essays on the Reality of Science Studies* (Cambridge, Mass.: Harvard University Press, 1999).

8. In another chapter (PH, 80ff.), Latour traces the way that Frédéric Joliot succeeded in bringing about the first artificial nuclear chain reaction before the

Germans did by entering into a complex series of negotiations with politicians, neutrons, Geiger counters, a Belgian mining company, telegrams, and laboratories, all mobilized together and gotten to mutually support each other, a collective of both human and non-human agents ("actants"), through which the system gains in realism and the realism gains in being realistic (PH, 109–10). Human actants (formerly distorted as disconnected "subjects") and non-human actants (formerly distorted as disconnected "objects"), neutrons and diplomats, enter into complex connections in order to produce the desired result.

9. BT, 226–27 (§44c).

10. Don Ihde, "ANT Meets Postphenomenology," 4/S (2008): http://www.4sonline.org.

11. Edmund Husserl, *Cartesian Meditations,* trans. Dorion Cairns (Dordrecht: Kluwer, 1999), 39–41 (§17).

12. Latour himself writes off all phenomenology as a philosophy of "consciousness," thereby depriving it of the very ongoing history he otherwise asserts belongs democratically to everything (else!). I myself think that Latour would be unable to differentiate what he calls "nonmodernism" from the "postmodernism" he belittles—if he actually consulted it, citing chapter and verse from the full history of the movement, instead of scorching it, *pace* the peace he says he prefers. See Ihde, "ANT meets Postphenomenology." The new realists would do well to pay attention to Ihde, in particular his exchanges with Latour and his critique of Heidegger, in Don Ihde, *Heidegger's Technologies: Postphenomenological Perspectives* (New York: Fordham University Press, 2010). See also *Postphenomenology: A Critical Companion to Ihde,* ed. Evan Selinger (Albany: SUNY Press, 2006).

13. There is not the least opposition, in principle, between reality and mediation. As an Aristotelian, Thomas Aquinas rejected this disdain of images but as a realist he said that while we are really related to God, God's relation to us is not real but only an *ens rationis.* The counterpart to the warrior realists in theology is Karl Barth. The counterparts to the "friends of interpretation" are Aristotelians like Aquinas and Hegelians like Paul Tillich, whence the theological analogy to the two types of philosophy of religion with which I began.

14. See ch. 8.

15. Graham Harman, *Prince of Networks: Bruno Latour and Metaphysics* (Melbourne: re.press, 2009), 163–64. Harman studied Heidegger at DePaul and uses the obviously realist elements in Heidegger as a point of departure for what he calls "object-oriented ontology," replacing the subject/object relation with an object/object relation. This was first proposed by Michel Serres, who calls objects "quasi-subjects," and it has long been a prominent feature in the phenomenology of technology in philosophers like Don Ihde. Harman's *Towards Speculative Realism: Essays and Lectures* (Winchester, UK: Zero Books, 2009), an interesting record of his renunciation of "correlationism," reads like a journal of a recovering fundamentalist denouncing the church he was raised in, by which he had been rejected for his heresies. I also emphasize Harman's interest in Alphonso Lingis,

with whom he studied at Pennsylvania State University, in connection with the interesting role played by Levinas among the new realists. Lingis was Levinas's first English translator.

16. One can say of Lyotard and Derrida something quite similar to what Gary Gutting says about Foucault: "he never questioned the objective validity of mathematics and the natural sciences. He does show how the social sciences (and the medicalized biological sciences) are essentially implicated in social power structures, but does not see such implication as automatically destroying the objective validity of a discipline's claims. Sometimes a discipline's role in a power regime is in part due precisely to its objective validity (if, for example, objectivity is a social value)." Gary Gutting, "Introduction: What is Continental Philosophy of Science?" in *Continental Philosophy of Science*, ed. Gary Gutting, Blackwell Readings in Continental Philosophy (Oxford: Wiley-Blackwell, 2005), 11.

17. For the most part Latour has in fact set out, guided by his own lights, down pretty much the same path as Derrida, and they share a common thematic, of which I note a few features here: hybridism, contamination, and anti-essentialism; contextualism, relationalism, and differentialism (*différance*); the critique of humanism; the aporias of mediation and representation (the dangerous supplement) and the critique of pure immediate presence; concatenations of translations and chains of signifiers; the politics of democracy as a politics of rogues; the unpredictable and the surprise of being overtaken by events; the critique of Rousseauianism, of pure and noble savages; the love of puns and neologisms; the autonomy of what I have constructed (the decision of the other in me); recasting truth in terms of practice (*facere veritatem*). What Latour calls non-modernism is indistinguishable from the basic framework of deconstruction. For mainstream continentalists, the great importance of Latour is to have carried out these analyses in a field, science studies or the history of science, in which they like Derrida have little or no competence, but in the end Latour reaches conclusions that are exactly the ones that deconstruction would have predicted and would find congenial. I am complaining not that he stole all this from Derrida but that he has never backed up his criticisms of Derrida. In so doing, Latour exposes the enormous missed opportunity and the terrible misjudgment continental philosophy has made in marginalizing the analysis of the natural sciences and hiding behind Heideggerian slogans like "science does not think" (which Derrida rejects). What Latour does not do is substantiate his criticism of the continental philosophers whom he castigates, while being content to repeat slogans about deconstruction—which includes repeating the ridiculous cliché of locking us in a prison house of language—that commonly circulate in hotel conference bars and carry about that much weight. I can imagine a certain Derrida having written a book that would have reached very much the same conclusions as *Pandora's Hope*, with the same love of puns but without the drive-by shootings of imaginary enemies in the ironic name of "peace." Why is it that when philosophers like Latour, Levinas, and Milbank speak of "peace" they become insufferably pugnacious? Unfortunately, in Latour's work deconstruction is forced to play the straw Callicles to Latour

himself, who enjoys making deconstruction look absurd while suppressing all the obvious replies Derrida would make to such absurd objections, if they even merit the dignity of being called objections. The irony is that the defense Latour makes on behalf of Science Studies, in defense of his own good name (299–300), against the same charges of vicious subjectivizing, applies almost without exception to deconstruction and Derrida's own good name. In general, whenever Latour writes "Science Studies," read "deconstruction." His own naive belief in the naiveté of this fantasy he calls "postmodernism"—"everything is just so much illusion, storytelling, and make believe" (PH, 275)—and the joy he takes in smashing this idol, are themselves a perfect instantiation of his own critique of iconoclasm and of the naive belief in naive belief. Why does it not hit Latour at some point that, in virtue of his own analyses, something is going on in what he himself would describe as a massive collective of connected thinkers, texts, seminars, conferences, arguments and studies, something more than "illusion and naive belief"? Derrida can repeat verbatim what Latour says at the end of PH: his critics have been attacking someone named "Derrida" who these critics say "defends all the absurdities I have disputed for twenty-five years" (PH, 299). My thanks to Michael Norton for pointing out to me an early text in which Latour writes more sensibly of Derrida: "Exegesis and hermeneutics are the tools around which the idea of scientific production has historically been forged. We claim that our empirical observations of laboratory activity fully support that audacious point of view; the notion of inscription, for example, is not to be taken lightly (Derrida, 1977)." Bruno Latour and Steve Woolgar, *Laboratory Life: The Construction of Scientific Facts* (Princeton, N.J.: Princeton University Press, 1986), 261n24. Norton also brought to my attention Latour's essay "Thou Shall Not Take the Lord's Name in Vain: Being a Sort of Sermon on the Hesitations of Religious Speech," *RES: Anthropology and Aesthetics,* no. 39 (Spring, 2001): 215–34, which links Derrida with Whitehead, calling them somewhat whimsically "Fathers of the Church" who provide us with a more sensible account of what religion is. For robust presentations of the realist elements in Derrida by philosophers who have in fact studied Derrida carefully, see the various writings of Christopher Norris. In response to Norris's notion that Derrida is a "transcendental realist," Derrida said that deconstruction has "always come forward *in the name of the real,* of the irreducible reality of the real—not the real as an attribute of the *thing* (*res*), objective, present, sense-able or intelligible, but the real as coming or event of the other. . . . In this sense, nothing is more 'realist' than deconstruction." Jacques Derrida, *Paper Machine,* trans. Rachel Bowlby (Stanford, Calif.: Stanford University Press, 2005), 96. For a closely argued presentation of Derrida and realism which labors under the unfortunate confusion that such realism comes as the cost of the ethical and religious elements in Derrida, see Martin Hägglund, *Radical Atheism: Derrida and the Time of Life* (Stanford, Calif.: Stanford University Press, 2008). For my response to Hägglund on ethics and religion, see "The Return of Anti-Religion: From Radical Atheism to Radical Theology," *Journal of Cultural and Religious Theory* 11, no. 2 (Spring, 2011), 32–125, http://www.jcrt.org/archives/11.2/caputo.pdf

18. Answering the question, "where were Pasteur's microbes before 1864?" by way of a diagram that is strikingly similar to Husserl's chart of the flow of retention and protention, Latour says that in the years before 1864 there was a conflict between spontaneous generation and ferments, and only after 1864 could we then say that before 1864 there was fermentation and not spontaneous generation (PH, 171–72). The point is identical with Heidegger's observation about Newton's laws in BT (226–27, §44c) and the reason is that they are both talking about the object qua known, which does not come at the expense of the object as if we were dead but simply adds a new stratum to reality known as "science." Science is not only about reality but adds a new stratum to reality.

19. The materialism that Žižek finally defends is not very materialistic, not because like Milbank it is supported by an analogical distribution of being from created material beings up through uncreated immaterial being, but because no theoretical physicist today thinks the physical world is all that grossly physical. The particles and quanta of energy, the waves and impulses of contemporary physics, make a mockery of the "crude" materialism of billiard-ball atoms bouncing around in empty space according to fixed and predetermining laws. In quantum physics, the world is "incomplete" and indeterminate, like a Google map that is determinate only at the level of the observer, which can in turn become more or less determinate as the need arises, when we zoom in or out. The critical point, Žižek points out, is that this is not a merely epistemological observation about the observer, but an ontological point about the "ontological incompleteness" or indeterminate status of physical reality itself (90). So Žižek speaks of a "spectral materialism," which includes the digitalization of information, the genetic code, and quantum physics. A true materialism rejoices in the disappearance of matter into the void; see Slavoj Žižek and John Milbank, *The Monstrosity of Christ: Paradox or Dialectic*, ed. Creston Davis (Cambridge, Mass.: MIT Press, 2009), 91–92. Žižek thinks the metaphysics that best fits this physics is Badiou's, who is the true materialist, precisely because Badiou's ontological-mathematical formalism steers clear of an ontology of life or *élan vital* of the sort we find in Bergson or Deleuze. Badiou is for the same reason the true atheist. As Milbank points out (*Monstrosity*, 150), any qualitative intensification of being—like *élan vital*, Deleuze's "crowned virtuality," or Heidegger's mysterious *Sein*—represents a failure of atheistic nerve and a drift toward a kind of *Ersatz* divinity. (I would simply call it the life-world.) This is confirmed by Hallward's argument that there is nothing to stop us from understanding the plane of immanence as the field of a theophany in which the creative forces are realized in created actualities, which actualize their virtualities; see Peter Hallward, *Out of This World: Deleuze and the Philosophy of Creation* (New York: Verso, 2006). Of course it is a curious Hegel that Žižek thinks Badiou incarnates since it represents exactly what Hegel criticized under the name of the "prose of the world" in the *Lectures on the Philosophy of Religion*, the prosaic world, natural things divested of their divinity, various collections of neutral grey empirical objects. Žižek's materialism, unlike its nineteenth-century antecedents, is not reductionistic. Material forces are all

there are, but there is always more to the material world than matter, which bears the structure of the "non-all." There are always phenomena like "consciousness" which have a positive non-being or non-materiality, not because consciousness is an angelic or an immaterial substance, but because there is always an incompleteness in reality, a subjective point of view on reality.

20. Catherine Malabou, *What Should We Do with Our Brain,* trans. Sebastian Rand (New York: Fordham University Press, 2008), 69.

21. That does not mean that there cannot be many universes *in* or *of* space and time.

22. Ray Brassier, *Nihil Unbound* (London: Palgrave Macmillan, 2007), 230–34; see n. 15, above, on Harman and Lingis. Credit ultimately goes to the fact that Harman studied with Alphonso Lingis.

23. If I experienced the other person's conscious experiences, they would be my experiences and the other person would not be the other person. The speculative realists themselves acknowledge that in this matter of "reality" Levinas was, at least in this analysis, on to something. Derrida too applauded Levinas on this point but he refined the position: (1) not even the "wholly other" is wholly unmediated, since it comes through "language" (*Bonjour!*); (2) it applies much more widely than Levinas appreciated, since there is an irreducible alterity to everything, not simply other persons. The Derridean point is an expanded Martha: hospitality ought to be extended not only to humans but to non-humans, and we ought to take a more gracious, generous, welcoming and hospitable relationship with the world to which we humans belong, in which and of which we are but a part, animals that we are. Derrida argued against Levinas that Heidegger and Husserl were right to insist that none of this could take place, that the event of the *tout autre* would not happen, entirely without mediation, so that the *tout autre* is not quite, not absolutely *tout autre*. See Jacque Derrida, "Violence and Metaphysics," *Writing and Difference,* trans. Alan Bass (Chicago: University of Chicago Press, 1978), 114–16, 147–48; there is no absolute peace; even ethical peace requires the pre-ethical transcendental violence of mediation (128–29).

24. Husserl, *Ideas I,* 155.

25. A point confirmed by physics: given the infinitesimal amount of time it takes for the light reflected off the face of the other to reach us, even the face-to-face encounter in the living present is an encounter with the past.

26. If, as some theorize, life originated in meteoric fragments coming from Mars, then we are all Martians or at least relatives of Martians or descendants, perhaps, not merely of monkeys but of Martians.

27. Writing, Derrida argues, is the anonymous, subject-less transcendental field, constitutive of both subjects and objects; see Jacques Derrida, *Edmund Husserl's Origin of Geometry,* trans. John Leavey (Boulder, Colo.: John Hays, 1978), 88–89.

28. Jacques Derrida, "*As If* I Were Dead: An Interview with Jacques Derrida," in *Applying: To Derrida,* ed. John Branningan, Ruth Robbins, and Julian Wolfreys (London: Macmillan, 1996), 216.

29. Husserl held that a sign is perfected by its intuitive fulfillment in the presence of the signified, as when I visit Budapest for the first time, having previously only read about or seen photographs of it. Derrida argued the contrary: the precise value of the sign is its capacity to operate in the *absence* of intuitive fulfillment, to extend our knowledge and signification well beyond the empirical limits of what we could ever traverse. The "ancestral" testifies to our capacity to "signify" a past in which we were not present, not merely in fact but in principle, since it concerns the time before human beings existed at all. So, far from offering a refutation of Derrida, Meillassoux owes a footnote to Derrida on the "archive" and the "absolute past." The impossibility of fulfillment is not a factual matter but a structural one, a venerable distinction in phenomenology about which Meillassoux seems innocent. Even so, we can imagine ("imaginatively fulfill") a world (in paintings, films, etc.) in which humanity does not yet or no longer exists. So ancestrality is a weaker phenomenon than Meillassoux thinks. It is a good example but an even better example is mathematical equations for which there is not even a possible imaginative fulfillment, like the assumption of parallels lines that meet, or of electrons that are both waves and particles. Far from posing some sort of humanistic threat to mathematical science, Derrida's critique of Husserl's intuitionism is cut to fit the most abstract achievements of mathematics and the paradoxes of quantum physics. Finally, Derrida does not criticize rationality as such. He says it should be enlarged beyond the rationality that proceeds from *logos,* meaning that there is a rationality that functions without the intuitive givenness demanded by *nous* and *logos* and proceeds by means of signifiers deprived of intuitive redemption, which is provided for by his grammatology (Jacques Derrida, *Of Grammatology,* corrected ed., trans. Gayatri Spivak [Baltimore: Johns Hopkins University Press, 1997], 10). Steven Shakespeare makes an excellent argument in this regard in "The Persistence of the Trace: Interrogating the Gods of Speculative Realism" (unpublished paper).

30. Of course, I am treating Meillassoux as a continental philosopher of a religion to come, but one that pales in comparison to Derrida's subtle feeling for the rhythms of a certain messianic faith irreducible to belief. The best example of this is his dubious speculation on "eternal recurrence" in Quentin Meillassoux, "Spectral Dilemma," *Collapse,* IV (May, 2008): 261–75; accessed April 2011, http://www.scribd.com/doc/23792245/Quentin-Meillassoux-Spectral-Dilemma. Meillassoux does not here engage a "perhaps" that puts pressure on the present, but engages in the wildest metaphysical speculation, of just the sort Kant tried to talk us out of, running around in endless circles, chasing after one's own tail. Derrida is a much colder "realist" than Meillassoux, since Derrida does not think that anything is going to come along and right the wrongs done to the dead. Mourning is impossible. On the impossibility of mourning, see Jill Peterson Adams, "Acts of Irreconcilable Mourning: Post-Holocaust Witness and Testimony" (unpublished paper). Compared to the urgency of Derrida's "to come," Meillassoux's argument seems idle.

31. Friedrich Nietzsche, *The Will to Power,* no. 447, trans. Walter Kaufman and R. J. Hollingdale (New York: Viking Press), 246–47.

32. What he calls non-philosophy or, in this case, non-theology, plays a similar role to what I am calling here a "theopoetics." Laruelle advances his argument in the name of a radical thought of immanence, as opposed to the Gnostic world which he is trying to "retrieve" or "reinvent." His construction of "heresy" and "Christ" as categories of immanence, his attempt to find their human meaning, is, if punishingly and unnecessarily opaque, on the mark and belongs to the work of what I would call a "radical" theology—whatever reservations I have about his metaphysics of life in the tradition of Michel Henry.

11. A NIHILISM OF GRACE

1. Ray Brassier, *Nihil Unbound: Enlightenment and Extinction* (London: Palgrave, Macmillan, 2007). I contract here the argumentative point of a complex book into a single paragraph.

2. *Kierkegaard's Writings,* trans. and ed. Howard Hong and Edna Hong, vol. 12.1, *Concluding Unscientific Postscript to* Philosophical Fragments (Princeton, N.J.: Princeton University Press, 1992), 83.

3. Gilles Deleuze, *The Logic of Sense,* ed. Constantin V. Boundas, trans. Mark Lester with Charles Stivale (New York: Columbia University Press, 1969), 149.

4. *The Complete Mystical Works of Meister Eckhart,* trans. and ed. Maurice O'C Walshe (New York: Crossroad, 2009), 110 ("In hoc apparuit caritas dei in nobis").

5. I say the "condition" but not precisely the "reason." We live because we live, not because we die. The reason we hold life dear is that life is life and life is its own "why." My claim is that the mortality of life, far from undermining the value of life, intensifies that value. Mortality is an enabling or intensifying condition not a disabling one, that the condition under which it is impossible, is what makes it possible. What we hold dear, precisely speaking, is life/death, *vita mortalis.*

6. This is dramatized in a haunting novel by Simone de Beauvoir, *All Men are Mortal,* trans. Leonard M. Friedman (New York: Norton & Norton, 1992).

7. Even though reincarnation remains within the horizon of the material world, it still seeks a way around the finality of death, trying to elude what gives the concept of "materialism" real teeth.

8. Of course, it is always possible to say, "death, perhaps," meaning that death is only apparently final. That belongs to what I called in chapter 5 an abridged or attenuated postmodernism, where we deny knowledge in order to make room for faith. For all the reasons I gave above, I take that to be a kind of fideism, an escape clause in our contract with life, a means of mounting an apologetic defense for the old two-worlds theory which, it is my hypothesis, has run out of steam. I am simply trying to construct a colder, cooler hermeneutics than that. The old apologetics is an easier sell in the churches on the grounds that the priests have a genius for explaining almost anything. Apart from saying that it was never my intention to start up a new church, of which we have a few too many already, I do think a theology of "perhaps" can "preach," but only to more progressive outlying

congregations who are fed up with the old dualism and feed on the promise of the world. See Phil Snider, *Preaching After God: Derrida, Caputo and the Language of Postmodern Homiletics* (Eugene, Oreg.: Cascade Books, 2012).

9. Jacques Derrida, *The Gift of Death,* trans. David Wills (Chicago: University of Chicago Press, 1995), 49.

10. Hélène Cixous, "Promised Belief," in *Feminism, Sexuality, and the Return of Religion,* ed. Linda Alcoff and John D. Caputo (Bloomington: Indiana University Press, 2011), 154–59.

11. This story, found only in a Gospel so idiosyncratic as to be called the "Fourth Gospel," is a vintage piece of strong theology, which even risks painting Jesus in a bad light to make its point. There is likely no authentic tradition behind it, but there is a fabulous tradition that its true author, the "beloved disciple" traditionally identified with the apostle John of Zebedee, is actually the risen Lazarus himself. I do not think such an authorship explains the high Christology; I think the high Christology explains the story! See Ben Witherington, "Was Lazarus the Beloved Disciple?" January 2007, http://benwitherington.blogspot.com/2007/01/was-lazarus-beloved-disciple.html; *The Gospel of John and Christian Theology,* ed. Richard Bauckham and Carl Mosser (Grand Rapids, Mich.: Eerdmanns, 2008); and John D. Caputo, "The Promise of the World," *Transfiguration: Nordic Journal of Christianity and the Arts* 10 (2010/11): 13–32.

12. Gilles Deleuze, *Pure Immanence: Essays on A Life,* trans. Anne Boyman (New York: Zone Books, 2001), 25–34.

13. The following five excerpts are from Charles Dickens, *Our Mutual Friend,* in *The Oxford Illustrated Dickens* (Oxford: Oxford University Press, 1989), 3:443–48, chapter 3.

14. Deleuze, *Pure Immanence,* 27; see the superb commentary on "A Life" by Giorgio Agamben, *Potentialities,* trans. Daniel Heller-Roazen (Stanford, Calif.: Stanford University Press, 1999), 220–39. See also Augustine, *De trinitate,* 13:20.

15. Deleuze, *Pure Immanence,* 29.

16. In doing so I am departing from the usage but not the point of the distinction between joy and *beatitude* in Marguerite Porete according to a splendid analysis by David Kangas, where *beatitudo* refers to an end of life after mortal life has ended, eternal life, which according to Augustine and Aquinas can alone satisfy our desire for happiness. Such transcendent *beatitudo,* Porete thinks, undermines the immanent joy of life, which is love, which is the life of God within us, which is "without why." See David Kangas, "Dangerous Joy: Marguerite Porete's Good-Bye to the Virtues," *Journal of Religion* 91, no. 3 (2011): 299–319. There is a good argument to be made that the language of "without why" and a certain amount of the framework of Meister Eckhart's work were inherited by him from Porete and Hadewijch. See Bernard McGinn, ed., *Meister Eckhart and the Beguine Mystics* (New York: Continuum, 1994), in particular, Maria Lichtmann, "Marguerite Porete and Meister Eckhart: *The Mirror of Simple Souls* Mirrored," 65–86; and Paul Dietrich, "The Wilderness of God in Hadewijch II and Meister Eckhart and his Circle," 31–43.

17. Martin Heidegger, *The Principle of Reason,* trans. Reginald Lily (Bloomington: Indiana University Press, 1991), 36–37.

18. Dylan Thomas, "Do Not Go Gentle into That Good Night," in *The Poems of Dylan Thomas* (New York: New Directions, 1953), 239.

19. Richard Kearney, "Epiphanies of the Everyday: Toward a Micro-Eschatology," in *After God,* ed. John Manoussakis (New York: Fordham University Press, 2006), 3–20.

20. Giorgio Agamben, *Nudities,* trans. David Kishik and Stefan Pedatella (Stanford, Calif.: Stanford University Press, 2011), 100–103.

21. For an excellent study of the history and significance of the saintly willingness to be consigned to hell (*resignatio ad infernum*), see Clark West, "The Deconstruction of Hell: A History of the *Resignatio ad Infernum* Tradition," (PhD diss., Syracuse University, 2013).

22. See David Kangas, "Dangerous Joy: Marguerite Porete's Good-Bye to the Virtues."

23. There is an excellent text in Deleuze's 1980 lectures on Spinoza, in which he says that it is too easy to say that philosophy has been compromised by "God," that philosophers have been blackmailed by the idea and forced to give it pride of place as the keeper of order and tranquility. For there is another, more anarchic and emancipatory side to the name of God as the very idea of the passage to the limits, of what drives our faculties to their limits, the drive to think the unthinkable, to represent the unrepresentable, to paint the unpaintable, to do the undoable, to say the unsayable. With God anything is possible. See *Les Cours de Gilles Deleuze,* "Spinoza: 25/11/1980," www.webdeleuze.com. That same motif or trope is in play when Derrida links God with the possibility of the impossibility and the art of learning how not to speak, another reason I am no party to the war between Deleuzeans and Derrideans.

12. THE GRACE OF THE WORLD

1. I trust it is by now clear that when I say "religion without religion" I do not mean a "good" religion without "bad" religion, as my critics sometimes say. I mean a risk without a safety net, a call without an identifiable source, a clear command or a guaranteed response—in short, an insistence without existence. I mean a religion of the promise of the world without some other fantastic world behind the scenes to make it all come true, a *foi* without a firm *croyance,* a risky faith up to its ears in unfaith and uncertainty without a firm belief in the rock of ages who will make all things turn out well. I mean praying without a prayer, without the books of common prayer handed down by the traditions.

2. Hélène Cixous, "Promised Belief," in *Feminism, Sexuality, and the Return of Religion,* ed. Linda Alcoff and John D. Caputo (Bloomington: Indiana University Press, 2011), 147. See also Jacques Derrida, *H. C.—for Life, That Is to Say . . . ,* trans. Laurent Milesi and Stefan Herbrechter (Stanford, Calif.: Stanford University

Press, 1998), 21; and Hélène Cixous, *Insister of Jacques Derrida,* trans. Peggy Kamuf (Stanford, Calif.: Stanford University Press, 2007), 179.

3. "Whoosh" is the term adopted as a descriptor for getting caught up in the rush of the sacred in Hubert Dreyfus and Sean Dorrance Kelly, *All Things Shining: Reading the Western Classics to Find Meaning in a Secular Age* (New York: Free Press, 2011). For a robust critique, see Garry Wills, "Superficial & Sublime," *New York Review of Books* (April 7, 2011); available at: http://www.nybooks.com/articles/archives/2011/apr/07/superficial-sublime/.

4. See Luce Irigaray, *Il mistero di Maria* (Rome: Paoline Editoriale Libri, 2010); and *Una nuova cultura dell'energia* (Torino: Bollati Boringhieri, 2011), which she wanted to publish under the title *After Buddha and Jesus,* according to Leonart Skof, "Silence and Hospitality in Irigaray: Towards a Culture of Nonviolence," *Breath of Hospitality: Intersubjectivity, Ethics, and Non-Violence* (Dordracht: Springer Publishing, forthcoming).

5. See Richard Bauckham, "Jesus and the Wild Animals (Mark 1:13): A Christological Image for an Ecological Age," in *Jesus of Nazareth: Lord and Christ: Essays on the Historical Jesus and New Testament Christology,* ed. J. B. Green and M. Turner (Grand Rapids, Mich.: Eerdmans, 1994), 3–21.

6. For a Deleuzean reading of the Christic body in Christian antiquity, see Francis Sanzaro, "The Immanent Body: A Thematic Study of the Logic of Immanence in Christology, Philosophy, and Aesthetics" (PhD diss., Syracuse University, 2012).

7. See John D. Caputo, *Against Ethics* (Bloomington: Indiana University Press, 1993).

8. *Slumdog Millionaire* is a 2008 film by director Danny Boyle. My thanks to Craig Keen for this comparison and for an astute commentary on my work from which I learned a great deal. See our exchange in John D. Caputo, "Praying for an Earthier Jesus: A Theology of Flesh," in *I More Than Others: Responses to Evil and Suffering,* ed. Eric R. Serverance (Newcastle, UK: Cambridge Scholars, 2010), 6–27, and Craig Keen, "Deferral: A Response to John D. Caputo's *The Weakness of God,*" 28–34.

9. So true is this that the authors of the gospels cannot make up their mind about whether flesh persists in the risen body. Jesus enjoys a breakfast of broiled fish with his disciples who have spent the night on the lake; he shares a meal with the disciples on the road to Emmaus who recognize him only when they sit down to table in an inn. Is the resurrected body a body of flesh? That is a conundrum for Christian theology, whether to include flesh, as in the gospel of Luke (24:50), or exclude it, as St. Paul says (1 Cor. 15:50). Dale Martin suggests that Paul's resolution of the unthinkable resurrected body is carried out completely within the parameters of the four elements of ancient cosmology. The resurrection has to do with producing a "pneumatic body," not with the separation of an other-worldly "soul" from a this-worldly "body" with which it is then rejoined, as in the later Hellenistic account that became canonical. Paul describes a permanent separation of one

body from another body, separating out the lower elements from the higher elements, the corruptible watery-earthy body from the lighter fiery-airy pneumatic one that lives on incorruptible, with a body like that of the sun and moon and stars, which it joins in the sky (*somata epourania*). See Dale Martin, *The Corinthian Body* (New Haven, Conn.: Yale University Press, 1995).

10. Giorgio Agamben, *Potentialities,* trans. Daniel Heller-Roazen (Stanford, Calif.: Stanford University Press, 1999), 220.

11. Peter Hallward, *Out of this World: Deleuze and the Philosophy of Creation* (New York: Verso, 2006).

12. It is quite interesting that the battle between the humans and the Cylons in *Battlestar Galactica* is also theological. What should we make of the fact that the humans are polytheists and the Cylons are monotheists, even though the Cylons are robots, albeit highly advanced robots made in the age after the "singularity" has been reached?

13. For the latest news on these developments, visit http://singularityu.org. See also Ray Kurzweil, *The Singularity is Near: When Humans Transcend Biology* (New York: Penguin Books, 2005); Hans Moravec, *Robot: Mere Machine to Transcendent Mind* (Oxford: Oxford University Press, 1999); Frank J. Tipler, *The Physics of Immortality: Modern Cosmology, God, and the Resurrection of the Dead* (New York: Anchor Books, 1994). For a good analysis and critique, see Cart Wolfe, *What Is Posthumanism?* (Minneapolis: University of Minnesota Press, 2010), xi–xxiv; N. Katherine Hayles, *How We Became Posthuman* (Chicago: University of Chicago Press, 1999); Thomas Carlson, *The Indiscrete Image: Infinitude and Creation of the Human* (Chicago: University of Chicago Press, 2008).

14. In the following seven paragraphs I redescribe "perhaps" as a kind of *khora*. This is a rewrite of a few pages excerpted from my "Before Creation: Derrida's Memory of God," *Mosaic: A Journal for the Interdisciplinary Study of Literature* 39, no. 3 (September 2006): 91–102.

15. Jacques Derrida, *Sauf le nom* (Paris: Galilée, 1993), 94–95; translated by David Wood, John P. Leavey Jr., and Ian McLeod as *On the Name,* ed. Thomas Dutoit (Stanford, Calif.: Stanford University Press, 1995), 75–76.

16. See Michael Naas's commentary and magnificent translation of "Khora s'enfout complètement" in *Miracle and Machine: Jacques Derrida and the Two Sources of Religion, Science and the Media* (New York: Fordham University Press, 2012), 179–80.

17. Jacques Derrida, *Politics of Friendship,* 4th ed. (New York: Verso, 2006), 29.

JOHN D. CAPUTO is Thomas J. Watson Professor of Religion Emeritus at Syracuse University and the David R. Cook Professor of Philosophy Emeritus at Villanova University. He is author of *The Weakness of God* (IUP, 2006), which won the American Academy of Religion's Award for Excellence in the Study of Religion in the Constructive-Reflective Studies category.

CPSIA information can be obtained at www.ICGtesting.com
Printed in the USA
LVOW10s1139070116

469341LV00009B/329/P